ANGELS LANDING P54

Welcome to Zion & Bryce Canyon National Parks

Connect with the mystery and mysticism of southern Utah in this fantastic and wild landscape of sand, stone and sky.

Geology

Perhaps nowhere else in the Southwest can compete with southern Utah when it comes to the sheer number of geological works of art. Soaring pinnacles and arches, dizzyingly deep canyons and rainbow-colored, alien-looking rocks are all par for the course. The bones of the earth – and the powerful natural processes that shape them – are laid bare. Take the time to observe the different-colored layers stacked one upon the other: Kayenta, Navajo, Temple Cap, Carmel. These are snapshots of the planet's distant past, and an amazing opportunity to take in the work of 240 million years in a single glance.

Adventure

There's no better way to get a feel for this red-rock wonderland than by having some fun. Serious fun. Whatever your sport, there's a good chance that Utah sets a pretty high standard. Hikes lead to majestic freestanding arches, secret oases, desert labyrinths and exposed traverses across narrow fins. Canyoneers rappel into the earth's wrinkles to explore dark, mystical passageways filled with adventure. Moab's slick-rock trails set the standard for mountain biking decades ago, while desert spires and mighty big walls are the envy of rock climbers around the world.

Scenic Drives

Though southern Utah's majestic parklands are hardly drive-by attractions, scenic roads abound. In fact, they're an essential part of your journey here in canyon country, whether you're driving, cycling, riding the park shuttles in Zion and Bryce or negotiating a teeth-rattling, nerve-wracking 4WD road in the rugged backcountry. And if there are moments when you feel as if you've seen that view before in a Hollywood film, it's because you probably have. Up that road less traveled, adventure awaits in one of America's last great wildernesses.

Wilderness

You could spend weeks immersed in the national parks and monuments. But then you'd be missing out on some of the most memorable places, from arty, alternative-minded towns like Moab to Native American tribal lands and sites where prehistoric denizens made their mark. Detours are always worthwhile here, whether for an earthy plate of organic, farm-fresh food or to capture another top-of-the-world vista. Local state parks (Snow Canyon, Goblin Valley) and wilderness areas (Paria Canyon-Vermilion Cliffs) deserve consideration, as do off-the-grid wild areas found in Grand Staircase–Escalante and Bears Ears National Monuments.

Why I Love Zion & Bryce Canyon National Parks

By Greg Benchwick, Writer

The desert of southern Utah has a magic to it that ignites the imagination and the soul in a way no other place on Earth can. When I come to Utah's national parks, I skip, I jump, I explore with the same fire, creativity and energy I had as a boy. It's my spiritual home, and I'm certain that somehow in the cosmic scheme of things, I was born from this vast, stark and beautiful land of towering sandstone cliffs, azure skies, mesas, prickly-sharp plants and soft red sand.

For more about our writers, see p288

Above: Canyonlands National Park (p178) with the La Sal Mountains in the background

Zion & Bryce Canyon National Parks

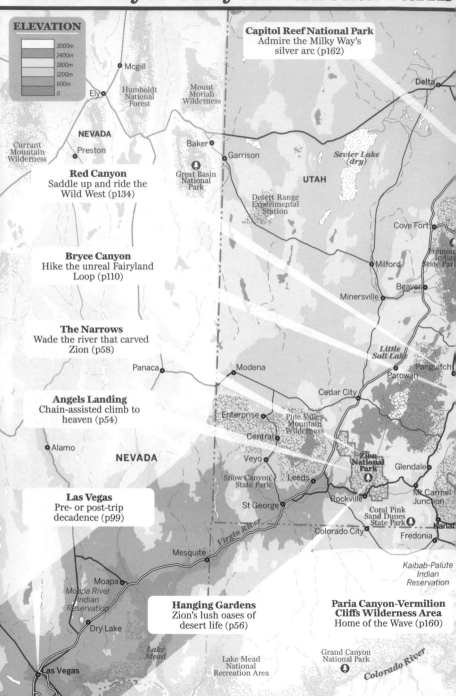

ELEVATION

	3000m
	2400m
	1800m
	1200m
	600m
	0

Capitol Reef National Park
Admire the Milky Way's
silver arc (p162)

Red Canyon
Saddle up and ride the
Wild West (p134)

Bryce Canyon
Hike the unreal Fairyland
Loop (p110)

The Narrows
Wade the river that carved
Zion (p58)

Angels Landing
Chain-assisted climb to
heaven (p54)

Las Vegas
Pre- or post-trip
decadence (p99)

Hanging Gardens
Zion's lush oases of
desert life (p56)

**Paria Canyon-Vermilion
Cliffs Wilderness Area**
Home of the Wave (p160)

NEVADA

UTAH

Mcgill

Ely

Humboldt
National
Forest

Mount
Moriah
Wilderness

Delta

Currant
Mountain
Wilderness

Preston

Baker

Garrison

*Sevier Lake
(dry)*

Great Basin
National
Park

Desert Range
Experimental
Station

Cove Fort

Fremont
Indian
State Park

Milford

Beaver

Minersville

*Little
Salt Lake*

Panaca

Modena

Parowan

Panguitch

Cedar City

Enterprise

Pine Valley
Mountain
Wilderness

Alamo

NEVADA

Central

Veyo

Snow Canyon
State Park

Leeds

**Zion
National
Park**

Glendale

St George

Rockville

Mt Carmel
Junction

Coral Pink
Sand Dunes
State Park

Kanab

Colorado City

Fredonia

Mesquite

Virgin River

*Kaibab-Palute
Indian
Reservation*

Moapa

*Moapa River
Indian
Reservation*

Dry Lake

*Lake
Mead*

Grand Canyon
National Park

Colorado River

Lake Mead
National
Recreation Area

Las Vegas

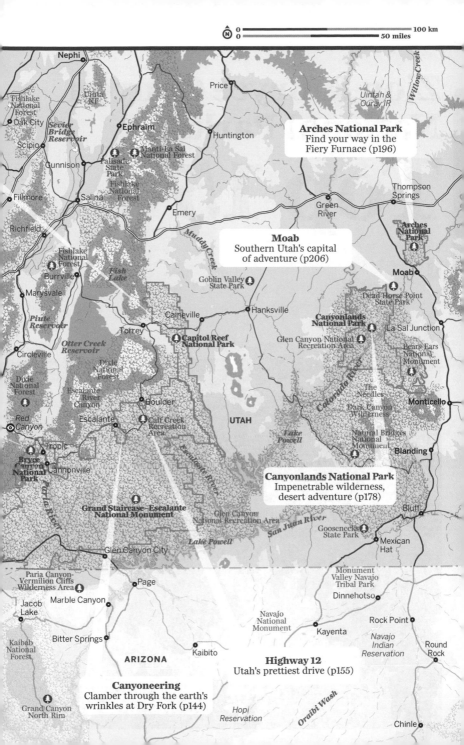

N

0 | 100 km
0 | 50 miles

Nephi

Price

Arches National Park
Find your way in the
Fiery Furnace (p196)

Uintah &
Ouray IR

Willow Creek

Fishlake
National
Forest
Oak City

Uinta
NF

Scipio

Ephraim

Huntington

Gunnison

Manti-La Sal
National Forest

Palisade
State
Park

Fillmore

Salina

Fishlake
National
Forest

Emery

Green
River

Thompson
Springs

Arches
National
Park

Richfield

Moab
Southern Utah's capital
of adventure (p206)

Moab

Burrville

Fishlake
National
Forest

Muddy Creek

Fish
Lake

Goblin Valley
State Park

Dead Horse Point
State Park

Marysvale

Hanksville

**Canyonlands
National Park**

La Sal Junction

Piute
Reservoir

Caineville

Torrey

Glen Canyon National
Recreation Area

Bears Ears
National
Monument

Circleville

Otter Creek
Reservoir

Dixie
National
Forest

**Capitol Reef
National Park**

The
Needles

Monticello

Dixie
National
Forest

Escalante
River
Canyon

Boulder

UTAH

Dark Canyon
Wilderness

Colorado River

Red
Canyon

Escalante

Calf Creek
Recreation
Area

Lake
Powell

Natural Bridges
National
Monument

Tropic

**Bryce
Canyon
National
Park**

Cannonville

Escalante River

Blanding

Paria River

**Grand Staircase–Escalante
National Monument**

Glen Canyon
National Recreation Area

San Juan River

Canyonlands National Park
Impenetrable wilderness,
desert adventure (p178)

Bluff

Glen Canyon City

Lake Powell

Goosenecks
State Park

Mexican
Hat

Paria Canyon–
Vermilion Cliffs
Wilderness Area

Page

Jacob
Lake

Marble Canyon

Monument
Valley Navajo
Tribal Park

Dinnehotso

Kaibab
National
Forest

Bitter Springs

Navajo
National
Monument

Rock Point

Round
Rock

ARIZONA

Kaibito

Kayenta

Navajo
Indian
Reservation

Highway 12
Utah's prettiest drive (p155)

Canyoneering
Clamber through the earth's
wrinkles at Dry Fork (p144)

Grand Canyon
North Rim

Hopi
Reservation

Oraibi Wash

Chinle

Zion & Bryce Canyon National Parks' Top 15

1

Angels Landing

1 The climb to Angels Landing (p54) in Zion Canyon is among the most memorable day hikes in Utah, if not North America. The 5-mile trail hugs the face of a towering cliff, snakes through a cool canyon and climbs up Walter's Wiggles (a series of 21 sharp switchbacks) before finally ascending a narrow, exposed ridge – where steel chains and the encouragement of strangers are your only friends. Your reward after reaching the 5790ft summit? A lofty view of Zion Canyon and some unreal photos of your vertigo-defying adventure.

The Narrows

2 One of Utah's most famous backcountry routes is this remarkably fun hike (p58) down the Virgin River. It's deceptively easy at first, but once you hit the confluence with Deep Creek, you'll be glad you brought that walking stick. By day two you'll be wading through chest-deep pools, the echoes of the rushing water growing louder and the dark canyon squeezing tighter until you reach Wall Street, where the sheer sandstone buttresses shoot up a neck-craning 1500ft. No permit? No worries: day hikers can get wet, too.

NIGEL MAY/SHUTTERSTOCK ©

GALYNA ANDRUSHKO/SHUTTERSTOCK ©

Mountain Biking in Moab

3 Moab is one of the mountain-biking capitals of the world, where the desert slickrock surrounding the town makes a perfect 'sticky' surface for knobbly tires. Challenging trails ascend steep bluffs, twist through forests and slam over 4WD roads into the wilds of canyon country. And you'll surely redefine adventure after treading the roller-coaster rock face of the Whole Enchilada (p207). There's a reason why some Moab hotels have a shower for bikes. One trip and you'll be hooked.

Las Vegas

4 As you awake from your in-flight nap – rested, content, ready for red-rock inspiration – here comes Vegas (p99) on the horizon, like a storm ready to swallow you and spit you out. As you leave the airport and glide under the neon of Vegas' Strip, the city puts on a dazzling show: dancing fountains, a spewing volcano, the Eiffel Tower. Its most dangerous charms lie in the gambling dens – seductive lairs where the fresh-pumped air and bright colors share one goal: separating you from your money. Step away if you can for fine restaurants and dazzling entertainment from the Cirque du Soleil.

Fairyland Loop

5 The sorbet-colored, castle-like spires and hoodoos of Bryce Canyon National Park pop like a Dr Seuss landscape. Though the smallest of Utah's national parks, this is perhaps the most immediately visually stunning, particularly at sunrise and sunset when an orange wash sets the otherworldly formations ablaze. Search for the perfect panoramic photo op from the Rim Trail, or let your imagination work overtime on the aptly named Fairyland Loop (p114), an all-day foray that gets up close and personal with wildly shaped hoodoos and millennial bristlecone pines.

Canyonlands

6 If Arches is Red Rock 101, then the Canyonlands (p178) is graduate school. Those looking for desert adventure, deep quiet, or a long, challenging backpacking trip will find it in the park's vast, impenetrable acres of arid wilderness. Distant mesas and sidewinder-like canyons, carved out by the mighty Colorado and Green Rivers, are visible from overlooks on the Island in the Sky, while more remote districts – the Needles, Horseshoe Canyon and the Maze – beckon backcountry veterans, on foot, bike or raft.
Mesa Arch (p184)

Fiery Furnace

7 Eroded over millions of years, Arches' namesake formations elegantly defy gravity and struggle against the passage of time. A hike through the desert to Delicate Arch – the unofficial state symbol – is de rigueur for any first-time visitor, but if you want to walk on the wild side, sign up for a guided tour through the sandstone labyrinth known as the Fiery Furnace (p200). Composed of giant fins and spectacularly narrow canyons, you'll be scrambling your way through one of the most improbable natural mazes on the planet.

Canyoneering

8 Canyoneering is a perfect combination of adventure and commitment. Once you rappel into a serious canyon, there is generally only one way out. Luckily, the remarkable diversity of chasms in Utah means that you don't always need a rope or wet suit to find yourself in some hidden corner of the earth. Get a taste at Escalante's Dry Fork (p145), which contains three nontechnical slots all within walking distance of one another, or head out to the lost slots of the Maze for a remote challenge.

7

JEFF GRENFORD/GETTY IMAGES ©

PUNG/SHUTTERSTOCK ©

Capitol Reef

9 The American West is known for its star-studded nights, but few destinations can compete with Capitol Reef's views of the heaven-spanning Milky Way. If you want to watch for shooting stars from your sleeping bag or contemplate the possibility of life in distant galaxies, this is certainly the spot: Capitol Reef (p162) is one of the last preserves of natural darkness in the United States, with over 7500 stars visible to the naked eye. Evening stargazing programs are held here and in Bryce Canyon; the latter also hosts organized moonlit hikes.

Highway 12

10 No American vacation is complete without a road trip, and there's no stretch of Utah asphalt more compelling than Highway 12 (p155). Stretching from Capitol Reef in the northeast to Bryce and Red Rock Canyon in the west, this byway traverses 124 remote miles, passing desert slickrock, colossal domes, photogenic buttes and cool forests of aspen and fir. Take a 4WD detour along Burr Trail Road, stop in Boulder for a bite at Hell's Backbone Grill, and remember to take it slow as you traverse razor-thin Hogback Ridge.

Climbing

11 There's no sport quite like rock climbing (p32). From a distance it appears to be a feat of strength, but balance, creativity, technical know-how and a Zen-like cool are all parts of the game. Clinging by your fingertips 1000ft up on one of Zion's internationally renowned big walls? Not the place to lose your cool. Experts dream of tackling the cracks at Indian Creek or the desert towers of Castle Valley, while beginners can get in on the action via a guided climb, learning the basics outside Moab or Springdale.

Climbing at Indian Creek (p216)

Views

12 Every park has its superlative viewpoints: the Canyonlands alone could form its very own top 10 list, Goblin Valley's surreal formations enchant those in the know, while few places can match the majesty or contrasting colors of Zion. If you had to pick just one spot for photography, however, the Wave (p160) – a mesmerizing swirl of red and white layers, seeming to ripple across the slickrock with all the sensuousness of flowing water – might be the winner, encapsulating all that is visually sublime in canyon country.

The Wave (p160)

JOHN & LISA MERRILL/GETTY IMAGES ©

JMWSCOUT/GETTY IMAGES ©

Hanging Gardens

13 If a mere five minutes in the Utah sun has you feeling as shriveled up as a raisin, you're going to find these lush desert oases all the more remarkable. Fed by mesa-top precipitation that has slowly percolated down through Navajo sandstone over millennia, these vertical gardens appear where dripping seeps exit shaded canyon walls, forced outward by a layer of harder Kayenta rock. Look for scarlet monkey flowers, mosses, golden columbines, maidenhair ferns and purple violets clinging marvelously to the rock face. Zion (p46) has some particularly lovely examples.
The Narrows (p58)

Rafting

14 Once the mercury starts to rise, nothing beats a fun day on the water to stay cool. And lucky for you, epic river trips (p213) abound outside Moab. If you're just looking for a lazy float, rent a canoe or kayak on the Green River. Ready to dial up the excitement a notch? The Colorado River's Westwater Canyon could be your go-to choice. The pick of the bunch, however, has to be a multiday trip through the Canyonlands to legendary Cataract Canyon, the hardest stretch of whitewater in Utah.
Rafting the Colorado River (p215)

Horseback Riding

15 What, come out West and not ride a horse? Saddle up, pardner! Several outfitters can get you on horseback (p135) for rides in Red Canyon, a former Wild West hideout of Butch Cassidy, while another takes you down into Bryce Canyon's hoodoo country. Grand Staircase–Escalante and Capitol Reef are other options with superb scenery. Nor will Moab outfitters and ranches disappoint; they can take you into the desert or the La Sal Mountains, and some run trips that combine horseback riding with river running – not at the same time, naturally. Bryce Canyon (p124)

Need to Know

For more information, see Survival Guide (p257)

Entrance Fees
Zion $35 per car; Bryce Canyon $35 per car; Arches $30

Number of Visitors
Zion 4.3 million; Bryce Canyon 2.6 million; Arches 1.5 million

Year Founded
Zion 1909; Bryce Canyon 1923; Arches 1929

Money
Bring cash. ATMs in Springdale and Zion Lodge (Zion); Panguitch, Bryce Canyon City (Bryce Canyon); Torrey (Capitol Reef); Moab (Arches).

Cell Phones
Minimal to nonexistent cell-phone coverage throughout most parks.

Driving
Zion: shuttle bus only in the main canyon; parking limited. Bryce: shuttle bus (free); parking limited for RVs. Arches: parking limited.

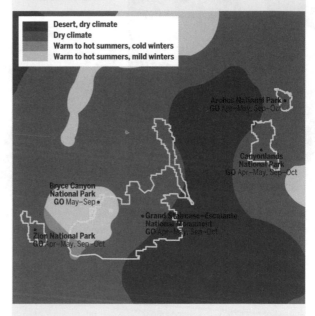

When to Go

Desert, dry climate
Dry climate
Warm to hot summers, cold winters
Warm to hot summers, mild winters

Arches National Park
GO Apr–May, Sep–Oct

Canyonlands National Park
GO Apr–May, Sep–Oct

Bryce Canyon National Park
GO May–Sep

Grand Staircase–Escalante National Monument
GO Apr–May, Sep–Oct

Zion National Park
GO Apr–May, Sep–Oct

High Season (May–Aug)

➡ Summer temperatures can soar above 100°F (38°C) and park traffic is at maximum capacity.

➡ July and August afternoon thunderstorms bring relief, but also create flash floods.

Shoulder (Mar & Apr, Sep–Nov)

➡ Spring is pleasant but unpredictable. At higher elevations, snow can linger into May or June.

➡ Fall is ideal: September is still hot, but days are clear, rivers remain warm and leaves begin to change.

Low Season (Dec–Feb)

➡ Businesses have shorter hours or close altogether, but the peace and quiet make it a great time to visit.

➡ Winters are generally mild at low elevations; expect snow and road closures at higher elevations.

Useful Websites

All Trails (www.alltrails.com) Great website and app for all of Utah's major trails.

CUSA (www.canyoneeringusa. com) Excellent resource for Utah canyoneering routes.

Lonely Planet (www.lonely planet.com/usa/southwest/ utah) Destination information, hotel bookings, traveler forum and more.

U.S. Forest Service (www. fs.fed.us) Tips for visiting the many forest service areas that offer great hiking and mountain biking.

Utah.com (www.utah.com) Utah's Office of Tourism; lots of free info.

Utah Mountain Biking (www. utahmountainbiking.com) Great tips and trails across the state.

Important Numbers

Emergency	☑911
Country code	☑1
International access code	☑011
Road conditions	☑511
Directory assistance	☑411

Exchange Rates

Australia	A$1	$0.76
Canada	C$1	$0.77
Europe	€1	$1.17
Japan	¥100	$0.91
Mexico	10 pesos	$0.49
New Zealand	NZ$1	$0.70
UK	£1	$1.34

For current exchange rates see www.xe.com.

Daily Costs

**Budget:
Less than $100**

➡ Tent or RV camping: $15–40

➡ Self-catering, cafe meals: $15–25

➡ Gas and entrance fees: $15–25

➡ Economy car rental: $30

**Midrange:
$100–$250**

➡ Mom-and-pop hotels, budget chains: $50–150

➡ Diners, local restaurants: $25–50

➡ Gas, entrance fees: $15–30

➡ Half-day hard-tail mountain bike rental: $25

➡ Standard car rental: $45

**Top End:
More than $250**

➡ Upscale hotels, B&Bs: from $150

➡ Upscale restaurants: $50–75

➡ Gas, entrance fees: $15–30

➡ Full-day full-suspension mountain bike rental: $75

➡ Guided horseback trail ride: $65–90

➡ SUV rental: $60

Opening Dates

All of Utah's national parks are open year-round, 24 hours a day. In winter, some roads will be impassable and some services reduced or closed. Most camp-sites are open year-round.

Park Policies & Regulations

Bicycles Generally permitted on park roads, but not on trails.

Campfires You may not gather wood in the park; campfires only permitted in designated sites;

when fire danger is high, no campfires permitted anywhere.

Driving Unless otherwise posted, the maximum speed limit in parks is 35mph.

Pets Generally not permitted on trails, in the backcountry or in park buildings.

Trail Etiquette & Safety Stay on the trail and do not take shortcuts. Do not throw rocks. Take only pictures and leave only footprints.

Wildlife & Cultural Artifacts Feeding wildlife is prohibited, as is touching or defacing cultural artifacts and sites.

Getting Around

Most travelers to Utah arrive by air or car. Major airports include Las Vegas and Salt Lake City; Denver and Phoenix are manageable but further away. Commercial service in Moab is starting up.

Car & RV Traveling with your own vehicle is the easiest and most rewarding way to explore the national parks. Car and RV rental is best in large cities such as Las Vegas or Salt Lake.

Bus Signing on to a bus tour such as Adventure Bus or Green Tortoise is the next best option. Greyhound serves several towns and cities in the state, but there is no public transportation to any national park in Utah.

Train Amtrak operates two major routes through the area (Chicago–San Francisco/Los Angeles). Use them to reach the region, but not for touring.

Shuttle A handful of private shuttles connect parks with large towns, such as St George–Zion.

For much more on **getting around**, see p268

PLAN YOUR TRIP NEED TO KNOW

If You Like...

Hiking

A wonderland of soaring red sandstone cliffs, surreal hoodoos and 240 million years of geological history on display, Utah is a paradise for hikers, whether you're a hardcore peak-bagger or just enjoy a casual daywalk.

Angels Landing Zion's iconic ascent – with chains and precipitous drop-offs – was cut into the cliffs in 1926. (p54)

Fiery Furnace Tour the third level of hell in this devilish maze of rock and stone. (p200)

The Narrows An incredible in-the-river experience, hiking and wading 16 miles down Zion's most impressive canyon. (p58)

Fairyland Loop Explore a pastel dream of towering hoodoos and martian landscapes on this challenging day hike. (p114)

Chesler Park Head into Utah's wilderness for a long tromp past desert wonderment on this Canyonlands National Park fave. (p188)

West Rim Two-day backpacking trip from high plateaus to Zion's canyon floor, with solitude and big views. (p55)

Hickman Bridge Cruise up from Capitol Reef's Fremont River to this gorgeous natural bridge. (p166)

Mountain Biking

The scenic slickrock playground outside Moab turned Utah into a mountain-biking hub decades ago.

Slickrock This moonscape ride near Moab is a roller-coaster of descents, curves and lung-busting cliffside climbs. (p20)

The Whole Enchilada Combine rides for an all-in-one descent to some of Moab's most distinctive riding features. (p207)

White Rim Road Go multiday on one of the continent's best mountain bike tours. (p191)

Gooseberry Mesa Technical slickrock fun with views back toward Zion. (p83)

Thunder Mountain Trail For great red canyon riding try this buffed-out trail just outside Bryce. (p134)

Scenic Drives

As amazing as Utah's national parks are, sometimes it's the drive between them you remember most.

Hwy 12 Utah's most stunning stretch of highway wends through canyons, desert slickrock and alpine forest. (p155)

White Rim Road Take on one of America's most iconic 4WD adventures. (p191)

Arches Scenic Drive Cruise through Arches for views of balanced rocks, delicate arches and the La Sal Mountains. (p204)

Cathedral Valley Loop Bump along Capitol Reef's desolate backcountry loop. (p173)

Hwy 14 The back road from Bryce to Zion climbs to 10,000ft, passing Cedar Breaks National Monument. (p97)

Colorado River Scenic Byway Follow the serpentine route of the Colorado River, stopping for hikes near the Fisher Towers. (p211)

Bryce Canyon Scenic Drive Travel by bike or shuttle for amazing views of the Bryce Amphitheater. (p122)

Canyoneering & Climbing

Squeezing your way through the twists and turns of a dark slot canyon or ascending a sheer, multipitch spire are just some of the ways to gain a new perspective on the planet.

The Subway Swim and rappel your way to one of Zion's most impressive geological formations. (p47)

Keyhole An excellent beginner's canyon in Zion, with thrills, watery chills and the occasional spill. (p71)

Dry Fork Slot Canyons Explore sandstone slot canyons for a taste of exquisitely sculpted landscape in remote Grand Staircase–Escalante. (p145)

Cohab Canyon Ascend Capitol Reef's Waterpocket Fold for secret slot canyons and amazing views. (p167)

Castle Valley Challenge your way up Castleton and other iconic towers outside of Moab. (p206)

Indian Creek The world's best crack climbing tests you with vertical lines in a sea of sandstone. (p216)

The Maze Go beyond the tourist track in the Canyonlands' forsaken district. (p193)

San Rafael Swell Don't get lost in the million and one slot canyons ripping through this reef-like rise. (p177)

Dramatic Views

Southern Utah is an unfurling tableau of sweeping panoramas that will defy your camera's wide-angled lens.

Observation Point Intensely rewarding hike to the top of Zion Canyon's cliffs, looking out over Angels Landing. (p57)

Grand View Point Take in the immensity of the Colorado Plateau at this Canyonland's overlook. (p186)

Landscape Arch Hike far into the backcountry for mind-blowing photo ops at this long-spanning sandstone arch. (p200)

Dead Horse Point State Park Revel in the best views of the Colorado River, like, ever. (p192)

Bryce Canyon Rim Trail No need to climb – the flat rim trail provides views of hoodoos and bristlecone forests. (p117)

Top: Dry Fork Slot Canyon (p145)

Bottom: Dead Horse Point State Park (p192)

Timber Creek Overlook Take in 270-degree views of finger canyons, plateaus, knobby buttes and Arizona on the horizon. (p67)

Cedar Breaks National Monument Wildly eroded natural amphitheater where sculpted cliffs and hoodoos glow like neon tie-dye. (p98)

Cycling

If you prefer a smooth, fast ride or just want to have some two-wheeled fun on a cruiser, try out these classics.

Zion Canyon Shuttle your bike up to the Temple of Sinawava and coast back amid spectacular scenery. (p71)

Red Canyon to Bryce Canyon Link two gorgeous parks with fiery hues of sculpted sandstone on this dedicated bike path. (p135)

Capitol Reef Head along the scenic drive for cool river views and plenty of sunshine. (p40)

Snow Canyon State Park Cycle from St George through red-rock scenery out to this gem of a park. (p94)

Water Adventures

The desert may be arid, but water plays a critical role in shaping the landscape here. Ride the rapids or float along in an inner tube while contemplating its importance.

Green River Look to the sky as you paddle flatwater stretches of the Green River. (p213)

Cataract Canyon Rip through class IV and V rapids on one of America's hallmark stretches of white water. (p206)

Lower Calf Creek Swim in the emerald pool beneath this ribbon-like cascade. (p138)

Willis Creek A great family-friendly slot hike that follows a flowing creek – wear water shoes or sandals. (p138)

Virgin River Grab an inner tube to beat the summer heat with a float downstream in Springdale. (p83)

Pool Parties Vegas pool clubs are just another example of Sin City–style decadence. (p99)

Film Locations

From glowing red buttes to scrubby desert plains to the twinkling lights of Vegas, the landscape glows with undeniable cinematic appeal.

Kanab John Wayne, Clint Eastwood and Charlton Heston have all appeared against this classic Western backdrop. (p157)

Las Vegas Sin City dominates the big screen in mainstream hits like *The Hangover* and *Ocean's Eleven*. (p99)

Grafton The ghost town location of the bicycle scene in *Butch Cassidy and the Sundance Kid*. (p83)

Moab & Around *Thelma & Louise* and *127 Hours* have dramatic scenes from Canyonlands and Dead Horse Point. (p206)

Moab Museum of Film & Western Heritage Discover the story lines that have made

this area a cinematographer's dream. (p207)

Wildlife

With the exception of scurrying lizards, wildlife in the desert tends to be fairly secretive, particularly during the blazing midday heat of summer. That said, if you look closely enough, you can find some unique creatures.

California Condors Biologists recently confirmed a condor couple was raising a chick in a Zion nest, the first-ever documented occurrence in Utah. The condor is the nation's largest bird. (p250)

Desert Tortoises A desert tortoise can live for up to 80 years and go for a year without drinking. They live in the Mojave Desert, which intersects with the Colorado Plateau at Zion. (p56)

Bighorn Sheep Depicted in rock art throughout the centuries, herds of bighorn sheep still inhabit the rocky terrain of the Canyonlands and Capitol Reef. (p245)

Gila Monsters & Roadrunners Some unusual inhabitants rule the roost in sandy Snow Canyon State Park. (p94)

Apex Predators There are some top-of-the-food-chain animals here too, including mountain lions and bears. (p245)

Month by Month

January

January is particularly slow and much of the tourism infrastructure surrounding the parks shuts down, but for nature lovers the peace and quiet can make for a fabulous visit.

☆ Sundance Film Festival

It may not be in southern Utah, but this is nonetheless the state's most famous event. Aspiring filmmakers, actors and half of Hollywood gather for a week of cutting-edge film in Park City.

🏃 Winter Bird Festival

Bird-lovers gather for three days in St George for walks, informative lectures and fun children's activities at the Winter Bird Festival (www.stgeorgebirdfest. com).

February

Lovers of snow and winter sports should check out high-altitude destinations such as Bryce Canyon, Cedar Breaks and the Brian Head ski resort.

🏃 Bryce Canyon Winterfest

Cross-country ski tours, ski archery, snowshoe races and lots of other snow-based activities and clinics. Held over President's Day weekend in mid-February. (p125)

March

March is spring-break season in the US. Hordes of college students and families with young kids are out exploring the Southwest's national parks. This can be a surprisingly busy time; reserve accommodation and be prepared for unpredictable weather.

🏃 Skinny Tire Festival

Four days of great cycling trips outside Moab in early March. Ride through Arches, along the Colorado River and to Dead Horse Point and back. (p217)

🏃 Jeep Safari

The week before Easter, about 2000 Jeeps and thousands more people overrun the town in the year's biggest event. Register early; trails are assigned. (p217)

April

The weather starts to warm up, but is still hard to gauge with wind, rain and snow alternating with wonderfully pleasant sunny days hitting temperatures in the 70s and 80s (over 21°C). Budding cottonwoods and blooming flowers brighten the landscape.

👁 Wildflower Viewing

Depending on rainfall and elevation, spring (April and May) is wildflower season in the desert. Check www. desertusa.com for wildflower bloom reports at your favorite national and state parks.

May

Summer gets started early in the desert, making this the beginning of the high season. Rafting and biking season swings into full gear.

✵ Moab Arts Festival

Held on Memorial Day Weekend, the Moab Arts Festival at Swanny City Park brings together fine artists with plenty of food vendors and music acts.

June

School's out for the summer! High season for road-tripping families is beginning and the blistering desert heat index is gradually inching up toward seasonal highs.

☆ Utah Shakespearean Festival

The play's the thing in Cedar City, where visitors can enjoy a dramatic Shakesperience, with Tony Award–winning performances, literary seminars and educational backstage tours from late June to September. (p95)

✵ Bryce Canyon Astronomy Festival

Some 7500 stars are visible to the naked eye at Bryce, and even more are on display during this festival when the Salt Lake Astronomical Society breaks out some huge telescopes. (p125)

July

Summer's in full swing with annual July 4 barbecues across the country. Despite 100+°F temperatures (over 38°C), it's one of the busiest months for most Utah parks. Beat the heat by scheduling activities for the early morning or late afternoon, or head to higher elevations.

✵ Independence Day

Cities and towns across the region celebrate America's birth on July 4.

🏃 Bryce Canyon Half Marathon

A wildly popular distance run that goes through the park, starting at Ruby's Inn and ending in Cannonville (www.brycecanyonhalf-marathon.com).

☆ Neil Simon Festival

American plays staged mid-July to mid-August (www.simonfest.org) in Utah's festival town, Cedar City.

🏃 GeoFest

Join Bryce Canyon park rangers for a weekend of guided hikes, family-friendly geology programs, bus tours with a geologist, evening programs and other activities. (p125)

August

Hotels and campgrounds are booked up and it's still off-the-thermometer hot, although afternoon thunderstorms bring some relief – as well as flash floods.

✵ Western Legends Roundup

Kanab lives for the annual Western Legends Roundup (www.westernlegends roundup.com) in late August. There are concerts, gunfights, cowboy poetry, dances, quilt shows, a film festival and more. Take a bus tour to all the film sites, or sign up for a Dutch-oven cooking lesson.

✵ Garfield County Fair

This Garfield County Fair in Panguitch hosts live bands and features parades, classic car shows, barbecues, livestock sales and rodeos for an entire week. (p135)

September

It's back to school for the kids, which means crowds begin to lessen. Fall is a particularly nice time to visit – weather is slightly cooler though the water is still warm, making it a good time to explore river canyons.

✵ Dixie Roundup

St George's mid-September weekend is full of Western-themed fun, including a parade and rodeo (www.stgeorgelions.com).

☆ Moab Music Festival

Each September, world-class classical, traditional and jazz musicians converge on the red-rock landscape around Moab for spectacular open-air concerts (www.moab musicfest.org).

☆ Zion Canyon Music Festival

One weekend in late September is filled with an eclectic lineup of bands, with everything from flatpickers to alternative rock (http://zioncanyonmusicfestival.com).

October

Lingering warm weather and less traffic makes this a particularly nice month to visit. Look for golden aspens at higher elevations.

🏃 St George Marathon

This highly acclaimed marathon takes over the town of St George (www.stgeorgemarathon.com), attracting 7400 runners from all 50 states and some 20,000 spectators. The route is regularly rated one of the country's most scenic.

November

The low season is beginning and some hotels and restaurants have shuttered up for the winter. The long Thanksgiving weekend sees a final burst of visitors to the region's parks.

☆ Moab Folk Festival

Folk music and environmental consciousness combine. This November festival is 100% wind-powered, venues are easily walkable and recycling is encouraged (www.moabfolkfestival.com). Big-name singer-songwriters take top billing.

Top: Snowshoeing in Bryce Canyon National Park (p125)

Bottom: Wildflowers (p254), Zion National Park

Itineraries

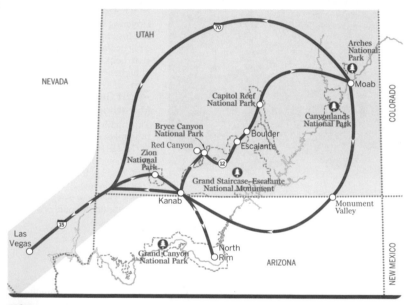

 Southern Utah's Parklands

See the best of Utah's parks, with possible detours to the Grand Canyon and Monument Valley.

Start off your trip with a bang in **Las Vegas**, but move on to **Zion National Park** by the second night so you can get an early start the next morning. See the highlights that day; the next morning hike Angels Landing and spend an afternoon in East Zion. Base yourself for the next two nights in **Kanab**, and detour for panoramic overlooks at the Grand Canyon's **North Rim**. Travel north to say hello to hoodoos in **Bryce Canyon National Park** and **Red Canyon**. Begin your drive down scenic **Hwy 12**, basing yourself in **Escalante** or **Boulder**, and squeeze through the slot canyons of **Grand Staircase–Escalante National Monument**. Continue down Hwy 12 to crack the geologists' code and go fruit-picking in the orchards of **Capitol Reef National Park**. Drive to **Moab** and spend three days in Arches, Canyonlands and on the mountain bike trails around town. It's a 6½-hour drive back to Vegas on the interstate or, if you want to take the scenic route, nine hours via cinematic **Monument Valley** in Arizona.

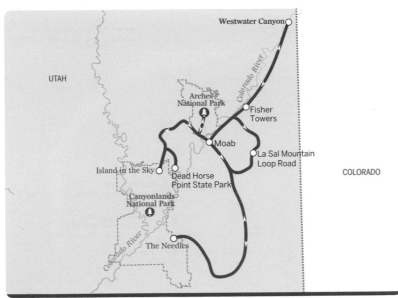

 ## A Week in Moab

Make the most of a week in the Moab area, visiting Arches and Canyonlands, interspersed with all the adventure sports for which the region is known.

On your first day visit **Arches National Park**, following our one-day itinerary. On your second day, load up with plenty of water and drive south to the Canyonlands' **Island in the Sky**, a 6000ft flat-topped mesa. Follow the Grand View Point Scenic Drive, picnic at the White Rim Overlook and try out some of the day hikes in the area. On the way back to Moab, stop at **Dead Horse Point State Park** (time it for sunset), taking in the spectacular views of the horseshoe bend of the Colorado River some 2000ft below.

Day three is devoted to the **Needles** area of the Canyonlands, named for the giant spires that rise from the desert. Hikes are longer here, and experienced backpackers will want to consider an overnight trip on the Chesler Park Loop (also doable in a long day). Devote day four to quintessential **Moab**: mountain biking. Good trails include Dead Horse Point for novices, Klondike Bluffs for intermediate riders and the famed Slickrock Trail for the hardcore who have already broken a bone or two. Scale back the adventure on day five and take a leisurely drive up into the aspens and firs of the high country on the **La Sal Mountain Loop Road**; picnic at Warner Lake. Alternatively, explore another of Moab's scenic byways, such as Potash Rd, where you'll find petroglyphs, dinosaur tracks and climbers.

Day six, get up early to take a full-day river trip; reserve well in advance to avoid disappointment. White-water lovers will gravitate toward **Westwater Canyon** (class III and IV). If you don't like navigating rapids, take a leisurely canoe, kayak or float along flatwater stretches. Also consider an overnight trip – this will give you a chance to experience the epic Cataract Canyon (class V) on a high-speed raft. On your last day, make it special and sign up for a canyoneering or rock-climbing trip out in the desert, or take a horseback ride in the La Sal Mountains.

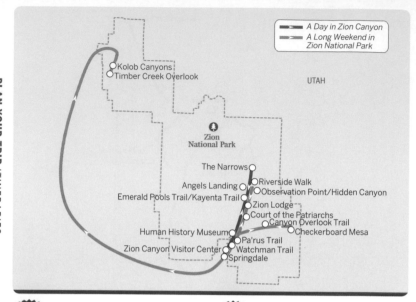

A Day in Zion Canyon

1 DAY

One day in Zion? It's not much, but a ride on the shuttle and a willingness to get your feet wet will give you a feel for this unique landscape.

Start early at the park's **visitor center** to get oriented and browse the introductory signage outside. Hop on the free shuttle, stopping off at Zion's **Human History Museum**. Ride the shuttle all the way up canyon to the Temple of Sinawava. Follow **Riverside Walk** and, if you're ready to get wet, plunge into the Virgin River and continue up the **Narrows** until your stomach begins to grumble. Picnic on the riverbank or catch the shuttle heading back down the canyon and have lunch beneath the giant cottonwood tree outside **Zion Lodge**. Hike the **Emerald Pools Trail** in combination with the quieter Kayenta Trail. Hop back on the shuttle, stopping at the **Court of the Patriarchs**. Hop off at Canyon Junction and follow the **Pa'rus Trail**, ideally around sunset. Alternatively, climb the peaceful hilltop **Watchman Trail**, which starts near the visitor center. Head back to **Springdale** for a hearty dinner and a peek at a gallery or two.

A Long Weekend in Zion National Park

3 DAYS

A long weekend is more like it: you'll be able to hit all the highlights as well as get off the beaten track.

On your first day, explore Zion Canyon, making time for the **Riverside Walk**, lunch by **Zion Lodge** and the **Emerald Pools Trail**.

Day two, get an early start on the hike up to **Angels Landing**, which will probably take most of the morning. Alternatively, try less-crowded hikes like **Observation Point** or **Hidden Canyon**. After a picnic with high-altitude views, return to your car and drive Hwy 9 through the Zion–Mt Carmel Tunnel to East Zion and Checkerboard Mesa. There's no end to the exploring here: go off trail and wander the slickrock, or hike the short but fun **Canyon Overlook Trail**. Return to **Springdale** for dinner.

On day three, sign up for a canyoneering trip, or head to the more remote **Kolob Canyons** up I-15. Explore the magnificent finger canyons, hiking up the Taylor Creek Middle Fork to an old cabin or two. Have lunch on the trail before continuing on to the magnificent **Timber Creek Overlook** at the end of the road.

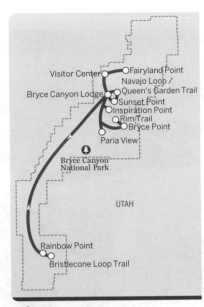

A Day in Bryce Canyon

Let your imagination run wild as you visit the planet's epicenter of hoodoos – unusual 'fairy chimneys' shaped by erosion. With a day to spare, tack on the Fairyland Loop hike or a visit to Mossy Cave.

See the free film and pick up information at the **visitor center**. Drive **Bryce Canyon Scenic Drive** all the way out to **Rainbow Point**. Hike the short **Bristlecone Loop Trail**, with its awesome vistas and ancient trees. Return along the Scenic Drive, stopping at the major sights along the way. Grab lunch at **Bryce Canyon Lodge** or snacks at the general store. Head to **Sunset Point** to glimpse the towering eroded hoodoos of Bryce Amphitheater. Descend into the canyon on the **Navajo Loop** and/or **Queen's Garden Trail**. Head down to **Inspiration Point** and **Bryce Point** by car or shuttle. Stroll along the **Rim Trail** and watch the light play on the hoodoos. Alternatively, drive to **Paria View** to watch the sunset. To really escape the crowds, detour out to serene, largely untrammeled **Fairyland Point**.

A Day in Arches National Park

Small in size but packed with over 2000 natural arches, this is a great park to explore, with plenty of opportunities to wander beyond the main sights for once-in-a-lifetime views of an enthralling geological process.

Get up early to beat the heat and stop at the **visitor center**. Take the park's **Scenic Drive**, which passes all the major sights. Walk among sandstone monoliths on the **Park Avenue Trail**, a highly trafficked trail best visited in the morning. Don't miss the viewpoint turnout where you can spy on the **Three Gossips**. Gawk at **Balanced Rock**, then stroll beneath natural arches off **Windows Road**. Pause for 360-degree views and a geology lesson at **Panorama Point**. Visit famous **Delicate Arch** at road's end; have a tailgate picnic afterward. With advance reservations, you can take a ranger-guided hike in the **Fiery Furnace**. With more energy to burn, hike to more arches from the **Devils Garden**. For solitude and sunsets, take Salt Valley Rd out to the **Klondike Bluffs**. Spend the evening eating, drinking, shopping and wandering around downtown **Moab**.

Zion National Park (p46)

Plan Your Trip
Activities

This is why you've come to Utah. Labyrinthine canyons, red rock spires, moonlit desert arches and slickrock playgrounds. It doesn't matter if you're a couch potato or hardcore thrill-seeker equipped with a GoPro. Grab a bike, rope or paddle, get out there and have fun.

Desert Etiquette

The desert is an exceedingly fragile environment, easily damaged by feet, tires and fires, and slow to heal.

Stay on the trail

Whether hiking, biking or driving, stay on the trail. If it's muddy, either be willing to get dirty or don't go – it's better than creating wider, braided trails.

If there is no trail

Stay on slickrock, gravel or sand; never step or ride on plants or cryptobiotic soil.

Pack it in, pack it out

Bring resealable plastic bags to contain trash and toilet paper.

Protect all water sources and riparian areas

Camp 200ft from any water, never wash yourself or dishes in creeks or springs and use minimal or no soap.

Backcountry fires

Usually prohibited.

Never touch artifacts

Don't move or take any cultural or archaeological artifacts.

Hiking & Backpacking

Hiking is the main and most accessible activity in the national parks and can be done at any time of year. Walks can be as short or long as you like, but remember this when planning: you need to be prepared. The wild desert may be unlike anything you have ever experienced, and designating certain parcels as 'national parks' has not tamed it.

The weather is extraordinary in its unpredictability and sheer force. The summer sun is blazing hot, sudden thunderstorms can drop enough water in 10 minutes to create deadly flash floods, and ferocious windstorms can rip or blow away your poorly staked tent all the way back to camp.

Number one on your packing checklist is water: a gallon (3.8L) of water per person per day is the recommended minimum in hot weather. Sun protection (hat, sunblock and sunglasses) is also vital. While the danger of dehydration and heat exhaustion is obvious enough, don't forget that violent downpours and strong winds can cause temperatures to quickly plummet. Always consider a waterproof shell and even a warm layer outside of summer.

After the elements, getting lost is the next major concern. Most day hikes are well signed and visitors are numerous, but nevertheless you should always take some sort of map. If you plan on going into the backcountry, definitely take a topographic (topo) map and a compass. You can pick up detailed maps in most visitor centers. All travelers, solo or not, should always remember the golden rule: let someone know where you are going and how long you plan to be gone.

When to Hike

Though southern Utah is a year-round destination, variations by location and season are extreme. As the majority of parks, monuments and other hiking destinations are in the desert, spring and fall are often the best times to hike. Summer – the height of tourist season – can be the worst, as temperatures routinely top 100°F. One smart summertime strategy is to hike the big canyons only very early or late in the day, planning your hike for the side that will be in shade.

Elevation also plays a factor. At over 8000ft, Bryce Canyon's rim stays a bit cooler, as do other spots in the mountains. However, in the fall certain roads and trails at higher elevations may be closed until April, May or even into June, and some canyon hikes are not safe in spring, when runoff from snowmelt can dangerously raise water levels. If you're planning on hiking the Narrows in Zion Canyon in April or May, for example, you'll need to check the river flow to ensure that levels are low enough.

Day Hikes

The majority of hikes in the region are day hikes, taking anywhere from 20 minutes to eight hours. On steep trails that lead from canyon floors to rims, or vice versa, a general guide is that it takes twice as long to ascend as to descend. For people who want to test themselves, or who don't have time for a full hike, it's always possible to tackle just the first few miles of a day or backcountry hike.

Backcountry Hikes

People can and do spend weeks hiking in the southern Utah desert, but it's something to build up to, once you get to know the place better. Backcountry hikes in the area lean toward the easier ones, usually involving one to three nights out. When you're ready for more, park rangers and local outfitters can help you find new challenges. In general, Zion, Bryce Canyon and Capitol Reef offer a good selection of easy to moderate backpacking trips, while Canyonlands and Grand Staircase–Escalante are famous for their difficulty.

The most important consideration on any backcountry hike is water. Will there be any on your route, and of what quality and quantity? Many blue squiggles marked on topo maps are not rivers at all, but washes, only flowing during a rainstorm or with spring runoff. Always check with rangers or knowledgeable locals before trekking into the unknown.

Scrambling the exposed ridgeline of Angels Landing (p54)

Canyoneering

Canyons can be secret, mystical destinations, with an eerie, unsettling beauty that sometimes gives the feeling that you're wandering the sacred ruins of an ancient civilization – although the smooth, scalloped walls and strange, sculpted dimples and pockmarks aren't the creations of any human culture, but the echoes of a much older visitor: water.

The thrill of squeezing yourself into a dark narrow slot, rappelling over the lip of a 70ft chute or swimming across a cold subterranean pool is obvious enough. The real question isn't whether or not you want to go, but rather what sort of experience you are looking for. For many people, a

nontechnical hike is a perfect intro, and if you're short on time or don't have the gear, a guided canyoneering trip or intro course may be the solution. For others, nothing short of full-on immersion will do.

For the latter group, a solid understanding of technical skills – how to tie knots, set up an anchor, use a rappelling device, unsnag a stuck rope and so on – is required but, unlike rock climbing, you don't need years of practice (though the recent flood of inexperienced canyoneers has been largely responsible for an increase in the number of rescues at Zion and elsewhere). Rappelling is a particularly easy way to put yourself into situations you may not be able to get out of, especially if you get hurt. Talk to any local guide, and they'll immediately tell you the number one rule of canyoneering: no jumping (this is in stark contrast to European canyoning). Jumping is among the leading causes of injury in the Utah wilderness.

Canyoneers must also be especially mindful of flash floods and high water levels (wet suits are required for some routes, regardless of the season). Being inside the cogs and wheels of Earth's geological

Hiking in Zion National Park (p50)

machinery is very cool – until they switch on. Always check the day's flash-flood forecast before you go out.

Canyoneering in Zion

Zion and its environs are the sport's epicenter in southern Utah – there are over 30 routes in the area. Before attempting any of the park's canyoneering routes unaided, take a basic skills course. If you need to rent equipment, such a course is obligatory for liability reasons. The most famous routes for beginners are the **Subway** and **Keyhole Canyon**. **Orderville Canyon** is another classic, which dumps you out in the Narrows. Canyoneers with more experience and the necessary technical skills can tackle **Mystery Canyon**, which also drops dramatically into the Virgin River. If you don't want to bother with the gear, explore **Hidden Canyon** or **Kanarra Canyon** instead.

Southern Utah's Other Canyons

You'll find more fantastic slot canyons along the Escalante River and Hole-in-the-Rock Rd in **Grand Staircase–Escalante National Monument**. Routes include canyons for all skill levels, with or without gear, but getting lost is fairly easy, so consider going with a guide. The Paria Canyon-Vermilion Cliffs Wilderness Area is another awesome place for experienced canyoneers to explore, whether you're looking for the premier 16-mile **Buckskin Gulch** challenge or an epic 38-mile backpacking adventure through **Paria Canyon** to Lee's Ferry, Arizona (permit required). Ask outfitters in Moab about more slot canyons in eastern Utah, including the wonderland of the **San Rafael Swell**, northwest of Moab off I-70, just west of the town of Green River.

Canyoneering Guides & Outfitters

In addition to recommended outfitters, the American Canyoneering Association (ACA; www.canyoneering.net) offers lots of information online, from technical forums and canyoneering primers to guide referrals. ACA also runs a multitude of certification courses across southern Utah.

For detailed route descriptions, browse CUSA (www.canyoneeringusa.com).

Canyoneering 1, 2 and *3* by Steve Allen are three top-notch guidebooks that cover southern Utah, particularly Grand Staircase–Escalante National Monument and the San Rafael Swell. *Zion: Canyoneering,* by Tom Jones, is an excellent guide to the Zion area.

Mountain Biking & Cycling

The fat-tire crowd already knows about Moab, a mountain-biking mecca for decades. The original **Slickrock Bike Trail** is there, among many others. If you're a novice rider, try the **Bar-M Loop**. For slickrock virgins who have mountain-biking experience, the **Klondike Bluffs Trail** awaits. When the summer sun is baking the desert lowlands, riders can escape to the cool forests of the La Sal Mountains outside town, where the **Moonlight Meadow Trail** is a high-altitude downhill challenge, or the flat single-track of the **Intrepid Trail** at Dead Horse Point State Park.

What mountain bikers might not know is that southwest Utah offers equally good trails in places outside St George and Zion, including at Gooseberry Mesa and Wire Mesa, and on national forest land in Red Canyon, west of Bryce Canyon. Even though mountain biking is prohibited on national park trails, it's permitted on dirt roads. In Canyonlands, Island in the Sky's **White Rim Rd** and the labyrinth of 4WD roads in the Maze are awesome

experiences, as is **Cathedral Valley Loop** in Capitol Reef and backcountry roads in Grand Staircase–Escalante. All mountain bikers should observe desert conservation guidelines, particularly rules about staying on trail.

Road cycling the paved scenic drives in Zion, Bryce Canyon and Capitol Reef is an excellent way to take in the parks' sights. The steeper, longer and more challenging paved roads in Arches and Canyonlands are best left for experienced cyclists in good shape. Recreational cycling paths are uncommon in southern Utah, with the notable exception of the St George area. The **Snow Canyon Loop** is the longest of the area trails (18 miles) connecting the town with the state park. Shorter paths are the Zion's **Pa'rus Trail** and the **Red Canyon Bike Path**, on USFS land outside Bryce Canyon.

You'll find outdoor outfitters and bicycle shops offering rentals and guided trips outside all of the national parks. If you want to rent a mountain bike, expect to pay $35 to $65 for a full day, plus $20 for a car rack or shuttle.

Rock Climbing

If Dr Seuss designed a rock-climbing playground, it would look a lot like this: a surreal landscape filled with enormous blobs, spires, soaring cliffs and canyon walls in kaleidoscopic colors. Some of the country's best rock climbing lies in southern Utah, though many routes are for moderate to expert climbers. Zion is famous for

---

EXTREME SPORTS

Need a thrill? Try these:

➡ Climb Prodigal Sun, Space Shot or one of Zion's other big walls.
➡ Through-hike the Subway in Zion.
➡ Raft Cataract Canyon on the Colorado River.
➡ Four-wheel drive Elephant Hill in Canyonlands' Needles district.
➡ Mountain bike Moab's Whole Enchilada Trail (p207).
➡ Backpack the Narrows of the Virgin River.
➡ Four-wheel drive the Cathedral Valley Loop in Capitol Reef.
➡ Canyoneer and backpack Buckskin Gulch (p161) in Paria Canyon.
➡ Skydive out of an airplane in Moab.

Top: Canyoneering near Moab (p206)

Bottom: Rafting the Green River (p213)

big-wall climbs, while the St George area, particularly Snow Canyon State Park, offers dozens of shorter bolted sport routes. You'll find great climbing in Arches, Canyonlands and Capitol Reef, although restrictions apply. Several popular routes for all abilities await near Moab: Indian Creek is known for its premier sandstone cracks, while Castleton and other desert towers offer superb multipitch adventure. Outdoor outfitters in Moab and Springdale offer rock-climbing classes for beginners and sell climbing gear.

Climbing in summer can get exceptionally hot. When the air temperature reaches 100°F, the cliff face could top 115°F, and the rocks hold the heat all night. Spring, fall and even winter are better times to climb; if you do climb in summer, start early in the morning. Some parks enforce seasonal route closures to protect nesting or breeding wildlife. All parks prohibit power drills, discourage excess bolting and ask climbers to use subdued colors for hangers and slings. Ask at park visitor centers about the latest regulations and

TIPS FOR SHUTTERBUGS

Nothing is more disappointing than coming home from the desert and uploading your digital photos or getting your rolls of film developed to find dozens, if not hundreds of washed-out horizons, with tiny friends and family squint-smiling in the distance.

You're not alone. Even the best photographers can't get the whole desert in their pictures. But you can improve the quality and composition of your photos, whether your camera is a top-shelf digital masterpiece or a disposable throwaway.

➡ If you have a digital camera, bring extra batteries and a charger; the instant gratification of your LCD preview screen will run the battery down fast.

➡ For print film, use 100 ASA film for all but the lowest light situations; it's the slowest film and will enhance resolution. Color slide film is the best, though it's more expensive.

➡ A zoom lens is extremely useful; most SLR cameras have one. Use it to isolate the central subject of your photos. A common composition mistake is to include too much landscape around the person or feature that's your main focus. Sacrifice background for foreground, and your photos will be more dramatic and interesting.

➡ Morning and evening are the best times to shoot. The same sandstone bluff can turn four or five different hues throughout the day, and the warmest hues will be at sunset. Because of the way a camera reads color (as grays), underexposing the shot slightly (by a half-stop or more) can bring out richer details in red tones.

➡ When shooting red rocks, a warming filter added to an SLR lens can enhance the colors of the rocks and reduce the blues of overcast or flat-light days. You can achieve the same affect on any digital camera by adjusting the white balance to the automatic 'cloudy' setting (or by reducing the color temperature).

➡ As a rule, don't shoot into the sun or include it in the frame; shoot what the sunlight is hitting. This is especially important when photographing people, who will turn into blackened silhouettes with the sun behind them. On bright days, move your subjects into shade for close-up portraits.

➡ A tripod is useful for low-exposure dusk shots but is cumbersome on hikes.

➡ Some digital cameras have waterproof cases that are worth the investment for canyoneers and river runners.

➡ That endless horizon? Move people out of the way and shoot it at sunset's last gasp. Check the weather report for sunset times, as well as when the moon rises. If you're traveling during a full moon, it can be fairly easy to arrange yourself in front of an iconic arch at dusk for that million-dollar shot.

For an in-depth regional photography guide, *Photographing the Southwest, Volume 1: Southern Utah* by Laurent Martres will take you around the national parks and off the beaten path.

Mountain biking near Moab (p207)

permits, which are usually required for overnight bivouacs. Even if you don't need a permit, stop by Zion's backcountry desk, where the rangers and volunteers are often climbers themselves, full of great local tips and advice.

Horseback Riding & Pack Trips

Canyon Trail Rides runs horseback and mule rides at Zion (p72), Bryce Canyon (p124) and the Grand Canyon's North Rim. One- and two-hour rides and half-day trips cost from $45 to $90 per person. Some rides are offered year-round, although the famous Grand Canyon trips are only available from mid-May to mid-October. You'll need to make reservations in advance in high season. Children must be at least seven years old for two-hour rides, and at least 10 for half-day rides. The weight limit is 220 pounds per rider fully dressed.

Several outfitters can get you on horseback for rides in Red Canyon, in the Dixie National Forest west of Bryce Canyon, as well as around Capitol Reef and into Grand Staircase–Escalante starting from Boulder and Kanab. Moab outfitters and ranches will take you into either the desert or the La Sal Mountains.

Red Rock Ride (☑435-679-8665; www.red rockride.com) offers week-long all-inclusive guided horseback trips visiting Zion, Bryce Canyon and the Grand Canyon's North Rim, Red Canyon in the Dixie National Forest and Paria Canyon in Grand Staircase–Escalante National Monument. Trips usually depart in spring and fall.

Water Sports
Rafting & Kayaking

Folks with white-water fantasies should head directly to Moab. The main rafting season runs from April to September (jet-boating season lasts longer), with peak water flow usually occurring in May and June. Whatever your skill level, outfitters in Moab stand ready to provide everything you might need, from rental equipment, permits and shuttles to guided tours and lessons.

Moab offers a number of river trips, from family-friendly floats and mellow flatwater canoe trips to daredevil rapid-rafting and jet-boating tours. For the calmest trips, rent equipment and paddle the upper portion of the Green River through **Labyrinth Canyon**, starting from the town of Green River, or the **Daily**, aka Fisher Towers, a section of the Colorado River alongside Hwy 128.

More adventurous trips through Canyonlands National Park require a permit, and the easiest way to get one is to join a guided trip. **Stillwater Canyon** is a calm section of Green River that allows you to float through the park. Just past the confluence of the Green and Colorado is **Cataract Canyon**, the region's ultimate challenge when it comes to technical white water.

For a shorter white-water rafting excursion, try **Westwater Canyon** for a one-day trip.

Swimming & Tubing

Zion's **Virgin River** is the best option for swimming. While generally shallow and cold, it does offer lots of swimming holes and warms up just enough later in summer to enjoy a dip. Tubing is prohibited within the park, but outfitters in Springdale rent inner tubes for local floats in summer, unless water levels are too low. You'll find more summer swimming holes along creeks in **Capitol Reef**, as well as at **Calf Creek Recreation Area**, where families can splash around and take a break from Grand Staircase–Escalante's dusty 4WD tracks.

Rappelling, Zion National Park (p46)

Fishing

Utah is an anglers' paradise, offering scads of mountain lakes and rivers and oodles of stocked reservoirs; unfortunately, not too many options exist in southern Utah, and the national parks are awful for fishing. C'mon, what'd you expect? It's a desert.

The mountains surrounding Zion harbor several good reservoirs stocked mostly with trout, including **Kolob Reservoir**,

---

COOL ESCAPES

It's the desert – you know it's gonna be hot. To beat the heat, escape to the following:

➡ Swimming holes on the Virgin River

➡ The Narrows of Zion Canyon

➡ High-elevation Cedar Breaks National Monument

➡ Pine Valley Mountains outside St George

➡ Calf Creek Recreation Area, especially Lower Calf Creek Falls

➡ Creeks winding through Capitol Reef National Park

➡ The shady pioneer-planted orchards of Fruita, in Capitol Reef National Park

➡ Moab's lofty La Sal Mountains

➡ Lazy float trips or white-water rafting near Moab

Exploring the Subway (p64), Zion National Park

off Kolob Terrace Rd; **Navajo Lake** and **Duck Creek** on Hwy 14, between Cedar City and Bryce Canyon; the reservoir in the **Pine Valley Mountains**, outside St George; and **Panguitch Lake**, between Panguitch and Cedar Breaks National Monument, in the Dixie National Forest. Off Hwy 12 north of Boulder, **Boulder Mountain** is a popular fly-fishing destination; you'll find outfitters in Torrey. Near Moab, the La Sal Mountains (p209) have a few good trout-fishing lakes, while fly fishers can cast lines into small Mill Creek, which runs out of the mountains.

Wherever you fish, including in the national parks, you'll need a Utah fishing license. Be sure to familiarize yourself with each fishing spot's particular restrictions. These vary and can be strict, limiting the type of bait or lure and the catch, sometimes to only one fish. Seasonal restrictions may also apply. All park visitor centers and public lands information offices in southern Utah should have the fishing information you'll need, including local regulations.

Contact the Utah Division of Wildlife Resources (DWR; https://wildlife.utah.gov) for up-to-date fishing regulations, including the state's annual fishing guidebook, available online as a free downloadable PDF. A resident/nonresident Utah fishing license costs $16/24 for three days and $20/40 for seven days. Children under the age of 12 do not need a fishing license, although they must still obey all regulations. Licenses may be bought online or over the phone directly from DWR, or from local businesses near busy fishing spots.

Four-wheel Driving

Southern Utah boasts dirt roads aplenty and a 4WD vehicle is useful on all of them. The region also has many dirt roads – some of which are legendary – that are only manageable via 4WD. Yet if there's one thing that can get the inexperienced into trouble faster than a static canyoneering rope, it's a 4WD vehicle. A rental 4WD is not a magic bullet; sometimes it's just a means for getting as far away from help as possible.

Before heading into the desert, know the capabilities of your vehicle. If you don't have the winches and experience to free

Four-wheel drive trail in the Needles (p192), Canyonlands National Park

a stuck vehicle, don't take chances on unknown roads. And before heading out, get current road and weather conditions from visitor centers and public lands information offices. GPS is delightful, but it's useless in a muddy wash with a storm coming. Expect that 4WD roads may be muddy and inaccessible for at least a day or two after even light rains, so wait until the road thoroughly dries out to tackle it. In winter, many 4WD roads in southern Utah may be impassable. If you've never driven back roads in Utah before, consider taking a guided tour first – it's a good reality check.

Remember, nothing ruins the desert's fragile cryptobiotic soil – which holds the entire ecosystem together – faster than car tires, and a single off-road joyride leaves harmful scars that can last decades.

Winter Sports

Several spots offer cross-country skiing and snowshoeing. Among the most popular is Bryce Canyon, which features 10 miles of cross-country trails atop the canyon's rim, plus 20 additional miles in the surrounding Dixie National Forest. During winter, park rangers offer guided snowshoe hikes, with free snowshoes loaned to participants. Otherwise, you can rent snowshoes and skis at Ruby's Inn, which also offers winter sleigh and horseback rides and snowmobiling tours outside the park. For the most fun in the snow, show up for the Bryce Canyon Winterfest, held annually in mid-February, featuring outdoor sports clinics, tours, ski races and competitions, as well as snow sculptures and sledding.

If you have your own skis, cross-country skiing is popular in the mountains east of Cedar City along Hwy 14, particularly the scenic amphitheater rim at Cedar Breaks, where a volunteer-staffed seasonal yurt lets you warm up with a cup of hot cocoa.

The La Sal Mountains outside Moab feature great snowshoeing and cross-country skiing and even a hut-to-hut system. Outdoor outfitters in Moab rent equipment, sell maps and cold-weather gear, and can arrange self-guided overnight trips.

Plan Your Trip
Travel with Children

Southern Utah's national parks feature inconceivable landscapes that seem like one ginormous playground, with wild rock formations to clamber upon, canyons to squeeze into, creeks to splash in and a variable level of adventure that can be easily tailored to every family's needs.

National Parks for Kids

The desert can be a magical experience, though expect it to be relatively physical and hands-on. Make sure to budget for some special activities – canyoneering, horseback riding, rafting and the like – in order to break up the time spent driving, posing for family photos at scenic viewpoints and (not again!) hiking.

Parents will often find themselves trying to balance risk and reward: how much room should you be giving your children to climb around and explore this amazing place, and when should you be stepping in to ensure their safety? Planning a ranger-led walk or a guided activity early on in your trip can be a good opportunity for kids to learn responsible behavior from a local expert, rather than the in-one-ear-out-the-other warnings of Mom or Dad.

Junior Ranger Programs

All of southern Utah's national parks offer **junior ranger programs** (www.nps.gov/learn), which focus on do-it-yourself activity books that kids can complete to get a special certificate and the all-important junior ranger badge. Of course, there's no age limit, and even adults can learn something and have fun doing the activities

Best Regions for Kids

Zion
Particularly good for families, with free shuttle buses, great ranger programs, river access and all levels of hikes and adrenaline-piqued activities.

Moab
Moab is awash in things to do: mountain biking, lazy river floats, white-water rafting and guided rock climbing. Arches is fabulous for families while Canyonlands appeals to adventure-loving teens.

Bryce
Kids will love finding resemblances in the hoodoos; a free park shuttle makes navigation hassle-free. There are also astronomy programs, guided full-moon hikes and horseback rides.

Grand Staircase–Escalante
Rugged Escalante is best for teens with outdoors experience, though adventurous youngsters will also enjoy squeezing through slots.

Capitol Reef
Earn a junior geologist badge at the Ripple Rock Nature Center, then visit pick-your-own-fruit orchards.

DEHYDRATION

One important thing to remember is that children are particularly vulnerable to the heat: they dehydrate faster, and symptoms can turn severe more quickly. Make sure they drink plenty of water at regular intervals. To keep salts from being flushed out of the body when it is particularly hot, add a pinch of sea salt or electrolyte powder to drinking water. A wide-brimmed hat, sunglasses and sunscreen are absolutely essential.

with their kids. For younger children, easier activity sheets may be available.

Most parks have free ranger-led educational activities and short walks during the peak season. Zion, for example, features such talks as Amazing Animals, Wild Waters, Eco Explorers, Gigantic Geology and even Music Makers. Evening family programs, scheduled after dinner, are usually a hit.

Also look for nature centers. In summer, Zion offers a drop-off junior ranger program at the Zion Nature Center, where children join instructor-led activities, hikes and games. Capitol Reef has its own Ripple Rock Nature Center (p174), which hosts ranger-led programs for kids; borrow a free activity backpack for families here or at the park's main visitor center. Canyonlands also lets families borrow activity-based 'Explorer Packs.'

Children's Highlights

Hiking

➡ **Zion** (p46) Easy destinations include the hanging gardens of Emerald Pools and Riverside Walk. More challenging walks include the Narrows, Hidden Canyon and the famously exposed climb up to Angels Landing.

➡ **Bryce Canyon** (p110) Descend into the canyon on Queen's Garden Trail.

➡ **Grand Staircase–Escalante National Monument** (p138) Better suited for older kids; hike to Lower Calf Creek Falls or try squeezing into the slot canyons on Willis Creek.

➡ **Capitol Reef** (p162) Spot petroglyphs along Capitol Gorge and pass giant domes and a towering arch at Hickman Bridge.

➡ **Goblin Valley State Park** (p177) Melted rock formations turn into goblins before your eyes.

➡ **Canyonlands** (p178) Pass an abandoned cowboy camp at Cave Spring or watch for passing condors at Grand View Point.

➡ **Arches** (p196) Most of the classic hikes here are family friendly, including Landscape Arch, Delicate Arch and Sand Dune & Broken Arches.

Cycling & Mountain Biking

You can rent bikes and car racks in several park gateway towns.

➡ **Zion Canyon Scenic Drive** (p68) A fun bike ride in reverse; whenever you get tired, just hop on the park shuttle (maximum two bicycles per bus).

➡ **Pa'rus Trail, Zion** (p52) This is one of the few park trails open to bikes.

➡ **Bryce Canyon** (p71) A paved recreational cycling path running from the middle of Bryce to Red Canyon.

➡ **Capitol Reef** (p173) Head along the scenic drive for cool river views.

➡ **Bar-M Loop, Arches** (p207) If the older kids are itching to go off-road, try out this mountain-biking trail outside Moab.

➡ **Snow Canyon State Park, St George** (p94) You can bike down the main road or take a gravel 'mountain bike' trail through the desert.

Horseback Riding

Note that the minimum age for kids is usually seven or 10 years old. Trips range from one hour to full-day treks.

➡ **Canyon Trail Rides, Zion** (p72) Ride on the Sand Bench Trail along the Virgin River.

➡ **Canyon Trail Rides, Bryce Canyon** (p124) Short trips to the canyon floor or a half-day ride through dramatic hoodoos.

➡ **Red Canyon Trail Rides, Bryce Canyon** (p124) Ride on private and public lands outside Bryce, including Red Canyon.

➡ **Scenic Rim Trail Rides, Red Canyon** (p135) Head out to Thunder Mountain and other locations.

➡ **Hell's Backbone Ranch & Trails, Boulder** (p157) Perfect for starring in your own Western.

➡ **Hondoo Rivers & Trails, Torrey** (p170) Guide service offering Capitol Reef–area rides.

→ **Red Cliffs Lodge, Moab** (p216) Gorgeous scenery north of Moab in Castle Valley.

Museums & Historical Sights

→ **Little Hollywood Land, Kanab** (p158) Western movie sets, costume shop and mock gunfights.

→ **Children's Museum, St George** (p91) Fun, hands-on museum; best for ages two to 10.

→ **Dinosaur Discovery Site, St George** (p91) Huge collection of fossilized tracks.

→ **Petroglyphs** Native American sites abound in southern Utah, though locations are not always advertised – ask at park visitor centers for more information.

→ **Best Friends Animal Sanctuary, Kanab** (p158) Animal lovers will adore this rescue center, one of the largest in the country: take a tour, spend the night or volunteer.

→ **Bryce Wildlife Adventure** (p134) Displays dioramas of over 800 animals from around the world and live fallow deer, as well as Indian artifacts and butterfly and giant-bug exhibits.

Water Sports

In the desert, kids will love cooling off and splashing around in the many rivers and reservoirs around Southern Utah. Never enter a creek or river if there is a chance of a flash flood. Storms can be miles away and completely out of sight; check the day's forecast and remain vigilant.

→ **Zion** (p82) Wade in the Virgin River, hike part of the Narrows or float downstream on a tube when water levels are high enough. Great even for young swimmers, but bring a PFD (personal flotation device).

→ **Moab** (p206) Canoe or raft down the Colorado or Green Rivers outside of town. Guides run both flatwater and white-water trips. Flatwater trips are good for all ages; white water is better for stronger swimmers.

→ **Capitol Reef** (p173) Both Pleasant Creek and Sulphur Creek offer delightful spots for wading. Great for any age.

→ **Escalante Petrified Forest State Park** (p154) Has a small reservoir for swimming; located off Hwy 12.

Planning
Be Prepared

→ Traveling with children, especially during summer in southern Utah, means taking it easy. The hot sun, dry climate and occasionally high altitude can quickly turn into sunburn, dehydration and fatigue.

→ Break up long car journeys with frequent stops; be realistic and try not to jam too much activity into the day.

→ Remember that the best times for outdoor activities in summer are early in the morning or late afternoon.

HIKING TIPS

→ Start the day with an educational ranger activity – you can then leverage the desire to show off newfound knowledge into a hike.

→ Most younger children are not goal oriented when hiking, and trying to reach a destination can cause no end of frustration for everyone. Pack a picnic, find some shade and plan on letting the kids climb on rocks, run after lizards, scoop up sand or play in a stream indefinitely.

→ Many of the most famous hikes are physically demanding, but not impossible for older children. If you plan on tackling a harder hike, make sure you start with a few easy warm-ups so you can first get used to the desert environment.

→ Bring some kid gear: binoculars, an inexpensive digital camera, compass and an appropriately sized daypack will up the fun level.

→ Older children might be interested in geocaching (www.geocaching.com), an outdoor 'treasure hunt' using a smartphone.

→ Sandstone is notoriously brittle and flaky; watch for loose rocks on the trail, when scrambling over boulders and especially near cliff edges.

Zion National Park (p46)

➡ Keep in mind that most of southern Utah's park gateway towns do not have large supermarkets or chain stores. Plan ahead and stock up on supplies for babies and toddlers at the start of your trip in urban areas like St George, Las Vegas or Salt Lake City.

➡ For all-round information and advice, check out Lonely Planet's *Travel with Children*.

Lodging & Camping

Hotels and motels typically offer rooms with two beds, which are ideal for families. Some have cribs and rollaway beds, sometimes for a minimal fee (usually portable cribs that may not work for all children). Ask about suites, adjoining rooms and appliances such as microwaves and refrigerators. Some hotels offer 'kids stay free' deals for children up to 12, and sometimes up to 18. Many B&Bs do not allow children, so ask before booking.

If it's late and you just need to crash, you should be able to find a national chain without a problem. Motel 6 and Super 8 are the least expensive, while Hilton is at the high end of the scale.

No trip to Utah's national parks would be complete without at least one night in a tent – most kids love it. Make sure you look for a campground that has designated fire rings so that you can have the obligatory campfire and trip-highlight s'mores. Seasonal fire restrictions in the West are very serious and not all campgrounds allow fires, so do some research ahead of time. If you do plan on camping, do note that you won't be alone. Campsites are much harder to find than hotel rooms, particularly in national parks. Reserve ahead of time to avoid spending hours fruitlessly searching for an open site. Most parks have at least one first-come, first-served campground, if you can marshal the troops to hit the road early enough, show up around 8am, wait for somebody to leave and cross your fingers you get there first. If you don't mind primitive sites, ask rangers about free dispersed camping on nearby BLM (Bureau of Land Management, i.e. public) land.

Plan Your Trip
Travel with Pets

It's only natural to want to explore the great outdoors with your pet, but you'll want to ensure they stay healthy and safe. Expect to encounter a lot of restrictions in national parks; state parks are a better bet if you want to spend the day on the trail together.

Park Regulations

Pets are allowed in southern Utah's national parks, but under a lot of restrictions (exceptions made for service animals). Pets aren't allowed on any trails (Zion's Pa'rus Trail is the lone exception), at scenic viewpoints or in the backcountry. Remember that these rules are in place to protect the park's flora and fauna, and also to keep your best friend from getting hurt.

Pets are not allowed on any park shuttles. They *are* allowed in national park campgrounds and outside of cars on main roads. Dogs must remain on a 6ft-long leash and be accompanied by a person at all times. If you leave your dog tied up unattended at a park campground, you'll be cited by rangers. Pets may be left alone inside RVs during the day (keep those windows open!), but they may not be left in cars; summer temperatures can quickly become lethal.

Some of southern Utah's national parks are located near kennels, where dogs and cats can be boarded for a day or overnight, including in Springdale (p78), Bryce Canyon City and Moab. Contact park visitor centers and tourist information offices for more referrals, including to local veterinarians. If you're spending a long day in the car, vets recommend stopping at least every two hours to let your dog pee, stretch its legs and have a long drink of water.

Hotel Policies

Costs
Expect extra accommodation costs of anywhere from $10 to $50 per night. Some hotels might make you put down a hefty credit-card deposit when checking in.

Weight & Breed Restrictions
Some hotels will not take pets weighing more than 40lb, or accept what they call 'aggressive' breeds (eg pit bulls, rottweilers). You may be able to obtain a waiver if you contact the hotel in advance.

Call Ahead
To avoid any unpleasant surprises, call in advance to check a property's pet policies, especially at independently owned lodgings.

Chains
Best Western is one of the most dog friendly of the chains, often with no weight limits. Motel 6 and La Quinta typically charge no extra fees.

Day Care
Most hotels will not let unaccompanied pets stay in a room. Make sure there is a kennel nearby if you won't be with your pet during the day.

Dog-friendly Areas

In Grand Staircase–Escalante and Bears Ears National Monuments, Utah's state parks, national forests and Bureau of Land Management (BLM) lands, dogs are usually allowed on hiking trails and in the backcountry, except in specially designated wilderness areas. That said, think twice before taking your pets on desert hikes in the summer – excruciatingly hot sand can burn tender paws – and always bring a water bowl. If you're camping, you'll need extra blankets year-round, as desert nights can be cold even after scorching summer days.

Outside the parks, southern Utah can be a pet-friendly travel destination, as long as you pay attention to a couple of rules. Don't immediately tie your dog up outside the first restaurant or cafe that you see. Instead, ask about local laws, to avoid ending up with a ticket. Some shops do allow dogs (often they'll post a note on the door or window saying so), or they might have a water bowl for customers' four-legged friends waiting outside.

In southern Utah, Kanab is easily the most pet-friendly town. It's home to Best Friends Animal Sanctuary (p158), a no-kill rescue center that's become famous for rehabilitating Michael Vick's pit bulls and for being featured on the popular National Geographic TV show *DogTown*. Many hotels and even a few restaurants allow dogs, while Willow Canyon Outdoor Co (p159) sells outdoor gear for your four-legged friend. Moab is another pet-friendly town, with dog-friendly hiking trails like Corona Arch, Negro Bill Canyon and Fisher Towers.

You won't see too many dogs in Las Vegas but the city has dozens of doggy day-care, canine spa and boarding facilities; contact the city's tourist information office or your hotel concierge for referrals. Otherwise, you'll likely have the best luck getting your dog a bed at one of the budget chains – Motel 6 has multiple locations, including near the Strip.

Horse Trails & Equestrian Facilities

You can bring horses, mules and burros into most of southern Utah's national parks, including Zion, Bryce Canyon, Capitol Reef and Canyonlands. Usually private stock are limited to specially designated trails and/or dirt roads. Stock may not be allowed at all during spring thaws and other periods when they could cause excessive trail damage. In canyon areas, watch out for descents that are steep, rocky and treacherous. Stock must be fed certified weed-free hay for at least 48 hours prior to their trip. Day rides in the national parks usually don't require permits (except in Canyonlands), but overnight backcountry trips do. Maximum group size is usually six to 12 animals. Consult each national park's website or call their visitor center or backcountry desk directly for updated regulations regarding private stock.

Throughout much of southern Utah, the Dixie National Forest (p124) offers excellent riding opportunities with some trails open to horses and miles of dirt roads, as well as specially designated horse camps. Only certified hay is allowed within the forest. Some tour companies and pack-trip outfitters allow customers to bring along their own stock – be sure to ask when making reservations.

If you're traveling with a horse, only a few lodgings will accept your four-legged friend. These include **Sandcreek RV Park** (☏435-425-3577; www.sandcreekrv.com; 540 Hwy 24; tent sites $20, RV sites $33-40, cabins $60; ☉Mar-Oct; ☏🐾) and Cowboy Homestead Cabins (p176) in Torrey, outside Capitol Reef. Horse-boarding facilities in southern Utah are offered at Red Cliffs Lodge (p216) in Moab.

On the Road

Zion National Park

Best Hikes

➡ The Narrows (p60)

➡ Angels Landing (p54)

➡ Emerald Pools (p53)

➡ Hidden Canyon (p56)

➡ The Subway (p64)

➡ West Rim Trail (p55)

Best Experiences

➡ Canyoneering (p71)

➡ Backpacking the Narrows (p58)

➡ Hanging Gardens (p56)

➡ Mountain Biking (p71)

➡ Exploring East Zion (p76)

Why Go?

From secret oases of trickling water to the hot-pink blooms of a prickly pear cactus, Zion's treasures turn up in the most unexpected places. That's not to say that the soaring majesty of 2000ft sandstone cliffs won't leave you awestruck, but it's the finer details that really make Zion stand apart. You don't need to be an amateur photographer to enjoy all that the park has to offer, though it is likely you'll fill your phone's memory with pictures by trip's end.

Whether you're capturing the play of shadows along the canyon walls, sharing the satisfaction of pulling over the final ledge of Angels Landing, admiring the echoes of water in the curves of a slot canyon or wading knee-deep in the adventure-fueled fun of the Narrows, Zion will continue to leave you breathless, every step of the way.

Driving Distances (Miles)

	Bryce Canyon National Park (Park Entrance)	Grand Canyon North Rim (Park Entrance)	Kolob Canyons (Park Entrance)	Las Vegas	Springdale
Grand Canyon North Rim (Park Entrance)	145				
Kolob Canyons (Park Entrance)	110	140			
Las Vegas	260	250	150		
Springdale	85	110	40	160	
Zion National Park (Springdale Entrance)	85	100	40	160	1

Entrances

Zion encompasses roughly 148,000 acres of land, though the vast majority of visitors head straight for Zion Canyon, the park's main attraction. Zion Canyon is closest to the south (main) entrance, outside the town of Springdale on Hwy 9. This supremely scenic highway continues 11 miles east through the park and the Zion–Mt Carmel Tunnel to the east entrance, where visitors from Bryce and other Utah parks will likely arrive. The park has two other entirely separate access points: Kolob Terrace Road, which climbs from the town of Virgin over 4000ft up to the canyon-top area west of the main canyon, and Kolob Canyons, 40 miles (one hour) northwest of the main canyon, reached via I-15.

WHY 'ZION'?

One of the park's first Mormon settlers called the canyon 'Little Zion,' referring to it as a place of refuge. The original Paiute name was Mukuntuweap, meaning 'straight-up land.'

Fast Facts

➜ **Entrance fee (valid 7 days)** vehicle/motorcycle/individual $35/30/20

➜ **Total area** 148,000 acres

➜ **Elevation range** 3660–8700ft

➜ **Average July temperature** 100°F (38°C)

➜ **Age of water seeping into the Emerald Pools** 12,000 years old

DON'T MISS

Zion's unique landscape has to be seen to be believed – it may be smaller than the Grand Canyon, but in a way this makes it easier to handle, with perspectives that are both monumental and yet still manageable at the same time. Hop on the shuttle (p79) for the best park overview, as it transports you the length of the main canyon.

Check out the oasis-like hanging gardens at the Emerald Pools (p53) or Weeping Rock (p56), where plants like scarlet monkey flowers and golden columbine grow from shaded seeps, clinging to the canyon walls.

Adventure lovers will want to make the white-knuckle climb up to Angels Landing (p54), the park's legendary vertigo-inducing trail up the canyon walls and out across a narrow fin of sandstone, with precipitous drop-offs nearly 1500ft down to the canyon floor.

Equally famous is the hike down – or up – the Virgin River, known as the Narrows (p58). Wading through chest-deep water with your backpack hoisted overhead and sheer walls closing in is a quintessential Zion experience.

If you prefer an even tighter squeeze, then Zion's slot canyons are a must. Hidden Canyon (p56) is a good intro as you won't need any gear; other descents like Keyhole (p71), Mystery (p71) and the Subway (p64) all require rope, harnesses, permits and wet suits.

Reservations

Zion's two main campgrounds require reservations. Watchman (p77) should be booked six months ahead; South Campground (p77) can only be booked two weeks ahead. Likewise, if you plan on backpacking or canyoneering, you should reserve your permits three months in advance.

Resources

➜ **Zion National Park** (www.nps.gov/zion)

➜ **Zion Natural History Association** (https://zionpark.org)

➜ **Zion Canyoneering Routes** (www.canyoneeringusa.com)

When You Arrive

➜ Zion National Park is open 24/7 year-round. Park passes can be purchased at the south (main) and east entrance stations and at Kolob Canyons Visitor Center (p79). Remember to hold on to your receipt if you are traveling to both the Zion Canyon and Kolob Canyons sections.

➜ If you are traveling between the south and east entrances and have a vehicle over 11ft 4in tall or 7ft 10in wide, you will need to pay an additional RV tunnel escort fee.

Zion National Park

ZION CANYON

The park's crème de la crème: sheer sandstone cliffs, secret hanging gardens, leg-busting adventure-filled hikes and enough heart-stopping scenery to make a photographer out of anyone. (p52)

ZION'S BACKCOUNTRY

Zion covers 229 sq miles, and most visitors only lay eyes on a tiny sliver. Buck the trend and face the wilderness along the West Rim Trail or Trans-Park Connector. (p55 & p70)

KOLOB CANYONS

The park's quieter northwestern corner, with dramatic finger canyons and the world's second-largest freestanding arch. One hour's drive from Springdale. (p65)

Bear Creek

Big Spring

Deep Creek

Goose Creek

Crystal Creek

Kolob Creek

Horse Pasture Plateau

West Rim Trail

Oak Creek

Sawmill Spring

UTAH

Blue Springs Reservoir

Lava Point Campground

Wildcat Canyon Trail

Kolob Reservoir

Kolob Creek

Upper Kolob Plateau

Kolob Plateau

Pine Spring Wash

Firepit Knoll (7265ft)

Hwy 14 (20mi)

Spring Creek

Camp Creek

Locust Creek

Taylor Creek

Horse Ranch Mountain (8726ft)

Finger Canyons

La Verkin Creek

Beartrap Canyon

Beatty Spring

Kolob Arch

Burnt Mountain (7069ft)

Hop Valley

Currant Creek

Lower Kolob Plateau

Smith Creek

Cedar City (14mi)

Kanarra Creek

Exit 40

Kolob Canyons Visitor Center

Kolob Canyons Viewpoint

Timber Creek Overlook

Kolob Canyons Road

Ash Creek

St George (24mi)

5 miles

10 km

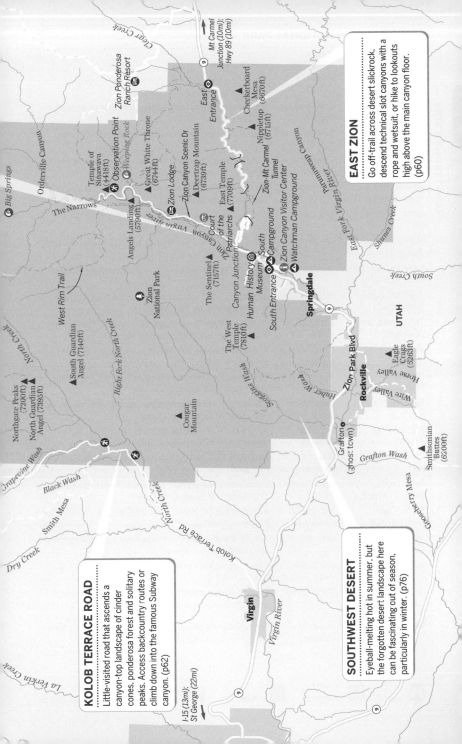

EAST ZION

Go off-trail across desert slickrock, descend technical slot canyons with a rope and wetsuit, or hike to lookouts high above the main canyon floor. (p60)

KOLOB TERRACE ROAD

Little-visited road that ascends a canyon-top landscape of cinder cones, ponderosa forest and solitary peaks. Access backcountry routes or climb down into the famous Subway canyon. (p62)

SOUTHWEST DESERT

Eyeball-melting hot in summer, but the forgotten desert landscape here can be fascinating out of season, particularly in winter. (p76)

Mt Carmel Junction (10mi);
Hwy 89 (10mi)

East
Entrance

Checkerboard
Mesa
(6670ft)

Nippletop
(6715ft)

Zion-Mt Carmel
Tunnel

Pine Creek Canyon

East Fork Virgin River

Shanes Creek

South Creek

UTAH

Zion Canyon Visitor Center

South
Campground

Watchman Campground

Zion Canyon Visitor Center

Human History
Museum

South Entrance

Canyon Junction

Springdale

Court
of the
Patriarchs

East Temple
(7709ft)

Deertrap Mountain
(6739ft)

Great White Throne
(6744ft)

Zion Canyon Scenic Dr

Zion Lodge

Weeping Rock

Observation Point
(6418ft)

Temple of
Sinawava

Angels Landing
(5790ft)

The Narrows

Big Springs

Orderville Canyon

Clear Creek

Mt Carmel (10mi);

9

Zion Ponderosa
Ranch Resort

The Sentinel
(7157ft)

The West
Temple
(7810ft)

Zion
National Park

West Rim Trail

South Guardian
Angel (7140ft)

North Guardian
Angel (7395ft)

Northgate Peaks
(7200ft)

Right Fork North Creek

North Creek

Cougar
Mountain

Kolob Terrace Rd

Grapevine Wash

Black Wash

Smith Mesa

Dry Creek

Virgin

Virgin River

I-15 (13mi);
St George (22mi)

9

9

Huber Wash

Coalpits Wash

Zion Park Blvd

Rockville

Wire Valley

Horse Valley

Eagle
Crags
(5263ft)

Grafton
(ghost town)

Grafton Wash

Crossberry Mesa

Smithsonian
Buttes
(6200ft)

La Verkin Creek

HIKING IN ZION NATIONAL PARK

NAME	START LOCATION	DESCRIPTION
Angels Landing (p54)	Grotto	Legendary Zion hike traversing a rock fin with precipitous drop-offs and chain-assisted scrambles
Cable Mountain Trail (p62)	Zion Ponderosa Ranch	A mesa-top jaunt that ends at a historic cable works overlooking Zion Canyon
Canyon Overlook (p60)	East of Zion–Mt Carmel Tunnel	A quick, elevated hike across slickrock to panoramic vistas
East Mesa Trail (p61)	Zion Ponderosa Ranch	Wanders through upcountry woods and then descends to incredible Observation Point views
Emerald Pools & Kayenta Trails (p53)	Zion Lodge	Popular series of trails leads up to three pools, hanging gardens and trickling waterfalls
Grotto Trail (p54)	Zion Lodge	Shady, even trail that connects Zion Lodge with the Grotto picnic grounds
Hidden Canyon Trail (p56)	Weeping Rock	Trace a trail carved into the cliff face to reach a gem of a hanging canyon
La Verkin Creek Trail to Kolob Arch (p66)	Lee Pass	Backcountry hike along a desert river to views of a giant arch
The Narrows: From the Bottom (p60)	Riverside Walk	A Zion icon: hikers walk, wade and swim up the Virgin River through spectacular canyon scenery
The Narrows: Top Down (p58)	Chamberlain Ranch	A backcountry in-the-river experience, swimming and hiking through the park's most famous canyon
Northgate Peaks Trail (p62)	Wildcat Canyon trailhead	A pine-and-meadow trail leads to a lava outcrop; option to summit an easy peak
Observation Point (p57)	Weeping Rock	Strenuous hike climbs steeply, traversing a hanging chasm before reaching a rewarding overlook
Pa'rus Trail (p52)	Zion Canyon Visitor Center	A paved, pet-, wheelchair- and bike-friendly path meandering along the river in lower Zion Canyon
Riverside Walk (p58)	Temple of Sinawava	An end-of-the-canyon trail follows the Virgin River past hanging gardens, weeping seeps and waterfalls
The Subway (p64)	Wildcat Canyon trailhead	Adventure-filled canyoneering route to the famous Subway formation
Taylor Creek Middle Fork (p65)	Kolob Canyons Rd	Creekside trail passes historic cabins en route to the natural amphitheater of Double Arch Alcove
Timber Creek Overlook (p67)	End of Kolob Canyons Rd	A short trail to 270-degree views of Kolob's finger canyons and the varied landscape beyond
Trans-Park Connector (p70)	Lee Pass	Linking strenuous and varied trails allows backpackers to span Zion, northwest to southeast
Watchman Trail (p53)	Zion Canyon Visitor Center	A short ascent leads to fine views; great at sunset
Weeping Rock Trail (p56)	Weeping Rock	Hanging gardens and falls that sometimes seep, sometimes weep, at the end of a short hike
West Rim Trail (p55)	Lava Point trailhead	Backcountry trail affords primo views while descending from Zion's high country to the canyon floor

 Views Great for Families Waterfalls Rock Climbing Flush Toilets

ZION NATIONAL PARK

DIFFICULTY	DURATION	DISTANCE	ELEVATION CHANGE	FEATURES	FACILITIES
difficult	3-4hr	5.4 miles	1488ft		
moderate	3hr	7.2 miles	250ft		
easy-moderate	45min	1 mile	163ft		
moderate	3hr	6.4 miles	500ft		
easy-moderate	1-2½hr	1.2-2.3 miles	400ft		
easy	15min	0.5 miles	35ft		
moderate-difficult	2½-4½hr	2.4 miles	850ft		
difficult	8hr-3 days	14 miles	800ft		
difficult	up to 8hr	up to 10 miles	334ft		
difficult	2 days	16 miles	1220ft		
easy-moderate	2hr	4.4 miles	110ft		
difficult	5hr	8 miles	2150ft		
easy	1-1½hr	1.7 miles	50ft		
easy	1½hr	2 miles	100ft		
technical	8hr	9.5 miles	1850ft		
moderate	3hr	5 miles	450ft		
easy	30min	1 mile	100ft		
difficult	4 days	36.3 miles	4000ft		
easy-moderate	1½-2hr	3.3 miles	368ft		
easy-moderate	30min	0.5 miles	100ft		
difficult	2 days	14.5 miles	3600ft		

 Drinking Water   *Backcountry Camping*   *Public Transportation to Trailhead*   *Swimming*

🏃 DAY HIKES

Zion has a fantastic diversity of hikes, from 15-minute excursions to hanging gardens to multiday quad-burning trips through sinuous river canyons and up relentless switchbacks that ascend the canyon walls. Though each area of the park offers hiking opportunities, the majority of trails depart from Zion Canyon and are only accessible via the park shuttle. These front-country trails are generally well signposted, paved and busy.

❶ Wilderness Permits

Permits are required for all overnight backpacking trips, all through-hikes of the Virgin River (the Narrows top-down hike) and the Left Fork (the Subway bottom-up), and any canyoneering or climbing routes requiring ropes. The best way to secure these permits is online (www.nps.gov/zion; search for *backpacking, canyoneering* or *climbing*); however, for each trip a certain number of walk-in permits are also available. Permit fees (which are in addition to the online reservation fee) are $15 for one to two hikers, $20 for three to seven hikers, and $25 for eight to 12 hikers. Note that the group size limit for most trails is 12 people; for technical canyons it is generally six people. If you are taking a backpacking trip, your permit will be arranged together with your campsite reservation.

ONLINE PERMITS

Online permit/campsite reservations cost $5 and can be made up to three months in advance (permits become available on the fifth day of each month, so, for example, for a June permit you should begin the process on April 5). Permits remain available online up until 5pm the day before your trip unless all spots have been taken. Note that a reservation is not the permit itself, which you must pick up *in person* at the Wilderness Desk or the Kolob Canyons Visitor Center. If you plan on applying for a lot of backcountry permits (eg you'll be canyoneering for several days in a row), it's best to become a **Zion Express Member**, which allows you to obtain your permits online.

Note that the two most popular backcountry permits, the Subway and Mystery Canyon (both technical routes), have special rules from April through October. Rather than reserve your permit directly, you must instead submit an advance lottery application on which you can request three possible dates for your trip. Applications are submitted three months in advance and cost $5. If any spaces remain open after the lottery, they will become available online. Note that the reservation fee is not the permit fee; these are paid separately.

LAST-MINUTE DRAWINGS

If all online permits for a technical canyoneering route have already been booked, you can apply online for a last-minute drawing. Last-minute drawings open up one week before the desired date; the drawing is held two days before the trip date at 1pm.

WALK-IN PERMITS

About one-third of all permits remain reserved for walk-in visitors the day before or the day of a trip. Out of season you shouldn't have too much trouble getting a permit this way. However, trying to get a next-day walk-in permit on a busy weekend can be like trying to get tickets to a rock concert; lines form outside the Wilderness Desk by 6am. Any campsites or routes that are not reservable online can only be obtained as a walk-in permit.

Zion Canyon

These trails are listed here according to the order you'll encounter them on the shuttle, beginning with the visitor center and ending with the Narrows.

🏃 Pa'rus Trail

Duration 1–1½ hours

Distance 1.7 miles one way

Difficulty Easy

Start Zion Canyon Visitor Center

Finish Canyon Junction

Nearest Town Springdale

Transportation Zion Park Shuttle

Summary A paved, wheelchair-, dog- and bike-friendly trail that meanders along beside and across the Virgin River, passing the South Campground and the Human History Museum.

Starting at the visitor center, the Pa'rus (*pah*-roos, meaning 'bubbling waters' in Paiute) is one of Zion's busiest thoroughfares. Paved, wheelchair-accessible and open to both bikes and dogs (leashed only), it's a pleasant stroll along the **Virgin River** and across the open canyon floor.

Here the widely spread canyon walls are stately and majestic rather than awesome and overpowering. The trail is the perfect place to contemplate the Towers of the Virgin, the Streaked Wall, Bridge Mountain and the Watchman. Four **footbridges** along the way crisscross the river, and numerous dirt paths lead down to the water where you can play. You can exit at the Human History Museum shuttle stop, or continue to trail's end, the Canyon Junction shuttle stop. There's little shade, so dress appropriately.

Zion Canyon – Day Hikes

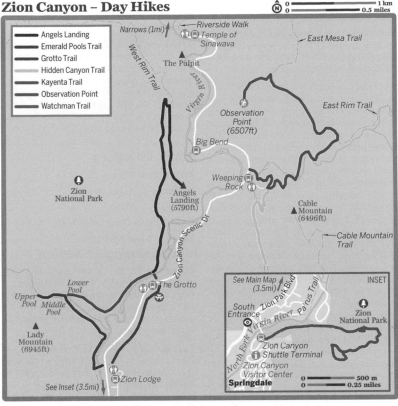

⚲ Watchman Trail

Duration 1½–2 hours

Distance 3.3 miles round-trip

Difficulty Easy–moderate

Start/Finish Zion Canyon Visitor Center

Nearest Town Springdale

Transportation Zion Park Shuttle

Summary The sunset trail of choice in Zion Canyon; ascend a mere 368ft to a short loop that provides fine views of the park's mountaincsque formations.

Don't be put off by the name; you're not climbing the monumental Watchman spire, but overlooking it. Wait until the midday heat has waned, then start off across the road from the visitor center on the same trailhead as Pa'rus. At first a dusty path along the **Virgin River**, the trail gently ascends to a small canyon at the base of **Bridge Moun-**

tain. Continue your ascent on several long switchbacks past moderate drop-offs to the top of a foothill, where the trail emerges to wide views. The pungent scent of sagebrush and spring blooms of prickly pear cactus make this an enjoyable ramble.

At the end a 0.3-mile loop trail skirts the foothill, leading to several prime **overlooks** of the Towers of the Virgin and the town of Springdale. Rising alone to the south you'll see the ragged Eagle Crags. The angular Watchman is the last formation to catch the fading light of sunset; bring a headlamp for the return hike.

⚲ Emerald Pools

Duration 1–2½ hours

Distance 1.2–2.1 miles round-trip

Difficulty Easy–moderate

Start/Finish Zion Lodge

Nearest Town Springdale

Transportation Zion Park Shuttle

Summary An extremely popular trail leads to a series of bucolic ponds, stunning desert-varnished rocks and a beautiful example of Zion's hanging gardens.

Short and sweet, this is a superb introduction to Zion's unique ecology. Regardless of your hiking ability or age, it's worth finding time to explore this area opposite the Zion Lodge.

From Zion Lodge, cross the road and bridge to get to the trailhead. The gradually rising trail leads to the **Lower Emerald Pool**, though it's not the pool that's the attraction but rather the refreshing water sprays cascading over the sandstone lip above. Wildflowers dot the wall of the hollowed-out alcove along the trail, seeming to subsist on nothing at all. Even when packed with admirers, it still feels like a secret oasis.

If that was enough walking for you, this is a good spot to turn around. Otherwise, follow the dirt trail as it ascends 150ft to the **Middle Pool** that feeds the waterfalls below.

From here, a steep, rocky half-mile spur leads to the **Upper Pool**. This is the loveliest grotto of all, surrounded by the impossibly sheer skirts of Lady Mountain. If you're lucky, you'll get to watch the canyon wren at play. But please stay out of the ecologically sensitive water.

ALTERNATIVE ROUTE: KAYENTA TRAIL

Once you've backtracked down from the Upper Pool, you could return to Zion Lodge the way you came. But we recommend continuing in the opposite direction, northwest on the Kayenta Trail. This path affords spectacular views down valley. Expect to be picking your way among rocks along the mile-long trail before you descend to the Grotto picnic grounds and shuttle stop. Following this route would bring the hike's total distance to 2.3 miles.

Grotto Trail

Duration 15 minutes

Distance 0.5 miles one way

Difficulty Easy

Start Zion Lodge

Finish Grotto shuttle stop

Nearest Town Springdale

Transportation Zion Park Shuttle

Summary A short walk through the trees beneath the canyon wall en route from the lodge to a picnic table in a grove of leafy cottonwoods.

If you don't feel like picnicking with the masses on the lawn of Zion Park Lodge, grab your sandwich and take this easy-peasy stroll through the trees to the **Grotto** picnic area and shuttle stop. A tiny old brick building there was the first Zion National Park visitor center and is now an artist retreat. Terrain is unpaved and unsuitable for wheelchairs.

Angels Landing

Duration 3–4 hours

Distance 5.4 miles round-trip

Difficulty Difficult

Start/Finish Grotto shuttle stop

Nearest Town Springdale

Transportation Zion Park Shuttle

Summary The best known of Zion's canyon hikes ascends 1000ft before the main attraction – a razor's-edge traverse and a final 488ft elevation gain on the chain-assisted scramble to the top. Grippy shoes are a must.

'How far did you get?' is the question asked every morning at coffee shops all over Springdale, as hikers compare notes on Angels Landing. This strenuous hike is not just a physical challenge, but a mental one for those with a fear of heights. While some will find this trail too unnerving to finish, adventure lovers will have a blast – the exposed scrambling and unrivaled panoramas ensure that Angels Landing lives up to the hype. By all means, start as early as possible, not only to avoid the heat, but because the number of people on the trail by noon causes frequent bottlenecks at the narrowest, chain-assisted sections. Not sure if you're willing to brave it? Check out the national park's virtual 'eHike' at www.nps.gov/zion/photosmultimedia/virtualtour.htm.

At the trailhead across the road from the Grotto picnic area, bear right. From here to Scout Lookout, you're tracing part of West Rim Trail. At first the trail meanders along the desert floor, then ascends gradually but relentlessly, becoming steeper as you begin climbing long, paved switchbacks up the canyon wall. The last switchback crosses beneath a rock overhang. Beyond it, the trail levels out, running deep into the narrow, slightly cooler **Refrigerator Canyon**.

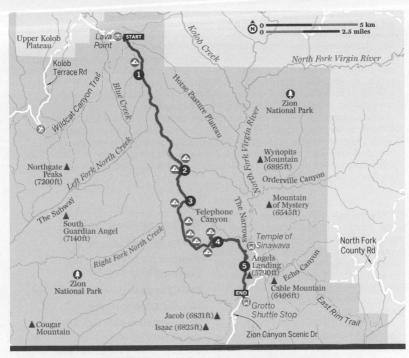

Overnight Hike
West Rim Trail

START LAVA POINT TRAILHEAD (KOLOB TERRACE RD)
END GROTTO SHUTTLE STOP
LENGTH 14.5 MILES; 2 DAYS

Starting on a high plateau, climbing down past Angels Landing, this is Zion's most popular backcountry trail. Permits are issued with campsite reservations; four are available online, while the rest are available for walk-ins. Get info on which springs are running, as these are your only water sources and will affect how much water you will need to carry.

Arrange a shuttle up to Lava Point trailhead, about 21 miles north of Virgin on Kolob Terrace Rd. There's a primitive campground here. The trail descends the Horse Pasture Plateau oh-so-gently for about 5 miles. After the first mile, you'll reach the spur trail to the seasonal **①Sawmill Spring** and campsite 9.

The first big view west opens up at around 4 miles, stretching across the valley of the Left Fork of North Creek. A mile or so further you'll descend into the grassy meadows of

②Potato Hollow, where a spur leads to a decent (though seasonal) spring. If it's running, this is the best place to get water. Campsites 7 and 8 are located here as well.

The hike up and out of the hollow is a bit of a workout, but the views are great. After about 2 miles, you'll reach the junction with **③Telephone Canyon Trail**, a shorter route to West Rim or Cabin Spring, but don't take it. The next 2-mile stretch is an incredible experience and is the primary reason for this trail's enduring popularity. Campsites 3 through 6 are spread along this edge of the mesa; reserve one if you can. It can get windy, so bring guylines for your tent.

Soon the trail descends steeply all the way to the Grotto. **④Cabin Spring** (also known as West Rim) is a major junction. From there, short spur trails lead to the spring itself (a trickle) and campsite 2. Telephone Canyon connects here, and campsite 1 is not far along it.

About 12.5 miles from Lava Point, you get to **⑤Scout Lookout** and the junction for Angels Landing. Beyond the junction, it's a 2-mile drop to the canyon floor and your shuttle ride back to the visitor center.

SLOW: DESERT TORTOISE CROSSING

One of the most endangered park residents is the tortoise, which inhabits the Mojave and Sonoran deserts. Though slow moving, a desert tortoise can live for up to 80 years, munching on wildflowers and grasses. With its canteen-like bladder, it can go up to a year without drinking. Using its strong hind legs, it burrows to escape the summer heat and freezing winter temperatures, and also to lay eggs. The sex of the hatchlings is determined by temperature: cooler for males, hotter for females.

Disease, predation and shrinking habitat have decimated the desert tortoise population. They like to rest in the shade, including under parked cars, so take a quick look around before driving away. They are often hit by high-speed and/or off-road drivers. If you see a tortoise in trouble, call a ranger. Do not pick it up, as a frightened tortoise may often pee on what it perceives to be an attacker, possibly leading to it dying of dehydration before the next rains come.

Once through the canyon, you'll ascend a few more switchbacks before reaching **Walter's Wiggles**, one of the park's engineering marvels. This set of 21 short, steep stonework zigzags is named after the early superintendent of Zion who constructed them. You emerge atop **Scout Lookout** at a sandy bench with a pit toilet and a turnoff for the West Rim.

If you've made it this far, you should really continue at least the next 70ft or so to see the incredible views. To do so, you'll have to brave the first part of the scary stuff – a **cliff-face climb** using carved-out footfalls and anchor-bolted chains. Afterwards, you get your first good look at **Angels Landing**. Seeing the thin saddle you have to cross – with some 1000ft of precipitous drop-offs on either side – stops many people in their tracks. Once across, the last half-mile of the 'trail,' such as it is, gets much steeper and rockier. Chains are bolted into the rock for much of the way. Trail's end, a sloping 30ft-wide flat rock surface at the top, is abundantly clear. Sit and take in the stunning 360-degree view of nearly all of Zion Canyon. You've earned it.

SIDE TRIP: WEST RIM TRAIL

If you want to make a day of it, escape the crowds or avoid the vertigo, try out the West Rim Trail. From Scout Lookout you can follow it into a landscape of surrealistic domes, desert wildflowers and sulfur-streaked rock. It's 6 miles round-trip up to and back from the canyon rim and **Cabin Spring**, and the latter half is a real quad burner, with another 1000ft of climbing. You don't have to go the whole way, though – a simple half-mile in will provide you with plenty to admire and photograph, and often in complete solitude.

Weeping Rock Trail

Duration 15–30 minutes

Distance 0.5 miles round-trip

Difficulty Easy

Start/Finish Weeping Rock shuttle stop

Nearest Town Springdale

Transportation Zion Park Shuttle

Summary Cool even in summer, a short-but-steep climb leads to an impressive alcove and hanging garden with water that sometimes seeps, sometimes weeps.

For a trail that's over almost before it's begun, this one is surprisingly memorable. The enormous, cool alcove at trail's end contains the park's largest **hanging garden** and an incredible amount of plant diversity. Interpretive signs identify and provide context for much of the flora along the way. The popular, mostly paved trek climbs 100ft (some stairs) to a romantically framed view of the White Throne and Zion Canyon. When the water is really running, it forms a veil from above; in all temperate seasons, expect to get a bit damp. In winter the weep can form giant icicles that may cause trail closure.

Hidden Canyon Trail

Duration 2½–4 hours

Distance Minimum 2.4 miles round-trip

Difficulty Moderate–difficult

Start/Finish Weeping Rock shuttle stop

Nearest Town Springdale

Transportation Zion Park Shuttle

Summary Exposed panoramas await as

you trace a trail carved into the cliff face to reach a gem of a canyon. You'll need to ascend 850ft in elevation to get there, though.

Get here early enough and you might have this cool hanging canyon all to yourself. Often overlooked by visitors en route to more well-known trails, Hidden Canyon is a great first-time canyoneering experience. There are no technical aspects to this hike, but if you enter deep enough into the canyon, you'll be presented with several fun, problem-solving challenges that require rock scrambling and route-finding skills.

Just getting to the canyon is something of an adventure. The initial ascent up a series of switchbacks is steep but mercifully short – definitely start early in the day while this section is in the shade. After passing the turnoff for Observation Point, the trail continues to climb, skirting a cliff face with vertiginous views as it winds around toward the mouth of the canyon. Chains are bolted into the rock at the most exposed points: although not as extreme as the Angels Landing trail, make use of these handholds – from the thin ledges, it's nearly 1000ft straight down.

Soon after you'll reach a series of pools and a (usually dry) waterfall, which mark the entrance to **Hidden Canyon** itself. With rippled red-and-cream rock on one side and a steep gray slab on the other, the sandy confines here beg for exploration. As you proceed deeper into the canyon, you'll pass shady pockets of maidenhair ferns and false Solomon's seal, while bigtooth maples stretch upwards, their brilliant green leaves contrasting marvelously with the rich ochers of the sandstone walls. Eventually you'll come to a small **standing arch**: from here the trail requires a fair amount of climbing up and around rock falls and giant boulders, and it can become a game of sorts to see how far you can go before having to turn back. A word of caution: only proceed if you're comfortable climbing back down what you originally came up.

🏃 Observation Point

Duration 5 hours

Distance 8 miles round-trip

Difficulty Difficult

Start/Finish Weeping Rock shuttle stop

Nearest Town Springdale

Transportation Zion Park Shuttle

Summary An intensely rewarding, and strenuous, hike to some of the best views in the park. In the course of 4 miles, the trail climbs switchbacks and crosses a canyon to reach an unsurpassed overlook.

Yeah, we know, you want to climb Angels Landing. That's great, but don't overlook Observation Point: fewer people, an incredible hanging-chasm canyon and the best views in the park at day's end. Be warned though, this is one of the most difficult day hikes in Zion, rising 2150ft in total. Bring plenty of water and food. You have two choices: start really early so that the initial challenging mile of switchbacks is sheltered from the sun, or make it a late-afternoon hike so the steepest ascent, out of Echo Canyon, lies in blessed shade. The trail is paved part of the way up, before turning into a combination of rock, dirt and sand.

Starting from the Weeping Rock stop, the first half-mile of the trail is the same as for Hidden Canyon, ascending long, steep, leg-burning switchbacks. After you branch left at a signed junction, the switchbacks continue for another half-mile until you make a turn north and enter **Echo Canyon**, a beautiful hanging chasm. Here the trail levels out briefly, hugging the serpentine cliff as the water-eroded chasm yawns below. The sculptural walls close in to almost arm's length. Towering above, the flat face of Cable Mountain is truly a sight to behold. After the canyon floor rises, you're trekking through a sandy wash that turns into a bowl and, before you realize it, you're climbing again. In spring, purple penstemon and crimson paintbrush flowers dot the slickrock crevices; lizards skitter about year-round.

At the 2-mile point, you reach a junction with the East Rim Trail, which also leads to Cable and Deertrap Mountains. After this, a long series of tough switchbacks draw you up the mountain. The trail is exposed to a long drop, but it's wide – no chains necessary. That plus having a mountain on one side makes it much less dizzying than the Angels Landing ascent. After about a mile, you'll reach the mesa top, and the trail is fairly level as it skirts the rim. Bear left at the signed junction with the East Mesa Trail.

For the final half-mile, you'll traverse a sandy piñon and juniper forest to **Observation Point**. From this perch at 6508ft, you can peer 600ft down to the knife-edge of Angels Landing and 2150ft to the Virgin

River – an incredible perspective of an iconic hike. The raven's-eye view down the canyon also includes a nice perspective of Red Arch Mountain. To the west, you're level with white Cathedral Mountain as the whole Zion world seems to spread out before you.

Observation Point has some great views, but climbing up from the canyon floor requires serious stamina. An alternative is to actually make a descent to the Point from the East Mesa Trail. According to one ranger, that's the 'sneaky' way.

🚶 Riverside Walk

Duration 1½ hour

Distance 2 miles round-trip

Difficulty Easy

Start/Finish Temple of Sinawava

Nearest Town Springdale

Transportation Zion Park Shuttle

Summary A popular paved path follows the river at the end of the canyon, accessing seeps, hanging gardens and wading spots – a must on any visit to Zion.

Shadowed from the slanting sun by towering walls, this fun walk parallels the slippery cobblestones of the **Virgin River** and is a kids' favorite. Interpretive signs explain the geology and ecology of the corridor, and various minispur trails lead to the river itself. The water is a great place to play, though it can be be chilly. Starting from the **Temple of Sinawava** at the end of Zion Canyon Rd, the crowded trail also serves as a feeder for the Narrows hike.

Look up and around when you set off; the canyon walls around Temple of Sinawava are popular rock-climbing sites. From the start, the pavement undulates up and down over roots and in and around water-carved alcoves. Park literature describes the walk as 'wheelchair accessible with assistance.' We think someone fairly strong would have to be doing the pushing; strollers work fine though. The paved trail ends where the **Narrows** begin, at a raised cul-de-sac with benches. Steps lead down to a rocky fan at the river's edge. Wear shoes you don't mind getting wet; you may not be able to resist the river, which beckons all – even those not hiking further up-canyon.

🏃 Overnight Hike
The Narrows: Top Down

START CHAMBERLAIN'S RANCH (EAST ZION)
END TEMPLE OF SINAWAVA
LENGTH 16 MILES; 2 DAYS

If there's one route that's made Zion famous, it's the wade down the Virgin River through a 1000ft sheer gorge known as the Narrows. Soaring walls, scalloped alcoves and wading through chest-deep pools with your backpack lifted over your head make it truly memorable. Overnight camping is by far and away the best experience, though you can hike from the top in one *very* strenuous, long day (90 minutes driving from Springdale to Chamberlain's Ranch; up to 12 hours hiking). Remember that the most difficult sections are at the end of the hike, when you'll be the most tired; we don't recommend this unless you have ironman stamina and have done the hike before. You can also day-hike the Narrows from the bottom, the most popular approach and the only one that doesn't require a permit.

The Narrows permits are some of the most sought-after in the park and are attached to campsites, except for through-hikers. Only 40 permits per day are issued: six campsites are available online; the other six are reserved for walk-ins at the Wilderness Desk (p79). Permits are not issued any time the river is flowing more than 120 cubic feet per second, so this hike may be closed at times between March and June. The optimum time to hike is late June through September. Flash floods (p275) are not uncommon in late summer, when, again, the park may close the route. Outside of summer, wet or dry suits are often necessary, as hypothermia is a real danger. The Wilderness Desk carefully tracks weather, and Springdale outfitters rent all the appropriate gear. A summer-season checklist includes a walking stick or trekking poles, synthetic clothing (no cotton!), extra fleece layers and at least one dry bag, in addition to all the usual camping gear. Canyoneering shoes and neoprene socks are useful, but not necessary outside spring. Overnight hikers are required to use human-waste

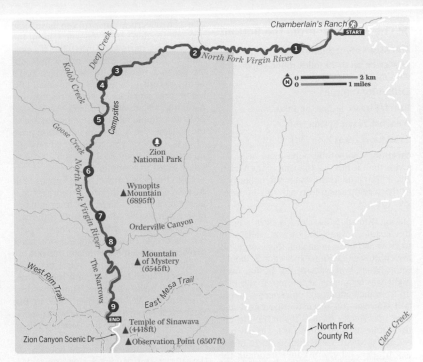

Chamberlain's Ranch
START

North Fork Virgin River

② ①

Deep Creek

Kolob Creek

③

④

Campsites

⑤

Goose Creek

North Fork Virgin River

ⓘ Zion National Park

⑥

Wynopits
▲ Mountain
(6895ft)

⑦

Orderville Canyon

⑧

Mountain
▲ of Mystery
(6545ft)

West Rim Trail

The Narrows

East Mesa Trail

⑨
END Temple of Sinawava
▲ (4418ft)

Zion Canyon Scenic Dr

▲ Observation Point (6507ft)

North Fork
County Rd

Clear Creek

N 0 — 2 km
0 — 1 miles

disposal (WAG) bags, which are given free to permit holders.

The trail begins at Chamberlain's Ranch, on the east side of the park, 90 minutes' drive from the south entrance. This is a one-way hike, so make reservations for a hiker shuttle, unless you have two cars and drivers. Shuttles usually leave Springdale at 6:15am; a second may leave around 9am if there are enough people. Past the ranch gate, a dirt road leads to the river, where you'll find an NPS trailhead marker.

The first day is the quietest, the flowing water and undulating walls casting a mesmerizing spell. The first 3 miles are out of the river and the least interesting – power through so you can spend more time with the fun stuff, exploring side canyons and taking photographs. Once you see ❶**Bulloch's Cabin**, an old homestead about an hour from the trailhead, you'll know that soon enough, the trail becomes the river. The ❷**First Narrows**, about 3½ hours into the hike and near the park boundary, is an early highlight and provides a taste of what's to come.

From here the hike is quite photogenic, with the canyon walls gradually coming closer together. A little over four hours from the trail-head, you'll reach a log-jam ❸**waterfall** that appears impassable. Upon closer inspection you'll soon pick out the trail that skirts around to the left. Depending on what time you started, this could be a good lunch spot.

❹**Deep Creek** is the first major confluence, doubling the river's volume. In the subsequent 2-mile stretch, expect secretive side canyons and faster water, sometimes waist deep and involving swims. Almost six hours from the trailhead is ❺**Kolob Creek** (generally dry), an interesting side canyon to explore. This area is the location of the 12 overnight campsites, each on a sandy outcrop far from the others.

On day 2 you'll pass ❻**Big Springs**, a good place to fill water bottles. After this are the 5 miles open to day hikers and plenty of deep pools and fast-moving water. In 2 miles you'll reach well-known ❼**Wall Street**, certainly one of the most memorable parts of all of Zion. Save some energy for ❽**Orderville Canyon**, a narrow side canyon that is lots of fun to explore. Orderville is about three hours downstream from Big Springs; you can follow it upstream for a half-mile. From here your company will steadily increase until you're just one of the crowd on the ❾**Riverside Walk**.

🚶The Narrows: From the Bottom

Duration up to 8 hours

Distance up to 10 miles round-trip (including Riverside Walk)

Difficulty Difficult

Start/Finish Temple of Sinawava

Nearest Town Springdale

Transportation Zion Park Shuttle

Summary Sometimes a bit more of a swim than a hike, as the trail is the Virgin River. You'll be in the water the majority of the way upstream through this impressive canyon.

Hiking through fa fast-flowing river in knee- to chest-deep water, the canyon walls seem to grow and press in on you: this is arguably *the* quintessential Zion experience. Although some hikers will want to do the full overnight trip beginning at the top, if you hike up from the bottom, you don't need a permit and you can still reach the narrowest and most spectacular section. If you trek the entire 5 miles to Big Springs (as far as day hikers are allowed), you'll outpace most of the day trippers – but don't underestimate the distance: this is a long way to hike upstream!

Preparation and timing are the keys to a successful Narrows adventure. Always, and we mean always, check conditions with a ranger before hiking. Find out what the day's flash-flood forecast is and make sure you're aware of the dangers. When the river is running more than 150 cubic feet per second, sometimes the case during spring runoff, the Narrows is closed. Runoff depends on the amount of winter snowfall: some years there is little change in the water level, other years the Narrows may be closed in April, May or June. Outside of summer, wet or dry suits may be necessary (p86). A hiking or trekking pole is always useful, as is a dry bag.

The 'trail' begins at the end of the **Riverside Walk**, where you enter and start following the river. Around the first bend you'll find **Mystery Falls**, the exit point for Mystery Canyon. You may catch canyoneers on their last rappel here. As you hike, each alcove, bowl, hollow, crack and arch seems its own secret place. Ravens glide over the water, and you can sometimes hear waterfalls spilling down from inside the rock.

It's about 2.5 miles to the junction with **Orderville Canyon**, which is another pop-

ular canyoneering route. If you have time and energy, don't miss the side trip up the smaller and narrower Orderville. It's possible to follow the canyon half a mile upstream to a waterfall, beyond which you'll need a permit. (There are several small falls before this; you'll know you've reached the main one when you see a park service sign or by the simple fact that it is impassible to most.) However, there is an admission price of sorts to the canyon: about a quarter-mile upstream is a small pool that you'll need to swim across to continue.

Past Orderville Canyon is the famous **Wall Street**, where the sheerness, nearness and height of the cliffs shatter whatever remains of your perspective. After this section, the canyon opens slightly again, the water gets periodically deeper (usually requiring swimming in places), and your fellow hikers thin out.

After the 4-mile point, you'll negotiate a series of huge boulders, and the canyon, though gorgeous, becomes somewhat less otherworldly. At 5 miles you come to **Big Springs**, a fern-fringed rush of water much larger than anything so far. Here day hikers are required to turn around.

While it can take up to eight hours to do the full round-trip to Big Springs, set aside a minimum of five hours so you'll at least have time to reach Wall Street. Don't forget you also have to hike the Riverside Trail back to the Temple of Sinawava.

East Zion

The following trails start on the east side of the Zion–Mt Carmel Tunnel, on Hwy 9.

🚶Canyon Overlook

Duration 45 minutes

Distance 1 mile round-trip

Difficulty Easy–moderate

Start/Finish East of Zion–Mt Carmel Tunnel

Nearest Town Springdale

Transportation Private

Summary A convenient stop off Hwy 9, Canyon Overlook is a relatively quick hike that rewards with fun desert scrambling and ends in a much-photographed panoramic vista.

Although this is not a particularly strenuous hike, the slickrock terrain is somewhat

East Zion – Day Hikes

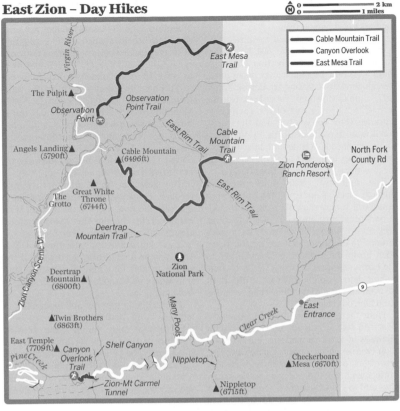

N   0   2 km
   0   1 miles

- Cable Mountain Trail
- Canyon Overlook
- East Mesa Trail

Virgin River

East Mesa Trail

The Pulpit▲

Observation Point Trail

Observation Point

East Rim Trail

Cable Mountain Trail

North Fork County Rd

Angels Landing (5790ft)▲

Cable Mountain (6496ft)

Zion Ponderosa Ranch Resort

The Grotto

Great White Throne (6744ft)▲

East Rim Trail

Deertrap Mountain Trail

Zion National Park

Zion Canyon Scenic Dr

Deertrap Mountain▲ (6800ft)

▲Twin Brothers (6863ft)

Many Pools

Clear Creek

East Entrance

9

East Temple (7709ft)▲

Canyon Overlook Trail

Shelf Canyon

Pine Creek

Nippletop

Checkerboard ▲Mesa (6670ft)

Zion–Mt Carmel Tunnel

Nippletop▲ (6715ft)

---

rugged, with exposed ledges and a pretty rocky trail – most kids will enjoy this one, though grandparents may be relatively less enthused.

At the east end of the Zion–Mt Carmel Tunnel, park and cross the road to the trailhead near the tunnel ranger booth. (If the small lot is full or if you're coming from Mt Carmel, park in the overflow lots 100 yards east of the tunnel.)

After an initial staircase ascent, the trail clings to the cliff walls, passes beneath overhangs sheltering hanging gardens, and bridges over sheer drops. Peer into the dark, narrow recesses below as you cross **Pine Creek Canyon**, a favorite technical canyoneering route.

After you cross the slickrock, you'll arrive at the final sweeping **Canyon Overlook**, with views of lower Zion Canyon and the West Temple, Altar of Sacrifice and the Sentinel. The Great Arch, visible from the west

side of the tunnel, is directly below you, though you won't be able to see it.

East Mesa Trail

Duration 3 hours

Distance 6.4 miles round-trip

Difficulty Moderate

Start/Finish Zion Ponderosa Ranch, Beaver Rd

Nearest Town Springdale

Transportation Private

Summary The sneaky, backcountry approach to Observation Point. The trail starts off a 4WD road on the east side of Zion and traverses upcountry ecosystems before dropping down to the overlook.

It feels deliciously like cheating to wander through the woods and then descend (500ft elevation change overall) to Observation

Point instead of hiking 2000ft uphill from Zion Canyon. Either way, you get some of the park's best perspectives.

Getting to the trailhead requires navigating a dirt road for the last few miles, but most vehicles should be fine as long as there is no rain. Finding it may be an issue, though. First drive to Zion Ponderosa Ranch (p77), 5 miles north up North Fork Rd; the turnoff is 2.5 miles east of the park's east entrance. Once you've arrived at the ranch, you'll want to continue north on dirt roads to the trailhead. You should take a topographic map, and don't be shy about asking for directions at the ranch's front desk.

The first two trail miles meander through open stands of tall ponderosa pines, which may show signs of the periodic park-prescribed burns. In May and June, keep an eye out for showy upcountry wildflowers. To the right you'll see canyon views open up in the distance before you get to the cairns marking **Mystery Canyon**. Take a short detour up the slickrock to the right to overlook the white, fingerlike canyons stretching out below.

From there the main trail turns southwest and starts gradually descending, with glimpses of Echo Canyon on your left and Zion Canyon on your right. Further descent down slickrock and loose stones, shaded by juniper and piñon, leads past some sandy sites and to the Observation Point spur at 3 miles. Sharing the last 0.2 miles of the trail with so many other people can be jarring. But just think how much easier it was for you to get here.

🐾 Cable Mountain Trail

Duration 3 hours

Distance 7.2 miles round-trip

Difficulty Moderate

Start/Finish Zion Ponderosa Ranch Resort, West Pine Rd

Nearest Town Springdale

Transportation Private

Summary An upcountry hike through ponderosa pines leads to your choice of Zion Canyon overlooks. Best of all, you'll encounter few fellow hikers on this trail, which is long but has little elevation change.

Seeking solitude? The route to Cable Mountain is an easy way to escape the crowds, and for those who want to make a long day of it, it can be combined with a hike to Deertrap Mountain. Even in season, you may not see a soul. Both are mainly plateau hikes that end at staggering viewpoints over Zion Canyon.

Like the East Mesa Trail, you'll first need to drive to Zion Ponderosa Ranch Resort (p77). Enter the ranch, and in half a mile, turn left at the signed junction for Cable Mountain onto Buck Rd. After 0.6 miles, turn left at an unsigned junction, and in 100 yards turn right onto West Pine Rd. In half a mile, this road dead-ends at the fence for the national park. There is no parking area; try not to block the gate.

The clear dirt trail starts by threading through ponderosa pine forest and in a quarter-mile passes a signed junction with a trail to Echo Canyon. After ascending for a steady half-mile through scrub forest, you'll reach a signed junction with the East Rim Trail. A mile further bear northward at the signed turnoff for Cable Mountain (Deertrap Mountain is another 2 miles straight on from this point).

The trail soon tops out and descends a final mile to the **historic cable works**, once used to haul down lumber. The wooden structure is rickety; don't climb on it. Instead, enjoy the panorama, overlooking the Big Bend of the Virgin River and the Oxbow containing Angels Landing. On a clear day you can see north to pink cliffs and Cedar Breaks (p98).

Kolob Terrace Road

Most of the trails along the scenic road that bisects the park are considered backcountry or technical routes, but Northgate Peaks is one notable exception.

🐾 Northgate Peaks Trail

Duration 2 hours

Distance 4.4 miles round-trip

Difficulty Easy–moderate

Start/Finish Wildcat Canyon trailhead, Kolob Terrace Rd

Nearest Town Springdale

Transportation Private

Summary An overlooked canyon-top gem: traipse through meadows and pine forest to reach a lava outcrop with a view of 7000ft-plus peaks.

Looking for a cool retreat on a hot summer day? Starting at 6500ft makes a big temperature difference. And since this area sees so little traffic, this pleasant trail remains largely uncrowded. The trailhead is located about 16 miles north of Hwy 9 on Kolob Terrace Rd. The dirt path starts at the end of the parking area.

For about a mile, you'll wander through an open meadow of sage and scrub. At the first junction, stay straight, following the sign for the West Rim Trail. (The Wildcat Connector Trail branches right and connects with the Hop Valley Trail). A hundred yards further, look for the signed Northgate Peaks Trail junction and turn right. The ponderosa pines, manzanita and wildflowers (June through early July) are a welcome rest for rock-weary eyes. You soon crest a rise to a final Y junction. Here, the trail for the famous canyoneering route, the Subway, branches left. Keep going straight.

The aptly named White Cliffs tower to the east as you gently ascend and descend to a **lava-rock outcrop** at trail's end – a good perch to admire the stunning terrain. On either side, seemingly close enough to touch, are the pale, crosshatched Northgate Peaks. Front and center is **North Guardian Angel**, with an arch so deep it's more of a cave. Framed amid these in the distance is the heart of Zion Canyon, including the East and West Temples and Deertrap Mountain, on the East Rim.

SIDE TRIP: EAST NORTHGATE PEAK

Although the Northgate Peaks trail officially ends at the outcrop, summiting **East Northgate Peak** (on the left) provides fantastic 360-degree views and is a fun way to extend the hike if you're game. A fairly clear social trail extends down from the lava outcrop to the base of the peak; follow this until you reach the slickrock. From here, ascend the rocky north face up to the vegetated area,

Kolob Terrace Road – Day Hikes

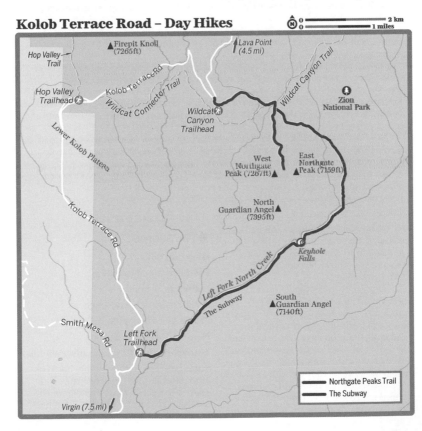

WORTH A TRIP

KOLOB TERRACE ROAD

Even in season you'll see relatively few other cars on this subtly scenic high-plateau road, where striking rock formation views alternate with pastoral rangeland. It's free to drive Zion's narrow waist, but if you do stop to picnic or hike, be ready to show your park pass or entrance receipt to rangers. There are no services up here besides some pit toilets at trailheads – the road is 22 to 33½ miles long one way, so make sure you have a full tank of gas before starting out. The upper reaches of the road often close due to snow during winter.

In the tiny burg of Virgin, just shy of 14 miles west of Zion's south entrance, turn north off Hwy 9 onto Kolob Terrace Rd – keep your eyes peeled as this road is very easy to miss! A quarter-mile past the technical Grapevine trailhead is the turnoff for **Smith Mesa Rd**. This well-graded dirt road (passable to cars when dry, impassable to all when wet) leaves the park after a mile as it winds along the top of Smith Mesa. The first few miles are worth the detour for the views back toward Tabernacle Dome, South Guardian Angel and Cougar Mountain. Past the Smith Mesa turnoff is the **Left Fork trailhead**, the end point for the popular canyoneering route the Subway.

From there you start ascending until you're 3000ft above where you started. The white and red Navajo sandstones you see at eye level up here are the same as those seen at the top of Zion Canyon. A series of turnouts offer views of Spendlove and Firepit Knolls, cinder cones that are reminders of the volcanism that once dominated this region. About 13 miles from Hwy 9, the **Hop Valley trailhead** takes off across sandy rangeland toward the park's Kolob Canyons section. This point in the road is also about as far as snowplows go in winter.

Three miles past Hop Valley is the **Wildcat Canyon trailhead**, the start of the Subway and the Northgate Peaks Trail. Just past this turnoff is one of the largest scenic turnouts along the road, with benches.

Some 21 miles from Hwy 9, you reach the junction for the graded gravel road to **Lava Point**. Don't make this journey without visiting the point, 1.8 miles further on. At 7890ft, this one-time fire lookout (the tower was removed in 2000) is one of Zion's highest and best vantage points. A virtual diorama of the park spreads before you, with views south to Arizona on clear days. There's also a six-site primitive campground (p78) here, and pit toilets. A half-mile further on you reach the trailhead for the West Rim Trail.

Lava Point is a good place to turn around. However, you can continue along Kolob Terrace Road to the **Kolob Reservoir**, 33.5 miles north of Hwy 9. It's a popular spot with local anglers and also offers free dispersed camping. Beyond the reservoir, the road reverts to dirt and continues 20 miles farther to Hwy 14, outside Cedar City. Lingering snow and runoff make this stretch wet and hazardous through late June. If you plan on going this way, check road conditions with the visitor center (p79) first.

after which you'll be able to follow cairns the rest of the way. It's much easier than it appears from afar, though it is certainly steep and you should be comfortable doing off-trail scrambling.

Looking south from the summit (left of North Guardian Angel Peak), you'll be able to pick out a shadowy cleft on the canyon floor – this is the upper part of the Subway.

All in all, figure on anywhere between one and two hours to get up to the top and back. Note that you can also climb the **West Peak**, though this is a Class 3 route with loose rock and some serious exposure. It is not recommended unless you have mountaineering or rock climbing experience.

🚶 The Subway

Duration 8 hours

Distance 9.5 miles one way

Difficulty Technical

Start Wildcat Canyon trailhead

Finish Left Fork trailhead

Nearest Town Springdale

Transportation Private or hiker shuttle

Summary The unique tunnel-like rock formations on this canyoneering route make it the park's most photographed backcountry feature. The fun-filled trail requires up to three rappels and descends more than 1800ft, generally in the water.

Though the Left Fork of North Creek – better known as the Subway – is technically a canyoneering route, we've included a description here because of its incredible popularity. The whole sculpted canyon is full of surprises, beauty and camera-worthy moments, including the curving walls that form the tunnel-like subway formations and hard-to-find dinosaur tracks. Along the way, the creek – the only trail – tumbles scenically over waterfalls, collects in deep pools, gives way to boulders and meanders in and out of the stream bed. You'll be swimming, scrambling, rappelling, sliding on your butt and whatever else you have to do to continue on.

This is unquestionably the hardest backcountry permit to get, involving an advance lottery system. If you can't get a permit for the technical top-down route, consider trying to hike it from the bottom up; a permit is also required, but it is somewhat easier to obtain. While the Subway is easy by canyoneering standards – three short rappels of 20ft or less – you still need to know what you're doing; people do get hurt here every year. Seek technical advice, get a good map and route description, and all the gear you'll need (including a wet suit outside of summer), and arrange a hiker shuttle. The one-way trail starts at the Wildcat Canyon trailhead, about 16 miles north of Hwy 9 on Kolob Terrace Rd.

At first, the route follows the Northgate Peaks Trail. Once you get to the signed spur to the Subway, the real adventure – and route-finding – begins. Keep your eyes peeled for cairns as you parallel, then cross **Russell Gulch** to an amazing bowl of slickrock. After about 2 miles and a final steep, downhill plunge, you'll reach the Left Fork of North Creek.

From here, you enter the streambed. After your first rappel, the canyon narrows and you find yourself faced with your first swim through a long corridor filled with icy water. From here it's one obstacle after another, including the famous **bowling ball chockstone**, **Keyhole Falls** and the final waterfall rappel. Just after final rappel is where you'll find the eerie **Subway** tunnel.

After passing through the Subway, you'll begin the lower portion of the hike. Although not as spectacular as the first half, there is still plenty to take in here. Two photogenic **cascades** and a set of **dino prints**

are the highlights. Eventually the valley begins to open up and vegetation becomes more desert-like, with yucca and prickly pear beginning to dot the trail. This is your cue to start looking for the exit trail on the right-hand side of the creek: if you go into autopilot and just wander along the streambed without paying attention, you can easily miss the sign indicating the way out – an all-too-frequent occurrence.

From here, the steep trail climbs sharply up before it reaches the volcanic rock of the plateau and meanders to the Left Fork trailhead parking lot. Figure on one hour to climb out of the canyon.

ALTERNATE ROUTE: BOTTOM UP

Although the approach is long and the trail not quite as spectacular as the top-down route, there's no arguing that the Subway and Keyhole Falls are awesome destinations – anywhere else and this hike would be a highlight. It's 7 miles round-trip; expect to spend six to nine hours hiking. As you start and finish at the Left Fork trailhead, you won't need a shuttle; you will need a permit, though.

When descending from the trailhead, make sure to follow the cairns; if you find yourself walking through a dry wash at any time, you've probably missed the turnoff somewhere and should retrace your steps until you find it. Likewise, take note of where the trail enters the canyon floor as you'll need to find it on your way back out. From the bottom of the canyon, simply follow the creek until you reach the Subway. You'll be hiking in ankle to knee deep water most of the time, so dress appropriately.

Kolob Canyons

Zion's northwest section, about 40 miles from Springdale, includes only three maintained trails. Want a challenge? Also consider day-hiking La Verkin Creek Trail.

🏃 Taylor Creek Middle Fork

Duration 3 hours

Distance 5 miles round-trip

Difficulty Moderate

Start/Finish Kolob Canyons Rd

Nearest Town Cedar City

Transportation Private

Summary A refreshing trip that

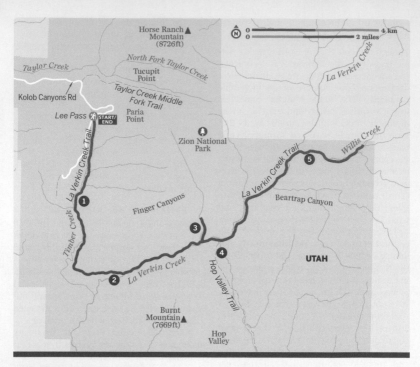

🏃 Overnight Hike
La Verkin Creek Trail to Kolob Arch

START/END LEE PASS (KOLOB CANYONS)
LENGTH 14–23 MILES, 8HR–3 DAYS

Hiking along Timber, La Verkin and Willis creeks is lovely in spring and fall. Early summer, biting goat flies can hound hikers and high-season temperatures are discouraging. It's a hard day hike due to length, sand and elevation changes (800ft overall); an overnight is both easier and allows time to explore the remote Willis Creek area. Permits are issued with campsite reservations; six are available online, while the remaining seven are available for walk-ins. Day hikers do not need a permit.

The trailhead is just south of the Lee Pass parking area on Kolob Canyons Rd. For the first 2 miles or so, you descend an open ridge with fine views of the finger canyons. Eventually, you'll skirt the spire of ❶ **Shuntavi Butte** and descend more steeply through piñon-juniper forest along Timber Creek.

The trail then turns east to the north bank of ❷ **La Verkin Creek**, a permanent, vigorous stream lined with the most convenient camp-

sites (numbers 4 through 10 are closest). The trail is sandy and slow going here.

After about 6.25 miles, follow the signed Kolob Arch Trail turnoff. The half-mile ❸ **Kolob Arch Spur** is as far as day hikers should travel. Some scrambling and route finding is required. When you reach a sign advising against further travel up-canyon, look high on the west wall for Kolob Arch. Though its 287ft opening is the second-largest in the world, the distant arch is so dwarfed by massive walls that it at first seems strangely anticlimactic. Spend some time watching the sun cloak the rock in ever-shifting shadows, however, and it soon makes a satisfying destination after all.

Just beyond the spur lies the signed junction for the ❹ **Hop Valley Trail**, which you can use as part of the Trans-Park Connector. Two miles past the arch is the turnoff for Beartrap Canyon, with a lovely waterfall half a mile in. The trail eventually turns up ❺ **Willis Creek**, a rarely visited section with towering sheer walls that open up near the park boundary. Don't leave the park limits, as private-property owners have been known to run off stray hikers.

crisscrosses Taylor Creek, passing through juniper, sage and piñon to get to two historic cabins. The real payoff is at the end: views of Double Arch Alcove, a natural amphitheater.

From the parking lot start, the path quickly drops down stairs and sand to creek level; the overall elevation change is 450ft.

After about a mile, you come to the 1930 **Larson Cabin** and a sign identifying the Taylor Creek Trail. As the trail enters a **finger canyon** between Tucupit and Paria Points, the walls narrow, and your steady ascent grows steeper still. A mile further **Fife Cabin** appears. It, like its predecessor, is too fragile to enter.

The last half-mile leads to **Double Arch Alcove**, where the seep-stained red rock glows and echoes with dripping water and swirling wind. It's a cool, refreshing break before your return trip.

🏃 Timber Creek Overlook

Duration 30 minutes

Distance 1 mile round-trip

Difficulty Easy

Start/Finish End of Kolob Canyons Rd

Nearest Town Cedar City

Transportation Private

Summary A short dirt trail to a promontory with 270-degree views of canyons and mountains. The track gets a bit steep and rocky, but unless the elevation affects you, it isn't difficult.

The shortest of the Kolob Canyon hiking options provides a chance to stretch your legs at the end of the scenic drive, but it's not the best of the park's overlooks. Remember that you're above 6300ft here, so the elevation may wind you more than the 100ft ascent. Start at the end of Kolob Canyons Rd; about 100 yards along the trail, you'll find picnic benches nestled beneath the Gambel oaks and junipers. The view at trail's end encompasses the ragged, fingerlike Kolob Canyons to the east and the flat mesas of the Lower Kolob Plateau to the south. From here, Zion Canyon is a wispy haze, unrecognizable as the mighty trench and inspiration of majestic homilies that it is.

🏃 Kanarra Creek

Duration 2–4 hours

Distance 3.5–4.5 miles round-trip

Difficulty Moderate

Start/Finish Kanarraville

Kolob Canyons – Day Hikes

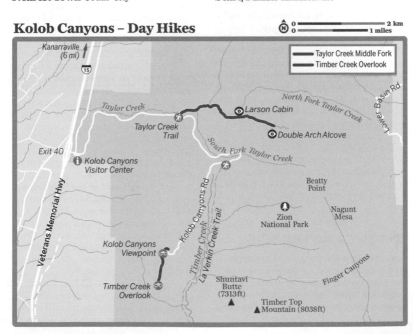

Nearest Town Kanarraville

Transportation Private

Summary Photogenic and extremely popular slot canyon offers a fun hike to two waterfalls, with makeshift log ladders adding to the thrill for first-time canyoneers and families.

This is the most famous hike in the Kolob Canyons area, even though it's not actually within the park boundaries. To get here, you'll need to drive 7 miles north of the park entrance to the town of Kanarraville, where you'll find a parking lot at the end of E 100 N St. From here the trail leads through open hills and scrub along the first mile of the canyon.

Soon after, you'll need to plunge into the stream, and the scenery becomes decidedly more picturesque. Once your feet are good and wet, you'll reach the first slot section, beyond which is the first waterfall – an iconic sight that's been captured in thousands of photographs. There is usually a log ladder of some sort here, allowing you to climb up the waterfall and continue on: inspect the quality of the rungs, ropes and webbing before you ascend; it all degrades quickly and may no longer be safe.

If you choose to continue on (many people turn around here), you'll need to climb past some smaller cascades and proceed through more slot sections before eventually reaching the second waterfall, also ascended via a ladder. Again, assess the quality before you climb – on our last visit this ladder was in particularly bad shape (with loose and missing rungs) and since you will be climbing through the rushing water, the risks are compounded. The hike continues upstream for another mile or so before the canyon eventually opens up again, a sign that it is time to turn around.

Make sure to don appropriate footwear (ie no flip-flops) and expect crowds. Reserve permits online ($8; www.kanarrafalls.com), or pick them up at the trailhead; note that payment is by credit card only.

🏃 OTHER ACTIVITIES

Besides hiking, the most popular activity in Zion is canyoneering – a world-class experience. There are also opportunities for cycling, horseback riding and wading/swimming. It is not a successful spot for anglers. Note that

🚗 Driving Tour
Zion Canyon Scenic Drive

START SOUTH ENTRANCE
END TEMPLE OF SINAWAVA
LENGTH 6.2 MILES ONE WAY;
45 MINUTES

The premier drive in the park leads between the towering red-rock cliffs of Zion's incredible main canyon and accesses all the major front-country trailheads. If you only have time for one activity in Zion, this is it – combined with a few of the hikes along the way.

Note that most of the road is actually closed to private cars from March through October; you'll be traveling aboard the excellent park shuttle instead.

Leaving from the visitor center, the first stop is the ❶ **Human History Museum** (p75), where you can catch a 22-minute intro film.

Just past the museum on Hwy 9 are a few turnouts that overlook the Streaked Wall. In spring, with binoculars, scan the rim for nesting peregrine falcons. Officially, the scenic drive begins where you turn north, and cars are restricted, at ❷ **Canyon Junction**. This stop marks one end of the Pa'rus Trail, which follows the Virgin River downstream to the visitor center.

Continuing up the canyon, you'll pass the Sentinel Slide on the left. About 7000 years ago, a big chunk of the cliff face sloughed off and blocked the water flow, turning the canyon into a big lake. (That's why the up-canyon features you see are more rounded and sculptural than in a typical river-cut gorge like the Grand Canyon.) The water eventually carved its way through the blockage and carried on.

Next, the ❸ **Court of the Patriarchs** stop fronts the shortest trail in the park, a 50-yard, staircase of a walk uphill to a view of the namesake peaks. Named by a Methodist minister in 1916, from left to right are Abraham, Isaac and Jacob, while crouching in front of Jacob is Mt Moroni (named for a Mormon angel).

Ahead on your right, ❹ **Zion Lodge** (p76) houses the park's only cafe and restaurant. The lodge was first built in the 1920s, but burned down in 1966. The wide grassy front lawn – shaded by a giant cotton-wood tree – is a favored place for a post-hike ice cream and nap. Across the road from the lodge is the corral for horseback rides and the trailhead for the Emerald Pools.

The **5 Grotto**, barely a half-mile north, is a large, cottonwood-shaded picnic area with plenty of tables, restrooms and drinking water. From the picnic area, the Grotto Trail leads south to Zion Lodge. Across the road from the picnic area, the West Rim Trail leads north toward Angels Landing. Those who'd rather admire Angels Landing than climb it should stroll the first flat quarter mile of the West Rim Trail to a stone bench for the perfect vantage.

Make sure you spend some time at **6 Weeping Rock** (p56). There's a lot to see at this bend in the river, a great example of an 'incised meander.' Pause to admire Angels Landing, the Organ, Cable Mountain, the Great White Throne and looming Observation Point. A short detour up the bucolic Weeping Rock Trail to a sheltered alcove and hanging garden is a worthwhile driving diversion. Two other great trails are accessed from here: the chain-assist Hidden Canyon Trail and the Papa Bear of workouts, Observation Point.

There are no trailheads at **7 Big Bend**, but rock climbers get out here on their way to some of Zion's famous walls. Others just soak up the view, which is a different vantage of the features seen from Weeping Rock. It's a good place to bring binoculars and scan the skies for California condors.

If you're using the shuttle, the only way to the next two sights is to walk. As you continue north, on a ledge up to the right look for a reconstructed granary. Although ancient Native American in origin, it was rebuilt in the 1930s by the Boy Scouts. After about a half-mile, you get to **8 Menu Falls**, so-named because it was pictured on Zion Lodge's first menu cover. The multilevel deck with overlook is the most popular place to get married in the park. From there it's easier to backtrack to Big Bend shuttle than to hoof it all the way up to the last stop. The canyon narrows near the cliff face that forms a natural amphitheater known as the **9 Temple of Sinawava**, at the road's end. Across the road the rock called the Pulpit does indeed look a bit like a giant lectern. From here you can take the popular Riverside Walk to the ultimate Zion experience, the Narrows.

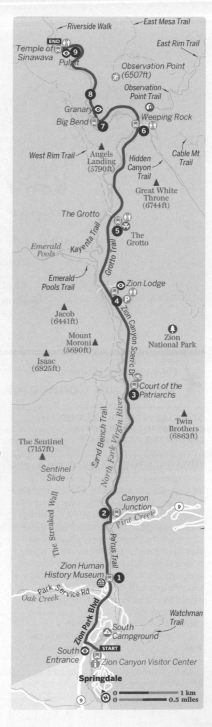

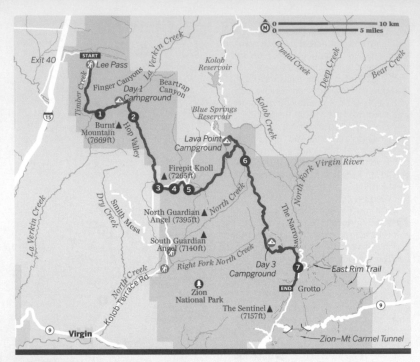

Overnight Hike
Trans-Park Connector

START LEE PASS (KOLOB CANYONS)
END GROTTO SHUTTLE STOP
LENGTH 36.3 MILES; 4 DAYS

The most popular way to traverse Zion is to hike northwest to southeast. Always check with rangers when planning, and bring detailed topo maps. There's very little water along this route, so you may need to carry it. Generally reliable springs can be found along La Verkin Creek, Wildcat Canyon and on the West Rim Trail. Spring is your best bet for water, while fall brings spectacular colors. Summer is hot, and parts of the trail may be closed because of snow December through March. You will likely need a hiker shuttle, and to arrange permits via campsite reservations for the La Verkin Creek Trail and the West Rim Trail.

Day one follows the **1 La Verkin Creek Trail**, which begins off Kolob Canyons Rd. Campsites 7 through 12 are all reasonably close to the next leg and are good choices to spend the night. Rest up because day two covers a lot of ground – over 15 miles in total.

Begin by heading south on the 6.7-mile **2 Hop Valley Trail**, which climbs up about 1000ft to a scenic open canyon and long, hot, sandy stretches, emerging at **3 Kolob Terrace Rd**. The 3.4-mile **4 Wildcat Connector Trail** links Hop Valley with the 4.7-mile **5 Wildcat Canyon Trail**. Together, the Wildcats comprise an uneven ascent of another 1000ft. Lava Point Campground (p78) and Sawmill Springs (on the West Rim Trail) are the usual campsites of choice.

Day three is somewhat less strenuous, with a gradual descent along the canyon top and a total distance of only 7 to 10 miles along the **6 West Rim Trail**. The ideal spot to spend the night is in campsites 3 through 6, which provide fabulous views.

Your last day follows the West Rim Trail steeply down into the canyon, past **7 Angels Landing**, and then down again to emerge at the Grotto shuttle stop in Zion Canyon. The truly hardcore can actually extend this hike another day to climb up out of the canyon along the East Rim trail (10 miles, 2000ft elevation gain), finishing at the east entrance.

classes and ranger-led programs are available too.

🏃 Canyoneering

If there's one sport that makes Zion special, it's canyoneering. Rappelling over the lip of a sandstone bowl, swimming icy pools, tracing a slot canyon's curves...canyoneering is daring, dangerous and sublime all at once. Zion's slot canyons are the park's most sought-after backcountry experience; reserve far in advance.

Don't be discouraged if you lack the necessary equipment or experience; beginners can join the fun too. The easiest way is to take a guided trip from any of the outfitters in Springdale. While these trips won't actually be inside park boundaries, the canyons in the immediate area are every bit as beautiful and exciting. Expect to spend roughly $190 per person (two-person minimum, if you're solo you'll pay closer to $350); options include family, regular and more extreme adventure trips. Gear and transportation are included.

Otherwise, if you're eager to strike off on your own, take a course instead. Courses cover all the basic knowledge you'll need – setting anchors, rappelling, problem-solving – and allow you to rent gear the day after so you can explore famous routes like the Subway or Keyhole on your own. Expect to spend from $170 to $210 per person (two-person minimum); some courses include gear rental in the price. For liability reasons, outfitters will not be able to rent you any gear unless you've taken a course first.

There are dozens of fantastic canyons in the Zion area, the most popular technical route being the Subway (p64). Get a guidebook (Tom Jones' *Zion Canyoneering* is a good one) or look online at www.canyoneeringusa.com for more information.

Keyhole Canyon ADVENTURE SPORTS
Off Hwy 9 east of the Zion–Mt Carmel Tunnel, Keyhole is a gem of a narrow slot that drops down three short rappels, interspersed with several cold, dark swims. Local canyoneering outfitters describe it as the route that offers the most bang for your buck. Relatively short (roughly two hours), it's a great beginners' canyon.

Orderville Canyon ADVENTURE SPORTS
Accessed off North Fork Rd on the park's east side, this is a classic beginners' canyon-

---

ⓘ FLASH FLOODS

If you plan on entering a slot canyon or the Narrows, make sure you check the daily flash-flood forecast at the visitor center or with the national weather service (www.weather.gov) before you go. Even when the weather seems clear, you should watch for signs of a flash flood (p275) as a storm upstream can still lead to flooding. A September 2015 afternoon downpour raised the volume of water in Keyhole Canyon from 55 cubic ft per second to 2,630 in 15 minutes, resulting in the deaths of seven canyoneers. Late summer is the primary time for floods, but they can happen at any time of the year.

---

eering route (added bonus: it feeds into the Narrows at the canyon's end). You'll need 60ft of rope, a wet suit outside summer and a permit. Experienced canyoneers can turn this into an epic day by starting in Birch Hollow above Orderville. Hiker shuttle necessary.

★ Mystery Canyon ADVENTURE SPORTS
Mystery Canyon lets you be a rock star: the last rappel drops straight into the Virgin River before admiring crowds hiking the Narrows. With multiple rappels of up to 120ft, this is one of Zion's best, but it's not for beginners. Advance lottery permit required; hiker shuttle necessary. It's accessed off Zion Ponderosa Ranch roads in East Zion.

Pine Creek Canyon ADVENTURE SPORTS
A popular canyoneering route with moderate challenges and rappels of 50ft to 100ft, Pine Creek has easy access from near the Canyon Overlook Trail (p60) in East Zion. A backcountry permit and wet suit are required.

🏃 Cycling

In the park, cycling is only allowed on the Zion Canyon Scenic Drive (p68) and on the Pa'rus Trail (p52), both of which are very pleasant and popular. In fact, the lack of cars from April through October makes cycling a great way to see the canyon. We recommend that you shuttle your bike up to the Temple of Sinawava and then bike Zion Canyon Scenic Drive going downhill. Being

---

IT'S A BIRD, IT'S A PLANE, IT'S A CONDOR!

With a wingspan of up to 10ft, the endangered California condor is the largest bird in North America. In the past decade, captive-bred birds released around the Grand Canyon have moved north. In 2014, biologists confirmed that a couple were raising a chick in a Zion nest – the first-ever documented occurrence in Utah. Condors seem to like to circle above Angels Landing and other tall park features. The Big Bend shuttle stop is a good vantage point from which to look for them, and they have also been spotted around Lava Point. Condors are basically big vultures, and they can be hard to differentiate from the common variety. To identify the real thing, look for all-black wings with a triangle of white at the tip underneath, visible when they fly.

---

under your own steam allows you to stop at turnouts where the shuttle doesn't. Do note that the park requires that you pull over and let shuttles pass. In practice this is not really much of an inconvenience and it keeps the majority of park visitors on the road, so be courteous.

Mountain biking is prohibited in the park, but there are other public land trails nearby. For more information on local trails or to arrange a rental, head to one of the bike shops (p83) in Springdale. The Zion Lodge (p77) gift shop also has rentals (half-day per adult/child $25/15).

Horseback Riding

Horses are allowed on most trails in the backcountry, though you'll need your own horse. Permits are not required for day trips; maximum group size is six animals. The only overnight stock camp is on the Hop Valley Trail, off Kolob Terrace Rd.

Canyon Trail Rides　　　HORSEBACK RIDING
(☑435-679-8665, 435-772-3810; www.canyon rides.com; 1hr/half-day trips $45/90; ☺Mar-Oct) Zion's official horseback-riding concessionaire operates across from Zion Lodge (p77). Ride on the Sand Bench Trail along the Virgin River. Minimum age of seven to 10 for the one-hour/half-day trips.

Rock Climbing

Zion Canyon contains some of the most famous big-wall climbs in the country, including Moonlight Buttress, Prodigal Sun, Touchstone and Space Shot. These are epic multipitch climbs that draw the best of the best for their challenge and beauty. However, there's not much for beginners or those who like single-pitch sport climbs. If you're interested in trying out rock climbing, you can sign up for a class or trip with a Springdale outfitter (p84).

If you are climbing, note that day climbs in Zion do not require a permit, though all overnights and bivouacs do.

Kids' Activities

With its can't-lose combo of rushing water, giant boulders to climb on and a landscape that looks like the backdrop for any number of fantasy novels, Zion is sure to keep children entertained. Do note that some of the more spectacular hikes require an arduous initial climb off the valley floor, so have your bag of tricks ready to keep everyone entertained. Also remember that some of the activities in Zion have a real element of danger; don't attempt anything beyond your children's ability levels, and if you're starting to feel anxious, don't hesitate to turn around.

Late May through late August, Zion National Park offers a series of children's programs for various age groups. Many are based at **Zion Nature Center** (Map p84; ☑435-772-3256; South Campground, off Hwy 9; ☺1-6pm late May-Aug; 🚻) **FREE**, but some take place at Zion Lodge (p76) or on trails. You might hunt for animal habitats along the Virgin River or hear stories about the life of the first pioneer settlers in the area. For schedules, check online (www.nps.gov/zion) or in the summer park newspaper.

Year-round, children five to 13 can earn a badge and become a Junior Ranger by completing the activity-filled *Junior Ranger Handbook* available at both visitor centers and the Human History Museum (p75). If you have little ones under five, pick up the *Junior Ranger Helper Activity Sheet* so they can earn a pin. The bookstores also sell *Zion Canyon Adventure*, a fun and informative illustrated 'guidebook' to the park.

Outside of these programs, wading in the Virgin River along Riverside Walk (p58) or the Pa'rus Trail (p52) is a good bet; in Springdale, tubing can make for a fun

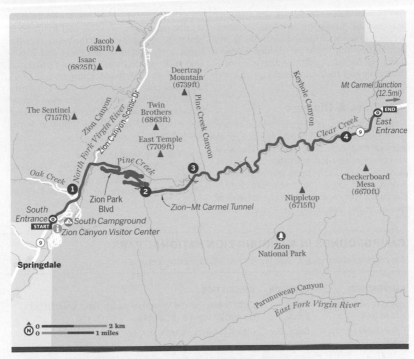

Driving Tour
Zion–Mount Carmel Highway (Highway 9)

START SOUTH ENTRANCE
END EAST ENTRANCE
LENGTH 12 MILES ONE WAY; 45 MINUTES
TO 2 HOURS WITH STOPS

As far as Zion's scenic drives go, Hwy 9 certainly rivals the main canyon, with a series of magnificent overlooks followed by a landscape of multicolor slickrock, culminating at Checkerboard Mesa. You can start this drive at either the south (main) entrance or, if you're coming from Bryce Canyon or elsewhere, the east entrance near Mt Carmel.

If you begin at the south entrance, follow the main road about 1.5 miles into the park, passing the **❶ Human History Museum** (p75), until you reach Canyon Junction, where the Zion Canyon drive splits off from the highway. Follow the highway east, climbing up a series of six tight switchbacks. This picturesque stretch offers superb views both back to the main canyon and ahead to the Great Arch. Make sure to stop at one of the turnouts before you get to the **❷ Zion–Mt Carmel Tunnel**.

At the time of its completion, the 1.1-mile tunnel was the longest in the United States. Engineers had to construct an aerial tramway just to create a workers' base camp. During the three years of construction (from 1927 to 1930), more than 146 metric tons of dynamite were used to move 72,000 cu yds of stone.

At the tunnel's east entrance is a small parking lot and the trailhead for the **❸ Canyon Overlook** (p60), which leads to the top of the canyon wall you were just admiring. After a second, smaller tunnel, don't miss the numerous turnouts that provide easy access to the slickrock. Although there are no official trails in this area, it's quite rewarding to simply wander around and explore.

After about 3.5 miles, you get your first glimpse of Checkerboard Mesa, a huge sloping face of beige slickrock, etched with both horizontal cross-bedding layers and vertical stress fractures caused by freeze-thaw cycles.

It's another mile to the official **❹ Checkerboard Mesa viewpoint**, your last must-see stop. About a quarter-mile further on is the east entrance, marking the park boundary.

way to cool down. Teenagers will definitely enjoy the adventure involved in Zion's premier hikes such as the Narrows (p58), Angels Landing (p54) or Hidden Canyon (p56). Springdale outfitters also offer canyoneering and rock climbing trips tailored to families.

 ## Tours & Classes

From fascinating geological forces to extreme desert flora and fauna, there's a lot to learn around Zion National Park. The wide variety of ranger-led activities are a great place to start. Daily talks (more frequent June through August) at the Human History Museum cover topics such as the survival of species in the desert and the culture of the area's ancients. Guided hikes explore topics like the power of water and indigenous plant life along some of the most popular trails, including Emerald Pools and Riverside Walk. Occasionally, evening programs are held at Watchman Campground (p77) and Zion Lodge, and **Kolob Canyons** hosts limited talks and walks of their own. Visitor centers post lists of each week's programs and a schedule is available online at www. nps.gov/zion.

Zion Canyon Field Institute TOURS
(☑435-772-3264; www.zionpark.org; programs $45-85) Explore Zion by moonlight, take a wildflower photography class, investigate

---

CAMPGROUNDS IN & AROUND ZION NATIONAL PARK

For wilderness camping in Zion you'll need a backcountry permit.

CAMPGROUND	LOCATION	DESCRIPTION
Point Supreme Campground (p98)	Cedar Breaks	Cedar Breaks National Monument campground. Beautiful but remote; 1hr from Kolob Canyons.
Cedar Canyon (p97)	Cedar City area	Closest campground to Cedar City.
Duck Creek Campground (p97)	Hwy 14	Pine-shaded sites at a blissfully cool 8400ft, east of Cedar City. Water; no showers, no hookups. Remote.
Lava Point Campground (p78)	Kolob Terrace Rd	Tiny, primitive NPS ground high in the upcountry. Tents only, no water. One hour from Springdale.
Pine Valley Recreation Complex (p95)	St George area	Escape the heat in the mountain wilderness an hour north of St George.
Snow Canyon State Park Campground (p95)	St George area	Fabulous red-rock formations but little shade. Hot showers, water and electrical hookups. One hour from Springdale.
South Campground (p77)	Zion Canyon	Top choice in Zion. No electricity, no showers. First-come, first-served only.
Temple View RV Resort	St George	Attracts St George snowbirds who live here all winter. One hour from Springdale, lots of services. Not for tents.
Watchman Campground (p77)	Zion Canyon	Top choice in Zion. Some electric hookups, no showers.
Zion Canyon Campground & RV Resort (p86)	Springdale	Crowded, friendly Springdale site with pool and river access. Full hookups, hot showers, wi-fi. Convenient to Zion.
Zion Ponderosa Ranch Resort (p77)	East Zion	Upcountry mesa-top camping at activity-oriented ranch. Wi-fi, showers. 45 minutes from Springdale.
Zion River Resort (p88)	Virgin	Fancy RV campground with 70ft pull-throughs and river sites. Loads of amenities. Convenient to Zion; not great for tents.
Zion Mountain Trading Post (p78)	East Zion	East-side campground convenient to the park. Showers, laundry and full hookups.

 Drinking Water   *Flush Toilets*   *Ranger Station Nearby*   *Great for Families*   *Wheelchair Accessible*

Kolob Canyons' geology or help clean up the Narrows. All activities include some hiking.

Ride Along with a Ranger TOURS
(Map p84; www.nps.gov/zion; Zion Canyon Visitor Center; ☉Jun-Sep) FREE The entertaining, ranger-led Zion Canyon shuttle tour (90 minutes) makes stops not on the regular route. It's a great nonhiking alternative for those with limited mobility.

⊙ SIGHTS

Human History Museum MUSEUM
(☉9am-7pm late May–early Sep, shorter hours rest of year) FREE A half-mile from the park's southern entrance station, the Human History Museum presents a modest exhibit of the geological and human history of Zion. A 22-minute introductory video is shown every half-hour, along with occasional ranger talks. The paved Pa'rus Trail (p52) parallels the road for 2 miles from South Campground (p77) to the main canyon junction, passing the museum on the way.

The building itself was built on the site of an original Mormon homestead settled by the Crawford family. Outside the museum, look for signs that point out the park's tallest sandstone cliffs, including the West Temple (7810ft) and the Towers of the Virgin.

NUMBER OF SITES	ELEVATION (FT)	OPEN	RESERVATIONS AVAILABLE?	FACILITIES
25	10,350	Jun-Sep	yes	
13	8100	late May–Sep	yes	
87	8400	mid-May–Sep	yes	
6	7900	Jun-Oct	no	
55	6900	mid-May–Sep	yes	
30	3200	year-round	yes	
127	3940	year-round	yes	
260	2800	year-round	yes	
184	3940	year-round	yes	
200	3898	year-round	yes	
18	6500	Mar-Nov	yes	
122	3552	year-round	yes	
22	5000	year-round	yes	

 Dogs Allowed (On Leash)   *Grocery Store Nearby*   *Restaurant Nearby*   *RV Dump Station*

Zion Lodge
HISTORIC BUILDING

(☑435-772-7700; www.zionlodge.com; Zion Canyon Scenic Dr) Whether you plan to stay at the Zion Lodge or not, a visit to this historic lodge, smack in the middle of Zion Canyon, is a must. Although the architecture itself pales in comparison to some of its counterparts in other national parks, its location is incomparable. Stunning red-rock cliffs surround you on all sides, and views of Lady Mountain, Heaps Canyon and the Virgin River are simply stunning. Evening nature programs and talks are also hosted on the grounds.

🛏 SLEEPING

Zion itself has just one lodge and a few basic campgrounds, which generally fill up from mid-March through November. The majority of visitors sleep in Springdale (p86), just outside the park's south entrance. If you are tent camping, be forewarned that there are not a lot of great sites in the immediate area; many campsites are essentially RV parking lots. See our tips for free public land camping (p89). Note that pets are allowed in RVs only.

ZION: OFF THE BEATEN PATH

In season, when the Zion Park Shuttle is standing-room only, popular trails can be a great place to meet travelers from around the world. But you do have choices if you want to get away from them all.

Outside of summer, you can explore the area of Zion known as the **Southwest Desert**. Rarely visited, there are two hikes here, the Chinle and the unofficial Coalpits Wash. Six campsites are located 5.5 miles in. Access is off Hwy 9, just south of Springdale on the north side of the road.

Perhaps the best option of all, however, is to do some **slickrock hiking**. East of the Zion–Mt Carmel Tunnel, anyone with a sense of adventure will be tempted to park at every turnout along the way and start scrambling around (do remember to stay on the rock though, and not step on the fragile cryptobiotic soil). Some trails end after 50ft; others traverse the desert slickrock for miles. It's easy to find some very narrow slots here, which you can peer down into from the top; indeed, some classic canyoneering routes such as Keyhole (p71) and Pine Creek Canyon (p71) are located this way. While there are few official trails in East Zion, here are a few unofficial destinations to give you some ideas of what's out there. Remember that it can get very hot here, so bring plenty of water, a hat and sunscreen, and don't hike at midday in summer.

The **Many Pools** trail follows an open wash up the hillside, beginning with a string of dry cascades and lovely pools, some of which hold some interesting critters (such as tadpoles) depending on the water level and season. You can follow the wash up through the slickrock for about a mile, until you eventually reach the mouth of a canyon.

To get here, park at the first major turnout east of the second (small) tunnel on Hwy 9; it's about a mile away. The wash is on the other side of the road from the parking lot, but it's not immediately visible. You'll either need to hike over a small hill heading slightly east, or cross under the road using the tunnel to the east, which will put you directly on the path.

Shelf Canyon is a fun little scramble to a secret canyon just east of the main tunnel. Short and sweet, it involves lots of low-grade bouldering and is definitely not for casual hikers. As you follow the canyon further back it gets increasingly narrow, eventually ending in a cave-like formation filled with narrow ledges that you can clamber up.

To get here, park at the overflow lot just east of the main tunnel on the north side – ie not the lot with the bathrooms. From here you'll need to figure out how to get into the drainage (walk up the road a bit) and then it's up, up and away.

Hiking up **Nippletop** (6715ft) is a great way to experience Zion's east-side wilderness. The hike is relatively short (3 miles round-trip) and only ascends about 1500ft – steep, but not too steep. The summit is class III (exposed but nontechnical), so you should only attempt this if you have climbing or mountaineering experience.

While spotting the Nipple shouldn't prove too difficult, finding the trail can be tricky, so it's recommended you study trip reports online together with a topo map in order to orient yourself before you go. The turnout for Nippletop is 1.9 miles east of the second (smaller) tunnel.

SACRIFICE ROCK

Spend a week in Zion and you may not realize that ancient peoples had much of a presence here. The National Park Service does its best to protect and preserve the natural and cultural resources under its care. But when it comes to the rock art and ruins left by ancestral inhabitants, there's only so much they can do. The **South Gate Petroglyphs**, aka 'Sacrifice Rock,' is a case in point. The handful of intriguing designs and animals are a few steps from the road near the south entrance. What strikes one most, however, is not the petroglyphs themselves but the overwhelming amount of modern graffiti surrounding them. 'Jayrod' may indeed rock, but did he need to let everyone know right here, for all eternity?

So you'll understand if Zion rangers do not advertise rock-art locations, and ruins are strictly off-limits. Ask a general 'I've heard there are petroglyphs in the park?' and you'll get a purposely obtuse 'Yes, I've heard that too' in response. There is at least one other rock art site close to a road. If you do your research and ask a specific question, the rangers can answer. But please remember to regard all ancient sites as you would a museum. These locations are both priceless artifacts and spiritual sites for the modern-day tribes whose ancestors created them.

🛏 Zion Canyon

Just inside Zion's south entrance are the park's two main campgrounds. Both are adjacent to the visitor center. Neither has showers, laundry facilities or a general store; these are available in Springdale. There is a maximum stay of 14 days from March through November. Up to two vehicles and six people are allowed per site. Ask about last-minute availability if you can't get a site; sometimes people cancel.

South Campground CAMPGROUND $

(Map p84; ☑ 435-772-3256; www.recreation.gov; Hwy 9; tent & RV sites $20; 🐾) The South Campground sits north of the visitor center (p79) beside the Pa'rus Trail (p52). Campsites can only be reserved starting two weeks in advance, for a maximum stay of three nights. They fill up immediately, so get ready to book online at exactly 8am EST. The campground has no electrical hookups for RVs; there's a dump station, however.

Watchman Campground CAMPGROUND $

(Map p84; ☑ 877-444-6777; www.recreation.gov; Hwy 9; tent sites $20, RV sites with hookups $30; 🐾) Towering cottonwoods provide fairly good shade for the 184 well-spaced sites at Watchman, located south of the visitor center. Sites are by reservation (six months in advance; 14-day maximum stay) and you should book as far in advance as possible, otherwise it's unlikely you'll get a spot. Fire grates, drinking water, RV hookups and flush toilets; no showers.

★ Zion Lodge LODGE $$

(☑ 888-297-2757, 435-772-7700; www.zionlodge.com; Zion Canyon Scenic Dr; cabins/r $260/225; 🌡@🛜) We love the stunning surrounding red-rock cliffs and the location in the middle of Zion Canyon (along with the red permit that allows you to drive to the lodge in shuttle season). But be warned: today's reconstructed lodge is not as grand as other national park lodges (the 1920s original burned down in 1966). Nevertheless, you'll need to reserve months ahead.

Although they're in wooden buildings with balconies, the motel rooms are just motel rooms: nothing fancy. Carved headboards, wood floors and gas fireplaces do give Western cabins more charm, but paper-thin walls are all that separate you from neighbors. There are two eateries and a big lawn for lounging outside. No room TVs; wi-fi speed is very slow as the signal comes via dish.

🛏 East Zion

Although not technically in the park, East Zion offers both a closer proximity to Bryce and Escalante and a higher elevation, meaning cooler temperatures in summer.

Zion Ponderosa Ranch Resort RANCH $

(☑ 800-293-5444; www.zionponderosa.com; Twin Knolls Rd; luxury tent $119, RV site $55, cabin $139-199; 🛜🛁🐾) Families love this activity-rich ranch on 4000 acres on Zion's eastern side. Guests can hike, bike, canyoneer, climb, swim, play sports, ride four-wheelers and horses, and eat three meals a day right here (packages available). Wi-fi-enabled camping sites and cabins (linens included) are served by huge showers and bathrooms.

Zion RV & Campground
CAMPGROUND $

(Zion Mountain Trading Post; ☑ 877-290-5756; http://zionrv.com; Hwy 9; tent sites $49, RV sites with hookups $69-79; 🛜) If you're simply looking for a place to pitch your tent, this isn't a bad spot, though rates are comparatively high. Sites are more spacious here than in the RV parks around Springdale; public showers and laundry are welcome additions. It is close to the road, however, and not all sites have shade. It's located just outside of Zion's east entrance.

Zion Mountain Ranch
CABIN $$$

(☑ 866-648-2555, 435-648-2555; www.zmr.com; Hwy 9; cabins $230-940; ❄ @) Six different cabin types and a variety of larger lodges are available at this luxury ranch. Buffalo roam, though it is a bit closer to the highway than might be expected. Activities, including horseback riding (available to nonguests, one hour $45) and fly-fishing, can be arranged through the resort. It's about 3 miles from Zion's east entrance.

🛏 Kolob Terrace Road

Kolob Terrace Rd is not the most convenient location, but you will certainly escape the crowds up here. There is some free dispersed camping on public land along the road on the way up; ask at the visitor center for tips (you cannot camp on private land or in the national-park boundaries).

Lava Point Campground
CAMPGROUND

(Lava Point Rd; ⊙ May-Sep) FREE Six first-come, first-served park sites 35 miles up Kolob Terrace Rd at 7900ft (1¼ hours from the main entrance). Pit toilets, no water.

Under Canvas Zion
TENTED CAMP $$$

(☑ 435-359-2911; www.undercanvas.com; 3955 Kolob Terrace Rd; tents $239-549; 🛏) If you love the idea of camping but are less enthused about actually sleeping on the ground, Under Canvas could be for you. Ringed by red mesas and distant sandstone peaks, these secluded luxury tents off Kolob Terrace Rd sleep up to four and come equipped with woodburning stoves and private bathrooms – some have star-gazing windows, too!

🛏 Kolob Canyons

There are no accommodations in this part of the park; most people stay in or around Cedar City. If you're camping, however, you may be able to get a backcountry site on the La Verkin Creek Trail (minimum 2-mile hike).

✗ EATING

Castle Dome Café
CAFE $

(Zion Canyon Scenic Dr, Zion Lodge; mains $5-12; ⊙ 7:30am-6pm Mar-Oct) This counter-service cafe serves sandwiches, pizza, breakfast snacks and ice cream. A beer garden serving local suds is located on the patio from May through mid-October.

Red Rock Grill
AMERICAN $$

(☑ 435-772-7760; Zion Canyon Scenic Dr, Zion Lodge; breakfast & sandwiches $6-17, dinner $16.50-30; ⊙ 6:30-10am & 11:30am-9pm Mar-Oct, hours vary Nov-Feb) Settle into your replica log chair or relax on the big deck with magnificent canyon views. Though the dinner menu touts its sustainable-cuisine stance for dishes like roast pork loin and flatiron steak, the results are hit-or-miss. Dinner reservations recommended. Full bar.

IS ZION FIDO-FRIENDLY?

We can't say that Zion is the canine-friendliest park in the area. Dogs are only allowed on one trail, the Pa'rus, and perhaps because of that, few motels in the area allow pets. If you want to take your furry friend hiking, you can try the **Bureau of Land Management (BLM)** land south of Rockville; the small **Springdale River Park** also allows dogs. But honestly, you have more hiking options in Grand Staircase–Escalante National Monument, and lots of Kanab hotels put out the doggie welcome mat.

About 4 miles west of Zion Canyon, **Doggy Dude Ranch** (☑ 435-772-3105; www.doggyduderanch.com; Hwy 9, btwn Rockville & Springdale; overnight/day boarding $36/26; ⊙ 8am-6pm) will keep your canine friend overnight.

ℹ Information

If you plan to do any serious hiking or exploring, a good map is essential. National Geographic (www.natgeomaps.com) puts out a colorful, waterproof *Trails Illustrated* map for Zion. The less snazzy park map from Zion Natural History Association (www.zionpark.org) also gets the job done. Both are available at park visitor centers.

Zion Canyon Visitor Center (Map p84; ☑435-772-3256; www.nps.gov/zion; Hwy 9, Zion National Park; ⊗8am-7pm Jun-Aug, shorter hours rest of year) Several rangers are on hand to answer questions at the main visitor center by the south entrance; ask to see the picture binder of hikes to know what you're getting into. Find out about ranger-led activities, river flow information and weather reports here.

Wilderness Desk (Map p84; ☑435-772-0170; www.nps.gov/zion; ⊗7am-7pm Jun-Aug, reduced hours rest of year) Issues permits for backcountry camping, canyoneering and rock climbing. Located at the Zion Canyon Visitor Center.

Kolob Canyons Visitor Center (☑435-586-0895; www.nps.gov/zion; Kolob Canyons Rd; ⊗8am-6pm late May-Sep, shorter hours rest of year) Small visitor center in the Kolob Canyons section of the park.

Zion Natural History Association (Map p84; ☑435-772-3264; www.zionpark.org; ⊗8am-8pm Jun-Aug, shorter hours rest of year) Runs the excellent Zion Canyon Visitor Center bookstore. Good online book selection.

National Park Rangers Emergency (☑435-772-3322) Call for emergencies.

ℹ Getting Around

SHUTTLE BUSES

How you get around Zion depends on the season. From March through early November passenger vehicles are not allowed on Zion Canyon Scenic Drive (p68). The park operates two free, linked shuttle loops.

The Zion Park Shuttle makes nine stops along the canyon, from the main visitor center to the Temple of Sinawava (a 45-minute round-trip).

The Springdale Shuttle also makes nine stops along Hwy 9 between the park's south entrance and the Majestic View Lodge in Springdale, the hotel furthest from the park. You can ride the Springdale Shuttle to the Zion Canyon Brew Pub and walk across a footbridge into the park. The visitor center and the first Zion shuttle stop lie on the other side of the kiosk.

> ### ℹ SHUTTLE WAIT TIMES
>
> During spring break and in the summer, you'll want to arrive at the visitor center no later than 8am (ideally 7am), otherwise you're looking at a wait time of an hour or more just to board the shuttle (not to mention the impossibility of finding a parking spot if you're in a car). If you do find yourself faced with a long line, consider walking a half-mile up the Pa'rus Trail (p52) to the Human History Museum, the shuttle's first stop. At the visitor center, passengers are only allowed to board if there are seats available. Once the shuttle is en route though, you're allowed to stand in the aisle, so your chances of getting on board are greatly increased. Bonus: the trail is a lovely way to start your day!

The propane-burning park shuttle buses are wheelchair-accessible, can accommodate large backpacks and carry up to two bicycles or one baby stroller. Schedules change, but generally high-season shuttles (mid-May to September) operate from 6am to 9:15pm, every five to 15 minutes.

PRIVATE VEHICLE

If you arrive via the south entrance, you should expect traffic jams of 30 minutes or more just to pass the kiosk – arrive well before 8am (or after 4pm) to avoid the worst of the traffic and increase your odds of getting a coveted parking spot.

Arriving from the east on Hwy 9, you have to pass through the Zion–Mt Carmel Tunnel.

If your RV or trailer is 7ft 10in wide or 11ft 4in high or larger, it must be escorted through, since vehicles this big need both lanes. Motorists requiring an escort pay $15 over the entrance fee, good for two trips.

Between April and October, rangers are stationed at the tunnel from 8am to 8pm daily; at other times, ask at the entrance stations. Vehicles prohibited at all times include those more than 13ft 1in tall or more than 40ft long.

HIKER SHUTTLES

In Springdale, outfitters run daily shuttles to transport hikers to backcountry and canyoneering trailheads. Zion Adventure Company (p84), **Red Rock Shuttle** (☑435-635-9104; www.redrockshuttle.com), and Zion Rock & Mountain Guides (p83) are all dependable. Expect to pay $20 to $42 per person, depending on your destination; reservations required.

BEN COOPER/GETTY IMAGES ©

NICKOLAY STANEV/SHUTTERSTOCK ©

1 The Narrows (p58)

Sometimes as much a swim as a hike, this trail follows the Virgin River though Zion Canyon.

2. Big Bend from Angels Landing (p54)

Angels Landing is the best known of Zion's hikes, ascending a 1000ft before the main attraction – a razor's-edge traverse and a final 488ft climb to the summit.

3. Virgin River (p58)

Riverside Walk along the Virgin River is one of the park's most popular and accessible hikes.

4. Rock climbing (p72)

Zion is home to some of the USA's best and biggest big-wall climbing, although there is not much for beginners within the park's boundaries.

JUSTIN REZNICK PHOTOGRAPHY/GETTY IMAGES ©

Around Zion National Park

Best Places to Stay

➡ Under the Eaves Inn (p86)
➡ Desert Pearl Inn (p87)
➡ Seven Wives Inn (p93)
➡ Red Rock Inn (p86)

Best Places to Eat

➡ King's Landing (p89)
➡ Bit & Spur (p89)
➡ Riggatti's Wood Fired Pizza (p93)
➡ Painted Pony (p94)
➡ Centro (p97)

Why Go?

You may be tempted to speed out of Vegas with your foot on the gas and Zion firmly in your sights – after all, the park is less than three hours away via the interstate. But once you cross the state line, consider slowing down to explore the vast wilderness that surrounds you: Snow Canyon State Park, St George and Cedar Breaks National Monument are all worthy detours, with their own superb views and an array of fun activities, including mountain biking, cycling, climbing and cross-country skiing.

Even if time is short, it's likely you'll be based outside the park anyway, unless you've got a coveted park campsite. As far as towns go, Springdale is the pick of the bunch, with easy access and a range of accommodations and restaurants. For something a bit more off the beaten path, consider sleepy Cedar City for Kolob Canyons access, or idyllic Glendale, perfectly situated in between Zion, Bryce and Kanab.

When to Go
Zion National Park

May–Aug
Soaring heat; rains increase the risk of flash floods in July and August.

Sep–Nov
Clear, warm days; festivals in Cedar City and St George.

Dec–Apr
Snow at higher elevations; some trails may be closed.

Springdale

POP 570 / ELEV 3898FT

When the cottonwoods are budding against the red cliffs, Springdale is the perfect little park town, though more frequently, it's a bottleneck of traffic entering Zion National Park. The main drag – well, the only drag – features eclectic cafes, galleries and restaurants touting local produce and organic ingredients. Many residents were drawn here for the surroundings, but you will occasionally run into a lifelong local who thinks they're 'just rocks.'

⊙ Sights

Grafton Ghost Town   GHOST TOWN

The freely accessible Grafton ghost town, outside Rockville, achieved its 15 minutes of fame in 1969 as the setting for the bicycle scene in *Butch Cassidy & the Sundance Kid*. Originally settled in 1859, the town never amounted to much. Today, a restored 1886 school and church, a well-maintained cemetery and some pioneer cabins remain.

In Rockville, 3.5 miles west of Springdale, take Bridge Rd south; cross the bridge and turn right on Grafton Rd. After half a mile follow the main road, which bears left and becomes gravel. A mile further, bear right at the sign. After another 2 miles, you'll pass the cemetery on your left, then drive a quarter-mile further to the ghost town. Park at the red gate.

La Verkin Overlook   VIEWPOINT

West of Virgin on Hwy 9, before La Verkin, a 1.5-mile gravel-and-dirt road leads south to La Verkin Overlook. Stop for a fantastic 360-degree view of the surrounding 40 sq miles, from Zion to the Pine Valley Mountains. Trails lead along the ridge above the Virgin River. This is a great sunset perch.

🏃 Activities

Mountain Biking

The area around Zion has a handful of heart-pumping mountain bike trails through the desert – these are wicked-fun rides. The three most famous trail systems are the **JEM Trail**, fast beginner-level single track through desert scrub along the canyon rim; **Wire Mesa**, intermediate-level slickrock riding with tremendous views; and **Gooseberry Mesa**, a technical slickrock route similar to what you'll find in Moab. Note that Wire and Gooseberry Mesa ac-

cess is rugged; you don't absolutely need high-clearance 4WD, but it is recommended. Further afield, the area around St George is another good spot for road and mountain bike trails. Ask at the bike stores for maps and more information.

Zion Cycles   MOUNTAIN BIKING

(☑ 435-772-0400; www.zioncycles.com; 868 Zion Park Blvd; half-/full-day rentals from $28/38, car racks from $20; ⊙ 9am-6pm Feb-Nov) Next to Zion Mountain School (p85), this is the most helpful bike shop in town, with lots of info on local trails and road, hard-tail and full-suspension mountain bike rentals. Shuttle available, no tours.

Bike Zion   MOUNTAIN BIKING

(☑ 435-772-3303; www.bikingzion.com; 1458 Zion Park Blvd; half-/full-day rental from $25/35, car racks half-/full day $12/15; ⊙ 8am-8pm) **Zion Rock's** (www.zionrockguides.com; canyoneering day $195; ⊙ 8am-8pm Mar-Oct, hours vary Nov-Feb) on-site sister cycle shop; has a variety of rentals and does tours. We never saw anyone in the store, so it's best if you call ahead.

Tubing

The Virgin River is swift, rocky and only about knee-deep; more of a bumpy adventure ride than a leisurely float, but tubing (outside the park only) is popular in the summer. Note that from June to August, the water is only 55°F to 65°F (13°C to 18°C). Zion Outfitters (p85) rents out river tubes ($20 per day), unless the water level is too low (or too high). The float stretches about 2.5 miles, and lasts from 90 minutes to two hours depending on the water flow.

Spa

Deep Canyon Adventure Spa   SPA

(☑ 800-765-7787; www.deepcanyonspa.com; 450 Zion Park Blvd, Flanigan's Inn; 1hr treatments from $99) After a hard day's hike, the river-stone massage will be your muscles' new best friend.

👉 Tours & Outfitters

If you're eager to try out canyoneering or rock climbing but don't have the gear or necessary experience, stop in at one of the following outfitters to sign up for a trip or a course. Most outfitters offer half-day, full-day, family and adventure-level tours. Outfitters with storefronts also offer gear rental for the Narrows (wetsuits, dry suits, neoprene booties, etc). There are also a few off-road 4WD tours available.

Springdale

★ **Zion Adventure Company**   ADVENTURE SPORTS

(☏435-772-1001; www.zionadventures.com; 36 Lion Blvd; canyoneering day from $189; ⊙8am-8pm Mar-Oct, shorter hours Nov-Feb) The main outfitter in town and certainly the most organized. The focus is on renting gear for the Narrows (p58; $25 to $55), but it also offers a good selection of canyoneering and climbing trips and courses. Solo travelers looking to bring the price down for guided trips by hooking up with others should try here first.

Springdale

Canyoneering and camping equipment for sale.

Zion Guru
ADVENTURE SPORTS
(☑ 435-632-0432; www.zionguru.com; 792 Zion Park Blvd; canyoneering day from $265; ⊙8am-9pm May–mid-Sep, hours vary rest of year) Guests rave about this holistic outfitter offering wellness programs as well as adventures in canyoneering, climbing and hiking, photography tours and park shuttles. Rental gear for the Narrows ($24 to $52) is in top condition.

Zion Mountaineering School
ADVENTURE SPORTS
(☑ 435-319-0313; www.guidesinzion.com; 868 Zion Park Blvd; canyoneering day course from $190; ⊙9am-7pm Mar-Oct, hours vary Nov-Feb) Local outfitter located behind the Zion Noodle Company, offering Narrows gear rental ($23 to $44), courses and guided trips. It also has public showers ($5).

Zion Outfitters
ADVENTURE SPORTS
(☑ 435-772-5090; http://zionoutfitter.com; 95 Zion Park Blvd; day bike/tube rentals $35/20; ⊙8am-7pm Mar-Oct, hours vary Nov-Feb) Ideally located at the park entrance, Zion Outfitters is particularly handy for cruiser bikes, tube rentals and gear for the Narrows ($24 to $45). It also has public showers ($4).

Red Desert Adventures
ADVENTURE SPORTS
(☑435-668-2888; www.reddesertadventure.com; canyoneering day from $195) A small company with experienced area guides; provides private guided hiking, biking, climbing and canyoneering. Prices drop with more participants.

Zion Outback Safaris
ADVENTURE
(☑435-668-3756; www.zionjeeptours.com; 2400 Zion Park Blvd, Majestic View Lodge; 3hr tour from $80) Backroad 4WD tours in a 12-seat modified truck. Private Jeep tours also available.

✦ Festivals & Events

Zion Half Marathon SPORTS
(https://vacationraces.com; ⊙Apr) On your marks, get set...four superb races in the Zion area make the end of April a very popular time for trail runners. There's a half-marathon, a 50k, a 100k and a 100-miler. It usually sells out, so reserve your spot early.

🛏 Sleeping

Springdale has a good selection of mid-range to boutique hotels, upscale chains and smaller B&Bs, plus one campsite. The lower the address number on Zion Park Blvd, the closer it is to the park entrance; all lodgings are near shuttle stops.

Just 4 miles southwest is Rockville, which has a further selection of cheaper B&Bs. Do note that many of the area B&Bs do not serve breakfast, but instead provide guests with a restaurant voucher in town, in order to cater to those who want an early start.

🛏 Springdale

★ Under the Eaves Inn B&B $
(☑435-772-3457; www.undertheeaves.com; 980 Zion Park Blvd; r $109-209; 🅿️❄🛜) From colorful tractor reflectors to angel art, the owners' collections enliven every corner of this quaint 1930s bungalow. The fireplace suite is huge; other character-filled rooms are snug. Hang out in the arts-and-crafts living room or on Adirondack chairs and swings in the gorgeous gardens. The best room is the upstairs suite with claw-foot tub. Local restaurant coupon for breakfast.

Zion Canyon Campground & RV Resort CAMPGROUND $
(☑435-772-3237; www.zioncamp.com; 479 Zion Park Blvd; tent/RV sites with hookups $39/49; @🛜❄🛜) Water and tubing access at this 200-site campground are just across the Virgin River from the national park. It is attached to the **Quality Inn** (☑435-772-3237; www.zioncamp.com; 479 Zion Park Blvd; r from $180; @🛜❄🛜) motel, and shared amenities include heated pool, laundry, camp store, playground and restaurant. It's mainly for RVs, though it can be a handy backup for tent campers if you can't get a spot in the park.

Not all sites have shade. Pets are allowed in RVs only.

Zion Park Motel MOTEL $
(☑435-772-3251; www.zionparkmotel.com; 865 Zion Park Blvd; r $79-189; ❄🛜❄) It's a wonder what a coat of paint can do for old wood-paneled rooms. Microwaves and minirefrigerators are the main perks at this family-owned and supremely central budget option.

HIKING THE NARROWS: DO YOU NEED THE GEAR?

All outfitters in town feature a Narrows rental package, which generally includes some combination of canyoneering shoes, neoprene socks, hiking stick and a wet or dry suit. But if you find yourself balking at the price tag that comes with most of these packages ($25 to $55 depending on the season), the next thought that pops into your head will probably be, 'Do I really need all this stuff anyway?' This is a fair question to ask, and the answer depends largely on your own experience, current river conditions and how far you plan on going.

The short answer is that you don't need anything in the package – you will see people in all sorts of attire trying to hike the Narrows, some of which is quite comical – but what you are wearing will greatly influence your comfort level and thus your overall enjoyment. To help you decide, remember the following:

➡ You are going to get wet, and when the water temperature is below 50°F (10°C), hypothermia is a real danger.

➡ It is cooler and shadier in the Narrows than elsewhere in Zion.

➡ You will be walking through fast-moving currents on slippery rocks – a strong hiking stick (or trekking poles) is like having a third leg.

➡ If you are carrying electronics, you obviously don't want them to get wet; a dry sack is very handy.

If you're still unsure, go to an outfitter the day before and talk to both employees and customers returning gear. Most hikers will be eager to share their opinions with you.

SMITHSONIAN BUTTE BACKCOUNTRY BYWAY

Stratified buttes, slickrock pinnacles and balancing rocks are all part of the attraction on this challenging 9-mile backcountry drive. Though rated for regular passenger vehicles, the road is not always well maintained – ruts can be giant and a high-clearance 4WD vehicle is preferable. In Rockville, turn south on Bridge Rd and cross the river. The road will veer before you get to the left-hand turn for Smithsonian Butte Rd. (Follow signs to the right and you'll reach Grafton Ghost Town (p83).

Start your trip counter here. Once you turn south, you'll be winding your way up with **Wire Valley** on your right and **Horse Valley** on the left: this initial 1-mile ascent is locally known as Cry Baby Hill and is the steepest and hardest part of the drive. The raggedly eroded formation to the southeast is **Eagle Crags**. Make sure to look around as you ascend. About a mile up the road the first panorama of Zion National Park formations unfolds; stop along the way to look at the other angles that follow.

At 4.5 miles, the road to **Gooseberry Mesa**, a premier mountain-biking destination, branches off to the right. Shortly after, you're rounding **Smithsonian Butte** on BLM (Bureau of Land Management) land to your left, in an area known for petroglyphs. The drive is almost over as you descend onto a plain and into **Apple Valley**. From there Hwy 59 leads toward Hurricane in one direction, and Arizona in the other.

★**Red Rock Inn**   B&B **$$**
(☑ 435-772-3139; www.redrockinn.com; 998 Zion Park Blvd; cottages $209-309; ❋ ☎) Eight romantic country-contemporary cottages spill down the desert hillside, backed by incredible red rock. One suite features an outdoor hot tub; others feature full or partial kitchen and pull-out beds. Breakfast vouchers included.

★**Desert Pearl Inn**   HOTEL **$$**
(☑ 435-772-8888, 888-828-0898; www.desertpearl.com; 707 Zion Park Blvd; r from $239; ❋ @ ☎ ❋) How naturally stylish: twig sculptures decorate the walls and molded metal headboards resemble art. Opt for a spacious riverside king suite to get a waterfront patio. The most sophisticated design in town and popular with hip Angelenos. Rooms include sink, toaster oven and microwave.

Driftwood Lodge   HOTEL **$$**
(☑ 435-772-3262, 888-801-8811; www.driftwoodlodge.net; 1515 Zion Park Blvd; r $169-299; ❋ ☎ ❋) Rich textures and dark leathers mold the upscale style of thoroughly remodeled rooms at this eco-minded lodging. Some of the contemporary suites have pastoral sunset views of field, river and mountain beyond. With an expansive pool on the grounds.

Canyon Vista Lodge   B&B **$$**
(☑ 435-772-3801; www.canyonvistabandb.com; 2175 Zion Park Blvd; ste $189-249; ❋ ☎) All the homey comfort of a B&B, coupled with the privacy of a hotel. Individual entrances lead out from Southwestern or Old World–style rooms onto a wooden porch or a sprawling patio and lawn with river access. Breakfast coupons; hot tub on-site.

Novel House Inn   B&B **$$**
(☑ 800-711-8400, 435-772-3650; www.novelhouse.com; 73 Paradise Rd; r $199-209; ❋ ☎) Incredible detail has gone into each of the 10 author-themed rooms: Rudyard Kipling has animal prints and mosquito netting, and a pillow in the Victorian Dickens room reads 'Bah humbug.' Breakfast coupons.

Zion Canyon Bed & Breakfast   B&B **$$**
(☑ 435-772-9466; www.zioncanyonbnb.com; 101 Kokopelli Circle; r $159-215; ❋ ☎) Deep canyon colors echo the scenery and over-the-top Southwestern styling. Everywhere you turn there's another gorgeous red-rock view framed perfectly in an oversized window. Full gourmet breakfasts and minispa.

Flanigan's Inn   HOTEL **$$**
(☑ 435-772-3244, 800-765-7787; www.flanigans.com; 450 Zion Park Blvd; r from $199, ste from $309; ❋ @ ☎ ❋) Rejuvenate your spirit by indulging in a seaweed and mineral mud wrap, walking the hilltop meditation labyrinth and sinking into your king-size bed in front of a crackling fire. Suites are deliciously plush with vaulted ceilings, bold color schemes and tasteful art; most sleep up to six. Standard rooms vary, so check out a few first. There are also two villas.

THE ART OF THE CANYON

With such incredible natural surrounds, it's no wonder that so many artists find inspiration in the canyon. You'll see the results hanging all over town in Springdale: in restaurants, hotels and B&Bs. A number of galleries in town carry the work of various local photographers, painters and sculptors, including: David Pettit, David West, Anna Weiler Brown and Deb Durban. Gallery hours can be as mercurial as their owners.

David J West Gallery (☏435-772-3510; www.davidjwest.com; 801 Zion Park Blvd; ⊙10am-9pm) Iconic local landscape photography; sells some photo gear.

De Zion Gallery (☏435-772-6888; www.deziongallery.com; 1051 Zion Park Blvd; ⊙10am-9pm Mar-Nov) Large studio with many Utah artists represented.

LaFave Gallery (☏435-772-0464; http://secure.lafavegallery.com; 1214 Zion Park Blvd; ⊙9am-8pm) Large collection of ceramics, jewelry, sculpture and paintings, but pride of place here goes to the work of local photographer David Pettit. Also sells signed prints.

Worthington Gallery (☏435-772-3446; https://worthingtongallery.com; 789 Zion Park Blvd; ⊙9am-8pm) Represents 20 different potters from across the Southwest.

Harvest House   B&B **$$**
(☏435-772-3880; www.harvesthouse.net; 29 Canyon View Dr; r $145-175; ✳☎) Modern B&B with four rooms, full breakfast and an outdoor hot tub.

Cliffrose Lodge   HOTEL **$$$**
(☏800-243-8824, 435-772-3234; www.cliffrose lodge.com; 281 Zion Park Blvd; r from $311-411; ✳☎≋) Kick back in a lounge chair or take a picnic lunch to enjoy on the five gorgeous acres of lawn and flower gardens leading down to the river. High-thread-count linens and pillow-top mattresses are among the upscale touches. Suites sleep up to six and feature full kitchens. This is a good high-end choice for families.

🛏 Rockville & Around

★2 Cranes Inn   INN **$**
(☏435-216-7700; http://2craneszion; 125 E Main St, Rockville; r $125-150) 🍽 In this quiet Buddhist home Lisa and Lizette have created a luxury hostel feel, with lovely rooms featuring original art and a shared kitchen where you can cook dinner away from the crowds and make breakfast to hit the trail early. There's good insider hiking information, an extensive garden and massage on-site. Not for partying: quiet hours start at 10pm.

Zion River Resort   CAMPGROUND **$**
(☏888-822-8594, 435-635-8594; www.zionriver resort.com; Hwy 9, Virgin; tents $45, RVs $58-72, cabins $105-259; @☎≋🐾) The massive RV resort outside Virgin, 12 miles west of Spring-

dale, caters to upscale big rigs with long pull-throughs and phone and cable hookups. There are only a handful of tent sites and camping cabins (no linens). Quality shower rooms, coin laundry, barbecue pavilion, guest kitchen, heated pool, and games and media room are tops. Pets in RVs only.

Desert Thistle Bed & Breakfast   B&B **$$**
(☏435-772-0251; www.thedesertthistle.com; 37 W Main St; r $155-170; ✳☎≋) A big backyard pool makes the romantic, modern Desert Thistle Bed & Breakfast a top choice on hot summer days. Rooms are posh and the Scottish owner, Maureen, is the consummate host. Rates include a breakfast voucher for use in Springdale; two-night minimum stay.

🍴 Eating

Springdale has plenty of cheerful options geared at the high visitor population. Few are outstanding. Most restaurants open for dinner serve beer and wine. Note that many places in town limit hours – or close entirely – off-season (November to February). To stock up on groceries, head 22 miles west to Hurricane.

Café Soleil   CAFE **$**
(☏435-772-0505; http://cafesoleilzionpark.com; 205 Zion Park Blvd; mains $10-13; ⊙6am-9pm May-Sep, 7am-8pm Oct-Apr; ☎🍽) The food is every bit as good as the free-trade coffee. Try the Mediterranean hummus wrap or giant vegetable frittata; there is pizza and salads, too. It's a good spot to grab sandwiches for hiking. Breakfast served till noon.

Whiptail Grill
SOUTHWEST **$**

(☑435-772-0283; www.whiptailgrillzion.com; 445 Zion Park Blvd; mains $12-17; ☺noon-9pm Mar-Nov, shorter hours rest of year; 🛜🖕) The old gas-station building isn't much to look at, but deep shade and fresh tastes abound: think gorgeous *chiles rellenos* (stuffed poblano chilies) and *carne asada* tacos grilled to perfection. Desserts are rich with a kick. Outdoor patio tables fill up quick.

MeMe's Cafe
CRÊPES **$**

(☑435-772-0114; www.memescafezion.com; 975 Zion Park Blvd; mains $11-18; ☺7am-10pm) For a coffee and sweet crêpes, make MeMe's Cafe your first stop of the day. It also serves salads, savory crêpes, burgers, brats and vegan meatloaf.

Park House Cafe
CAFE **$**

(☑435-772-0100; http://parkhousecafezion.com; 1880 Zion Park Blvd; breakfast $6.50-13.50; ☺8am-2pm Mar-Oct; 🛜) Wake up as late as you like: Park House Cafe serves its Asiago bagel with egg and avocado – along with organic coffee and other breakfast items – until 2pm. It's a sweet little spot on the edge of town with an artsy vibe.

Zion Park Gift & Deli
DELI **$**

(☑435-772 3843; http://zionparkgiftanddeli.com; 866 Zion Park Blvd; sandwiches $8.50; ☺8:30am-8:30pm) Sharing a space with a souvenir shop, this one-counter wonder turns out good sandwiches (including boxed lunches for the park), breakfasts, chocolates and ice cream, all to go.

Thai Sapa
ASIAN **0**

(☑435-772-0510; www.thaisapazion.com; 198 Zion Park Blvd; mains $12-15; ☺11:30am-9:30pm) This mix of Thai, Chinese and Indian cuisine is the best Asian-cuisine option in town.

Zion Pizza & Noodle
ITALIAN **$**

(☑435-772-3815; www.zionpizzanoodle.com; 868 Zion Park Blvd; pizza & pasta $11-17; ☺4-9pm) No need to reinvent the wheel here – the can't-lose combo of pizza and pasta remains Zion's go-to choice for families. Specialty pizzas tend toward the unusual (Thai chicken, Southwest burrito) while cheese and pepperoni sates the less adventurous. Counter service only, with to-go options available.

Sol Foods Downtown Supermarket
MARKET **$**

(☑435-772-3100; www.solfoods.com; 995 Zion Park Blvd; ☺7am-11pm Apr-Oct, 9am-8pm Nov-Mar) Springdale's grocery store has a decent selection, with organic items and camping-friendly meals. There's also a salad bar and deli with $8 sandwiches. Groceries are pricey, however.

Oscar's Cafe
SOUTHWEST **$$**

(☑435-772-3232; www.cafeoscars.com; 948 Zion Park Blvd; mains $12-20, breakfast $6-13; ☺7am-9pm) From green-chili-laden omelets to pork *verde* burritos (with a green salsa), expect big servings of Southwestern spice. There's also smoky ribs, garlic burgers and beer on tap. The Mexican-tiled patio with twinkly lights (and heaters) is a favorite hangout in the evening. The breakfast is quite popular, which might mean a late start in the park.

Bit & Spur Restaurant & Saloon
SOUTHWEST **$$**

(☑435-772-3498; www.bitandspur.com; 1212 Zion Park Blvd; mains $14-30; ☺5-11pm Mar-Oct, 5-11pm Fri-Sun Nov-Feb; 🛜) Sweet-potato tamales and chili-rubbed rib-eyes are two of the classics at this local institution. Inside, the walls are wild with local art; outside on the deck it's all about the red-rock sunset. Full bar.

★ King's Landing
AMERICAN **$$$**

(☑435-772-7422; www.klbzion.com; 1515 Zion Park Blvd, Driftwood Lodge; mains $18-38; ☺5-9pm; 🖕) With a lauded Las Vegas chef and his pastry chef wife at the helm, this hotel-restaurant surpasses expectations. Bison fettuccine with truffle oil, charred octopus and verdant greens entice. Locals love its intimacy. There

AROUND ZION NATIONAL PARK SPRINGDALE

---

❶ DISPERSED CAMPING

Can't get a coveted spot at one of the park's two main campgrounds? We've been there. Luckily, there is beautiful public land in the area where you can pitch a tent or park your RV for free (no water or bathrooms). The Zion NPS website has a detailed map of public camping (www.nps.gov/zion; run a search for campgrounds south of Hwy 9) or you can ask at the ranger desk; most sites are roughly 30 minutes away from Springdale. The best and closest sites for tent campers is off the Smithsonian Butte Hwy south of Rockville, though depending on the season you may need a 4WD car to access this area. Websites like www.campendium.com and http://freecampsites.net are also useful resources.

are also good burgers, vegetarian fare that does not bore and beautiful desserts. Reserve ahead.

Spotted Dog · · · · · · · · · · · · · · · AMERICAN $$$
(☑435-772-0700; www.flanigans.com; 428 Zion Park Blvd; breakfast $9, mains $15-35; ☺7-11am & 5-9pm Mar-Nov) One of the more inventive top-end dining choices in Springdale, the Spotted Dog has a seasonal menu with a focus on regional specialties. Expect delicacies like Cedar Mountain lamb shank, wild game meatloaf and Rocky Mountain trout. Spacious dining areas plus two outdoor patios.

♟ Drinking

If you just want a beer, remember you'll also have to order at minimum an appetizer (eg chips and salsa) per Utah state law. You can grab six-packs at Sol Foods (p89).

★ Deep Creek Coffee Co · · · · · · · · · · · CAFE
(☑435-767-0272; www.deepcreekcoffee.com; 932 Zion Park Blvd; ☺6:30am-2pm; ☎) The town's best coffee, with espresso drinks and fresh pastries daily.

Zion Canyon Brew Pub · · · · · · · · · · BREWERY
(☑435-772-0336; www.zionbrewery.com; 95 Zion Park Blvd; ☺11:30am-9pm; ☎) The local brewery has a killer location, with an outdoor patio that cozies up to the Virgin River and the park entrance. Nine varieties of suds are on tap, from Red Altar to Delusion Ale. It does have a full food menu, but all you really need are the pretzel sticks and you're good to go.

Jack's Sports Grill · · · · · · · · · · · · SPORTS BAR
(☑435-772-3700; 1149 Zion Park Blvd; ☺noon-10pm) Jack's has a full bar and serves sandwiches, rice bowls and all-day breakfast, but the real reason you're here is to catch the big game on one of the many big screens.

☆ Entertainment

OC Tanner Amphitheater · · · · · · · · · · THEATER
(☑box office 435-652-7800; www.octannershows.com; 300 Lion Blvd; ☺mid-May–Aug) Outdoor amphitheater surrounded by red rock; stages classical, bluegrass, country and other concerts and performances.

❶ Information

Springdale Visitor Center (☑435-429-1555; www.zionnationalpark.com; 1101 Zion Park Blvd; ☺7am-10pm) If nothing else is open, this private visitor center can be helpful, although it's mostly a gift shop.

Zion Canyon Visitors Bureau (☑435-772-3434; www.zionpark.com; 118 Lion Blvd; ☺9am-5pm Mon-Fri) Offers comprehensive accommodations listings of family-friendly motels and hotels, as well as boutique inns and B&Bs.

Zion Canyon Medical Clinic (☑435-772-3226; http://zioncanyonclinic.com; 120 Lion Blvd; ☺9am-5pm Tue-Sat Mar-Oct, shorter hours Nov-Feb) Walk-in urgent-care clinic.

Zion Park Laundry (865 Zion Park Blvd; ☺7am-10pm) Unstaffed, self-service laundromat on main street; soap available.

❶ Getting Around

PRIVATE VEHICLE
If you're staying in Springdale, it's best to use the shuttle as finding a parking spot in town can quickly turn into a Herculean task. If you're just passing through, arrive before 8am to secure a parking space at the park's visitor center and avoid the lengthy traffic jams at the entrance.

In town, you can park for free along the main road. Town lots cost $20 per day; there is also a slightly cheaper **pay lot** (Lion Blvd; per day $15) behind the Zion Adventure Company.

SHUTTLE
From March through early November the free **Springdale Shuttle** runs through town every 10 to 15 minutes, from 7am to 10pm (seasonal hours vary). It runs from the Majestic View Lodge to the park's south entrance, with nine stops in total. At the park entrance, you can walk across a footbridge to the visitor center and Zion shuttle.

St George

POP 77,000 / ELEV 2860FT

Nicknamed 'Dixie' for its warm weather and southern location, St George has long been attracting winter residents and retirees. Brigham Young, second president of the Mormon church, was one of the first snowbirds in the one-time farming community here. An interesting-if-small historic downtown core holds some interest, but it's the area outside of town, where you're quickly immersed in magnificent desert scenery, that's most appealing. Snow Canyon State Park is a great place to go cycling, rock climbing and hiking.

The abundant and affordable lodging makes this an oft-used stop between Las Vegas and Salt Lake City – or en route to Zion National Park after a late-night flight. The town lies about 41 miles (up to an hour) from Zion National Park's south entrance and 33 miles (30 minutes) from the Kolob Canyons' entrance on I-15.

◉ Sights

Pick up a free, full-color, historic-building walking tour brochure at the visitor center (p94). The intersection of Temple and Main Sts is at the heart of the old town center.

Dinosaur Discovery Site   MUSEUM
(☑435-574-3466; www.utahdinosaurs.com; 2180 E Riverside Dr; adult/child under 12yr $6/3; ☺10am-6pm Mon-Sat, shorter hours Oct-Feb) St George's oldest residents aren't retirees from Idaho, but Jurassic-era dinosaurs. Entry gets you an interpretive tour of the huge collection of tracks, beginning with a video. The casts were first unearthed by a farm plow in 2000 and rare paleontology discoveries, such as dinosaur swim tracks, continue to be made.

Brigham Young Winter Home   MUSEUM
(☑435-673-2517; 67 W 200 N; ☺9am-5pm Mon-Sat) FREE A tour of the Mormon leader's seasonal home and headquarters illuminates a lot about early town and experimental-farming history.

St. George Children's Museum   MUSEUM
(☑435-986-4000; www.sgchildrensmuseum.org; 86 S Main St; admission per person $5; ☺10am-6pm Tue-Sat; ⚹) St George has plenty of 'No' signs: no touching this, no climbing that, no sitting here and definitely no skateboarding anywhere. So if the kids are starting to get a little antsy, let them loose here, where they can touch, climb and play to their hearts' delight. It's best suited for ages two to 10.

Daughters of Utah Pioneers Museum   MUSEUM
(McQuarrie Memorial Museum; ☑435-628-7274; www.dupstgeorge.org; 145 N 100 E; ☺10am-5pm Mon, Tue, Thu-Sat) FREE Two floors packed full of pioneer artifacts, furniture, photographs, quilts, guns and so on.

Jacob Hamblin Home   MUSEUM
(☑435-673-5181; 3325 Santa Clara Dr; ☺9am-6:30pm) FREE For an evocative picture of the Mormon pioneer experience, head 5 miles north of town to Santa Clara and the 1863 Jacob Hamblin Home, where orchards still grow.

🏃 Activities

Hiking trails crisscross St George. Eventually they'll be connected and the trail along the Virgin River will extend to Zion National Park; get a map at the visitor center (p94). And don't forget that Snow Canyon State Park (p94) is nearby.

Mountain bikers will want to check out the **Green Valley Trail** (also called Bearclaw Poppy) through the desert just west of town. Mountain-bike rental costs $30 to $45 per day. Road cyclists can follow popular bike paths all the way to Snow Canyon.

A handful of local golf courses are open to the public (many more are private). Reserve up to two weeks in advance at www.sgcity.org/golf.

Red Rock Bicycle Company   MOUNTAIN BIKING
(☑435-674-3185; www.redrockbicycle.com; 446 W 100 S; mountain bikes per 24hr from $35, car racks from $15; ☺9am-7pm Mon-Sat, 11am-5pm Sun) Rentals and servicing available.

Bicycles Unlimited   MOUNTAIN BIKING
(☑435-673-4492; www.bicyclesunlimited.com; 90 S 100 E; mountain bike rentals per 4hr $25-39, car rack $15-22; ☺9am-6pm Mon-Sat) Rentals available.

Desert Rat Outdoor Store   OUTDOORS
(☑435-628-7277; www.thedesertrat.net; 468 West St George Blvd; ☺9am-7pm Mon-Fri, to 6pm Sat) This outdoor store will outfit you for any activity and provide area advice. Also sells all the gear you might need.

Paragon Adventures   ADVENTURE SPORTS
(☑435 673-1709; www.paragonadventure.com; 955 N 1300 W) The offerings from this popular outfitter include road or mountain bike tours, rock climbing, small-group canyoneering, interpretive hikes and popular zipline adventures.

Arts to Zion   TOURS
(www.artstozion.org) Check the website for information about self-touring artist studios throughout St George.

🎆 Festivals

Dixie Roundup   SPORTS
(☑435-628-8282; ☺mid-Sep) A mid-September weekend full of Western fun, including a parade and rodeo.

St George Marathon   SPORTS
(www.stgeorgemarathon.com; ☺Oct) This October event takes over the town, attracting runners from all 50 states.

St George

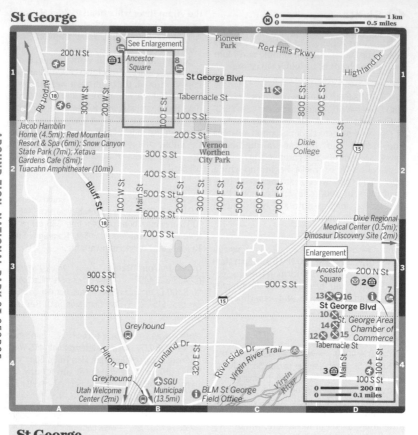

AROUND ZION NATIONAL PARK ST GEORGE

St George

◉ Sights
1 Brigham Young Winter Home	B1
2 Daughters of Utah Pioneers Museum	D3
3 St. George Children's Museum	D4

◯ Activities, Courses & Tours
4 Bicycles Unlimited	D4
5 Desert Rat Outdoor Store	A1
6 Red Rock Bicycle Company	A1

🛏 Sleeping
7 Best Western Coral Hills	D3
8 Dixie Palm Motel	B1
9 Seven Wives Inn	B1

✖ Eating
10 Bear Paw Cafe	D3
11 Bombay Cafe	C1
12 Judd's General Store	D4
13 Painted Pony	D3
14 Riggatti's Wood Fired Pizza	D4
15 Twenty-Five on Main	D4

◉ Drinking & Nightlife
16 George's	D3

🛏 Sleeping

St George offers the cheapest lodging near Zion and has a plethora of generic motels, some with rates that dip below $50 in the off-season. Rates listed are for high season.

Campers should check out sites in Snow Canyon State Park (p95). A bit further away,

there are campsites at Red Cliffs Recreation Area (near Hurricane), the Baker Dam Recreation Area (north up Hwy 18) and the USFS campground in Pine Valley (p95).

Dixie Palm Motel MOTEL $
(☎866-651-3997, 435-673-3531; www.dixiepalms motel.com; 185 E St George Blvd; r from $62;

❋☎☲) It may not look like much outside, but regular maintenance and TLC put the Dixie Palm at the head of the low-budget pack. The 15 rooms have minirefrigerators and microwaves; some have full kitchens.

America's Best Inn & Suites MOTEL $
(☑435-652-3030, 800-718-0297; www.bestzion. com; 245 N Red Cliffs Dr; r from $85; ❋@☎☲) Well positioned for fast out-of-town access off I-15, this economic choice is also surprisingly quiet. Minirefrigerators and microwaves come standard in the tidy rooms.

★ Seven Wives Inn B&B $$
(☑435-628-3737, 800-600-3737; www.seven wivesinn.com; 217 N 100 W; r $120-185; ❋@☎☲) Two 1800s homes and a cottage feature lovely bedrooms and suites surrounded by well-tended gardens and a small pool. The name comes from settler times, when one of the owners harbored fugitive polygamists in the 1880s. The cottage is pet-friendly.

Best Western Coral Hills MOTEL $$
(☑800-542-7733, 435-673-4844; www.coralhills. com; 125 E St George Blvd; r from $93; ❋@☎☲) You can't beat being a block or two from downtown restaurants and historic sights. Waterfalls and spiffed-up decor set this locally owned franchise apart.

Inn at Entrada RESORT $$
(☑435-634-7100; www.innatentrada.com; 2588 W Sinagua Trail; r/ste from $179/249; P🚭❋ ☎☲) Nestled in red rock and xeriscaped for low-water consumption, this private country club has luxury adobe cottages with hot tubs, gas fireplaces and ample amenities. It's primarily a golfing destination, and also has an on-site restaurant and spa. There's a $20 resort fee. It's located 6 miles north of town off Snow Canyon Pkwy.

Red Mountain Resort & Spa RESORT $$$
(☑877-246-4453, 435-673-4905; www.redmoun tainresort.com; 1275 E Red Mountain Circle; r from $179; ❋@☎☲☲) A Zen-chic sensibility pervades this low-profile yogacentric adobe resort, right down to the silk pillows that echo the copper color of surrounding cliffs. Full meals, guided hikes, spa services and yoga classes are generally included depending on the accommodation package. There's an additional $25 resort fee. It's located 7 miles northwest of town off Snow Canyon Pkwy.

Amira Resort & Spa RESORT $$$
(☑435-628-1370; www.amiraresort.com; 1871 W Canyon View Dr; r from $169; @☲) Luxury spa

and sports resort: 4000-sq-ft golf center, 14 tennis courts and six swimming pools. Hiking and weight-loss programs feature prominently. It's located 5 miles southwest of town.

🍴 Eating & Drinking

★ Riggatti's Wood Fired Pizza PIZZA $
(☑435-674-9922; www.riggattis.com; 73 N Main St; pizzas $8-14; ◷11am-9pm Mon-Sat) With a fanatical local following, this tiny pizzeria is a boon for travelers searching for thin-crust pizzas with bubbling mozzarella and pesto. Grab one of the very few counter seats and save room for hot cinnamon sticks.

Judd's General Store ICE CREAM $
(☑435-628-2596; 62 W Tabernacle St; ice cream from $3; ◷9:30am-5:30pm Mon-Sat) Stop for a sweet scoop of ice cream or piece of nostalgic candy.

Bear Paw Cafe CAFE $
(☑435-634-0126; 75 N Main St; mains $7-12; ◷7am-3pm; ♠) This homey cafe is St George's most popular breakfast spot, with patrons waiting curbside even in the low season. Try a half-order if your appetite isn't mammoth. There's an extensive kids' menu.

Bombay Cafe INDIAN $
(☑435-673-8888; http://bombaycafesg.com; 57 N 700 E; mains $8-14; ◷11am-2:30pm & 5-9pm Mon-Sat) This tiny hole-in-the-wall is run by Pakistani batik artist Shazad Sheikh and his wife, Rabia. You'll find chicken tikka masala, daal chana, naan and other classic dishes alongside a small collection of handmade saris and scarves for sale.

Twenty-Five on Main CAFE $
(☑435-628-7110; www.25main.com; 25 N Main St; mains $8-14; ◷8am-9pm Mon-Thu, to 10pm Fri & Sat) A hip, modern cafe with sidewalk tables. Homemade cupcakes are not all it does well – check out the breakfast panini, the warm salmon salad and the pasta primavera, overflowing with veggies.

★ Xetava Gardens Cafe AMERICAN $$
(☑435-656-0165; www.xetava.com; 815 Coyote Gulch Ct, Ivins; breakfast $7-13, lunch & dinner $13-17; ◷9am-5pm Sun-Thu, 9am-9pm Fri & Sat; ♪) We'd drive much further than 8 miles for the organic, locavore fare served here in a stunning red-rock setting. Expect small plates (mahi cake), salads, ciabatta sandwiches, gyros and burgers.

★ **Painted Pony**　　MODERN AMERICAN $$$
(☑435-634-1700; www.painted-pony.com; 2 W St George Blvd; lunch $8-14, dinner mains $25-36; ☺11:30am-10pm Mon-Sat, 4-10pm Sun) Think gourmet comfort food and great salads. At dinner you might choose a juniper-brined pork chop; at lunch, meatloaf with a port-wine reduction and rosemary mashed potatoes.

George's　　PUB
(☑435-216-7311; http://georgescornerrestaurant. com; 2 W St George Blvd; ☺8am-midnight; ☏) This central pub anchors historic Ancestor Sq. Local beers on tap and a reliable, if un-exciting, menu; weekend brunch is popular.

☆ Entertainment

Tuacahn Amphitheater　　THEATER
(☑435-652-3200; www.tuacahn.org; 1100 Tuacahn Dr, Ivins) Ten miles northwest in Ivins; hosts musicals in summer and other performances year-round.

❶ Information

Additional information is available at www. utahsdixie.com and www.sgcity.org.

St. George Area Chamber of Commerce
(☑435-628-1658; www.stgeorgechamber.com; 97 E St George Blvd; ☺9am-5pm Mon-Fri) The visitor center caters to relocating retirees, and has loads of city info.

Dixie Regional Medical Center (☑435-251-1000; https://intermountainhealthcare.org/ locations/dixie-regional-medical-center/; 1380 S Medical Center Dr; ☺24hr)

BLM St George Field Office (☑435-688-3200; www.blm.gov/office/st-george-field-office; 345 E Riverside Dr; ☺7:45am-5pm Mon-Fri, 10am-3pm Sat) Get interagency information on surrounding public lands: USFS, BLM and state parks. Topographic maps and guides available. Staff can also suggest where to camp for free on BLM land.

Utah Welcome Center (☑435-673-4542; http://travel.utah.gov; 1835 S Convention Center Dr, Dixie Convention Center; ☺10am-5pm) Statewide information 2 miles south of St George. There's a wildlife museum (think taxidermy) on-site with the same hours.

❶ Getting There & Away

Taxis ($15 to downtown) and all the big-chain car-rental companies are represented at the St George airport. Note that Las Vegas McCarran International Airport, 120 miles southwest, often has better flight and car-rental deals than Utah airports.

St George Municipal Airport (SGU; ☑435-627-4080; www.flysgu.com; 4550 S Airport Pkwy) Located 13.5 miles southeast of town.

St George Express (☑435-652-1100; www. stgeorgeexpress.com; 805 S Bluff St; 1-way Las Vegas $19-38) Shuttle service to Las Vegas, NV (two hours) and Zion National Park. Provides door-to-door service.

Greyhound (☑435-673-2933; www.grey-hound.com; 1235 S Bluff St; ☏) Buses depart from the local McDonald's en route to Salt Lake (5½ hours) and Las Vegas (two hours). With on-board wi-fi.

Snow Canyon State Park

Gila monsters, roadrunners and desert tor-toises populate a landscape of undulating slickrock and ancient lava flows in this pop-ular state park. **Snow Canyon** (☑435-628-2255; https://stateparks.utah.gov/parks/snow-canyon/; 1002 Snow Canyon Dr, Ivins; per person/vehicle $4/10; ☺day use 6am-10pm; ♿) is a 7400-acre sampler of southwest Utah's fa-mous land features, 11 miles northwest of St George. Easy trails – perfect for kids – lead to tiny slot canyons, petrified sand dunes, lava tubes and red-and-white domes. Sum-mers are blazing hot: visit in early morn-ing or come in spring or fall. The park was named after prominent Utah pioneers Lorenzo and Erastus Snow, not frozen pre-cipitation, but for the record it does very occasionally snow here.

Hiking trails loop off the main road. **Jen-ny's Canyon Trail** is an easy 1-mile round-trip to a short slot canyon. Wind through a cottonwood-filled field and past ancient lava flows to a 200ft arch on **Johnson Canyon Trail** (2-mile round-trip). A 1000ft stretch of vegetation-free sand dunes serves as a play-ground for the kiddies, old and young, near a picnic area.

The best hike, however, is a loop that combines several different trails. Depart-ing from the visitor center, follow the lovely **Hidden Pinyon** nature trail to the petrified sand dunes. From the top of the former dunes you descend to a 27,000-year-old lava flow via the Butterfly and Lava Flow trails – bring a headlamp to explore the lava tube along the latter. From here, follow the West Canyon trail south, returning to the visitor center by way of Three Ponds. The total dis-tance is roughly 3.5 miles.

Cycling is popular on the main road through the park, a 17-mile loop from St George (where you can rent bikes). There's also great **rock climbing** in the park, particularly for beginners, with over 150 bolted and sport routes, plus top-roping.

Apart from during the unrelenting summer, the 35-site **campground** (☑800-322-3770; http://utahstateparks.reserveamerica.com; 1002 Snow Canyon Dr, Ivins; tent/RV sites with partial hookups $20/25; 🐾) is great, and so scenic. You can reserve one of the 30 bookable sites (14 with electrical and water hookups) up to four months in advance. There are showers and dump station available. Campers do not pay the park's day-use fee.

Pine Valley Mountain Wilderness Area

Mountains rise sharply in the 70-sq-mile **Pine Valley Wilderness Area** (☑435-652-3100; www.fs.usda.gov/dixie; Pine Valley) in the Dixie National Forest, 32 miles northwest of St George off Hwy 18. The highest point, Signal Peak (10,365ft), remains snow-capped till July and rushing streams lace the mountainous area. The St George Field Office provides information and free backcountry permits.

When the desert heat blurs your vision, Pine Valley offers cool respite. Most hikes here begin as strenuous climbs. The 5-mile round-trip **Mill Canyon Trail** and the 6-mile **Whipple Trail** are most popular, each linking with the 35-mile **Summit Trail**.

Pine Valley Recreation Complex (☑877-444-6777; www.recreation.gov; Pine Valley Recreation Area Rd, Pine Valley; tent sites $17, RV sites without hookups $17-34; ☺mid May–Sep), 3 miles east of Pine Valley, has a few pine-shaded campgrounds at 6800ft and 55 sites in total. They all have water but no showers or hookups; bring mosquito repellent.

Cedar City

POP 28,860 / ELEV 5850FT

This sleepy college town comes to life every summer when the Shakespeare festival takes over. Associated events, plays and tours continue into fall. Year-round you can make one of the many B&Bs a quiet home base for exploring the Kolob Canyons section of Zion National Park or Cedar Breaks National Monument (p98). At roughly 6000ft, cooler temperatures prevail here than in Springdale (60 miles away) or St George (55 miles); there's even occasional snow in May.

◉ Sights & Activities

Frontier Homestead State Park Museum   MUSEUM
(☑435-586-9290; http://frontierhomestead.org; 635 N Main St; admission $4; ☺9am-5pm Mon-Sat; 🖝) Kids love the cabins and the brightly painted 19th-century buggies, as well as the garden full of old farm equipment to run through. Living history demos take place June through August.

Cedar Cycle   CYCLING
(☑435-586-5210; http://cedarcycle.com; 38 E 200 S; road/mountain-bike rental per day $35/39; ☺9am-5:30pm Mon-Fri, 10am-2pm Sat) After you rent a bike, the knowledgeable staff here can point you to local trails.

✪ Festivals

Utah Shakespeare Festival   THEATER
(☑435-586-7878; www.bard.org; 200 W College Ave; tickets from $20; ☺late Jun-Oct) Southern Utah University puts on three of the bard's plays and three contemporary dramas each summer season in Cedar City. Productions are well regarded, but don't miss the extras, all free: 'greenshows' with Elizabethan minstrels, literary seminars discussing the plays and costume classes. Backstage and scene-changing tours cost extra.

Neil Simon Festival   THEATER
(www.simonfest.org; ☺mid-Jul–mid-Aug) American plays staged mid-summer.

🛏 Sleeping

Weekends during the Shakespearean festival may cost more than the high season (March through October). A proliferation of good B&Bs is a boon for couples.

Iron Gate Inn   B&B $
(☑800-808-4599, 435-867-0603; www.theirongateinn.com; 100 N 200 W; r $129-149; 🅿@🛜) With an on-site winery, this distinct 1897 Second Empire Victorian house features large, modern-luxury guest rooms, rambling porches and a big yard. Enjoy your breakfast on the large shady patio.

Big Yellow Inn   B&B $
(☑435-586-0960; www.bigyellowinn.com; 234 S 300 W; r from $109; 🅿@🛜) This purpose-built Georgian Revival inn has room to roam, with a dining room, a library, a den and many porches. Upstairs rooms are elegantly ornate with period decor. Downstairs, the ground-floor walk-out rooms are simpler

Cedar City

Cedar City

and a bit more 'country.' The owners also oversee several adjunct B&B properties and vacation rentals around town.

Anniversary House   B&B **$**
(☑️435-865-1266, 800-778-5109; www.theanniver saryhouse.com; 133 S 100 W; r from $109; ❄️🛜🐾) Remarkably comfortable rooms, a great-to-talk-to host and thoughtful extras make this one of our faves. Savor freshly baked cake and complimentary beverages in the mission-style dining room or lounge around in the landscaped backyard with hot tub and grill. Outdoor kennel available.

Garden Cottage B&B   B&B **$**
(☑️435-586-4919, 866-586-4919; www.thegarden cottagebnb.com; 16 N 200 W; r from $119; ⊙May-Sep; ❄️🛜) Romantic vines climb up the steep-roofed cottage walls, and in season a fantasia of blooms grow in encompassing gardens. If you like antiques and quilts, you're going to love Garden Cottage. The

owner has done an amazing job displaying family treasures. No room TVs.

Amid Summer's Inn B&B **$**
(☑888-586-2601, 435-586-2600; www.amidsummersinn.com; 140 S 100 W; r $99-149; ☺May-Oct; ✳@☎) Tasteful additions have brought the guest room count to 10 at this 1930s home-based B&B. Common areas and some rooms have a Victorian feel; others are more over-the-top trompe l'oeil fantasies. Accommodating hosts; great breakfasts.

✗ Eating & Drinking

★Centro PIZZA **$**
(☑435-867-8123; www.centropizzeria.com; 50 W Center St; pizzas $10-15; ☺11am-10pm Mon-Sat) Serving wood-fired Neapolitan pizza and heaping bowls of fresh salad in a sleek atmosphere, Centro is a hub for hedonist appetites. Touches like hand-crushed tomato sauce and homemade fennel sausage up the ante. Though the wine list is basic, there's a good selection of brews. Good service.

Lonny Boy's BBQ BARBECUE **$**
(☑435-867-8010; http://sonnyboysbbq.com; 126 N Main St; mains $6-16; ☺11am-9pm Mon Thu, to 10pm Fri & Sat) Don't be fooled by the cookie-cutter shopping plaza setting. There's a huge meat smoker outside, rolls of paper towels on the tables and sticky barbecue on the menu. It's filled with international visitors looking for a slice of Americana and locals with their king cab pickups.

Grind Coffeehouse CAFE
(☑435-867-5333, 19 N Main St; ☺7am-7pm Mon-Sat; ☎) Hang out with the locals and have a barista-made brew, a great hot sandwich or a big salad. Sometimes there's music on the menu.

❶ Information

Cedar City & Brian Head Tourism & Convention Bureau (☑435-586-5124, 800-354-4849; www.visitcedarcity.com; 581 N Main St; ☺8:30am-5pm Mon-Sat; ☎) Area-wide info and free internet use. A tiny **Daughters of Utah Pioneers Museum** (☑435-586-8269; 581 N Main St; ☺10am-5pm Mon-Fri, to 1pm Sat May-Sep, shorter hr rest of yr) is located here.
Cedar City Ranger Station (☑435-865-3200; www.fs.usda.gov/dixie; 1789 N Wedgewood Lane; ☺8am-5pm Mon-Fri) Provides **Dixie National Forest** (p156) information and can advise on USFS campsites.

Valley View Family Medicine (☑435-868-5000; www.intermountainhealthcare.org; 1333 N Main; ☺24hr)

❶ Getting There & Away

Greyhound (☑800-231-2222; www.greyhound.com; 1495 W 200 N) Regional buses stop in Cedar City.

Highway 14

Scenic Hwy 14 leads 42 miles over the Markagunt Plateau, cresting at 10,000ft and offering awesome vistas of Zion National Park and Arizona to the south. This is essentially a backdoor route between Zion and Bryce or Escalante: it's not quite as stunning as Hwy 9, though it will be less crowded, and along the way you'll find several hiking trails, campgrounds and overlooks, as well as the main attraction, Cedar Breaks National Monument. Stop by the Cedar City Ranger Station for maps and information. Though Hwy 14 remains open all winter, you may want snow tires between November and April. The closest campsite to Cedar City is the pleasant USFS **Cedar Canyon** (☑877-444-6777; www.recreation.gov; Hwy 14; tent & RV sites $17-34; ☺late May-Sep; ✤), located 11 miles east of town and 31 miles from Zion's Kolob Canyons entrance at an elevation of 8100ft.

Hiking and cycling trails past the Cedar Breaks National Monument turnoff on Hwy 14 have tremendous views, particularly at sunset. They include the short (less than a mile one way) **Cascade Falls** and **Bristlecone Pine Trail** and the 32-mile **Virgin River Rim Trail**. A signed turnoff 24.5 miles from Cedar City leads to jumbled lava beds.

Boating and fishing are the activities of choice at Navajo Lake, 25 miles east of Cedar City. You can rent canoes ($25) or motorboats ($80 to $175) or stay over in a historic 1920s cabin at **Navajo Lake Lodge** (☑702-646-4197; www.navajolakelodge.com; Duck Creek Village; cabins from $89; ☺May-Oct; ✤). The rustic lodgings include fireplaces and bedding, but no refrigerators.

Five miles further east, **Duck Creek Visitor Center** (☑435-682-2432; www.fs.usda.gov/recarea/dixie/recarea/?recid=24854; Hwy 14; ☺10am-5pm late May-early Sep) provides information for nearby trails and fishing in the adjacent pond and stream. Here at 8400ft, the 87 pine-shaded sites at **Duck Creek Campground** (☑877-444-6777; www.recreation.gov; Hwy 14; tent & RV sites without hookups

$17-34; ☺mid-May–Sep; ☷) are blissfully cool in summer. The ever-expanding log-cabin town at nearby **Duck Creek Village** (www. duckcreekvillage.com) has more services, including a couple of restaurants, realty offices, cabin rental outfits, a laundromat and an internet cafe. The village area is big with off-road enthusiasts – ATVs in summer and snowmobiles in winter.

About 7 miles east of Duck Creek, a signed, passable dirt road leads the 10 miles to **Strawberry Point**, an incredibly scenic overview of red-rock formations and forest lands.

Cedar Breaks National Monument
ELEV 10,300FT

Sculpted cliffs and towering hoodoos glow like neon tie-dye in a wildly eroded natural amphitheater encompassed by **Cedar Breaks National Monument** (☑435-586-9451, 435-586-0787; www.nps.gov/cebr; Hwy 143 E, Brian Head; 7-day pass adult/child $7/free; ☺late May–mid-Oct). The majestic kaleidoscope of magenta, salmon, plum, rust and ocher rises to a height of 10,450ft atop the Markagunt Plateau. The compact park lies 22 miles east and north of Cedar City, off Hwy 14. There are no cedar trees here, by the way: early pioneers mistook the evergreen junipers for cedars.

BRIAN HEAD SKI RESORT
···

Did someone mention skiing in the desert? From Thanksgiving through April, snow bunnies come to test the closest slopes to Las Vegas. Advanced skiers might grow impatient with the short trails (except on a powder day), but there's lots to love for beginners and intermediates at **Brian Head Resort** (☑435-677-2035; www.brianhead.com; 329 S Hwy 143; 1-day lift ticket adult/child from $45/32), 35 miles northeast of Cedar City. Lines are usually short and it's the only resort in Utah within sight of red rock. Here's the lowdown: 1320ft vertical drop; base elevation, 9600ft; 640 acres and seven high-speed triple lifts. In summer, the mountain morphs into a premier biking destination and fun zone for children (think climbing wall, trampoline, ziplines etc).

This altitude gets more than a little snow, and the monument's one road, Hwy 148, is closed from sometime in November through to at least May. Summer temperatures range from only 40°F to 70°F (4°C to 21°C); brief storms drop rain, hail and even powdery white snow. In season, rangers hold geology talks and star parties at the small visitor center.

No established trails descend into the breaks, but the park has five viewpoints off Hwy 148 and there are rim trails. **Ramparts Trail** – one of southern Utah's most magnificent trails – leaves from the visitor center. The elevation change on the 3-mile round-trip is only 400ft, but it can be tiring because of the overall high elevation. **Alpine Pond Trail** is a lovely, though less dramatic, 4-mile loop.

The first-come, first-served **Point Supreme Campground** (☑435-586-9451; www. recreation.gov; 2390 Hwy 56 #11; tent & RV sites without hookups $24; ☺Jun-Oct; ☷) has water and restrooms, but no showers; its 28 sites rarely fill. It's about an hour's drive from Zion's Kolob Canyons.

Along Highway 89

Few linger here, but the tiny old towns along Hwy 89 have some restaurant and lodging gems hidden within (beware seasonal closings).

Independent motels and a few eateries line Hwy 89 in **Hatch**, 25 miles southwest of Bryce Canyon and 15 miles south of Panguitch.

Further south, 50 miles from Bryce and 26 miles to Zion, **Glendale** is a historic little Mormon town founded in 1871. Today it's an access point for Grand Staircase–Escalante National Monument (GSENM). From Hwy 89, turn onto 300 North at the faded sign for GSENM; from there it turns into Glendale Bench Rd, which leads to scenic **Skutumpah & Johnson Canyon Roads**.

At the turnoff for Hwy 9, **Mt Carmel Junction** has art galleries, two gas stations (one with a sandwich counter) and lodgings about 15 slow-and-scenic miles from the east entrance of Zion, and 18 miles north of Kanab.

◉ Sights

★**Maynard Dixon**
Living History Museum   MUSEUM
(☑435-648-2652; www.thunderbirdfoundation. com; 2200 S State St, Mt Carmel; self-guided/ docent tour $10/20; ☺10am-5pm Mar-Nov) In

Mt Carmel, the *Architectural Digest*–noted Maynard Dixon Living History Museum is where renowned Western painter Maynard Dixon (1875–1946) lived and worked in the 1930s and '40s. Docent-led tours are by appointment only. Look for the house at Mile 84 on Hwy 89 (called State St in town), about 6 miles south of Glendale; it's easy to miss.

🛏 Sleeping

Historic Smith Hotel   B&B **$**
(📞800-528-3558, 435-648-2156; www.historic smithhotel.com; 295 N Main St, Glendale; r from $89; ❄🐾🛜🐕) More comfortable than a favorite old sweater; don't let the small rooms turn you off. The proprietors are a great help in planning your day and the big breakfast tables are the place to meet other intrepid travelers from around the globe. Great back decks, and there is a hot tub and garden, too.

Arrowhead Country
Inn & Cabins   B&B **$**
(📞435-648-2569, 888-821-1670; www.arrow headbb.com; 2155 S State St; r from $109, cabins from $149; ❄🛜🐾🐕) The quilt-covered four-poster beds sure are comfy. The east fork of the Virgin River meanders behind the inn and a trail leads from here to the base of the white cliffs. It's located 2.5 miles north of Mt Carmel Junction and Hwy 9. Two cabins are pet-friendly.

Las Vegas

POP 594,294 / ELEV 2000FT

Las Vegas remains the ultimate escape. Where else can you party in ancient Rome, get hitched at midnight, wake up in Egypt and brunch beneath the Eiffel Tower? Double down with the high rollers, browse couture or tacky souvenirs, sip a neon 3ft-high margarita or a frozen vodka martini from a bar made of ice – it's all here for the taking.

Ever notice that there are no clocks inside casinos? Vegas exists outside time, a sequence of never-ending buffets, ever-flowing drinks and adrenaline-fueled gaming tables. In this never-ending desert dreamscape of boom and bust, once-famous signs collect dust in a neon boneyard while the clang of construction echoes over the Strip. After the alarming hiccup of the 2008 recession, the city is once more back on track, attracting well over 40 million visitors per year and bursting with schemes to lure even more in future.

WORTH A TRIP

PAROWAN GAP

People have been passing this way for millennia, and the **Parowan Gap** (https://parowan.org/parowan-gap/; Parowan Gap Rd, Parowan) petroglyphs prove it. Look closely as you continue walking along the road to find panels additional to those signed. Archaeo-astronomers believe that the gap in the rocks opposite the petroglyphs may have been used as part of an ancient, astronomically based calendar. Cedar City's tourism office (p97) has colorful interpretive brochures explaining site details.

Park travelers using Las Vegas as a jumping-off point may be more interested in the cheap flights and proximity to the great outdoors. Red Rock Canyon is just a fat-tire hop away, and even the Grand Canyon's South Rim is a doable day trip from the Strip.

👁 Sights

Vegas' sights are primarily concentrated along the 4.2-mile stretch of Las Vegas Blvd anchored by Mandalay Bay to the south (at Russell Rd) and the Stratosphere to the north (at Sahara Ave) and in the Downtown area around the intersection of Las Vegas Blvd (N Las Vegas Blvd at this point) and Fremont St. Note that while the street has the same name, there's an additional 2 miles between Downtown and the northern end of the Strip, with not much of interest in-between. It might look close if you decide to walk between the two, but you'll probably find yourself cursing in the desert heat if you do so. Ride-shares, the Monorail and Deuce bus services are by far the easiest ways to get around this spaced-out (in more ways than one) city.

👁 The Strip

★**New York–New York**   CASINO
(📞800-689-1797; www.newyorknewyork.com; 3790 S Las Vegas Blvd; ⏰24hr; 🅿) Opened in 1997, the mini-megalopolis of New York–New York remains a perennial hit with spring breakers. Tables in the casino's 'Party Pit' are set against a backdrop of go-go dancers and occasional live entertainers, while out front, perspective-warping replicas of the Statue of Liberty, Brooklyn Bridge, and Chrysler and Empire State buildings delight

Las Vegas Strip

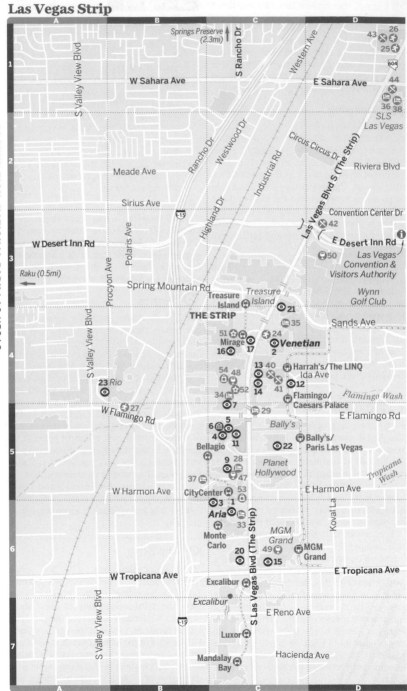

visitors from abroad. Tying it all together, the **Big Apple Arcade** and **Roller Coaster** are timeless hits with kids and big kids alike.

★**Aria**   LANDMARK
(CityCenter; www.aria.com; 3780 S Las Vegas Blvd; ⓟ) We've seen this symbiotic relationship before (think giant hotel anchored by a mall 'concept'), but the way that this futuristic-feeling complex places a small galaxy of hypermodern, chichi hotels in orbit around the glitzy **Shops at Crystals** is a first. The upscale spread includes the subdued, stylish **Vdara**, the hush-hush opulent **Mandarin Oriental** and the dramatic architectural showpiece **Aria**, whose sophisticated casino provides a fitting backdrop to its many drop-dead-gorgeous restaurants. CityCenter's hotels have in excess of 6700 rooms!

★**Cosmopolitan**   CASINO
(🖉702-698-7000; www.cosmopolitanlasvegas.com; 3708 S Las Vegas Blvd; ⊘24hr; ⓟ) Hipsters who thought they were too cool for Vegas finally have a place to go where they don't need irony to endure – or enjoy – the aesthetics of the Strip. Like the new Hollywood 'It' girl, the Cosmopolitan casino looks absolutely fabulous at all times. A steady stream of ingenues and entourages parade through the lobby (with some of the coolest design elements we've seen) along with anyone else who adores contemporary art and design.

★**Paris Las Vegas**   CASINO
(🖉877-796-2096; www.caesars.com/paris-las-vegas; 3655 S Las Vegas Blvd; ⊘24hr; ⓟ) This miniversion of the French capital might lack the charm of the City of Light, but its efforts to emulate Paris' landmarks, including a 34-story Hotel de Ville and facades from the Opera House and Louvre, make it a fun stop for families and anyone yet to see the real thing. Its vaulted casino ceilings simulate sunny skies above myriad tables and slots, while its high-limit authentic French roulette wheels, sans 0 and 00, slightly improve your odds.

★**Bellagio**   CASINO
(🖉702-693-7111; www.bellagio.com; 3600 S Las Vegas Blvd; ⊘24hr; ⓟ🐾) The Bellagio experience transcends its decadent casino floor of high-limit gaming tables and in excess of 2300 slot machines; locals say odds here are less than favorable. A stop on the World Poker Tour, Bellagio's tournament-worthy poker room offers kitchen-to-gaming-table

AROUND ZION NATIONAL PARK LAS VEGAS

Las Vegas Strip

delivery around-the-clock. Most, however, come for the property's stunning architecture, interiors and amenities, including the **Conservatory & Botanical Gardens**, **Gallery of Fine Art**, unmissable **Fountains of Bellagio** and the 2000-plus hand-blown glass flowers embellishing the hotel (p105) lobby.

★**Caesars Palace**   CASINO
(☑866-227-5938; www.caesars.com/caesars-palace; 3570 S Las Vegas Blvd; ◎24hr; Ⓟ) Caesars Palace claims that its smartly renovated casino floor has more million-dollar slots than anywhere in the world, but its claims to fame

are far more numerous than that. Entertainment's heavyweights Celine Dion and Elton John 'own' its custom-built **Colosseum** theater, fashionistas saunter around **The Forum Shops**, while Caesars hotel guests quaff cocktails in the **Garden of the Gods Pool Oasis**. By night, megaclub Omnia (p108) is the only place to get off your face this side of Ibiza.

High Roller   LANDMARK
(☑702-777-2782;   www.caesars.com/linq/high-roller; LINQ Promenade; adult/child from $22/9, after 5pm $32/19; ◎11:30am-1:30am; Ⓟ🚻; 🚌Flamingo or Harrah's/Linq) The world's largest

observation wheel towers 550ft above **LINQ Promenade**. Each of the 28 air-conditioned passenger cabins is enclosed by handcrafted Italian glass. Outside, 2000 colorful LED lights glow from dusk until dawn. One revolution takes about 30 minutes and each pod can hold 40 guests. From 4pm to 7pm, select pods host the adults-only (21-plus) 'happy half-hour' ($35, or $47 after 5pm) with an open bar (read all-you-can-drink) shared between your fellow riders. Things can get messy, fast.

Mirage Volcano LANDMARK
(☑702-791-7111; www.mirage.com; Mirage; ⊙shows 7pm, 8pm & 9pm daily) **FREE** When the Mirage's trademark artificial volcano erupts with a roar out of a 3-acre lagoon, it inevitably brings traffic on the Strip to a screeching halt. Be on the lookout for wisps of smoke escaping from the top, signaling that the fiery Polynesian-style inferno, with a soundtrack by a Grateful Dead drummer and an Indian tabla musician, is about to begin.

Venetian CASINO
(☑702-414-1000; www.venetian.com; 3355 S Las Vegas Blvd; ⊙24hr; **P**) The Venetian's regal 120,000-sq-ft casino has marble floors, hand-painted ceiling frescoes and 120 table games, including a high-limit lounge and an elegant non-smoking poker room, where women are especially welcome (unlike at many other poker rooms in town). When combined with its younger, neighboring sibling **Palazzo**, the properties claim the largest casino space in Las Vegas. Unmissable on the Strip, a highlight of this miniature replica of Venice is to take a **gondola ride** down its Grand Canal.

Viva Las Vegas Wedding Chapel CHAPEL
(☑702-384-0771; www.vivalasvegasweddings.com; 1205 S Las Vegas Blvd; **P**) Even if you're not contemplating tying the knot, it's worth a peek inside this little assembly-line wedding chapel of loooove to see if anyone is getting married. The public is welcome to attend the themed weddings: kitschy as all get-out, they range from Elvis' 'Blue Hawaii' and 'Pink Caddy' to 'Twilight,' 'Gangster' and 'Gladiator' themes. Book ceremonies in advance.

Downtown & Off-Strip

Mob Museum MUSEUM
(☑702-229-2734; www.themobmuseum.org; 300 Stewart Ave; adult/child $27/17; ⊙9am-9pm; **P**;

☐ Deuce) It's hard to say what's more impressive: the museum's physical location in a historic federal courthouse where mobsters sat for federal hearings in 1950–51, the fact that the board of directors is headed up by a former FBI special agent, or the thoughtfully curated exhibits telling the story of organized crime in America. In addition to hands-on FBI equipment and mob-related artifacts, the museum boasts a series of multimedia exhibits featuring interviews with real-life Tony Sopranos.

★**National Atomic Testing Museum** MUSEUM
(☑702-794-5151; www.nationalatomictestingmuseum.org; 755 Flamingo Rd E, Desert Research Institute; adult/child $22/16; ⊙10am-5pm Mon-Sat, noon-5pm Sun; ☐202) Fascinating multimedia exhibits focus on science, technology and the social history of the 'Atomic Age,' which lasted from WWII until atmospheric bomb testing was driven underground in 1961 and a worldwide ban on nuclear testing was declared in 1992. View footage of atomic testing and examine southern Nevada's nuclear past, present and future, from Native American ways of life to the environmental legacy of atomic testing. Don't miss the ticket booth (how could you?); it's a Nevada Test Site guard-station replica.

★**Springs Preserve** NATURE RESERVE
(☑702-822-7700; www.springspreserve.org; 333 S Valley View Blvd; adult/child $19/11; ⊙9am-5pm; **⊛**; ☐104) ✈ On the site of the natural springs (which ran dry in 1962) that fed *las vegas* ('the meadows'), where southern Paiutes and Spanish Trail traders camped, and later Mormon missionaries and Western pioneers settled the valley, this educational complex is an incredible trip through historical, cultural and biological time. The touchstone is the **Desert Living Center**, demonstrating sustainable architectural design and everyday eco-conscious living.

Red Rock Canyon National Conservation Area NATURE RESERVE
(☑702-515-5350; www.redrockcanyonlv.org; 1000 Scenic Loop Dr; car/bicycle $15/5; ⊙scenic loop 6am-8pm Apr-Sep, to 7pm Mar & Oct, to 5pm Nov-Feb; **⊛**) Red Rock's dramatic vistas are revered by Las Vegas locals and adored by visitors from around the world. Formed by extreme tectonic forces, it's thought the canyon, whose 3000ft red rock escarpment rises sharply from the valley floor, was formed

around 65 million years ago. A 13-mile, one-way scenic loop drive offers mesmerizing vistas of the canyon's most striking features. Hiking trails and rock-climbing routes radiate from roadside parking areas.

★ **Neon Museum –**
Neon Boneyard MUSEUM
(☑702-387-6366; www.neonmuseum.org; 770 N Las Vegas Blvd; 1hr tour adult/child $28/24; ⊙tours daily, schedules vary; 🚌113) This non-profit project is doing what almost no one else does: saving Las Vegas' history. Book ahead for a fascinating guided walking tour of the 'Neon Boneyard,' where irreplaceable vintage neon signs – Las Vegas' original art form – spend their retirement. Start exploring at the visitor center inside the salvaged La Concha Motel lobby, a mid-century modern icon designed by African American architect Paul Revere Williams. Tours are usually given throughout the day, but are most spectacular at night.

★ **Pinball Hall of Fame** MUSEUM
(☑702-597-2627; www.pinballmuseum.org; 1610 E Tropicana Ave; per game 25¢-$1; ⊙11am-11pm Sun-Thu, to midnight Fri & Sat; 🚐; 🚌201) You may have more fun at this no-frills arcade than playing slot machines back on the Strip. Tim Arnold shares his collection of 200-plus vintage pinball and video games with the public. Take time to read the handwritten curatorial cards explaining the unusual history behind these restored machines.

🏃 Activities

★ **Stratosphere**
Thrill Rides AMUSEMENT PARK
(☑702-380-7777; www.stratospherehotel.com/thrillrides; Stratosphere; elevator adult $20, incl 3 thrill rides $35, all-day pass $40; ⊙10am-1am Sun-Thu, to 2am Fri & Sat; Sahara) The world's highest thrill rides await, a whopping 110 stories above the Strip. Big Shot straps riders into completely exposed seats that zip up the tower's pinnacle, while Insanity spins riders out over the tower's edge. X-Scream leaves you hanging 27ft over the edge, 866ft above ground. For a real adrenaline rush, save your dough for **SkyJump**.

VooDoo ZipLine ADVENTURE SPORTS
(☑702-388-0477; www.voodoozipline.com; Rio; $28; ⊙11am-midnight) How does 'flying' between **Rio's** two hotel towers sound? The ride starts with you strapped into a seat on a 50-story tower. Four hundred feet below is the expansive pool area, and beyond is the cityscape. Once the operator sets you free, you'll whiz down metal lines to a lower tower, taking in the 800ft-long rush...then get pulled back!

Red Rock Climbing Center CLIMBING
(☑702-254-5604; www.redrockclimbingcenter. com; 8201 W Charleston Blvd; day pass $15, belay check $5, equipment rental $10; ⊙9am-9pm Sat & Sun, to 11pm Mon & Fri, 6am-11pm Tue-Thu) Run by climbers, this outdoor-adventure shop rents bouldering crash pads, carries all-weather apparel and brand-name hiking, rock-climbing, camping and backpacking equipment and has an indoor climbing wall on which you can prepare for the real thing.

👉 Tours

★ **Flightlinez Bootleg Canyon** OUTDOORS
(☑702-293-6885; www.flightlinezbootleg.com; 1644 Nevada Hwy; 3hr tour $159; ⊙8am-5pm) This thrilling aerial adventure is like ziplining, but with a paragliding harness. Morning tours see the coolest temps, while late afternoon tours may catch sunset over the desert. Riders must weigh between 75lb and 250lb (fully dressed) and wear close-toed shoes.

🛏 Sleeping

With over 150,000 hotel rooms and consistently high occupancy rates, prices in Vegas fluctuate constantly. Sometimes the best deals are found in advance; other times, at the last minute. As a general rule, if you find a good price on a place you trust, nab it. Decent rooms Downtown start from as low as $29, while the swankiest digs on the Strip can fetch upwards of $10,000 per night!

🛏 The Strip

★ **W Las Vegas** BOUTIQUE HOTEL **$**
(☑702-761-8700; www.wlasvegas.com; 2535 S Las Vegas Blvd; r from $107; P❄️📶🏊🐾) At the time of writing, the new W Las Vegas, occupying what was one of two towers belonging to sister property SLS, was the hottest ticket on the north Strip, offering excellent rates for a stylish brand-new product by this exciting world-recognized brand. If you like design and a cooler crowd, head north and hang here.

SLS HOTEL **$**
(☑702-761-7000; www.slslasvegas.com; 2535 S Las Vegas Blvd; d from $102; P❄️📶🏊) You

GOING TO THE CHAPEL

A blushing bride says 'I do' every five minutes in Sin City. Scores of celebrity couples have exchanged vows in Vegas, from Elvis Presley and Priscilla Beaulieu to Andre Agassi and Steffi Graf. Why not you, too? After all, the 50:50 odds of a marriage surviving 'til death do us part' start to look pretty good compared with the chances of hitting a royal flush on a video-poker machine.

If you're thinking of officially tying the knot in Las Vegas and want to know what's required, contact Clark County's **Marriage License Bureau** (www.clarkcountynv.gov/depts/clerk/services/pages/marriagelicenses.aspx), which gets jammed during crunch times such as weekends, holidays and 'lucky number' days.

can nab a room at Vegas' SLS (the Starwood Hotel Group's boutique brand) on the north Strip at a crazy rate compared to same-branded properties in other destinations. The hotel's quirky style is infectious: you'll have fun with the acronym within minutes.

★**Cromwell Las Vegas**   BOUTIQUE HOTEL **$**
(☑702-777-3777; www.caesars.com/cromwell; 3595 S Las Vegas Blvd; r/ste from $89/427; P☀☎☱☃) If you're 20- to 30-something, can hold your own with the cool kids, or you're just effortlessly stylish whatever your demographic, there are a few good reasons to choose Cromwell, the best being its location and frequently excellent rates on sassy, entry-level rooms. The others? You've got your sights set on partying at **Drai's** or dining downstairs at **Giada**.

★**Cosmopolitan**   CASINO HOTEL **$$**
(☑702-698-7000; www.cosmopolitanlasvegas. com; 3708 S Las Vegas Blvd; r/ste from $120/250; P☀@☎☱☃; ☐Deuce) With at least eight distinctively different and equally stylish room types to choose from, Cosmo's digs are the hippest on the Strip. Ranging from oversized to decadent, about 2200 of its 2900 or so rooms have balconies (all but the entry-level category), many sport sunken Japanese tubs and all feature plush furnishings and design quirks you'll delight in uncovering.

★**NOBU Hotel**   HOTEL **$$**
(☑800-727-4923; www.caesars.com/nobu-caesarspalace; 3570 S Las Vegas Blvd, Caesars Palace; d from $149) This exclusive boutique hotel within Caesars Palace (p102) is one for lovers of Japanese design from the traditional to the modern. Rooms are in high demand and suites are often the domain of celebrities.

★**Palazzo**   CASINO HOTEL **$$**
(☑702-607-7777; www.palazzo.com; 3325 S Las Vegas Blvd; ste weekday/weekend from $201/231; P☀@☎☱) Looking more like rival Bellagio than its older sister and neighbor the **Venetian**, from which it couldn't be more different outside, room sizes and appointments within Palazzo are on par with, if not practically identical to the Venetian's. Enormous suites come with the Venetian's signature sunken living rooms and Roman tubs, while Prestige Suites enjoy VIP check-in with complimentary champagne.

★**Bellagio**   CASINO HOTEL **$$$**
(☑702-693-7111; www.bellagio.com; 3600 S Las Vegas Blvd; r weekday/weekend from $179/249; P☀@☎☱☃) When it opened in 1998, Bellagio was the world's most expensive hotel. Aging gracefully, it remains one of America's finest. Its sumptuous oversized guest rooms fuse classic style with modern amenities and feature palettes of platinum, indigo and muted white-gold, or rusty autumnal oranges with subtle splashes of *matcha* green. Cashmere throws, mood lighting and automatic drapes complete the picture.

🛏 Downtown & Off-Strip

Many off-Strip casino hotels offer free guest shuttles to/from the Strip.

★**El Cortez**   CASINO HOTEL **$**
(☑702-385-5200; www.elcortezhotelcasino.com; 600 Freemont St E; r weekday/weekend from $45/85; P☀@☎) A wide range of rooms with all kinds of vibes are available at this fun, retro property close to all the action on Fremont St. Rooms are in the 1980s tower addition to the heritage-listed 1941 **El Cortez** casino and the modern, flashier El Cortez Suites, across the street. Rates offered

are generally great value, though don't expect the earth.

★ Hilton Grand Vacations on Paradise
HOTEL $

(☑ 702-946-9200; www.hiltongrandvacations.com/nevada/hgvc-paradise; 455 Karen Ave; ste from $75; P✳☀🛱🏊) The spacious studio suites and one- and two-bedroom apartments of this well-maintained resort-style facility, less than a mile from the center Strip, offer excellent value, especially for traveling families.

★ Hard Rock
CASINO HOTEL $

(☑ 702-693-5000; www.hardrockhotel.com; 4455 Paradise Rd; r weekday/weekend from $60/120; P✳☀🛱🏊) Sexy, oversized rooms and HRH suites underwent a bunch of refurbishments in 2016 and 2017, making this party palace for music lovers a great alternative to staying on the Strip – there's even a free shuttle to take you there and bring you back.

✖ Eating

The Strip has been studded with celebrity chefs for years. All-you-can-eat buffets and $10 steaks still exist, but today's high-rolling visitors demand ever more sophisticated dining experiences, with meals designed – although not personally prepared – by famous taste-makers. Flash enough cash and you can taste the same cuisine served at revered restaurants from NYC to Paris to Shanghai.

✖ The Strip

★ Tacos El Gordo
MEXICAN $

(☑ 702-982-5420; www.tacoselgordobc.com; 3049 S Las Vegas Blvd; small plates $3-12; ☺10am-2am Sun-Thu, to 4am Fri & Sat; P🚲🚶; 🚊Deuce, SDX) This Tijuana-style taco shop from SoCal is just the ticket when it's way late, you've got almost no money left and you're desperately craving carne asada (beef) or *adobada* (chili-marinated pork) tacos in hot, handmade tortillas. Adventurous eaters order the authentic *sesos* (beef brains), *cabeza* (roasted cow's head) or tripe (intestines) variations.

★ Umami Burger
BURGERS $

(☑ 702-761-7614; www.umamiburger.com; SLS, 2535 S Las Vegas Blvd; burgers $12-15; ☺10am-10pm Sat & Sun, from 1pm Mon & Fri; P) The SLS (p104) burger offering is one of the best on the Strip, with its outdoor beer garden, extensive craft-beer selection and juicy boutique burgers made by the chain that won *GQ* magazine's prestigious 'burger of the year' crown.

★ Jaburrito
SUSHI $

(☑ 702-901-7375; www.jaburritos.com; LINQ Promenade; items $10-13; ☺11am-11pm Sun-Thu, to midnight Fri & Sat) It's simple: hybridize a nori (seaweed) sushi roll with a burrito. What could go wrong? Nothing actually...they're awesome!

★ Guy Fieri's Vegas Kitchen & Bar
AMERICAN $$

(☑ 702-794-3139; www.caesars.com/linq; LINQ Casino; mains $19-35; ☺9am-midnight) *Diners, Drive-ins and Dives* celebrity chef Guy Fieri has opened his first restaurant on the Strip at **LINQ Casino**, dishing out an eclectic menu of his own design, inspired by so many years journeying America's back roads for the best and fairest down-home cooking.

Lemongrass
ASIAN $$

(☑ 702-590-8670; www.aria.com; Aria; mains $14-32, tasting menus $39-59; ☺11am-2am; 🚲🚶) Visually high impact, this Thai and pan-Asian kitchen offers a satay bar and quasi-authentic soups, curries and noodle dishes, from *tom kha* chicken to drunken noodles with seafood. Use caution when ordering spice level 10 – it's mouth-searing.

ℹ VEGAS PLANNING

Vegas refuses to play by the rules of most cities, so working out how best to tackle your adventures can be a little overwhelming when you arrive. Although parking is widely free, it's rarely cost-effective to rent a car unless you'll be doing a lot of day trips. Stick to tour buses, taxis/rideshares and the local bus/monorail system when exploring the city. Walking around Vegas (especially in the sweltering summer heat) can have its downsides.

Once you've got your bearings, worked out what you want to see and do and how to get there, you'll generally need dinner reservations and show tickets. Casino and hotel concierges are your best bet here. Be sure to pack some fancy threads as many high-end destinations enforce strict dress codes.

★ **Joël Robuchon**   FRENCH $$$

(☑702-891-7925; www.mgmgrand.com/en/res taurants.html; MGM Grand; tasting menus $120-425; ☉5:30-10pm) The acclaimed 'Chef of the Century' leads the pack in the French culinary invasion of the Strip. Adjacent to the **MGM Grand's** high-rollers' gaming area, Robuchon's plush dining rooms, done up in leather and velvet, feel like a dinner party at a 1930s Paris mansion. Complex seasonal tasting menus promise the meal of a lifetime – and they often deliver.

★ **Morimoto**   FUSION $$$

(☑702-891-3001; www.mgmgrand.com/en/res taurants.html; MGM Grand; mains $24-75; ☉5-10pm Sun-Thu, to 10:30 Fri & Sat) Iron Chef Masaharu Morimoto's latest Vegas incarnation is in his eponymous showcase restaurant, which pays homage to his Japanese roots and the cuisine of this city that has propelled him to legend status around the world. Dining here is an experience in every possible way and, we think, worth every penny.

★ **Twist by Pierre Gagnaire**   FRENCH $$$

(☑702-590-8888; www.mandarinoriental.com/ las-vegas; Mandarin Oriental, CityCenter; mains $67-76, tasting menus $170-295; ☉6-10pm Tue-Thu, to 10:30pm Fri & Sat) If romantic Twist's sparkling nighttime Strip views don't make you gasp, the modern French cuisine by this three-star Michelin chef just might. Seasonal tasting menus may include squid-ink *gnocchetti* topped with carrot gelée or langoustine with grapefruit fondue, finished off with bubble-gum ice-cream with marshmallow and green-tea crumbles. Reservations essential; dress code is business casual.

✕ Downtown & Off-Strip

Get off the Strip for more reasonable prices.

Container Park   FAST FOOD $

(☑702-359-9982; www.downtowncontainerpark. com; 707 Fremont St; items $3-12; ☉11am-midnight Mon-Thu, 10am-2am Fri & Sat, 10am-midnight Sun; ☑; 🚊Deuce) With food-truck-style menus, outdoor patio seating and late-night hours, food vendors include the cutting-edge **Container Park** sell something to satisfy everyone's appetite. When we last stopped by, the ever-changing lineup included **Pinches Tacos** for Mexican flavors, Southern-style **Big Ern's BBQ**, raw-food and healthy vegan cuisine from **Simply Pure**, and salads and panini at **Bin 702** wine bar.

★ **Firefly**   TAPAS $$

(☑702-369-3971; www.fireflylv.com; 3824 Paradise Rd; shared plates $5-12, mains $15-32; ☉11:30am-1am Mon-Thu, to 2am Fri & Sat, 11am-1am Sun; 🚊108) Firefly is always packed with a fashionable local crowd, who come for well-prepared Spanish and Latin American tapas, such as *patatas bravas*, chorizo-stuffed empanadas and vegetarian bites such as garbanzo beans seasoned with chili, lime and sea salt. A backlit bar dispenses the house specialty sangria – red, white or sparkling – and fruity mojitos. Reservations strongly recommended.

★ **Raku**   JAPANESE $$

(☑702-367-3511; www.raku-grill.com/grill; 5030 W Spring Mountain Rd; shared plates $5-20; ☉6pm-3am Mon-Sat; 🚊203) At the place where LA chefs come to dine when they're in town, Japanese owner-chef Mitsuo Edo crafts small plates blossoming with exquisite flavors. You'll find yourself ordering just one more thing, again and again, from the menu of *robata*-grilled meats, homemade tofu and seasoned vegetables. Make reservations a few days in advance or angle for the tiny bar.

★ **Echo & Rig**   STEAK $$

(☑702-489-3525, www.echoandrig.com; 440 S Rampart Blvd; lunch $10-13, dinner $21-36; ☉11am-11pm Mon-Fri, from 9am Sat & Sun; 🅿❄) Check out the news tab of this restaurant's homepage for drool-worthy ways to season steaks and marinate meats, and to get a sense of this classy, original joint (pun intended). Sourcing the freshest cuts from its eponymous butcher, the idea is that customers will stop by the butcher and try it at home, once these talented folk have inspired them.

🍷 Drinking & Nightlife

You don't need us to tell you that Las Vegas is party central – the Strip is ground zero for some of the country's hottest clubs and most happening bars, where you never know who you'll be rubbing shoulders with. What you might not know is that Downtown's Fremont East Entertainment District is the go-to place for Vegas' coolest non-mainstream haunts.

🍷 The Strip

★ **107 SkyLounge**   LOUNGE

(☑702-380-7711; www.stratospherehotel.com; 2000 S Las Vegas Blvd, 107th fl, Stratosphere Tower; ☉4pm-3am) There's just no place to get any higher in Las Vegas – without the approval of an air traffic controller – than the lounge overlooking the revolving **Top of the World** restaurant. Come during happy hour (4pm to 7pm daily) for two-for-one cocktails, half-price appetizers and striking sunset views.

★**Chandelier Lounge** COCKTAIL BAR
(☑702-698-7979; www.cosmopolitanlasvegas. com/lounges-bars/chandelier; Cosmopolitan; ☺24hr; ◻Deuce) Towering high in the center of Cosmopolitan (p101), this ethereal cocktail bar is inventive yet beautifully simple, with three levels connected by romantic curved staircases, all draped with glowing strands of glass beads. The second level is headquarters for molecular mixology (order a martini made with liquid nitrogen), while the third specializes in floral and fruit infusions.

★**Double Down Saloon** BAR
(☑702-791-5775; www.doubledownsaloon.com; 4640 Paradise Rd; ☺24hr; ◻108) This dark, psychedelic gin joint appeals to the lunatic fringe. It never closes, there's never a cover charge, the house drink is called 'ass juice' and it claims to be the birthplace of the bacon martini. When live bands aren't terrorizing the crowd, the jukebox vibrates with New Orleans jazz, British punk, Chicago blues and surf-guitar king Dick Dale.

★**XS** CLUB
(☑702-770-0097; www.xslasvegas.com; Encore; cover $20-30; ☺10:30pm-4am Fri-Sun) XS is the hottest nightclub in Vegas – at least for now. Its extravagantly gold-drenched decor and over-the-top design mean you'll be waiting in line for cocktails at a bar towered over by ultra-curvaceous, larger-than-life golden statues of female torsos. Famous electronica DJs make the dance floor writhe, while high rollers opt for VIP bottle service at private poolside cabanas.

★**Wet Republic** CLUB
(☑702-891-3563; www.wetrepublic.com; MGM Grand; cover $20-40; ☺11am-6pm) Think of Wet Republic, the city's biggest 'ultra pool,' as a nightclub brought out into the sunlight. The mostly 20- and 30-something crowd in stylish swimwear show up for EDM tunes spun by megawatt DJs like Calvin Harris, fruity cocktails and bobbing oh-so-coolly around saltwater pools while checking out the bikini-clad scenery. Book ahead for VIP bungalows, daybeds and cabanas.

★**Hakkasan** CLUB
(☑702-891-3838; www.hakkasanlv.com; MGM Grand; cover $20-75; ☺10:30pm-4am Thu-Sun) At this lavish Asian-inspired nightclub, international jet-set DJs such as Tiësto and Steve Aoki rule the jam-packed main dance floor bordered by VIP booths and floor-to-ceiling LED screens. More offbeat sounds spin in the intimate Ling Ling Club, revealing leather sofas and backlit amber glass. Bouncers enforce the dress code: upscale nightlife attire (no athletic wear, collared shirts required for men).

★**Marquee** CLUB
(☑702-333-9000; www.marqueelasvegas.com; Cosmopolitan; ☺10:30pm-5am Mon, Fri & Sat) The Cosmopolitan's (p101) glam nightclub cashes in on its multimillion-dollar sound system and a happening dance floor surrounded by towering LED screens displaying light projections that complement EDM tracks hand-picked by famous DJs. From late spring through early fall, Marquee's mega-popular daytime pool club heads outside to a lively party deck overlooking the Strip, with VIP cabanas and bungalows.

★**Omnia** CLUB
(☑702-785-6200; www.omniaclubs.com/las-vegas; Caesars Palace; cover female/male from $20/40; ☺10:30pm-4am Tue & Thu-Sun) Hakkasan group's new Caesars megaclub offers Top 40/hip-hop DJs, plus bottle service and Strip views with a Miami Beach vibe. Residencies by Calvin Harris, Steve Aoki and Martin Garrix.

● Downtown & Off-Strip

★**Beauty Bar** BAR
(☑702-598-3757; www.beautybarlv.com; 517 Fremont St E; cover free-$10; ☺9pm-4am; ◻Deuce) Swill a cocktail or just chill with the cool kids inside the salvaged innards of a 1950s New Jersey beauty salon. DJs and live bands rotate nightly, spinning everything from tiki lounge tunes, disco and '80s hits to punk, metal, glam and indie rock. Check the website for special events such as 'Karate Karaoke.' There's often no cover charge.

★**Commonwealth** BAR
(☑702-445-6400; www.commonwealthlv.com; 525 Fremont St E; ☺7pm-late Tue-Sat; ◻Deuce) It might be a little too cool for school but, whoa, that Prohibition-era interior is worth a look: plush booths, softly glowing chande-

liers, Victorian-era bric-a-brac and a saloon bar. Imbibe your old-fashioned cocktails on the rooftop patio overlooking the Fremont East scene. They say there's a secret cocktail bar within the bar, but you didn't hear that from us.

☆ Entertainment

That sensory overload of blindingly bright neon lights means you've finally landed on Las Vegas Blvd. The infamous Strip has the lion's share of gigantic casino hotels, all flashily competing to lure you (and your wallet) inside, with larger-than-life production shows, celebrity-filled nightclubs and burlesque cabarets. Head off-Strip to find jukebox dive bars, arty cocktail lounges, strip clubs and more.

★ **Aces of Comedy**   COMEDY
(☑702-792-7777; www.mirage.com; Mirage; tickets $40-100; ☉schedules vary, box office 10am-10pm Thu-Mon, to 8pm Tue & Wed) You'd be hard pressed to find a better A-list collection of famous stand-up comedians than this year-round series of appearances at the **Mirage**, which delivers the likes of Jay Leno, David Spade and Tim Allen to the Strip. Buy tickets in advance online or by phone, or go in person to the Mirage's **Cirque du Soleil** box office.

★o   THEATER
(☑702-693-8866; www.cirquedusoleil.com/o; Bellagio; tickets $99-212; ☉7pm & 9:30pm Wed-Sun) Phonetically speaking, it's the French word for water (eau). With a lithe international cast performing in, on and above water, Cirque du Soleil's O tells the tale of theater through the ages. It's a spectacular feat of imagination and engineering, and you'll pay dearly to see it – it's one of the Strip's few shows that rarely sells discounted tickets.

ℹ Information

INTERNET ACCESS

Most casino hotels charge a fee of up to $15 per 24 hours (sometimes only wired access is available). Free wi-fi hot spots are more common off-Strip. Cheap internet cafes hide inside souvenir shops on the Strip and along Maryland Pkwy opposite the UNLV campus.

MEDICAL SERVICES

University Medical Center (UMC; ☑702-383-2000; www.umcsn.com; 1800 W Charleston Blvd; ☉24hr) Southern Nevada's most advanced trauma center has a 24-hour ER.

Walgreens (☑702-739-9645; 3765 S Las Vegas Blvd; ☉store 24hr, pharmacy 9am-7pm, clinic 10am-6pm) Has an in-store health-care walk-in clinic.

MONEY

ATM transaction fees inside casino gaming areas are high. Credit cards are widely accepted.

TOURIST INFORMATION

Las Vegas Convention & Visitors Authority (LVCVA; ☑702-892-7575; www.lasvegas.com; 3150 Paradise Rd; ☉8am-5pm Mon-Fri; Las Vegas Convention Center)

ℹ Getting There & Around

AIR

McCarran International Airport (LAS; ☑702-261-5211; www.mccarran.com; 5757 Wayne Newton Blvd; 🐕) is one of the USA's 10 busiest airports. Taxis to Strip hotels average $15 to $20 (cash only, plus tip); superslow airport shuttle buses charge half as much. **Airport shuttles** (p94) also run to/from St George, Utah.

BUS

Long-distance **Greyhound** (☑214-849-8100; www.greyhound.com) buses arrive at the **Las Vegas Bus Station** (☑702-384-9561; www.greyhound.com; 200 S Main St; ☉24hr; 🚌SDX) near the Fremont Street Experience.

Two routes run 24/7 between the Strip and Downtown: the double-decker Deuce, which stops more frequently, and the quicker SDX. A 24hr pass for both is $8.

CAR & MOTORCYCLE

Major car-rental agencies are based at the airport's rent-a-car center, accessible via a free shuttle from outside the main terminal. Free self-parking and valet (tip $3 to $5) are available at most casino hotels. From Las Vegas, it's less than a three-hour drive to Zion National Park via I-15 north to Hwy 9 east.

Bryce Canyon National Park

Best Hikes

➡ Fairyland Loop Trail (p114)

➡ Peekabo Loop Trail (p118)

➡ Navajo Loop Trail (p116)

➡ Queen's Garden Trail (p114)

Best Places to Stay

➡ Sunset Campground (p125)

➡ Bryce Canyon Lodge (p125)

➡ Bryce Canyon Resort (p127)

Why Go?

These sights are nothing short of otherworldly. Repeated freezes and thaws have eroded soft sandstone and limestone into a landscape that's utterly unique: sandcastle spires known as hoodoos, jutted fins, windows and deep narrows. Though it's the smallest of southern Utah's national parks, Bryce Canyon stands among the most prized.

Not actually a canyon, Bryce comprises the eastern edge of an 18-mile plateau. Its Pink Cliffs mark the top step of the Grand Staircase, a giant geologic terrace reaching to the Grand Canyon. Trails descend through 1000ft amphitheaters of pastel daggers into a maze of fragrant juniper and sculpted high-mountain desert.

High altitude means cooler temperatures than other Utah parks. Clean, dry air also means excellent visibility, reaching all the way into the Andromeda Galaxy 2.5 million light-years away.

Driving Distances (Miles)

	Bryce Canyon National Park (Park Entrance)	Kanab	Moab	Panguitch	Tropic
Kanab	75				
Moab	275	320			
Panguitch	25	70	250		
Tropic	10	80	280	30	
Zion National Park (East Entrance)	75	30	315	65	80

Entrance

The park's sole vehicle entrance is 3 miles south of Utah Hwy 12, via Hwy 63. The park gate is always open, though entrance booths are not staffed at night. Bryce Canyon is open 24 hours a day, 365 days a year.

Because of severe traffic issues, the park has implemented parking restrictions on RVs and trailer vehicles in high season. Those affected should check the park website for details on any restrictions between May and September. Given the crowds, it's best to enter the park by bike on the paved multi-use trail, or via the free shuttle.

Compared with the vast landscape that surrounds it, the park is relatively small, at 16 miles long and 4 miles across at its widest point.

DON'T MISS
....
➜ Best short canyon hike: Navajo Loop Trail (p116)

➜ Best colors: Bryce Amphitheater (p123) at sunrise

➜ Best long hike for solitude among the amphitheaters: Fairyland Loop Trail (p114)

➜ Most stunning hoodoos: Silent City from Inspiration Point (p123)

➜ Best overlooked sight: 1600-year-old trees on Bristlecone Loop Trail (p123)

➜ Best nightlife: night-sky programs (p125) offer stargazing with telescopes and expert insight

When You Arrive

➜ As you approach, tune your radio to AM 1590 for current general park information.

➜ The entrance booth distributes park brochures with a driving map and facilities information along with the park newspaper, the Hoodoo, which gives current information about opening hours, ranger-led activities, hiking trails, backpacking and shuttle information.

➜ Take advantage of the Bryce Canyon Shuttle, a free service that operates between Ruby's Inn and Bryce Point, with buses every 15 minutes between 8am and 8pm in high season.

➜ Hydration stations throughout the park offer free water bottle refills.

➜ Backcountry permits for overnight travel are issued at the visitor center on a first-come, first-served basis.

PARK POLICIES & REGULATIONS
....
It's important you don't feed the park's wild animals. Pets must be on a leash and are only allowed on paved surfaces (roads, parking lots, paved scenic overlooks and the Rim Trail between Sunset and Sunrise Points). They are not allowed on unpaved trails or in public buildings. While you can bike on the multi-use trail, mountain biking is prohibited on the trails.

Fast Facts

➜ **Entrance fee (valid 7 days):** Vehicle/motorcycle/individual $35/30/20

➜ **Area:** 56 sq miles

➜ **Elevation:** 7894ft to 6580ft

➜ **Average July temperatures:** high 80°F (27°C), low 46°F (8°C)

➜ **Oldest residents:** The park's bristlecone pines are up to 1600 years old.

Reservations

Reservations may be made up to six months in advance for North Campground (RV reservations on 13 sites) and Sunset Campground (reservations on 20 tent sites). Otherwise, it's a first-come, first-served basis.

Resources

➜ **Bryce Canyon National Park** (www.nps.gov/brca)

➜ **Bryce Canyon Natural History Association** (www.brycecanyon.org)

Bryce Canyon National Park

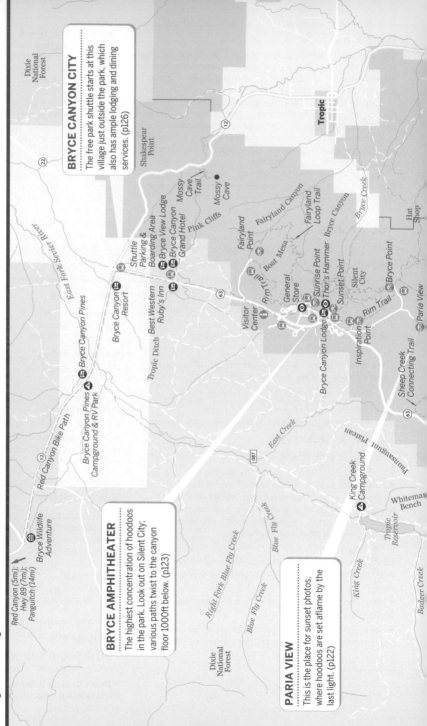

N 0 — 2 miles
0 — 4 km

BRYCE CANYON CITY

The free park shuttle starts at this village just outside the park, which also has ample lodging and dining services. (p126)

BRYCE AMPHITHEATER

The highest concentration of hoodoos in the park. Look out on Silent City; various paths twist to the canyon floor 1000ft below. (p123)

PARIA VIEW

This is the place for sunset photos, where hoodoos are set aflame by the last light. (p122)

Dixie National Forest

Tropic

Shakespear Point

Mossy Cave Trail

Mossy Cave

Pink Cliffs

Bryce View Lodge

Bryce Canyon Grand Hotel

Fairyland Canyon

Fairyland Loop Trail

Fairyland Point

Boat Mesa

Bryce Canyon

Bryce Creek

Hat Shop

Shuttle Parking & Boarding Area

Bryce Canyon Resort

Best Western Ruby's Inn

Tropic Ditch

Rim Trail

General Store

Sunrise Point

Thor's Hammer

Sunset Point

Silent City

Bryce Point

Paria View

Visitor Center

Bryce Canyon Lodge

Inspiration Point

Rim Trail

Sheep Creek / Connecting Trail

East Fork Sevier River

Bryce Canyon Pines

Red Canyon Bike Path

Bryce Canyon Pines Campground & RV Park

Red Canyon (5mi); Hwy 89 (7mi); Panguitch (14mi)

Bryce Wildlife Adventure

Dixie National Forest

Right Fork Blue Fly Creek

Blue Fly Creek

Blue Fly Creek

King Creek

King Creek Campground

Tropic Reservoir

Whiteman Bench

East Creek

Paunsaugunt Plateau

Badger Creek

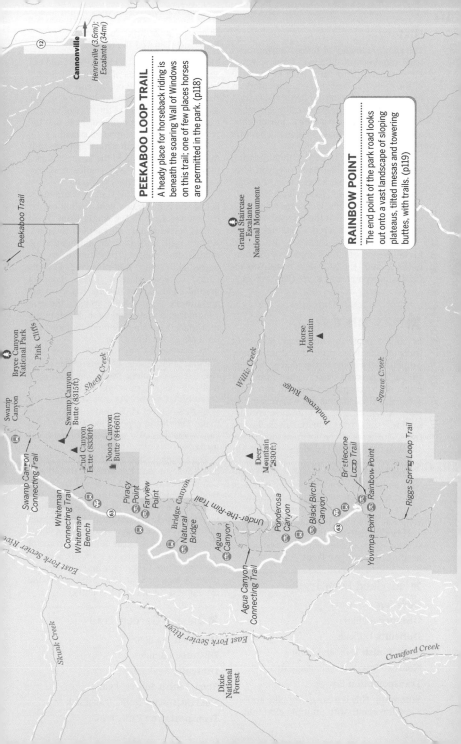

PEEKABOO LOOP TRAIL

A heady place for horseback riding is beneath the soaring Wall of Windows on this trail; one of few places horses are permitted in the park. (p118)

RAINBOW POINT

The end point of the park road looks out onto a vast landscape of sloping plateaus, tilted mesas and towering buttes, with trails. (p119)

Henrieville (3.6mi); Escalante (34mi)

Cannonville

(12)

Peekaboo Trail

Bryce Canyon National Park

Pink Cliffs

Swamp Canyon

Swamp Canyon Butte (8315ft)

Sheep Creek

2nd Canyon Butte (8330ft)

Noon Canyon Butte (8466ft)

Grand Staircase - Escalante National Monument

Willie Creek

Horse Mountain

Ponderosa Ridge

Squaw Creek

Swamp Canyon Connecting Trail

Whiteman Connecting Trail

Whiteman Bench

East Fork Sevier River

Piracy Point

Farview Point

(63)

Bridge Canyon

Natural Bridge

Under-the-Rim Trail

Deer Mountain 8330ft

Ponderosa Canyon

Black Birch Canyon

Bristlecone Loop Trail

Rainbow Point

Agua Canyon

Agua Canyon Connecting Trail

Yovimpa Point

(63)

Riggs Spring Loop Trail

Skunk Creek

East Fork Sevier River

Dixie National Forest

Crawford Creek

History

The geologic history of Bryce Canyon dates back hundreds of millions of years, while human history only dates back to the time of the Ancestral Puebloan cultures. Modern history was marked by the rise of the United States National Park System, the spread of Mormonism, conservationist movements, and new pressures that threaten the nation's public lands.

You can't enter the park without passing through the town-like Bryce Canyon City. Ruby's Inn (p127) has a lock on most operations in town, and for good reason. The motel has been part of the landscape since 1919, when it was located at the canyon's rim. After the area was declared a national monument in 1923, owner Rueben Syrett moved his business north to his ranch. It's still here today. In 2007 the 2300-acre resort was officially incorporated as Bryce Canyon City.

🏃 DAY HIKES

Bryce is a relatively small park, and most trails are day hikes around and into Bryce Amphitheater, home to the highest concentration of hoodoos. Hikes range from easy walks on paved paths along the rim (with some stretches suitable for wheelchairs) to steep switchbacks up and down sometimes muddy, sometimes dusty, packed-earth trails. Further south or north on the plateau you won't see as many hoodoos – or as many people.

Loose rocks act like marbles under your feet; ankle injuries are extremely common and can ruin your trip. Always wear well-fitting hiking boots with ankle support if you need it, and lace boots all the way up.

Hikes are listed in the order of approach, starting from outside the park entrance and heading toward Bryce Point.

🏃 Fairyland Loop Trail

Duration 4–5 hours

Distance 8 miles

Difficulty Difficult

Start/Finish Fairyland Point

Nearest Towns Tropic, Panguitch

Transportation Private

Summary This is a great day hike and a good workout, with multiple elevation changes. Unlike Bryce Amphitheater, Fairyland is spared the crowds.

This trail begins at **Fairyland Point** and circles the majestic cliffs of flat-topped, 8076ft Boat Mesa, emerging on the rim near Sunrise Point. There are fewer hoodoos in this area. The last 2.5 miles of the loop follows the Rim Trail back to the trailhead. Note that the park shuttle doesn't stop at Fairyland.

This trail is difficult primarily because it meanders – in and out of the hoodoos, down into washes, up and over saddles etc. Carry plenty of water, and pace yourself.

From the point, the trail dips gradually below the rim – watch your footing on the narrow sections. To the south, **Boat Mesa** stands between you and views of the park. A short walk leads past ancient bristlecone pines, some clinging precariously to the ragged cliffs, their 1000-plus-year-old roots curled up like wizened fingers. Looping around hoodoos that rise like castle turrets and towers, the trail soon drops to the canyon floor and a seasonal wash. Much of the north-facing terrain here holds its snowpack until May, sometimes June.

At **Fairyland Canyon**, 600ft below your starting point, towers of deep-orange stone rise like giant totem poles. The trail rises and falls before traversing a ridge toward **Campbell Canyon**. As you walk beneath Boat Mesa's great cliffs, notice how the formation comes to a point like the bow of a ship – you'll quickly understand how it got its name.

Zigzagging up and down, the trail eventually reaches a seasonal wash on the floor of Campbell Canyon. Keep an eye out for **Tower Bridge**, which connects three spires to two windows. To reach the base of the formation, take the clearly marked dead-end spur from the wash. From Tower Bridge it's a 950ft climb in 1.5 miles to the Rim Trail, some of it strenuous. En route, to your left, look for the long, white **China Wall** and its little windows. A look back at Boat Mesa shows the changing vistas of canyon country.

🏃 Queen's Garden Trail

Duration 1–2 hours

Distance 1.8 miles

Difficulty Moderate

Start/Finish Sunrise Point

Nearest Towns Tropic, Panguitch

Transportation Park shuttle

Bryce Canyon – Day Hikes

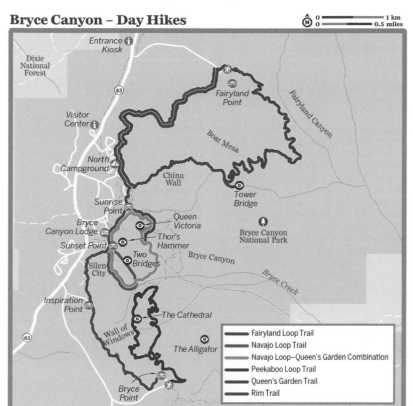

Legend
- Fairyland Loop Trail
- Navajo Loop Trail
- Navajo Loop–Queen's Garden Combination
- Peekaboo Loop Trail
- Queen's Garden Trail
- Rim Trail

Summary Good for kids, the easiest trail into the canyon makes a gentle descent over sloping erosional fins. It passes elegant hoodoo formations but stops short of the canyon floor.

The Queen's Garden Trail is not a loop, but an in-and-out hike. You can also add the Queen's Garden Connecting Trail, part of the Navajo Loop–Queen's Garden Combination.

From **Sunrise Point**, follow signs to the trailhead off the Rim Trail (p117). Views of the amphitheater as you descend are superb – a maze of colorful rock spires extends to Bryce Point, and deep-green pines dot the canyon floor beneath undulating slopes seemingly tie-dyed pink, orange and white. As you drop below the rim, watch for the stark and primitive bristlecone pines, which are thought to be about 1600 years old. These ancient trees' dense needles cluster like foxtails on the ends of the branches.

After a series of switchbacks, turn right and follow signs to the Queen's Garden Trail. The short spur from the main trail passes through a tunnel and emerges among exceptionally beautiful hoodoo castles in striking whites and oranges amid rich green pines. After looping around a high wall and passing through two more tunnels, bear right and follow signs to **Queen Victoria**. The trail's namesake monarch peers down from a white-capped rock, perched atop her throne.

Return to the rim or link with the Navajo Loop Trail via the Queen's Garden Connecting Trail, which drops to the canyon floor.

🚶 Navajo Loop–Queen's Garden Combination Trail

Duration 2–3 hours
Distance 2.9 miles
Difficulty Moderate

Start/Finish Sunrise Point

Nearest Towns Tropic, Panguitch

Transportation Park shuttle

Summary The most popular route in the park, and fairly gentle, it hits Bryce's signature features in a relatively short amount of time, despite the sometimes-steep grade.

Begin with **Queen's Garden Trail** to avoid the steep descent through Wall Street (which was closed when we last visited because of unstable rocks). Check ahead with rangers for trail closure information, particularly after winter.

From Sunrise Point, follow signs for the Queen's Garden Connecting Trail, which descends to the garden of spires and follows the canyon floor. Another advantage of taking this trail is time spent on the canyon floor, where tall pines provide shade and offer perspective on oversize hoodoos. The final push, a steep ascent through **Wall Street** and past the **Silent City**, is the more visually stunning of the two trails. If Wall Street is closed due to rockfall, opt to ascend to the rim via the Two Bridges side of the **Navajo Loop Trail**.

Before you top out on the rim, detour right a short distance to see **Thor's Hammer**. Then stroll back to Sunrise Point along the Rim Trail, gazing into the canyon for yet another perspective on the hoodoos.

🚶 Navajo Loop Trail

Duration 1–2 hours

Distance 1.3 miles

Difficulty Moderate–difficult

Start/Finish Sunset Point

Nearest Towns Tropic, Panguitch

Transportation Park shuttle

Summary This sometimes-steep hike is short but spectacular. From the trailhead at Sunset Point, you drop right into the canyon beneath towering hoodoos that dwarf onlookers.

This popular trail passes alongside Thor's Hammer, the park's most famous rock formation; beneath Two Bridges, a pair of small water-carved arches; and through Wall Street (which regularly closes because of rock falls), a narrow canyon with steep rock walls that reveal only a sliver of sky above. It's a steep ascent and descent, but the trail

HIKING IN BRYCE CANYON NATIONAL PARK

NAME	START LOCATION	DESCRIPTION
Under-the-Rim Trail (p119)	Bryce Point	Bryce's premier backcountry hike passes few hoodoos but promises solitude
Peekaboo Loop Trail (p118)	Bryce Point	The greatest variety of terrain and scenery in Bryce; horses allowed
Rim Trail (p117)	Fairyland Point, Bryce Point or any rim trailhead	Canyon rim hike with stellar overlook of hoodoos
Fairyland Loop Trail (p114)	Fairyland Point	Long hike away from crowds leads past castlelike formations
Riggs Spring Loop Trail (p121)	Rainbow Point	This strenuous hike drops off the plateau's southern tip through three ecological zones
Queen's Garden Trail (p114)	Sunrise Point	Gentlest descent into the canyon on eroding fins, passing myriad hoodoos
Navajo Loop–Queen's Garden Combination (p115)	Sunrise Point	Most popular route in the park; hits Bryce's signature features

 Wildlife Watching   *Views*   *Great for Families*

is clearly marked and fairly wide. Those in reasonably good shape won't have a problem. Rangers strongly recommend hiking it clockwise to avoid a steep descent through Wall Street, a notorious ankle-buster. To lengthen your hike by 30 minutes to an hour, you could also start at Queen's Garden Trail (p114).

From the wide, fenced-in viewing area at Sunset Point, follow signs for the Navajo Loop Trail. The trail drops immediately into a switchback, then forks about 100 yards ahead. Take the left fork, which leads past **Thor's Hammer** down a long slope to the canyon floor. Entering the canyon, you can follow the sign on your left to see **Two Bridges**.

At the canyon floor, turn right to continue the loop and ascend back to the rim. Sometimes closed due to rockfall (check ahead with rangers), **Wall Street** features 100ft walls which block much of the sunlight, keeping the canyon shady and cool. The giant Douglas fir trees towering between the walls are over 750 years old!

To the left of the Wall Street trail, the **Silent City** looms large. If the spur trail through the tunnel on your left is open, take a quick jaunt to look down on these eerie pinnacles. The trail finishes with a steep ascent and some 30 switchbacks that lead to the rim.

Rim Trail

Duration 2–3 hours

Distance 5.5 miles one way

Difficulty Easy–moderate

Start Bryce Point

Finish Fairyland Point

Nearest Towns Tropic, Panguitch

Transportation Park shuttle

Summary With great views, this trail hugs the canyon rim, stretching from the south end of Bryce Amphitheater at Bryce Point all the way to Fairyland Point (p114), near the northern park boundary.

Sections of this trail are level, particularly between Sunrise and Sunset Points, where the path is paved and wheelchair accessible. Log rail fences mark vertical drop-offs in many places. In other spots you'll ascend moderately steep, wooded rises to seek shade beneath the pines, watch wildlife or soak up vibrant displays of spring wildflowers. The colors in the rock pop out most when lit by the morning or afternoon sun.

BRYCE CANYON NATIONAL PARK DAY HIKES

DIFFICULTY	DURATION	ROUND-TRIP DISTANCE	ELEVATION CHANGE	FEATURES	FACILITIES
moderate-difficult	3 days	22.9 miles one way	1315ft		
difficult	3-5hr	5.5 miles	500-900ftV		
easy-moderate	2-3hr	5.5 miles one way	550ft		
difficult	4-5hr	8 miles	900ft		
difficult	4-5hr or overnight	8.8 miles	1675ft		
moderate	1-2hr	1.8 miles	320ft		
moderate	2-3hr	2.9 miles	521ft		

 Restrooms   *Drinking Water*   *Backcountry camping*

You can join the trail anywhere along its 5.5-mile route – just keep in mind that unless the shuttle is running or you arrange to be picked up, you'll have to walk back. If you plan on taking the shuttle, note that buses don't stop at Fairyland.

You'll find restrooms and drinking water at Sunset Point, and the general store (p128) and snack bar (both open spring through fall) near Sunrise Point, which is roughly the midpoint of the hike. You can also duck into Bryce Canyon Lodge (p125) for lunch, restrooms and drinking water.

Remember that Bryce sits atop a sloping plateau. The north end of the Rim Trail is lower than the south end, so it's downhill from Bryce Point to Fairyland Point, though the trail rises and falls in a few spots, particularly in its climb from Sunrise Point to North Campground.

During the walk, you'll leave behind Bryce Amphitheater and arrive above Campbell Canyon and Fairyland Amphitheater. You'll find fewer formations at this end of the park, but giant Boat Mesa and its high cliffs rise majestically to the north.

From Bryce Point to Inspiration Point the trail skirts the canyon rim atop white cliffs, revealing gorgeous formations, including the Wall of Windows. After passing briefly through trees, it continues along the ridge top to the uppermost level of Inspiration Point, 1.3 miles from Bryce Point.

The leg to Sunset Point drops 200ft in 0.75 miles, winding its way along limestone-capped cliffs. Below the rim the Silent City rises in all its hoodoo glory; the lower you go, the higher the rock spires rise beside you.

At Sunset Point you may wish to detour along the Navajo Loop Trail for a taste of the canyon; you can reemerge on the Rim Trail further ahead by adding the Queen's Garden Connecting Trail. Otherwise, stay the course and look for Thor's Hammer as you continue the 0.5-mile stroll along a paved path to Sunrise Point – the most crowded stretch of trail in the entire park. The views are worth it.

Past Sunrise Point, crowds thin as the trail climbs 150ft toward North Campground (p125). Fork left at the Fairyland Loop Trail junction, unless you'd like to follow the moderately difficult, 3-mile round-trip spur into the canyon (950ft elevation loss) to see the window-laced China Wall and Tower Bridge, twin arches between

chunky rock spires. Otherwise, watch for these features from the Rim Trail.

Topping out near North Campground, the path ambles across gently rolling hills on the forested plateau before rejoining the canyon rim at Fairyland Point, 2.5 miles from Sunrise Point.

🏃 Peekaboo Loop Trail

Duration 3–5 hours

Distance 5.5 miles

Difficulty Difficult

Start/Finish Bryce Point

Nearest Towns Tropic, Panguitch

Transportation Park shuttle

Summary An ideal day hike, Peekaboo Loop Trail sees the most variety of terrain and scenery in Bryce, with 1500ft to 1800ft of cumulative elevation changes.

Access to this circular trail is via either the Navajo Loop or the Queen's Garden Connecting Trail, which runs off the Queen's Garden Trail (p116). The following description starts from Bryce Point – if starting from Sunrise Point it's a 6.6-mile hike; from Sunset Point it's 5 miles.

The Peekaboo Loop Trail is also a horse trail, so expect to see occasional riders. They move slowly, so you'll have plenty of advance warning. Stock animals have right of way – step off the trail and let them pass undisturbed. If you don't want to navigate around horse droppings, consider another route. But views here are among the park's best, particularly of the Wall of Windows, the Silent City and the Fairy Castle. You'll also find shady spots to rest, a picnic area and pit toilets (the latter are on the loop, just west of its intersection with the connecting trail to Bryce Point, and only open during summer).

This trail rises and falls many times; be prepared for a workout. If you're afraid of heights, be forewarned that in places you'll pass sheer drops, though the trail is comfortably wide enough for a horse.

From Bryce Point follow signs to the Peekaboo Connecting Trail, just east of the parking area. Bear left at the fork where you'll descend 1.1 miles down the connecting trail. You'll pass through mixed conifers, then swoop out along a gray-white limestone fin beneath the Bryce Point overlook. Further down the trail, hoodoo columns take on a bright-orange hue. After passing through a human-made tunnel, look for the **Alligator** in the white rock ahead. As you work your way down the switchbacks, watch for the **Wall of Windows**, which juts above bright-orange hoodoos atop a sheer vertical cliff face perpendicular to the canyon rim. The windows line the top of this wall.

At the loop trail junction, bear right. As you pass beneath healthy fir and spruce trees, you'll spot a few blackened snags. They're victims of electrical storms, not forest fires – the plateau's high elevation and isolated trees attract lightning. Also look for ancient bristlecone pines; an inch of these trees' trunks represents 100 years' growth.

Climbing a saddle, you'll rise to eye level with the hoodoo tops before dropping over the other side to the cluster of delicate red spires at **Fairy Castle**. Midway around, just past the turnoff for the Navajo Loop, the trail climbs again to spectacular views of the **Silent City** and passes beneath the **Cathedral**, a majestic wall of buttresslike hoodoos. The rolling trail skirts the Wall of Windows, threads through a tunnel and switchbacks down. Notice the rapidly changing views as you pass the huge Wall of Windows. The trail turns west and climbs, then drops again amid more hoodoos. As you approach the Bryce Point trail, take the spur on your right to the lush green rest area near the horse corral for a cooldown or picnic before climbing out of the canyon.

🚶 OVERNIGHT HIKES

🚶 Under-the-Rim Trail

Duration 3 days

Distance 22.9 miles one way

Difficulty Moderate–difficult

Start Rainbow Point

Finish Bryce Point

Nearest Towns Tropic, Panguitch

Transportation Park shuttle

Summary Ideal for getting away from it all, this multi-day hike skirts beneath cliffs, through amphitheaters and amid pines and aspens. Originally fire trails, these paths lack some of the drama of backcountry hikes elsewhere.

If you start at **Rainbow Point** and end at Bryce Point, you can hike the park's primary

Under-The-Rim Trail

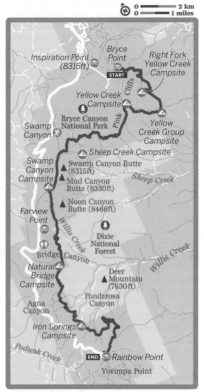

backcountry trail in two days, though three are recommended. In either direction you'll face a hefty ascent the last 3 miles. Rangers prefer visitors hike the trail south to north, but you can do it either way.

Running nearly the length of the park, the trail rises from the piñon juniper community (6600ft to 7000ft), through the ponderosa pine community (7000ft to 8500ft) to the fir-spruce community (8500ft to 9100ft), touching the rim only at the trailheads. There are spots along the way to filter water, so be sure to bring a pump and be conservative with your water use.

Descending from the scenic drive, four connecting trails link with the Under-the-Rim Trail, each near a backcountry campsite. These connecting trails allow hikers to approach any section as a day hike. Rangers can offer details on the connecting trails. You could also set up base camp at one of the sites and take day hikes in either direction.

If you have the time, extend your trek south along the 8.8-mile Riggs Spring Loop Trail.

This is a one-way hike, so consider leaving a car at one or both ends. A shuttle service to Rainbow Point may be available – inquire at the visitor center. Hitchhiking is prohibited in the park, but hikers can sometimes catch rides back to Bryce Point without much difficulty.

Permits ($5 per person for up to 14 days) are obtained at the visitor center between 9am and one hour prior to the center's closing time. You cannot place an advance order by phone or email, but you can make reservations in person up to 48 hours in advance. Campsites are assigned with the purchase of a backcountry permit. The maximum stay at any particular site is three nights.

Most backcountry trails are covered with snow from late October to March or April; even in May, snowpack sometimes obscures sections of trail. June and September are ideal times to hike, while in July and August you'll have to contend with thunderstorms. Mosquitoes are rare, but cedar gnats are annoying in early summer. In winter, backpackers must have an interview with the backcountry ranger to discuss hazards.

Beyond the usual safety preparations for hiking in the deserts of southern Utah, the primary concern is elevation. Take it slow until you're acclimated. For navigating, use the medium-scale National Geographic Trails Illustrated *Map of Bryce Canyon*. All water in the backcountry must be purified.

DAY 1: BRYCE POINT TO RIGHT FORK SWAMP CANYON CAMPSITE
4–6 HOURS / 10.5 MILES

From Bryce Point the trail descends steeply almost due east, then swings south. After 0.5 miles you'll wind down to a ridge, where the earth changes from gray to orange. Over the next 0.5 miles Rainbow Point comes into view above the ridge in the foreground.

As the trail traces a south-facing promontory, look north for a grand panorama of the Pink Cliffs. On the right (west) the Right Fork Yellow Creek forms a steep-sided drainage. Two miles in you'll pass the **Hat Shop**, its gray boulder caps perched atop spindly conglomerate stands.

At the base of this descent, 2.8 miles from Bryce Point, is the **Right Fork Yellow Creek campsite**, a good spot in a clearing beside the creek, which runs all year.

From the campsite, follow the left (east) bank of the creek for half a mile, then cross

it and bear south. Here the landscape is a semidesert, with little shade and plenty of pungent sage growing in the sandy soil. As the trail turns west, you'll pass the **Yellow Creek group campsite** on the left.

A quarter-mile beyond the campsite, you'll reach **Yellow Creek**. The trail follows the creek and climbs toward the Pink Cliffs at the head of the creek and **Paria View**, 1000ft above. The trail soon crosses the creek; cairns point the way.

Another quarter mile brings you to the **Yellow Creek campsite**, in plenty of shade beside the creek. It's a great spot to watch the sunset.

From here you'll turn southwest up a short, steep hill. The trail undulates for about 2 miles, crossing a slope between two amphitheaters. After 1.5 miles the trail drops into Pasture Wash. Follow cairns to the south edge of the wash and look for a sharp uphill turn, where the trail visibly zigzags up and out of the wash. The view (north to south) of Swamp Canyon, Mud Canyon and Noon Canyon Buttes will reward your effort.

Descend into the valley to the junction with the **Sheep Creek Connecting Trail**, which climbs 2 miles to the scenic drive. A well-marked spur leads 0.5 miles south to the **Sheep Creek campsite** (closed when we last visited due to bear activity), its beauty second only to the Yellow Creek site; you can usually find water here.

From the junction, the trail climbs 150ft – crossing from the Sheep Creek amphitheater to the Swamp Canyon amphitheater – then descends into Swamp Canyon amid a stand of large quaking aspens. On the left (southeast), in a clearing among large ponderosa pines, is the **Right Fork Swamp Canyon campsite**; water is sometimes available in upper Swamp Canyon, 100yd west of the campsite.

DAY 2: RIGHT FORK SWAMP CANYON CAMPSITE TO NATURAL BRIDGE CAMPSITE
1½–2½ HOURS / 4.6 MILES

Three hundred feet past the campsite is the junction with the mile-long Swamp Canyon Connecting Trail, which climbs north to the scenic drive. From the connecting trail junction, you'll climb steadily south, then turn west up switchbacks. Just beyond, at 8200ft, is the **Swamp Canyon campsite**. Although there's not much flat ground, and the site is near the trail, it's cool in summer. You'll sometimes find water 0.25 miles up the

Whiteman Connecting Trail, which climbs 0.9 miles to the scenic drive.

Beyond camp the trail passes aspens and pines, then descends to the base of Farview Cliffs. From here you'll skirt **Willis Creek** for a mile until it turns southeast. You may find it difficult to distinguish the trail from other small creeks; bear south and west.

The trail ducks into Dixie National Forest for 0.25 miles, then curves sharply east to climb an eroded sandstone slope southwest of Willis Creek. At the top, the sandy trail snakes around the east edge of a promontory for gorgeous views of the **Pink Cliffs**.

Descend to a southern tributary of Willis Creek and continue 0.5 miles (you may need to cross several times if the water is running high) to the **Natural Bridge campsite**, which lacks water.

DAY 3: NATURAL BRIDGE CAMPSITE TO RAINBOW POINT
3–5 HOURS / 7.8 MILES

Half a mile out of camp, the trail traverses a sage meadow toward Agua Canyon. Crossing this canyon may prove tricky: on older topo maps, the trail turns slightly west and cuts straight across the canyon, but due to floods you now need to hike up the canyon 0.75 miles, then switchback up the canyon's south ridge. When in doubt, follow the cairns. The switchbacks are snowed under until late spring. Atop this ridge, the Agua Canyon Connecting Trail climbs 1.6 miles to the scenic drive. This is one of the hardest stretches of the trail, with fallen trees and washouts.

From the connecting trail junction, you'll skirt a pink promontory, descend into Ponderosa Canyon, then zigzag up and down to South Fork Canyon. Just past the head of the canyon, you'll reach the **Iron Spring campsite** on your right; the east-facing ridge leaves little room to spread out. Amid a grove of aspens 600ft up canyon (southwest) from the campsite, **Iron Spring** supplies year-round water. The turnoff for the spring lies 100yd north of the campsite. The water here tastes bad (hence the name), so consider bringing some powdered juice to cover up the taste.

The trail continues its undulating rhythm, dipping to cross both arms of Black Birch Canyon, where directional cairns are sometimes obscured by debris. After clambering over the lower slopes of a northwest-jutting promontory, you'll enter the southernmost amphitheater of Bryce Canyon's Pink Cliffs.

The trail traces the hammer-shaped ridge below Rainbow Point, climbing steadily and offering unsurpassed views. Ascend the final 1.5 miles up the back (south) side of the amphitheater to the rim. You'll cross the Riggs Spring Loop Trail just beneath the rim, 100yd east of the Rainbow Point parking lot. If the urge to peer over the rim is irresistible, take extreme caution, as the edges are unstable.

🚶Riggs Spring Loop Trail

Duration 3–5 hours (or overnight)

Distance 8.6 miles

Difficulty Difficult

Start/Finish Rainbow Point

Nearest Towns Tropic, Panguitch

Transportation Park shuttle

Summary This trail loops from the tip of the Paunsaugunt Plateau, descending beneath the spectacular Pink Cliffs through spruce, fir and aspen, then through ponderosa pines to a desert habitat of sagebrush and scrub oak. Aside from the length, it's fairly moderate, and accessible for fit hikers.

If you choose to do this hike over two days you will need a **backcountry** permit. Permits ($5 per person for up to 14 days) are obtained at the visitor center between 9am and one hour prior to the center's closing time. You cannot place an advance order by phone or email, but you can make reservations in person up to 48 hours in advance. Campsites are assigned with purchase of a backcountry permit. The maximum stay at any particular site is three nights. Bear canisters are also

Riggs Spring Loop Trail

available at the visitor center and recommended for all backcountry hikes.

Make this loop clockwise, not counterclockwise; it's a safer way through steep terrain. Extend the hike to an overnight outing to ease your pace and soak up the solitude. Starting at Rainbow Point, follow the **Bristlecone Loop Trail** to the turnoff for the Under-the-Rim Trail and follow signs to the Riggs Spring Loop Trail.

The trail descends the Pink Cliffs onto the **Promontory**, a ridgeline that juts from the plateau in a sweeping arc south. Molly's Nipple rises to the southeast; Navajo Mountain is on the horizon 80 miles to the east-southeast.

After dropping off the Promontory along tree-lined slopes, you'll double back north for grand views of the Pink Cliffs, then descend to **Coral Hollow campsite**. This site lies beneath oak and pine trees 3.6 miles from, and 1200ft below, Rainbow Point; there's no water here, and it's buggy, so try to plan around it if you can.

From Coral Hollow you'll loop below Yovimpa Point on a gradual descent through pines to **Mutton Hollow**. **Riggs Spring campsite** (7480ft) sits amid pines at the base of this hollow. Of the three camps on this loop, this one is the most idyllic. You'll almost always find water at Riggs Spring, hemmed in by a log fence. This is the lowest point along the trail.

Onward, the increasingly steep trail climbs past towering ponderosa pines en route to **Yovimpa Pass**, which lies atop a plateau at 8360ft. The higher you get, the better the views of the approaching cliffs. Perched atop this plateau, the **Yovimpa Pass campsite** provides little shade but often has water.

The last 1.6 miles of the trail skirt the edge of the plateau through woods before rejoining the rim at Yovimpa Point. Breaks in the forest reveal views of the Grand Staircase and the hoodoos below Rainbow Point.

☂ OTHER ACTIVITIES

For a wonderful perspective on the park, take to the air with **Bryce Canyon Airlines and Helicopters** (📋 435-691-8813; www.rubys inn.com/scenic-flights; 1000 S Hwy 63, Ruby's Inn; $85-525).

Driving Tour
Bryce Canyon Scenic Drive

START BRYCE CANYON NATIONAL PARK VISITOR CENTER
END BRYCE CANYON NATIONAL PARK VISITOR CENTER
LENGTH 34 MILES; TWO HOURS

Spanning the length of the park, this out-and-back route hits all the park highlights.

The scenic drive winds south for 17 miles and roughly parallels the canyon rim, climbing from 7894ft at the visitor center to 9115ft at Rainbow Point, the plateau's southern tip at road's end.

Head directly to **❶ Rainbow Point** (p119; a 35-minute drive from the visitor center), then stop at the scenic overlooks as you return to avoid left-hand turns into the turnouts. Visit Rainbow Point via a short, wheelchair-accessible path.

At the other end of the parking lot another short, wheelchair-accessible trail leads to **❷ Yovimpa Point**. The southwest-facing view reveals more forested slopes and less eroding rock.

Just north of Mile 16, at 8750ft, the small **❸ Black Birch Canyon** overlook shows precipitous cliffs roadside.

Higher than the previous stop, **❹ Ponderosa Canyon** offers long vistas like those at Rainbow Point. Below, note the namesake giant ponderosa pines, some as tall as 150ft.

One of the best stops at this end of the park, the **❺ Agua Canyon** viewpoint overlooks two large formations of precariously balanced, top-heavy hoodoos.

The parking lot at **❻ Natural Bridge** is the biggest since Rainbow Point, and with good reason: a stunning span of eroded, red-hued limestone juts from the edge of the overlook.

The stop at **❼ Farview Point** offers a grand view of the tree-studded rises and benches, giant plateaus, blue-hued mesas and buttes.

The overlook at **❽ Swamp Canyon** sits in a forested dip between two ridgelines that extend into the canyon.

Three miles north of Swamp Canyon, turn right and follow signs to the **❾ Paria View** viewpoint, 2 miles off the main road.

Most of the hoodoo amphitheaters at Bryce face east and are best viewed at sunrise.

If you make just one stop, make it **10 Bryce Point**. You can walk the rim above **11 Bryce Amphitheater** for awesome views of the **12 Silent City**, an assemblage of hoodoos resembling figures frozen in the rock. Be sure to follow the path to the actual point, a fenced-in promontory that juts over the forested canyon floor, 1000ft below.

Bryce Point marks the beginning of the 5.5-mile **13 Rim Trail** (p117) and the **14 Peekaboo Loop Trail** (p118).

At **15 Inspiration Point** a short ascent up a paved path takes you to another overlook into Bryce Amphitheater. Inspiration Point sits lower than Bryce Point and provides much the same view, though the Silent City is most compelling from here. Inspiration Point is a great place to return for stargazing.

Views into Bryce Amphitheater at **16 Sunset Point** (p118) are as good as they get, but don't expect solitude. It's at the core of the park, near campgrounds, the lodge and all visitor services. Aside from great views of the Silent City, this point is known for **17 Thor's Hammer**, a big square-capped rock balanced atop a spindly hoodoo. This is the starting point for the **18 Navajo Loop Trail** (p116), the park's most popular hike, and you'll find restrooms, drinking water and picnic tables. Don't be fooled by the name of this point. Because it faces east, sunrises are better here than sunsets.

Marking the north end of Bryce Amphitheater, the southeast-facing **19 Sunrise Point** (p115) offers great views of hoodoos, the Aquarius Plateau and the Sinking Ship, a sloping mesa that looks like a ship's stern rising out of the water. Keep your eyes peeled for the **20 Limber Pine**, a spindly tree whose roots have been exposed through erosion, but which nonetheless remains anchored to the receding sand. Within walking distance or a one-minute drive are the Bryce Canyon General Store (p128), drinking water, restrooms, picnic tables and a snack bar; head north toward the campground on the loop road.

End your driving tour at the **21 visitor center** (p129) or head to **22 Fairyland Point** (p114). To reach the point, drive a mile north of the entrance gate, then a mile east of the main road. Fairyland Point is a less-visited spot with wooded views north toward the Aquarius Plateau. Here you can see hoodoos at all stages of evolution, from fin to crumbling tower, and start the **23 Fairyland Loop Trail** (p114).

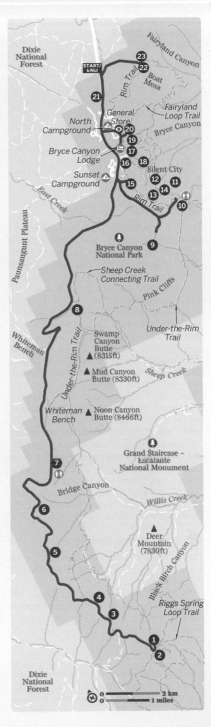

PRAIRIE DOGS

••

Although Utah prairie dogs once numbered in the billions across the West, a century of shooting and poisoning at the hands of ranchers drove them to near extinction by 1950. As a keystone species, the threatened animal is essential to the grassland ecosystem, improving soil quality, providing homes for other animals, prey and even maintaining meadow ecosystems. In 1974 scientists established a small prairie dog colony in the meadows at Bryce Canyon National Park and carefully monitored these small rodents (named 'dogs' by the Lewis and Clark Expedition for their barks). In March, as snows begin to melt, about 300 prairie dogs emerge from hibernation and begin a luxurious summer of calling, mating and fattening up on sweet grasses. Every June the park celebrates their continued presence with the Annual Utah Prairie Dog Day. The park asks that visitors stay out of the colonies and avoid the temptation to feed or pester the animals.

BRYCE CANYON NATIONAL PARK OTHER ACTIVITIES

🚴 Cycling

The best way into the park is on a bike via the multi-use trail. The paved trail runs for five miles within the park, connecting with the **Red Canyon Trail** FREE to take you all the way past Bryce Canyon City to the Red Canyon Visitor Center. The multi-use trail ends at Inspiration Point.

Road and mountain bikes can be rented in Bryce Canyon City. Hardtail mountain bike bicycle rental costs $10 hr, $25 half-day, $40 all day. Nice full-suspension models cost $20 hr, $55 half-day, $75 all day. You can't mountain bike on the park's trails; instead, head to Red Canyon and other spots in **Dixie National Forest** (☑ 435-865-3700; www.fs.usda.gov/recarea/dixie) FREE for amazing single-track rides. Several outfitters including **Backroads Bicycle Adventures** (☑ 800-462-2848; www.backroads.com; 6-day trip from $2500), **Rim Tours** (☑ 435-259-5223; www.rimtours.com; half-day from $90) and **Western Spirit Cycling** (☑ 435-259-8732, 800-845-2453; www.westernspirit.com; 6-day trip $1395) offer guided day and multi-day rides.

🐎 Horseback Riding

There are no overnight backcountry tours within the park. All outfitters have a limit of 220lb for riders.

To bring your own horse to Bryce, coordinate with Canyon Trail Rides. Contact the park for regulations. There are no backcountry campgrounds suitable for stock animals.

Canyon Trail Rides   HORSEBACK RIDING
(☑ 435-679-8663; www.canyonrides.com; Hwy 63, Bryce Canyon Lodge; 2hr/half-day tour $65/90) The national park's only licensed outfitter

operates out of the park lodge. You can take a short, two-hour trip to the canyon floor or giddy-up for a half day through the dramatic hoodoos on Peekaboo Trail (p118).

Red Canyon Trail Rides   HORSEBACK RIDING
(☑ 800-892-7923; www.redcanyontrailrides.com; Hwy 12, Bryce Canyon Pines; half-day ride $75; ☉ Mar-Nov) Ride for as little as a half-hour or as long as a whole day on private and public lands outside the park, including Red Canyon (p134).

🦌 Wildlife Watching

Bryce Canyon is home to 59 mammal species, 11 reptile species, four amphibian species and more than 1000 insect species. As many as 175 bird species pass through annually, though large, highly adaptable ravens are among the few birds found year-round. If you're lucky, you might also spot California condors or a peregrine falcon. Keep an eye to the ground for the threatened Utah prairie dog. Pronghorn antelope are plentiful and one of the largest animals you are likely to spot.

🚶 Ranger Programs

From early summer until fall, rangers lead rim walks, hikes amid the hoodoos, short geology lectures, evening programs, kids' ecology walks and astronomy talks, with telescopes. Ask at the visitor center for current schedules, or visit the park website for general information.

If you time your visit to coincide with the full moon (and clear skies), don't miss the **moon walk**, a popular two- to three-mile stroll among the hoodoos. A lottery for participation is held at the visitor center on the afternoon of the hike; treaded hiking boots are required.

🏃 Winter Activities

Snow blankets the park in winter, but the snowcaps on formations are stunning. Most roads are plowed; others are designated for cross-country skiing and snowshoeing. The best **cross-country skiing** and **snowshoeing trails** are on the Paria Ski Loop, the Rim Trail and Fairyland Road.

🎆 FESTIVALS & EVENTS

Astronomy Festival   LIGHT SHOW
(www.nps.gov/brca/planyourvisit/astrofest.htm; ☺mid-Jun) Bryce Canyon's annual four-day Astronomy Festival celebrates the exceptional viewing of the night skies at Bryce. It features talks, walks and stargazing with experts, the park's Astronomy Rangers and the Salt Lake Astronomical Society. A rocket-building workshop appeals to kids. Over 50 telescopes are available for viewing.

Bryce Canyon Winterfest   SPORTS
(www.rubysinn.com/bryce-canyon-winter-festival; ☺early Feb) Includes everything from cross-country skiing and snowmobiling to archery and snow sculpting.

GeoFest   FAIR
(www.nps.gov/brca/annual-geology-festival.htm; ☺late Jul) Join park rangers for guided hikes, family-friendly geology programs, bus tours with a geologist and evening programs. There are also exhibits and family-oriented activities.

Bryce Canyon Half Marathon   SPORTS
(www.brycecanyonhalfmarathon.com; registration $50; ☺Jul) A wildly popular distance run through the park, starting at Ruby's Inn (p127) and ending past Tropic in Cannonville.

🛏️ SLEEPING

The park has one lodge and two campgrounds. Most travelers stay just north of the park in Bryce Canyon City, near the Hwy 12/63 junction, or 11 miles east in Tropic (p133). Other lodgings and campsites are available along Hwy 12, and 24 miles west in and around the small town of Panguitch (p135). Red Canyon (p134), Dixie National Forest and Kodachrome Basin State Park

(p154) also have campgrounds. There are limited vacation rentals near the park, but extend your search by about 20 miles and you'll find plenty of options.

🛏️ In the Park

Sunset Campground   CAMPGROUND $
(☎877-444-6777; www.recreation.gov; Bryce Canyon Rd; tent/RV site $20/30; ☺Apr-Sep) Just south of Sunset Point, this 102-site campground offers more shade than North Campground but has few amenities beyond flush toilets. Inquire about availability at the visitor center (p129), and secure your site early. Twenty tent sites can be reserved up to six months ahead.

North Campground   CAMPGROUND $
(☎877-444-6777; www.recreation.gov; Bryce Canyon Rd; tent/RV sites $20/30) Near the visitor center (p129), the 101 sites at this enormous trail-side campground all have campfire rings. A short walk from the campground takes you to showers, a coin laundry and a general store. A fee-for-use sanitary dump station ($5) is available in summer months at the south end. RV reservations are available six months out.

Bryce Canyon Lodge   LODGE $$
(☎435-834-8700, 877-386-4383; www.brycecanyonforever.com; Hwy 63; r & cabins $213-270; ☺Apr-Oct; @🌐) Built in the 1920s, the main park lodge exudes rustic mountain charm, with a large stone fireplace and exposed roof timbers. Most of the 'sunrise' and 'sunset' motel rooms are in a two-story annex building with private balconies. In the perfect woodsy setting, the retro-cool 'western'

BRYCE CANYON NATIONAL PARK FESTIVALS & EVENTS

ℹ️ AVOID THE CROWDS

In the heat of high season, every parking lot and viewpoint in Bryce will be jam packed. Here are a few picks to (try to) beat the crowds.

Fairyland Loop (p114) For views that may make you feel like you've landed on the moon, with a fraction of the traffic.

Dixie National Forest The national forest surrounding the national park has amazing hiking and plenty of solitude.

Moon Walks FREE Ranger-led hikes on full-moon nights.

cabins have gas fireplaces and creaky porches – and are the best spot for families.

Bryce Canyon City

The village of Bryce Canyon City is located just outside the park. It's not an actual town, but a growing tourist center with minimarts, outfitters, a gas station and hotels.

If you're unable to secure a reservation or don't arrive early enough to get a site in the park, you could spend a night at a Bryce Canyon City campground and return early in the morning to grab a spot in the park.

Bryce Canyon Pines

Campground & RV Park   CAMPGROUND $

(📞800-892-7923; www.brycecanyonmotel.com; Hwy 12; tent/RV sites $38/50; ☺Apr-Oct) Across the street from the affiliated motel, 4 miles west of the Hwy 12/63 junction, this campground sits behind a gas station and general store. The roadside location is convenient, but not exactly ambient. Showers are avail-

able for guests. Note that at 7700ft it can be windy and cold in spring.

Ruby's RV Park

& Campground   CAMPGROUND $

(📞435-834-5301, 866-878-9373; www.rubysinn. com; 1000 S Hwy 63; tent sites $30, tipis $40, RV sites with partial/full hookups $42/48, cabins $64; ☺Apr-Oct; 🛜🐕) This crowded campground, 3 miles north of the Bryce visitor center (p129), has amenities, including flush toilets, showers, drinking water, a coin laundry, electrical hookups, a dump station, restaurant, general store and a hot tub. Both double-bunk cabins and tipis use shared bathroom facilities. Bring your own sleeping bag. Though over-the-top commercial, it's nonetheless convenient. Online reservations and walk-ins accepted.

Bryce View Lodge   MOTEL $

(📞888-279-2304; www.bryceviewlodge.com; d $120; ☺Apr-Oct; 🅿🐕🌐🛜🐕) Geared to budget travelers, the motel's 130 standard rooms are decent, though smaller than those

---

CAMPGROUNDS IN & AROUND BRYCE CANYON

CAMPGROUND	LOCATION	DESCRIPTION	NUMBER OF SITES
North (p125)	Bryce Canyon, in the park	Large, private and forested, recycling bins, good amenities and direct trail access	101
Sunset (p125)	Bryce Canyon, in the park	Shady, few amenities, best for last-minute availability in the park	102
Bryce Canyon Pines Campground	Bryce Canyon City	Convenient behind gas station minimart but bare and lacking ambience	24
Ruby's RV Park & Campground	Bryce Canyon City	Packed with amenities, near the park entrance; little privacy	200
Pine Lake	Clay Creek	Lovely and private, trailside in pine forest with good amenities	37
KOA of Cannonville	Hwy 12, east of Tropic	Great for families, ample amenities include pool and roadside ambience	80
Red Canyon	Hwy 12, Red Canyon	Pretty and forested with basic amenities, popular with off-road vehicles (ORVs)	33
Red Canyon RV Park	cnr Hwys 12 & 89	Friendly roadside RV village, convenient but with little privacy	24
King Creek	USFS Rd 287, near Tropic	Woodsy and well maintained, near river, popular with (loud) ORVs	37

 Drinking Water   *Flush Toilets*   *Great for Families*   *Wheelchair Accessible*   *Dogs Allowed (On Leash)*

of Ruby's Inn and a little bit musty. It has fewer amenities than most places in town, but guests enjoy free access to all the facilities across the street at Ruby's, including the pool and hot tub.

Bryce Canyon Pines MOTEL **$**
(☑800-892-7923; www.brycecanyonmotel.com; Hwy 12; r & cottage $140, ste $335; ☺Apr-Nov; P❄✿🛜🏊) If everything else is booked, check out this friendly motel, 4 miles west of the Hwy 12/63 junction. Standards may be a bit dreary and outdated – and the showers are downright Lilliputian – but deluxe rooms and cottages are smart. The attached restaurant is a favorite of locals. There's also a small campground.

Bryce Canyon Resort MOTEL **$$**
(☑800-834-0043; www.brycecanyonresort.com; cnr Hwys 12 & 63; r $189, cabins $250; P❄🛜🏊🍽) Four miles from the park, this is a great option. While the grounds leave much to be desired, there's a modernist-kitsch appeal to the rooms that blend all

that's great about the American motel, with modern treatments like huge murals and steampunk fixtures.

**Best Western Plus
Bryce Canyon Grand Hotel** HOTEL **$$**
(☑866-866-6634, 435-834-5700; www.brycecanyongrand.com; 30 N 100 E, Bryce Canyon City; d/ste $210/310; P✿@🛜🏊) This Best Western hotel earns its plus status with stylish, ample rooms featuring flat-screen TVs and a breakfast bar that spoils you for choice. Amenities include an outdoor swimming pool and hot tub, fitness center and coin laundry. It's a step up from the other hotels on the strip, but lacks the homegrown Americana character typical of the area.

Best Western Ruby's Inn HOTEL **$$**
(☑435-834-5341, 866-866-6616; www.rubysinn.com; 1000 S Hwy 63; RV sites $30, r $145-160, ste $220; P🐾✿@🛜🏊🍽) This is a gargantuan motel complex with ample facilities located just 1 mile north of the park entrance. Standard rooms feature two beds, either queen

ELEVATION	OPEN	RESERVATION REQUIRED?	DAY FEE	FACILITIES
8000ft	year-round	early May-late Sep	free	
8000ft	late spring-fall	May-Sep	free	
7700ft	Apr-Oct	yes	NA	
8000ft	Apr-Oct	partial	NA	
7400ft	mid-May–Oct 1	no	free	
6000ft	Mar-Dec	partial	NA	
8000ft	Jun-Sep	groups only	$4	
6500ft	Apr-Sep	partial	NA	
8000ft	mid-May–Oct 1	no	$4-6	

  Grocery Store Nearby

  Restaurant Nearby

 Pay-phone

 Summertime Campfire Program

 RV Dump Station

or king size, coffeemakers and hair dryers, and while they feel rather modular, they are highly serviceable. Reserve well in advance during high season, and ask for a room upstairs to avoid the noise.

The sprawling property includes a grocery store with camping supplies, a gas station, a post office, a coin laundry, an indoor pool and hot tub, showers, a currency exchange service, a perfectly kitsch onsite gallery and a liquor store (a rarity around here). There's plenty of room for kids to roam, and they'll love exploring the different little corners in the massive complex.

The tour desk can book helicopter tours and horseback riding. Ruby's also rents bicycles and ATVs. In summer there's a nightly rodeo (except Sunday), though we don't recommend it due to the animal welfare issues involved. Ruby's RV Park & Campground (p126) is just a few hundred feet south of here on the same side of the road.

✕ EATING

✕ In the Park

Bryce Canyon General Store & Snack Bar MARKET $
(Bryce Canyon Rd; dishes $3-9; ⊗noon-10pm) In addition to foodstuffs, sundries and tourist

---

RAILROAD DAYS

In the early 1920s, the Union Pacific Railroad saw dollar signs in starting tourism in the majestic but still-inaccessible canyons of southern Utah and northern Arizona. It built great lodges laden with modern comforts at the Grand Canyon, Zion, Cedar Breaks and Bryce Canyon. Trains reached Cedar City, where guests were shuttled via motor coach on a loop dubbed the Grand Circle Tour. Railroad brochures whetted travelers' appetites for Bryce, 'probably the most astonishing blend of exquisite beauty and grotesque grandeur ever produced by the forces of erosion. It is not to be described, however imperfectly, except in the language of fancy.' Today Bryce Canyon Lodge, the last of the original lodges, is the final remnant of the long-lost era of luxury rail travel in America.

---

kitsch, the general store near Sunrise Point (p115) sells hot dogs, cold drinks, packaged sandwiches, chili, soup and pizza.

★**Bryce Canyon Lodge Restaurant** AMERICAN $$
(⊘435-834-5361; Bryce Canyon Rd; breakfast & lunch $10-20, dinner $10-35; ⊗7am-10pm Apr-Oct) 🍴 While service may lag, meals deliver, with the excellent regional cuisine ranging from fresh green salads to bison burgers, braised portobellos and steak. All food is made on site and the certified green menu offers only sustainable seafood. The wine list is decent and, best of all, the low-lit room is forgiving if you arrive covered in trail dust.

✕ Bryce Canyon City

Ruby's Inn General Store SUPERMARKET $
(⊘435-834-5341; 1000 S Hwy 63, Best Western Ruby's Inn; ⊗7am-10pm) Sells groceries with a considerable mark-up, plus sundries, clothing and camping supplies. It also has a post office, showers ($6), free wi-fi and computer terminals ($1 for five minutes).

Bryce Canyon Pines Restaurant AMERICAN $$
(⊘435-834-5441; www.brycecanyonmotel.com/bryce-restaurant/; Hwy 12; breakfast & lunch $9.50-14, dinner mains $12-24; ⊗6:30am-9:30pm Apr-Oct) This supercute diner is classic Utah, with waitstaff that dote, Naugahyde booths and even a crackling fire on cold days. Expect hearty plates of meat and potatoes, perfect BLTs and meal-size soups. Locals come for towering wedges of homemade pie, such as the banana blueberry creme, and it's locally respected as the best breakfast joint around.

Best Western Ruby's Inn AMERICAN $$
(Cowboy's Buffet and Steak Room; ⊘435-834-5341; 1000 S Hwy 63; mains $8-34; ⊗6:30am-9pm, year round) Ruby's operates two restaurants: a full-service dining room and buffet off the hotel lobby, and an economical diner that serves pizza, burgers and fried food. Both deliver mediocre assembly-line cooking that's overpriced but convenient. For fresher food, order off the menu instead of the buffet. Expect a wait at dinner.

Cowboy Ranch House AMERICAN $$
(⊘435-834-5351; cnr Hwys 12 & 63; mains $14-30; ⊗7-11am & 5-10pm) Part of Bryce Canyon Resort (p127), this is a decent spot to grab a bite. Expect classic Americana fare like

flame-grilled steaks, trout and burgers, with some Mexican dishes and an emphasis on local produce. Breakfast is also available, and there's a small sports bar.

Ebenezer's Barn & Grill BARBECUE **$$$**
(☑800-468-8660; www.ebenezersbarnandgrill. com; 1000 S Hwy 63; dinner show $32-38; ☺7pm mid-May–Oct) A big BBQ dinner here comes with a kitschy but good-natured evening of country and western music (drinks not included). Options include salmon, steak, pulled pork or chicken served with beans and cornbread. Since it's wildly popular, reservations are necessary. It's run by Ruby's Inn and located across the street.

ℹ Information

Due to Bryce's high elevation, some visitors may experience altitude sickness. Avoid alcohol and strenuous physical exercise.

Backcountry permits for overnight travel are issued at the park's visitor center on a first-come, first-served basis.

Bryce Canyon National Park Visitor Center
(☑435-834-5322; www.nps.gov/brca; Hwy 63; ☺8am-8pm May-Sep, 8am-6pm Oct & Apr, 8am-4:30pm Nov-Mar; ☏) Check here for weather, hiking and road conditions and campground availability. Exhibits show plant, animal life and geologic displays and there's an excellent 20-minute orientation video. The park headquarters are here, as is first aid, and phones and wi-fi in the lobby. Families can pick up Junior Ranger Activity Guides. Located adjacent to the entrance station.

Parking here is limited to one hour, so consider taking the free **shuttle** (☑435-834-5290; ☺8am-7pm early spring to late fall).

Bryce Canyon Natural History Association
(☑435-834-4600; www.brycecanyon.org) A nonprofit that aids the park service with edu-

cational, scientific and interpretive activities. The association operates the bookstore, and staff answer questions in the visitor center. Its excellent online shop sells books, maps, videos, music and trip-planning packets tailored to the individual traveler's needs.

ℹ Getting Around

A private vehicle is the only transportation option from fall through early spring. From mid-April through September, the free shuttle keeps you from getting stuck without a parking spot. (Note: the park's visitor center parking lot fills up too, and parking is limited to one hour.) Leave your car at Ruby's Inn or Ruby's Campground stops, and ride the shuttle into the park. The shuttle goes as far as Bryce Point; buses come roughly every 15 minutes between 8am and 8pm, and a round-trip without exiting takes 50 minutes. The *Hoodoo* newspaper shows routes. Biking is a great (and green!) way to get around the park, and you can bike to every major trailhead. The off-road paved multi-use path is perfect for families.

No trailers are permitted south of Sunset Point. If you're towing, leave your load at your campsite or in the trailer turnaround lot at the visitor center.

DOG LODGING

Even picky pet owners laud **Pawz** (☑435-691-3696; 1460 E 4200 N, Panguitch), a down-home kennel located in rural sagebrush country. Features include indoor dog beds and yards with pools. It's 5 miles out of Panguitch but doggie pickups are available in town with advance notice. There's both day camp and overnight options.

JOE CORNISH/GETTY IMAGES ©

1. Thor's Hammer (p117)
At the end of the Navajo Loop Trail you'll find this improbable sight.

2. Silent City (p118)
Hot-air balloons float over Silent City, an assemblage of hoodoos resembling figures frozen in the rock.

3. Navajo Loop Trail (p116)
This short but spectacular trail passes many of the park's most iconic sights.

4. Inspiration Point (p123)
This viewpoint is one of the best places in the park to see Silent City.

Around Bryce Canyon National Park

Best Places to Stay

➡ Buffalo Sage (p133)

➡ Red Brick Inn (p136)

➡ Cottonwood Meadow Lodge (p136)

➡ Red Canyon Campground (p135)

Best Places to Eat

➡ Stone Hearth Grille (p134)

➡ Café Adobe (p136)

➡ Henrie's Drive-in (p137)

Why Go?

This is Butch Cassidy country, where legends of the outlaw abound. He's said to have ridden the trails in scenic Red Canyon, past the red limestone towers where a hiking route is named for him today. The gunslinger's boyhood home can be visited in tiny Circleville.

If you're looking for a base for visiting Bryce Canyon National Park, towns include the farming community of Tropic and tourist-friendly, old-fashioned Panguitch, the gateway to Bryce Canyon.

This is a great place to go cycling: unlike Bryce Canyon, Red Canyon has both paved bike paths and mountain-biking trails.

When to Go
Bryce Canyon National Park

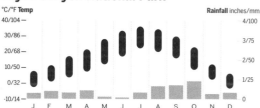

May–Aug
Moderately hot; afternoon thundershowers common in late summer.

Sep & Oct
Mild days; you'll still need a warm coat.

Nov–Feb
Very cold, with snow on the ground.

Tropic

POP 520 / ELEV 6309FT

Founded in 1891 by Mormon pioneers, the tiny town of Tropic is a satellite to Bryce Canyon National Park, located 10 miles east on Hwy 12. The farming community got its start with the creation of Tropic Ditch, which diverted water from Bryce Canyon to irrigate fields.

🏃 Activities

★ Mecham Outfitters
HORSEBACK RIDING
(☑435-679-8823; www.mechamoutfitters.com; half-day ride $75) Longtime locally run outfitter leading highly recommended half- and full-day horse rides, including through slot canyons, in nearby Dixie National Forest (p156) and on Grand Staircase–Escalante National Monument (p138) lands.

🛏 Sleeping

Bryce Pioneer Village
CABIN $
(☑800-222-0381, 435-679-8546; www.brycepioneervillage.com; 80 S Main St; tent/RV site $30/45, cabins from $115, d from $125; ❄) On the edge of town in 14 acres of land, these cabins are standard and a little cramped. There's also an RV campground featuring full electrical hookup and showers included in the camping fee.

Pine Lake Campground
CAMPGROUND $
(☑Escalante Ranger District 435-826-5400, group reservations 877-444-6777; www.recreation.gov; Dixie; sites $15; ❄Jun-Sep) This campground is located in a pretty pine forest near a reservoir, 11 miles north of the Hwy 12/63 junction then 6 miles east on unpaved Clay Creek. Powerboats aren't allowed, but expect ATVs. Only groups may reserve. There's no trash collection and amenities are limited to vault toilets and drinking water.

King Creek Campground
CAMPGROUND $
(☑435-676-2676, group reservations 877-444-6777; www.fs.usda.gov/main/dixie/home; King Creek Campground Rd, Bryce Canyon; site $15; ❄mid-May–Oct 1) Near Bryce's western boundary, 3 miles west of the Hwy 12/63 junction then 7 miles south via unpaved USFS Rd 087, this woodsy, well-maintained, first-come, first-served 37-site campground is adjacent to Tropic Reservoir and the Sevier River (bring bug spray). It's also popular with ATV riders (bring earplugs). Amenities include flush toilets, drinking water and a dump station.

KOA of Cannonville
CAMPGROUND $
(☑435-679-8988; http://koa.com/campgrounds/cannonville; 150 W 200 N, Cannonville; tent/RV site from $35/45, cabins from $79; ❄Mar-Dec; ❄❄) Particularly good for families, KOA of Cannonville provides lots of amenities (flush toilets, drinking water, dump station, electrical hookups, spotlessly clean bathrooms and showers). It's 5 miles east of Tropic, and has 80 sites and cabins.

★ Buffalo Sage B&B
B&B $
(☑435-679-8443; www.buffalosage.com; 980 N Hwy 12; d $120; ❄May-Sep; ❄❄) Up on a bluff west of town, three exterior-access rooms lead out to an expansive, upper-level deck or ground-level patio with great views. The owner's background in art is evident in the decor. Do note that the communal living area is shared with cats and a dog. The full breakfast accommodates vegetarians.

Bryce Country Cabins
CABIN $
(☑888-679-8643, 435-679-8643; www.brycecountrycabins.com; 320 N Main St; cabins $125; ❄Feb-Oct; ❄❄) Friendly and family run, these well-designed pine cabins are centered around an outdoor fire pit, perfect for stargazing around a bonfire. The only drawback is they're right on the main street. Deluxe cabins have cozy furniture and vaulted ceilings. Perks include TVs, coffeemakers, small porches and charm – it's among the best simple accommodations near Bryce.

Bullberry Inn
B&B $
(☑800-249-8126, 435-679-8820; www.bullberryinn.com; 412 S Hwy 12; r $135-145; ❄Apr-Oct, ❄) Though the home dates only to 1998, this farmhouse-style inn serves up traditional Utah, down to the Bullberry jelly, a recipe that's been in the family for generations. The family gives a warm welcome and the country-cozy theme goes far – from ample log- and bear-themed rooms to a full country breakfast. There's a two-night minimum stay.

America's Best Value Inn & Suites – Bryce Canyon
INN $
(☑435-679-8811, 800-442-1890; www.americasbestvalueinn.com; 199 N Main St; r from $89; ❄❄❄) These standard rooms in a boxy setting are competitively priced in off-season. Look online for discounts. Pets allowed with fee.

Bryce Trails B&B
B&B $$

(☑435-679-8200; www.brycetrails.com; 1001 W Bryce Way; r $170-195; ✹☎) Reticent toward walk-ins, this tidy lodging nonetheless offers bright and slightly kitsch Western-theme rooms, some with deck or Jacuzzi. It's located 1 mile from Main St.

Bryce Canyon Inn
INN $$

(☑800-592-1468, 435-679-8502; www.brycecan yoninn.com; 21 N Main St; r from $98, cabins from $175; ✹☎) These immaculate pine-scented, roadside rooms feature quilted beds and free continental breakfast. Cabins are tightly spaced, but feature a refrigerator, coffeemaker and TV. There's also an on-site pizzeria and espresso bar.

Stone Canyon Inn
INN $$$

(☑866-489-4680, 435-679-8611; www.stone canyoninn.com; 1220 Stone Canyon Lane; cabins $235-360; ✹☎) In a Wild West setting of scrub hills backed by Technicolor sunsets, this stately stone-and-wood lodging offers adventure out the back door – stroll or bike to your heart's content. Cabins are spacious and luxuriously private, though trumped by the charm of the main house, where a restaurant was recently added. There's a Finnish sauna. It's 1.3 miles from Main St.

✖ Eating

Pizza Place
AMERICAN $

(☑435-679-8888; 21 N Main St; pizza $8-16; ☺11am-9pm) Think wood-fired flatbread piled high with fresh ingredients. When locals eat out, they come to this family-owned joint with the pulse of Tropic. Hours vary seasonally.

Clarke's Country Market
MARKET $

(☑435-679-8633; 141 N Main St; sandwiches $5-8; ☺8am-9pm) Tropic's only grocery store has a deli sandwich counter and homemade baked goods.

Rustler's
AMERICAN $$

(☑435-679-8383; 141 N Main St; breakfast & lunch $4-15, dinner $14-26; ☺7am-10pm; ☎) A full-service American restaurant with outdoor deck seating. Portions are large though not very memorable. Beer and wine are available.

Stone Hearth Grille
AMERICAN $$$

(☑435-679-8923; www.stonehearthgrille.com; 1380 W Stone Canyon Lane; mains $26-38; ☺5-10pm Mar-Oct) In a lovely rural setting staring out at the bluffs, this upscale lodge restaurant serves rib-eye steaks, quinoa-stuffed peppers and satisfying green salads alongside a decent wine list. It's the best dinner option in the area. The deck seating offers a heavy dose of romance.

Red Canyon

Impressive, deep-ocher-red monoliths rise up roadside as you drive along Hwy 12, 10 miles west of the Hwy 63/Bryce Canyon turnoff. The aptly named **Red Canyon** (☑435-676-2676; www.fs.usda.gov/recarea/dixie; Scenic Byway 12, Dixie National Forest; park 24hr, visitor center 9am-6pm Jun-Aug, 10am-4pm May & Sep) provides super-easy access to these eerie, intensely colored formations. In fact, you have to cross under two blasted-rock arches to continue on the highway. A network of trails leads hikers, bikers and horseback riders deeper into these national-forest-service lands. Check out the excellent geologic displays and pick up trail maps at the visitor center.

◎ Sights & Activities

Bryce Wildlife Adventure
MUSEUM

(Bryce Museum; ☑435-834-5555; www.bryce wildlifeadventure.com; 1945 W Hwy 12; adult/child $8/5; ☺9am-7pm Apr–mid-Nov) This roadside attraction displays dioramas of more than 800 animals from around the world, as well as Native American artifacts and butterfly and giant bug exhibits. The dioramas and descriptions are actually pretty darned good. There are live deer out back that you can feed, though it's a bit sad seeing these beautiful creatures penned up.

Red Canyon Trails
HIKING

Several moderately easy hiking trails begin near the visitor center: the 0.7-mile (30-minute) **Arches Trail** passes 15 arches as it winds through a canyon, and the 0.5-mile (30-minute) **Pink Ledges Trail** passes red-rock formations. For a harder hike, try the 2.8-mile (two to four hours) **Golden Wall Trail**; you can extend it to a 5-mile round-trip by adding **Buckhorn Trail**.

Thunder Mountain Trail
MOUNTAIN BIKING

(🚲) The best trail in the region, the Thunder Mountain loop has 5 paved miles ideal for families; the other 7.8 miles are strenuous and involve sand and switchbacks (start the ride toward Bryce to ride uphill on the pavement and downhill on the dirt). Be aware that horses share the trail.

Red Canyon

Bicycle Trail
CYCLING

(🚲) This newish bike path runs 8.6 miles along Hwy 12 from Thunder Mountain trailhead to East Fork Rd. It's paved and perfect for families. There are plans to eventually extend the path all the way to Bryce.

Scenic Rim
Trail Rides
HORSEBACK RIDING

(📞435-679-8761, 800-679-5859; www.brycecanyon horseback.com; 1000 S Hwy 63, Ruby's Inn; 4hr ride $90) Guided horseback rides to Thunder Mountain and other Red Canyon locations. Based at Best Western Ruby's Inn.

🛌 Sleeping

More lodging choices are available in nearby Panguitch and Hatch. It's a 20-minute drive from Red Canyon to Bryce, and 10 minutes to Panguitch.

Red Canyon Campground
CAMPGROUND $

(📞435-676-2676; www.fs.usda.gov; Scenic Byway 12, Panguitch; tent & RV sites $20; ⊙mid-May–Sep) Surrounded by limestone formations and ponderosa pines, the 37 no-reservation sites here are quite scenic. Quiet-use trails (no ATVs) lead off from here, making this a good alternative to Bryce Canyon National Park camping. There are showers and a dump station, but no hookups. It's 10 miles west of the Hwy 12/63 junction.

Red Canyon Village
CAMPGROUND $

(📞435-676-2243; www.redcanyonvillage.com; cnr Hwys 12 & 89; sites $39, cabins $125; ⊙Apr-Oct) If you can't secure a site at the Red Canyon Campground, try this park, which also operates a small store. Options include tent sites, RV hookups and cabins. Cabins are micro-size, without private bathrooms.

ℹ️ Information

Red Canyon Visitor Center (📞435-676-2676; www.fs.usda.gov/recarea/dixie/recarea/?recid =24942; 5375 Hwy 12; ⊙9am-6pm Jun-Aug, 10am-4pm May & Sep) Check out the excellent geologic displays and pick up trail maps at the visitor center.

ℹ️ Getting There & Away

Red Canyon is in the **Dixie National Forest Powell ranger district** (p137). It's on Hwy 12, 1.5 miles from the Hwy 89 junction south of Panguitch, and 15 miles from Bryce Canyon.

Panguitch

POP 1500 / ELEV 6666FT

Founded in 1864, historically Panguitch was a profitable pioneer ranching and lumber community. Since the 1920s inception of the national park, the town has had a can't-live-with-or-without-it relationship with Bryce Canyon, 24 miles east. Lodging long ago became the number-one industry, as it's also used as an overnight stop halfway between Las Vegas (234 miles) and Salt Lake City (245 miles).

Other than some interesting turn-of-the-20th-century brick homes and buildings, it has few attractions. Main St has an antique store or two, but mostly people fill up with food and fuel, rest up and move on. In a pinch you could use it as a base for seeing Bryce, Zion and Cedar Breaks.

Panguitch is the seat of Garfield County and hosts numerous festivals.

👁 Sights

Nearby Red Canyon has gorgeous hiking and many locals enjoy Panguitch Lake in summer. Panguitch once hosted a brick factory and boasts a number of beautiful red-brick houses.

🎪 Festivals & Events

Panguitch Valley Balloon Rally
FAIR

(Chariots in the Sky; http://panguitch.com/event/panguitch-valley-balloon-rally/; ⊙late Jun) A huge hot-air balloon festival featuring music and family activities.

Garfield County Fair
STREET CARNIVAL

(📞435-676-1113; https://garfieldcountyfair.com; ⊙late Aug) Established in 1938 and now one of the most anticipated events of the year, this fair hosts live bands and features parades, classic car shows, barbecues, livestock sales and rodeos for an entire week.

🛌 Sleeping

Panguitch and the area around the Hwy 89/12 junction (7 miles south) feature a good selection of cute B&Bs and old-fashioned motels, with budget and midrange options. If you pull into town without a reservation, rates may be higher. Properties open in the off-season (November to March) reduce rates significantly. Motels that allow pets generally only keep a few pet-friendly rooms, best reserved in advance.

Camping

Hitch-N-Post
CAMPGROUND $

(☑435-676-2436; www.hitchnpostrv.com; 420 N Main St; tent/RV sites with hookups $20/36; 🕏🔊) Small lawns and trees divide RV spaces; tent sites are in a grassy field, but still have barbecue grills. RV wash and heavy-duty laundry on site.

Panguitch KOA
CAMPGROUND $

(☑800-562-1625, 435-676-2225; http://koa.com/campgrounds/panguitch; 555 S Main St; tent/RV site from $32/39; 🔊🕏🔊) Offers complete facilities, including a swimming pool. Showers cost $5 for nonguests.

Lodging

Purple Sage
MOTEL $

(☑800-241-6889, 435-676-2659; www.purplesagemotel.biz; 132 E Center St; r from $79; ⊖Mar-Oct; 🕏🔊🕏) Comfy, as motels go, this tidy spot slips in sweet extras such as pillow-top mattresses, new furnishings and coffeemakers. Staff are helpfully chatty. Pets may be allowed; check first in person.

Panguitch House
B&B $

(☑435-676-2574, 435-899-0190; www.panguitchhousebandb.com; 259 E Center St; r from $95; 🕏🔊) The nicely simple, new B&B rooms in this renovated red-brick home are an excellent alternative to a motel. The price is more than right and the friendly hosts provide a big breakfast and advice on area adventures.

THE QUILT WALK FESTIVAL

In quaint homes around Panguitch, quilters are working as feverishly as Penelope at the loom. This subculture owes its origin to an event in the settlers' first winter. With food scarce during the brutal winter of 1884, seven men set out on a 40-mile journey in a wagon pulled by oxen to find provisions. Impeded by deep snow, they would have perished but found that the quilts on which they prayed also served to compact the snow. Panguitch legend has it that they completed the journey by laying quilts across the snow and walking over them.

They are now honored by the annual Quilt Walk Festival (www.quiltwalk.org; ⊖mid-Jun), a week-long event that features historic home tours, theater shows and tractor parades. There are also races, quilt shows and an art fair.

Marianna Inn Motel
MOTEL $

(☑435-676-8844, 800-598-9190; www.mariannainn.com; 699 N Main St; r from $89; 🕏🔊🕏🕏) Rooms in the dollhouse-like motel with the large, shaded swing deck are standard. But the newest additions – deluxe log-style rooms – are worth splurging on. BBQ grill available for guests.

Hatch Station Motel
MOTEL $

(☑435-735-4015; 177 S Main St, Hatch; r from $69; ⊖mid-Mar–late Oct; 🕏🔊) Bargain rooms roadside.

Color Country Motel
MOTEL $

(☑435-676-2386, 800-225-6518; www.colorcountrymotel.com; 526 N Main St; r from $65; 🕏) An economical, standard motel with perks – a pool and outdoor hot tub.

★Red Brick Inn
B&B $$

(☑435-690-1048; www.redbrickinn.com; 161 N 100 W; r $130-220; ⊖May-Oct; 🕏🔊) Warm California native Peggy runs this 1919 charmer that once served as the town hospital. Rooms are cozy and comfortable, breakfasts are elaborate and outstanding, and stories abound. Chill out swinging in a garden hammock or pedaling a loan bike. Ask in advance about pets.

★Cottonwood Meadow Lodge
LODGE $$

(☑435-676-8950; www.brycecanyoncabins.com; Mile 123, Hwy 89; cottages from $185; ⊖mid-Apr–Oct; 🔊) Dubbed 'cowboy-licious' by a wizened ranch hand, this lodge delivers open-range dreams. Recycled from a Mormon saw town, the private ranch, 2 miles south of Hwy 12, near Panguitch, occupies acres of tawny grass and tumbling sagebrush. Cabins range from a rustic-chic bunkhouse with wooden plank floors to stylish farmhouses with gleaming kitchens, blazing hearths and porch rockers. There's a minimum two-night stay.

🍴 Eating & Drinking

The selection of restaurants is a little slim. Eateries in Hatch are also close by.

★Café Adobe
AMERICAN $

(☑435-735-4020; 16 N Main St, Hatch; mains $10-18; ⊖2-6pm Tue-Sat Apr-Nov) It's worth the 15-mile trek from Panguitch south to Hatch to sample this spot's gourmet hamburgers, creative sandwiches and decadent pies. Don't pass up the homemade tortilla chips and chunky salsa. Locals from the whole region congregate here.

ON BUTCH CASSIDY'S TRAIL

Nearly every town in southern Utah claims a connection to Butch Cassidy (1866–c 1908), the Old West's most famous bank and train robber. As part of the Wild Bunch, Cassidy (née Robert LeRoy Parker) pulled 19 heists from 1896 to 1901. Accounts usually describe him with a breathless romanticism, likening him to a kind of Robin Hood. Bring up the subject in these parts and you'll likely be surprised at how many folks' grandfathers had encounters with him. The robber may even have attended a dance in the old **Torrey Schoolhouse**, now a B&B. And many a dilapidated shack or a canyon, just over yonder, served as his hideout. The most credible claim for the location of the famous Robbers' Roost hideout is in the **Henry Mountains**.

In the wee town of **Circleville**, located 28 miles north of Panguitch, stands the honest-to-goodness boyhood home of the gun-slingin' bandit. The cabin is partially renovated but uninhabited, 2 miles south of town on the west side of Hwy 89. When reporters arrived after the release of the film *Butch Cassidy and the Sundance Kid* (1969), they met the outlaw's youngest sister, who claimed that Butch did in fact not die in South America in 1908, but returned for a visit after that. Writers have been digging for the truth to no avail ever since. You can see where they filmed Robert Redford's famous bicycle scene at the **Grafton ghost town**, outside Rockville.

Local lore holds that Cassidy didn't steal much in Utah because this is where his bread was buttered. Whatever the reason, the Wild Bunch's only big heist in the state was in April, 1897, when the gang stole more than $8000 from Pleasant Valley Coal Company in Castle Gate, 4 miles north of Helper on Hwy 191. The little **Western Mining & Railroad Museum** (☑ 435-472-3009; http://wmrrm.com; 296 S Main St, Helper; adult/child $2/1; ⊙10am-5pm Mon-Sat May-Aug, 11am-4pm Tue-Sat Sep-Apr), 8 miles north of Price, has exhibits on the outlaws, including photos, in the basement. For more, check out *The Outlaw Trail*, written by Charles Kelly.

Henrie's Drive-in   BURGERS $
(☑ 435-616-2355; 166 N Main St; burgers $5-8; ⊙11am-10pm Mar-Oct) Craving a deliciously greasy burger and fries? Look no further and don't forget the strawberry milkshake.

Joe's Main Street Market   MARKET $
(☑ 435-676-2361; www.joesmainstreetmarket. com; 10 S Main St; ⊙8am-9pm Mon-Sat) The town's main grocery store.

Cowboy's Smokehouse BBQ   BARBECUE $$
(☑ 435-676-8030; www.thecowboysmokehouse. com; 95 N Main St; breakfast & lunch $5-12, dinner $15-32; ⊙7am-10pm Mon-Sat) Sweet staff serve steaks and brisket with housemade sauce, but the food quality can be erratic. Portions are generous.

ⓘ Information

Powell Ranger Station (☑ 435-676-9300; 225 E Center St; ⊙8am-4:30pm Mon-Fri) Dixie National Forest (p156) camping and hiking info.

Garfield County Tourism Office (☑ 800-444-6689, 435-676-1160; www.brycecanyon country.com; 55 S Main St; ⊙9am-5pm) Provides regional travel and event information.

Garfield Memorial Hospital (☑ 435-676-8811; 224 N 400 E; ⊙24hr) A small hospital with trauma care services.

Garfield County Sheriff's Office (☑ 435-676-2678; https://gcutsheriff.com; 375 N 700 W)

Post Office (☑ 435-676-8853; 65 N 100 W; ⊙8:30am-5pm Mon-Fri, 9:30am-noon Sat)

ⓘ Getting There & Away

The main drag through town, Hwy 89, comes in on Main St from the north, then turns east on Center St. South of Center, Main St becomes Hwy 143 leading to Panguitch Lake.

There are no scheduled bus, air or train services to Panguitch.

Grand Staircase–Escalante National Monument

Best Hikes

➜ Slot Canyons of Dry Fork/ Coyote Gulch (p145)

➜ Willis Creek (p145)

➜ Lower Calf Creek Falls (p144)

➜ Escalante River Natural Bridge (p142)

➜ Boulder Mail Trail (p146)

Best Drives

➜ Burr Trail (p147)

➜ Hole-in-the-Rock Road (p148)

➜ Cottonwood Canyon Road (p148)

Why Go?

Grand Staircase–Escalante National Monument is one of the largest parks in the Southwest, with some of the least visited – yet most spectacular – scenery, including impossibly narrow slot canyons, rippled slickrock and pink dunes. Its name refers to the geological layers that begin at the bottom of the Grand Canyon and rise, in stair steps, 3500ft to Bryce Canyon. Tourist infrastructure is minimal and limited to surrounding towns.

Established amid controversy by former president Clinton in 1996, the monument was thrust back into the headlines in late 2017 when the Trump administration proposed to reduce its size from 1.9 million acres to 1 million acres. Land that was previously part of the monument is now considered public land and granted less protection. It remains to be seen how this will affect the visitor experience. A lengthy court battle disputing the changes is currently underway.

Driving Distances (miles)

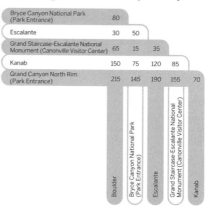

	Boulder	Bryce Canyon National Park (Park Entrance)	Escalante	Grand Staircase-Escalante National Monument (Canonville Visitor Center)	Kanab
Bryce Canyon National Park (Park Entrance)	80				
Escalante	30	50			
Grand Staircase-Escalante National Monument (Canonville Visitor Center)	65	15	35		
Kanab	150	75	120	85	
Grand Canyon North Rim (Park Entrance)	215	145	190	155	70

Entrances

There are no entrance stations; the monument is freely accessible 24/7. It encompasses three major geologic areas: the westernmost Grand Staircase, south of Bryce Canyon and west of Cottonwood Canyon Rd; central Kaiparowits Plateau, east of Cottonwood Canyon Rd and west of Hole-in-the-Rock Rd; and the eastern Escalante Canyons, southwest of the Burr Trail. In the north, scenic Hwy 12 skirts the boundary of GSENM, passing through the small towns of Escalante and Boulder.

In the south, Hwy 89 arcs east from the larger town of Kanab. Three unpaved roads cross the park between the highways, roughly north to south: Skutumpah and Johnson Canyon Rds, Cottonwood Canyon Rd and Smoky Mountain Rd. Hole-in-the-Rock Rd, a dead end, leads southeast from Hwy 12 toward Glen Canyon National Recreation Area. Partly paved Burr Trail crosses the monument's northeast corner from Boulder into Capitol Reef.

You can get a free permit to car-camp or backpack overnight from any visitor center, information kiosk or major trailhead. Only Calf Creek Recreation Area carries a day-use fee.

DON'T MISS

GSENM is so big that it is conducive to multiple visits. Start with a hike near Boulder (Lower Calf Creek or Escalante Natural Bridge) and explore some of the slot canyons on Hole-in-the-Rock Rd. If you have time, drive the Cottonwood Canyon Rd toward Kanab and enjoy the solitude of its lesser-known hikes.

When You Arrive

➡ Day use is generally free. Visitor centers in Escalante, Cannonville and Kanab offer free park bulletins and maps, and sell more detailed maps, like the USGS 7.5-quadrangles.

➡ Fill up on water at visitor centers; there is none at trailheads, nor at most campgrounds.

➡ Check with rangers at a visitor center about road conditions, the weather forecast and the type of vehicle suitable for the roads you plan to travel on. Much of the park is on 4WD roads and clay surfaces become impassable when wet.

➡ There is no comprehensive topographical map for the park, but the National Geographic Trails Illustrated (www. natgeomaps.com) map No 710, *Canyons of the Escalante*, covers the northeast corner of the park.

PARK POLICIES & REGULATIONS

All vehicles must stay on designated roads, which are open to mountain bikes, cars, 4WDs, all-terrain vehicles (ATVs) and other off-highway vehicles.

Campfires in developed campgrounds are restricted to fire rings; elsewhere you're allowed to use a fire pan. Do not light fires at archaeological sites or in rock shelters or alcoves. Banned in Coyote Gulch, dogs are allowed elsewhere, though they often must be leashed.

Fast Facts

➡ **Total area:** 2969 sq miles

➡ **Elevation:** 4900ft

➡ **Average high/low temperature** (at Escalante) in July: 91°F/55°F

Reservations

While GSENM campgrounds do not accept reservations, state park and private campgrounds do. You may camp for free on BLM land, following regulations and standard Leave No Trace ethics. Some popular hikes require permits based on a lottery system.

Resources

➡ **Grand Staircase–Escalante National Monument** (www.blm.gov)

➡ **Paria Canyon-Vermilion Cliffs Wilderness** (www. blm.gov)

GRAND STAIRCASE–ESCALANTE NATIONAL MONUMENT

Grand Staircase–Escalante National Monument & Around

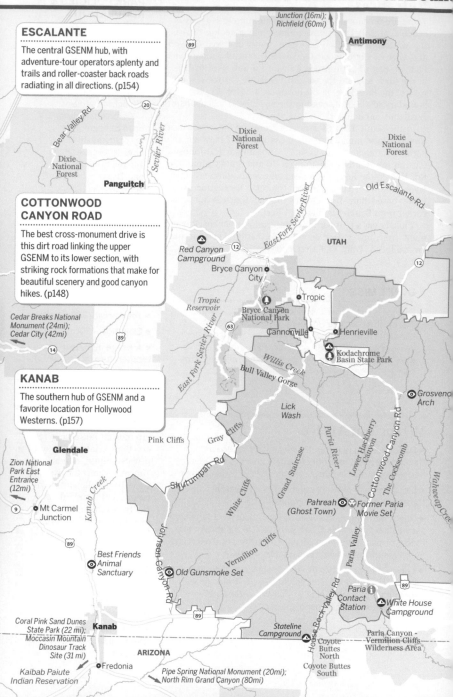

ESCALANTE

The central GSENM hub, with adventure-tour operators aplenty and trails and roller-coaster back roads radiating in all directions. (p154)

COTTONWOOD CANYON ROAD

The best cross-monument drive is this dirt road linking the upper GSENM to its lower section, with striking rock formations that make for beautiful scenery and good canyon hikes. (p148)

KANAB

The southern hub of GSENM and a favorite location for Hollywood Westerns. (p157)

Junction (16mi);
Richfield (60mi)

Antimony

89

Bear Valley Rd

20

Dixie National Forest

Dixie National Forest

Old Escalante Rd

Dixie National Forest

Panguitch

Sevier River

East Fork Sevier River

UTAH

Red Canyon Campground

12

12

Bryce Canyon City

Tropic

Cedar Breaks National Monument (24mi);
Cedar City (42mi)

89

Tropic Reservoir

East Fork Sevier River

63

Bryce Canyon National Park

Cannonville

Henrieville

14

Willis Creek

Kodachrome Basin State Park

Bull Valley Gorge

Grosvenor Arch

KANAB

The southern hub of GSENM and a favorite location for Hollywood Westerns. (p157)

Lick Wash

Pink Cliffs

Gray Cliffs

Paria River

Lower Hackberry Canyon

Cottonwood Canyon Rd

The Cockscomb

Wahweap Creek

Glendale

Zion National Park East Entrance (12mi)

Kanab Creek

Shurtumpah Rd

White Cliffs

Grand Staircase

9

Mt Carmel Junction

89

Johnson Canyon Rd

Pahreah (Ghost Town)

Former Paria Movie Set

Best Friends Animal Sanctuary

Old Gunsmoke Set

Vermilion Cliffs

Paria Valley

House Rock Valley Rd

Paria Contact Station

89

Coral Pink Sand Dunes State Park (22 mi);
Moccasin Mountain Dinosaur Track Site (31 mi)

Kanab

89

ARIZONA

Stateline Campground

White House Campground

Paria Canyon - Vermilion Cliffs Wilderness Area

Kaibab Paiute Indian Reservation

Fredonia

Pipe Spring National Monument (20mi);
North Rim Grand Canyon (80mi)

Coyote Buttes North

Coyote Buttes South

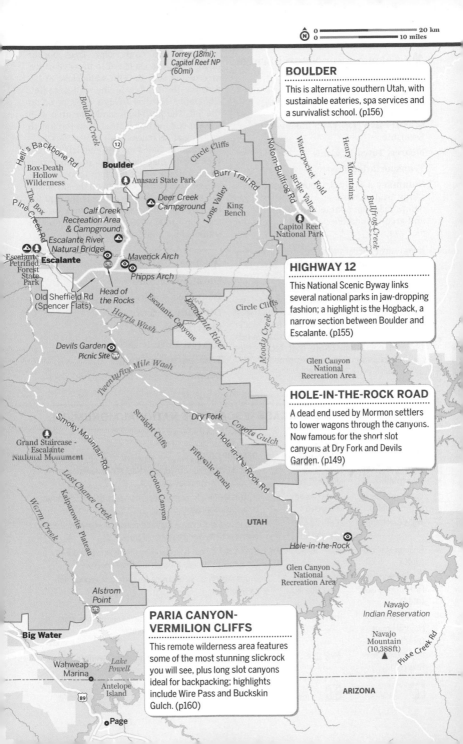

0 ⬆N **0**
20 km
10 miles

↑ Torrey (18mi);
Capitol Reef NP
(60mi)

BOULDER

This is alternative southern Utah, with sustainable eateries, spa services and a survivalist school. (p156)

Boulder Creek

(12)

Circle Cliffs

Notom-Bullfrog Rd

Waterpocket Fold

Strike Valley

Henry Mountains

Hell's Backbone Rd

Boulder

Box-Death
Hollow
Wilderness

Burr Trail Rd

Bullfrog Creek

The Box

Anasazi State Park

Long Valley

King Bench

Pine Creek Rd

Deer Creek
Campground

Calf Creek
Recreation Area
& Campground

Escalante River
Natural Bridge

Capitol Reef
National Park

Escalante

Escalante
Petrified
Forest State
Park

Maverick Arch

Phipps Arch

HIGHWAY 12

This National Scenic Byway links several national parks in jaw-dropping fashion; a highlight is the Hogback, a narrow section between Boulder and Escalante. (p155)

Old Sheffield Rd
(Spencer Flats)

Head of
the Rocks

Escalante Canyons

Circle Cliffs

Escalante River

Moody Creek

Harris Wash

Glen Canyon
National
Recreation Area

Devils Garden
Picnic Site

Twentyfive Mile Wash

HOLE-IN-THE-ROCK ROAD

A dead end used by Mormon settlers to lower wagons through the canyons. Now famous for the short slot canyons at Dry Fork and Devils Garden. (p149)

Smoky Mountain Rd

Dry Fork

Coyote Gulch

Grand Staircase -
Escalante
National Monument

Straight Cliffs

Hole-in-the-Rock Rd

Fiftymile Bench

Last Chance Creek

Kaiparowits Plateau

Croton Canyon

UTAH

Worm Creek

Hole-in-the-Rock

Navajo
Indian Reservation

Alstrom
Point

Glen Canyon
National
Recreation Area

Navajo
Mountain
(10,388ft) ▲

Piute Creek Rd

PARIA CANYON-VERMILION CLIFFS

This remote wilderness area features some of the most stunning slickrock you will see, plus long slot canyons ideal for backpacking; highlights include Wire Pass and Buckskin Gulch. (p160)

Big Water

Wahweap
Marina

Lake
Powell

Antelope
Island

(89)

●Page

ARIZONA

🚶 DAY HIKES

🚶 Escalante River Natural Bridge

Duration 3 hours

Distance 4.4 miles

Difficulty Easy–moderate

Start/Finish Hwy 12, 15 miles east of Escalante

Nearest Town Escalante

Transportation Private

Summary A fairly flat, but sometimes sandy, trail crisscrosses the river six times before reaching a large natural bridge and arch beyond. Be prepared to get your feet wet.

If you want a level walk with dramatic scenery, you've found it. The Escalante River hike is not as demanding as Lower Calf Creek Falls and it allows (requires) you to play in the water. Park at the trailhead by the Hwy 12 bridge over the Escalante River, just west of the Calf Creek Recreation Area. Water sandals are best for the alternating sandy and wet conditions. Note that biting flies can be bothersome in early summer.

Descend and cross the **Escalante River**. Walk through cottonwoods, then an exposed sagebrush and sand valley. Trees appear again when you get closer to the second river crossing, and the cliff walls close in before the third. After another full-sun stint, **Escalante Natural Bridge** appears off to the left. The 130ft-high sandstone arch with a 100ft span is best viewed from the fourth crossing at 1.8 miles.

Continue, and look up and left for the rock alcove that has a small **granary ruin**. You'll ford the river three more times before you get to **Natural Arch** up on the skyline to the southwest. Note that this is the end for the day hike, but you can continue on this trail for a total of 15 miles and end up at a trailhead back in Escalante town.

🚶 Upper Calf Creek Falls

Duration 1½ hours

Distance 2.2 miles

Difficulty Moderate

Start/Finish Hwy 12

Nearest Town Boulder

Transportation Private

Summary A short, but steep and stren-

HIKING IN GRAND STAIRCASE–ESCALANTE NATIONAL MONUMENT

NAME	START LOCATION	DESCRIPTION
Lower Calf Creek Falls (p143)	Calf Creek Recreation Area	A sandy, creekside canyon walk past Native American sites to a 126ft-tall waterfall and pool.
Lower Hackberry Canyon (p146)	Cottonwood Canyon Rd	A pleasant hike through a deep, narrow gorge that's cooled by a shallow stream.
Willis Creek (p145)	Cottonwood Canyon Rd	Accessible slot canyon that alternates between narrows and open sections along a seasonal creek.
Boulder Mail Trail (p146)	Hell's Backbone Rd	Hearty wilderness hike following the historic Boulder–Escalante mail route through Box-Death Hollow.
Slot Canyons of Dry Fork/Coyote Gulch (p144)	Hole-in-the-Rock Rd	Drops steeply down slickrock to reach four sinuous slot canyons.
Escalante River Natural Bridge (p142)	Hwy 12	A flat, sandy trail crisscrosses the river numerous times before reaching a large natural bridge.
Upper Calf Creek Falls (p142)	Hwy 12	A short but strenuous trail down slickrock leads to falls and two sets of pools.

 Views   *Flush Toilets*   *Great for Families*   *Waterfalls*

uous, trail down slickrock leads through a desert moonscape to an oasis. The two sets of pools and waterfalls at hike's end appear like a mirage.

Soaking your feet in a moss-covered pool while canyon wrens and mountain bluebirds dart about seems like an impossible dream when you first start your slickrock descent. The upper hike may not be as well known or dramatic as Lower Calf Creek Falls, but stick with it and you'll be rewarded with unexpected beauty. The quarter-mile unmarked dirt road to the trailhead is outside of Boulder, on the north side of Hwy 12 between mile markers 80 and 81.

Start at the rim, which overlooks all of **Calf Creek Canyon**, the **Straight Cliffs** beyond. From there the trail descends 550ft down steep white Navajo sandstone littered with dark volcanic boulders. Follow the cairns down until the incline levels off. The rock becomes more stratified and colorful just about the time you get a glimpse of treetops in the inner canyon to the west.

Shortly after, you'll come to a fork. Follow cairns down to the left and you'll reach the **lower pool** of the Upper trail – a vegetation-covered oasis beneath an 86ft waterfall. Follow the path up to the right for the **upper**

pools, where water cascades through shallow potholes and ponds before falling over the rim. Take the time to explore both pools: swim if it's warm, look over the canyon edge and appreciate the isolation.

Lower Calf Creek Falls

Duration 4 hours

Distance 6 miles

Difficulty Moderate

Start/Finish Calf Creek Recreation Area, Hwy 12, 14 miles east of Escalante

Nearest Town Escalante

Transportation Private

Summary The sandy track eventually follows a year-round running creek through a spectacular canyon before arriving at a 126ft waterfall, a joy on a hot day.

Lower Calf Creek Falls' beauty is no secret; this is easily the most heavily traveled trail in the entire monument. Its accessibility – right off Hwy 12 between Escalante and Boulder – makes it a perfect stopover. Though it doesn't climb much, the trail has long sandy stretches that can take a lot out

DIFFICULTY	DURATION	ROUND-TRIP DISTANCE	ELEVATION CHANGE	FEATURES	FACILITIES
moderate	4hr	6 miles	250ft		
easy-moderate	2-3hr	3-6 miles	100ft		
easy-moderate	up to 3hr	up to 4.4 miles	300ft		
difficult	2-3 days	16 miles one way	1800ft		
moderate-difficult	3hr	4.5 miles	600ft		
easy-moderate	3hr	4.4 miles	200ft		
moderate	1½hr	2.2 miles	600ft		

 Rock Climbing   *Swimming*   *Backcountry Campsite*

of you. Carry plenty of water (available at the trailhead); the creek is not safe for drinking.

Park at the **Calf Creek Recreation Area** (day use $5) and campground, between mile markers 75 and 76 on Hwy 12. As you work your way toward the creek, you'll pass honeycombed rocks and Navajo sandstone domes, an 800-year-old Native American **granary**, a box canyon where calves were once herded (hence the name Calf Creek), **prehistoric pictographs** and lush green wetlands.

Past the last bend, the trail ends in an amphitheater of rock with a 126ft-tall **waterfall** with a thin stream cascading into a large pool. The sandy shore and extended knee-deep wading area, before the deeper drop-off, make this a favorite with families. Remember, the sandy walk out is as strenuous as the walk in, so pace yourself.

Slot Canyons of Dry Fork/Coyote Gulch

Duration 3 hours

Distance 4.5 miles

Difficulty Moderate–difficult

Start/Finish Dry Fork Rd, off Hole-in-the-Rock Rd

Grand Staircase – Day Hikes

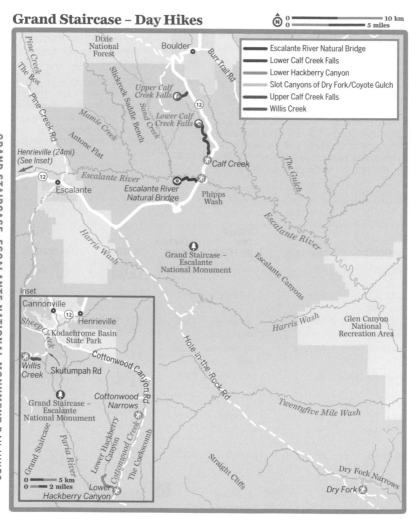

GRAND STAIRCASE–ESCALANTE NATIONAL MONUMENT DAY HIKES

Nearest Town Escalante

Transportation Private

Summary A remote but popular Hole-in-the-Rock Rd hike leads to four different slot canyons, complete with serpentine walls, incredible narrows and bouldering obstacles.

GSENM is famous for its sculpted slot canyons, spillways of brightly colored, weathered rock, and the four slots on this route are some of the most visited in the monument. Expect to encounter pools of water in some. From Hwy 12, drive 26 miles down Hole-in-the-Rock Rd to Dry Fork Rd (Rte 252), turn left, and drive 1.7 miles to the parking area, bearing left at all junctions.

From the parking area the route switchbacks steeply down the slickrock and you find yourself alternately sidestepping and pitching forward. An overabundance of willy-nilly rock cairns can lead you astray here. Look up and see where you're headed: toward the reddish-brown dirt hills with little vegetation to the north (leftish). You reach the bottom in **Coyote Gulch** wash. Follow it north, and when you emerge into an opening, **Dry Fork** slot canyon is immediately to the left (west). Dry Fork is often overlooked as not tight or physically challenging enough, but it's our favorite. You can walk for miles between undulating orange walls, with only a few small boulder step-ups.

Double back to Coyote Gulch and head downstream (east), keeping your eyes peeled for the first slot on the left, **Peek-a-Boo**. Even to get into this dramatic canyon, you have to climb up a 12ft handhold-carved wall (much easier if you're tall or not alone). From there the hanging slot tightens and passes under several arches. You may have to navigate some water, and scrambling is definitely required to the end point. Hikers have climbed up and over Peek-a-Boo to sneak up behind Spooky but it requires good orienteering skills, otherwise it's easy to get lost.

Retrace your steps to the main wash. A half-mile further downstream, veer left and hike through the sandy wash to **Spooky Gulch**, which is even narrower. The 0.3-mile slot is less technically challenging, but impassable for larger hikers. Turn back and return to the trailhead from here.

If you really want to lengthen your hike, you could continue to **Brimstone Gulch**, half a mile further.

🚶 Willis Creek

Duration up to 3 hours

Distance 4.4 miles

Difficulty Easy–moderate

Start/Finish Skumptah Rd, 6.9 miles southwest of Cannonville

Nearest Towns Cannonville, Escalante

Transportation Private

Summary A great little slot-canyon hike, accessible to young and old.

Unlike most of GSENM's slot canyons, the cliffs around Willis Creek are light beige, not red – an interesting contrast to the oftentimes orange mineral stream flowing through it. The trail starts 3 miles south of Cannonville on Skumptah Rd (access via Cottonwood Canyon Rd). Easy access and an almost-level canyon floor make this a great family route.

Across the road from the parking lot, follow the well-worn path down the hill and proceed left, down canyon. In less than five minutes the serpentine walls rise around you. There's no trail per se, you're just wandering from bank to bank following **Willis Creek**. Avoid drinking from the creek, there is sometimes horse manure about. The narrows open up after about half a mile, and this is where many people turn around. But you shouldn't.

Once you hike around, not slide down, the 11ft **pour-off**, the canyon walls grow taller. At times cliffs tower 200ft above, only 6ft apart.

Tight and narrow sections alternate until 2.2 miles along you reach the confluence with **Sheep Creek**, the end to this day hike.

🏃 Lower Hackberry Canyon

Duration 2–3 hours

Distance 3–6 miles

Difficulty Easy–moderate

Start/Finish Cottonwood Canyon Rd, 14 miles north of Hwy 89

Nearest Town Kanab

Transportation Private

Summary A pleasant hike through a cool gorge that flows with a shallow stream. Walk as much or as little as you like – Lower Hackberry continues for 26 miles.

This narrow gorge hike provides a welcome stretch for drivers on Cottonwood Canyon Rd. The marked trailhead takes about half an hour to reach from Hwy 89. From Cannonville and Hwy 12, the trailhead is 31 miles south. Wear long sleeves and pants to avoid deer flies in late spring.

Follow the dirt track to a typically dry wash. Past the corral you'll reach **Lower Hackberry Canyon**. Water often flows down the canyon, and many stream crossings are required, but it's not usually deep – normally a few inches. Wander as far as you like; the first few miles of the canyon are the most narrow and interesting. After a while, the canyon opens up; in early summer, clouds of gnats often choose this point to attack. Mostly only backpackers proceed from here.

🏃 OVERNIGHT HIKE

🏃 Boulder Mail Trail

Duration 2–3 days

Distance 16 miles one way

Difficulty Difficult

Start Boulder landing strip

Finish Upper Escalante River trailhead

Nearest Towns Boulder, Escalante

Transportation Hiker shuttle

Summary A hearty wilderness hike following the historic Boulder–Escalante mail route around rugged Box-Death Hollow. Detouring into the slickrock wilderness area provides an interesting extra day's adventure.

The monument is a mecca for hardcore backcountry adventurers, but significant route-finding skills are required (GPS skills don't count). Be sure to carry 7.5-minute USGS maps. The BLM recommends using portable waste containers (available at the BLM in Escalante); in the future these will be mandatory. Talk to rangers before heading out, and don't take unnecessary risks. In addition to this epic trail, ask rangers about Coyote Gulch, off Hole-in-the-Rock Rd, and the Gulch, off Burr Trail Rd. Escalante River Natural Bridge day hike can also be stretched into a 15-mile trek.

A free permit is needed for overnight hikes, and can be picked up at any visitor center, information kiosk or trailhead register. Beware: poison ivy abounds along creek banks.

This historic trail was once the supply and mail route between Boulder and Escalante. Much of it is unmarked or follows cairns. Most people do the one-way trip in two days, but a third day allows you to do some cross-country wandering and further explore Death Hollow, a world of gullies, grottoes, spires and other slickrock wonders perched on the east edge of your route.

There are serious ups and downs along the trail. We recommend beginning at the **Boulder landing strip**, off Hell's Backbone Rd outside of Boulder at 6800ft, and ending at the Upper Escalante River trailhead, less than a mile outside Escalante at 5800ft. Arrange a hiker shuttle to and from, or just back to your car from the endpoint. The following description is general and is not meant to be your sole route guide; get detailed maps such as the USGS *Escalante, Calf Creek and Boulder Town* quadrangles. Check with rangers for current conditions and descriptions.

The first leg takes you from the landing strip to Death Hollow (four to five hours, 5.5 miles). Don't start late: you'll want plenty of light for the final descent. A mile-long 4WD road leads from the parking lot to the sign marking the start of the Boulder Mail Trail and the flats atop New Home Bench. From there it's 450ft down to the **Sand Creek** drainage, where cottonwoods offer shade and there's water year-round. Then it's a 400ft trudge back up to the **Slickrock Saddle Bench** before making the precipitous 900ft drop into **Death Hollow**, a gorgeous, riparian canyon named for mules lost on the

Boulder Mail Trail

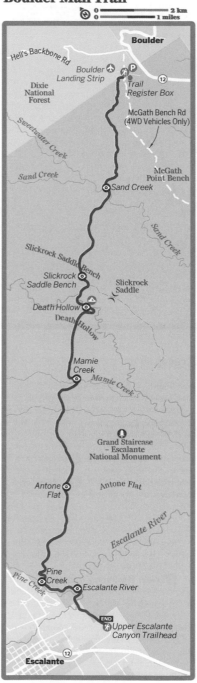

steep trip down. Death Hollow has several springs at the point where the Mail Trail traverses the canyon. Several campsites lie within 0.25 miles of where the trail meets the creek here; some of the best are 300yd downstream.

A strenuous 800ft ascent out of Death Hollow kicks things off on day two. The trail then crosses to a slickrock plateau, descends to the usually dry **Mamie Creek** and along and over a cracked sandstone formation resembling a giant cerebellum. At **Antone Flat** you come into open country, where a chalky-white slickrock draw may hold water in deep pockets.

After another 900ft slickrock descent, you climb down to **Pine Creek**. The creek's west bank is private, so follow its east bank to the **Escalante River**. To the west the canyon opens and the trail swings south through the brush, meeting a 4WD road and the Upper Escalante Canyon trailhead.

🚗DRIVING

Check road conditions before entering the monument and note that a high-clearance 4WD is recommended for some roads.

🚗Burr Trail

Duration 3 hours

Distance 60 miles

Start/Finish Hwy 12, Boulder

Summary This paved route provides an intro to all park formations – cliffs, canyons, buttes, mesas and monoliths – in colors from sandy white to deep coral red. Sweeping curves and steep ups and downs add to the attraction.

The most immediately gratifying, dramatic drive in the area, the Burr Trail heads east from Boulder as a paved road, crosses GSENM's northeast corner and, after 30 miles, arrives at Capitol Reef National Park (p162), where the road becomes loose gravel. This first section is quite a challenging road-bike ride, as well.

Once you enter the monument, it's not far to the two trailheads: the 7-mile-long **Deer Creek trail** and the 52-mile trek through **Grand Gulch**, popular with backpackers. Check with rangers for details about these spectacular hikes through riparian zones

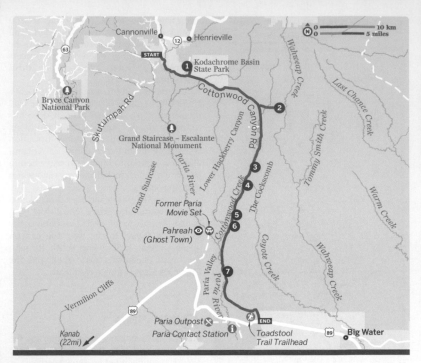

Driving Tour
Cottonwood Canyon Road

DURATION 3 HOURS
DISTANCE 46 MILES ONE WAY
START HWY 12, 34 MILES WEST OF
ESCALANTE
FINISH HWY 89, 45 MILES EAST OF KANAB
NEAREST TOWNS ESCALANTE, KANAB

Sculpted red sandstone monoliths, pale beige-
and-yellow towering arches and charcoal-gray
peaks: mile by mile, Cottonwood Canyon Rd
unfolds as a striking geology lesson. Don't
forget to get out and look around.

If you make only one of the three
cross-monument drives, we suggest it be
Cottonwood Canyon Rd, with its stunning
geological sights, interesting hikes and ever-
changing geography. The rough road is passable only when dry. Usually 2WD vehicles will
do, but 4WD is never a bad idea.

The first 9 miles of road to ❶ **Kodachrome Basin State Park** are paved. Stop
at the park to see a wonderland of red-rock
spires, balancing rocks and minibuttes. South
from here, the road gets bumpy. After about
20 miles, and a short side detour, you'll reach

the 90ft-high ❷ **Grosvenor Arch**. Follow
the level sidewalk to stand beneath this rare
yellow- and sand-colored stone double arch
towering so far above.

The main road continues south, weaving in
and among rock formations. You're traveling
along the west side of the ❸ **Cockscomb**, a
distinctive, long, narrow monocline caused by
a fold in the Earth's crust. ❹ **Cottonwood
Narrows** is a worthwhile 1.5-mile hike through
a sandstone slot canyon that takes about an
hour and a half. There are signposted parking
areas at both north and south entrances.

Soon after, stands of cottonwoods appear
in the wash on the right, and the rutted road
rises along a narrow shelf.

❺ **Lower Hackberry Canyon** is another
good day hike, right before ❻ **Yellow Rock**, a
tough, steep but climbable peak made of Navajo sandstone, with elaborate cross-bedding
and fracture lines. It's 2 miles round-trip.

From there, interesting features abound as
the landscape morphs from jagged rock into
coal-colored dirt hills before the road reaches
❼ **Paria Valley** and Hwy 89 beyond.

and red-rock desert. Deer Creek also has a tiny campground.

Just past the creek, the road enters **Long Canyon** beneath towering vertical slabs of red rock. At 11 miles look for an unmarked pullout on the road's left side. You'll see the opening for a side **slot canyon** north across a scrubby wash. Poke about the narrowing red-rock slot as far as you like.

Driving out of Long Canyon, stop at the crest for views beyond of the sheer **Circle Cliffs**, which hang like curtains above the undulating valley floor. Still snowcapped in summer, the **Henry Mountains** rise above 11,000ft on the horizon. **Wolverine Loop** is a 25-mile, 4WD road that circles south through an area riddled with scrubland, canyons and nearby cliffs. Several hiking trails lead off from there, and the area is popular with mountain bikers. Continuing on Burr Trail, you cross the **White Canyon Flat** plateau before the pavement ends and the road meets the giant, angled buttes of 100-mile **Waterpocket Fold** in Capitol Reef, the feature that blocked 19th-century settlers' passage west. Trailhead access to **Muley Twist Canyon** is nearby. Just ahead, the **Burr Trail Switchbacks** follow an original wagon route through the fold. You can continue onto **Notom-Bullfrog Rd** and north to Hwy 24 or south to Glen Canyon. But if you plan to turn around and return to Boulder, first drive the switchbacks – the magnificence and scale of the landscape will blow your mind.

🚗 Hole-in-the-Rock Road

Duration 8–9 hours

Distance 114 miles

Start/Finish Hwy 12, 5 miles east of Escalante

Nearest Town Escalante

Summary A much-traveled, washboard-rough road follows the route of a historic wagon trail, providing access to area attractions and trails. Expect to be sucking at least a little dust behind other cars.

The history is wilder than the scenery along this dust pit of a road. From 1879 to 1880, more than 200 pioneering Mormons followed this route on their way to settle southeast Utah. When the precipitous walls of Glen Canyon on the Colorado River blocked their path, they blasted and hammered through the cliff, creating a hole wide

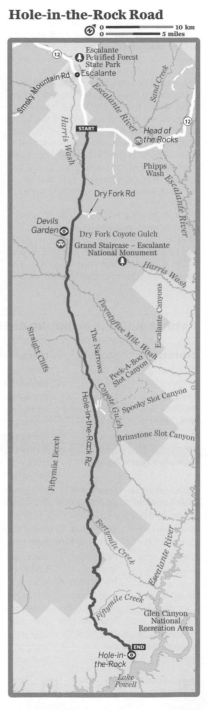

Hole-in-the-Rock Road

GRAND STAIRCASE–ESCALANTE NATIONAL MONUMENT DRIVING

enough to lower their 80 wagons through – a feat that is honored by the road's name today. The final part of their trail lies submerged beneath Lake Powell. History buffs should pick up Stewart Aitchison's *Hole-in-the-Rock Trail* for a detailed account.

The road is passable by ordinary passenger cars when dry, except for the last 7 miles, which always require 4WD. Even if you don't drive the entire route, at least visit the freely accessible **Devils Garden**, 12 miles in. Here rock fists, orbs, spires and fingers rise to 40ft above the desert floor. It's a sandy but fairly short walk from the parking lot to the formations. When climbing on, over and under the giant sandstone slabs, nature becomes your playground.

About 26 miles in, turn left for **Dry Fork** with the most well-known slot-canyon day hikes on the road. While there are no facilities on the road, dispersed camping is permitted with a free backcountry permit. The last section of this road may be really rough,

in which case you should park and walk the final half-mile to the trailhead parking lot.

The last 7 miles are so rugged, they can take almost as long to traverse as the first 50. The road stops short of the actual **Hole-in-the-Rock**, but hikers can trek out and scramble down past the 'hole' to **Lake Powell** in less than an hour. Sorry, no elevators for the climb back up.

Skutumpah & Johnson Canyon Roads

Duration 2½ hours

Distance 51 miles one way

Start Hwy 89, 9 miles east of Kanab

Finish Cannonville

Nearest Town Kanab

Summary A partially paved, partially dirt road crosses the monument beneath Bryce Canyon. En route it passes through the Vermilion, White, Gray and Pink Cliffs, the latter of which are particularly dramatic.

CAMPGROUNDS IN & AROUND GSENM

CAMPGROUND	LOCATION	DESCRIPTION	NUMBER OF SITES
Deer Creek (p152)	Burr Trail Rd	Primitive campground near Boulder: creek, trees and red rock. No water, no hookups.	7
Escalante Petrified Forest State Park (p154)	Escalante Petrified Forest State Park	By a swimmable reservoir and forest outside Escalante, with showers, and electrical and water hookups. Interpretive trail.	22
Calf Creek (p152)	Hwy 12	Popular canyon ground near year-round creek and the monument's only marked trail. No showers.	14
Hitch'n Post (p158)	Kanab	Shady little rustic campground in the center of Kanab. Full hookups, pull-through sites and wi-fi.	16
Kodachrome Basin State Park Campground (p154)	Kodachrome Basin State Park	Park service campground with well-spaced sites. Some shade; good hot showers.	26
Bryce View Campground (p154)	Kodachrome Basin State Park	New in 2015; sites have fire rings, vault toilet and water tap.	11
Stateline Campground (p161)	Paria Canyon-Vermilion Cliffs Wilderness Area	An excellent primitive campground near Wire Pass trailhead. Shade, pit toilets and picnic tables; no water.	6
White House Campground (p161)	Paria Canyon-Vermilion Cliffs Wilderness Area	Primitive campground at White House trailhead with pit toilets; no water, no trash collection. Tents only.	5
Coral Pink Sand Dunes State Park (p160)	Sand Dunes Rd	Near stunning pink dunes outside Kanab; can get windy, all-terrain-vehicle use noisy. Showers, no hookups.	22

 Drinking Water   *Flush Toilets*   *Ranger Station Nearby*   *Great for Families*   *Wheelchair Accessible*

Together these two roads comprise the monument's westernmost route. Paved Johnson Canyon Rd trundles north for 16 miles to intersect Skutumpah (*scoot*-em-pah) Rd. This very rutted dirt route (4WD recommended, and sometimes required) continues for 35 miles to Cannonville on Hwy 12. Driving south–north provides the best perspective.

Start out in very scenic **Johnson Canyon**, which has distant views of the coral **Vermilion Cliffs**. About 6 miles along, you'll see the crumbling wooden buildings of the old **Gunsmoke set**, where the TV Western was filmed. They are on private property, but are easily visible from the road. Soon after, the landscape changes color as the **White Cliffs** appear to the east.

Those who don't have the time, or a proper vehicle, to tackle Skutumpah Rd could turn off at the junction onto the 15-mile **Glendale Bench Rd**, a much easier 2WD dirt track that leads east to Glendale on Hwy 89.

Once on Skutumpah Rd, there are numerous old side roads, so pay attention and keep to the main road. Here the **Gray Cliffs** rise to the north and you pass through pastureland before reaching the trailhead for **Lick Wash**. It's 8 miles round-trip on this trail, turning around at Park Wash junction. Uneven stones line part of the way and it can be broiling hot in the canyon, but it's worth doing just the first section to see the scenery.

The road gets steep and rocky before **Bull Valley Gorge**. Stop at the wide spot in the road and walk left along the gorge rim; after about 50ft look back at the debris beneath the 'bridge' you're about to drive across. If you have good eyesight, or binoculars, you might make out a wheel or a window of the **1950s truck** that fell off the road and now forms part of the bridge base. Exploring the gorge itself requires rock-climbing skills.

Soon after, on the road north, is the trailhead parking lot (and pit toilet) for **Willis Creek**, an easy slot-canyon hike. The dramatic **Pink Cliffs** are the last thing you see

ELEVATION	OPEN	RESERVATION REQUIRED?	DAY FEE	FACILITIES
5800ft	mid-May–mid-Sep	no	$10	
5900ft	year-round	yes	$5	
5400ft	year-round	no	$15	
4900ft	year-round	yes	NA	
5800ft	year-round	yes	free	
5800ft	year-round	yes	free	
5040ft	year-round	no	free	
3000ft	year-round	no	free	
6000ft	year-round	yes	free	

 Dogs Allowed (On Leash)   Grocery Store Nearby   Restaurant Nearby   Pay-phone   RV Dump Station

before the sharp descent to the valley intersection with **Cottonwood Canyon Rd**, just south of Cannonville.

🏃 OTHER ACTIVITIES

Outfitters in Boulder, Escalante, Torrey and Kanab offer half-, full- and multiday guided treks into the monument. Horseback riding is available out of Boulder and Kanab; fly-fishing from Escalante.

Boulder Outdoor Survival School   OUTDOORS
(☑ 800-335-7404; www.boss-inc.com; 7-/14-/28-day courses from $1725/2995/4795) Learn how to survive in this forbidding wilderness. The school operates seven-day and longer courses in GSENM, with subjects including primitive living and hunter-gathering.

🏃 Cycling

Though the monument is laced with old ranching roads, such as **Wolverine Loop**, that could be used for mountain biking, the sport hasn't really caught on here.

Escalante Outfitters (p154) rents mountain bikes.

🛌 SLEEPING

Free, dispersed backcountry camping – outside wilderness study areas – is widely available in the monument, but you need a permit. Pick one up at any visitor center, where you can discuss locations with rangers, or at major trailheads.

Outside the monument, campgrounds at Kodachrome Basin, Escalante Petrified Forest and Coral Pink Sand Dunes State Parks have running water and hot showers. Area towns are the only option for lodgings with walls.

In the monument's two campgrounds you have to pack out trash, but leashed pets are allowed. Both are first-come, first-served.

Deer Creek Campground   CAMPGROUND $
(☑ 435-826-5600; www.reserveamerica.com; Burr Trail Rd; tent sites $30; ☉ mid-May–mid-Sep) This

campground, 6 miles southeast of Boulder, has few sites and no water, but does have pit toilets. It sits beside a year-round creek beneath tall trees.

Calf Creek Recreation Area   CAMPGROUND $
(☑ 435-826-5499; www.blm.gov/visit/calf-creek-recreation-area-campground; Hwy 12; tent & RV sites $15) Beside a year-round creek, this campground is surrounded by red-rock canyons (hot in summer) and has 14 incredibly popular, nonreservable sites. Drinking water is available; there are no hookups.

ℹ️ Information

Food, gas, lodging and other services are available in Boulder, Escalante, Torrey and Kanab.

Big Water Visitor Center (☑ 435-675-3200; www.blm.gov/visit/big-water-visitor-center; 100 Upper Revolution Way; ☉ 8:30am-5pm) Near Lake Powell.

Cannonville Visitor Center (☑ 435-826-5640; www.blm.gov/visit/cannonville-visitor-center; 10 W Center St, Cannonville; ☉ 8am-4:30pm Apr-Oct) Five miles east of Tropic.

Escalante Interagency Visitor Center (☑ 435-826-5499; www.fs.usda.gov/recarea/dixie/recarea/?recid=24978; 775 W Main St, Escalante; ☉ 8am-4:30pm daily Apr-Sep, Mon-Fri Oct-Mar) *The* source for information about area public lands; jointly operated by the BLM, the USFS and NPS. Ask here about trails, road conditions and camping.

GSENM Visitor Center (☑ 435-644-1300; www.blm.gov/visit/kanab-visitor-center; 745 E Hwy 89, Kanab; ☉ 8am-4:30pm) Provides road, trail and weather updates for the Grand Staircase–Escalante National Monument.

ℹ️ Getting There & Around

High-clearance 4WD vehicles allow you the most access, since many roads are unpaved and only occasionally bladed. (Most off-the-lot SUVs and light trucks are *not* high-clearance vehicles.) Heed all warnings about road conditions. Remember to buy gasoline whenever you see it.

Some outfitters in towns around the park have hiker shuttles or 4WD rentals. However, if you plan to do a lot of back road exploring, rent a car. Those arriving via Las Vegas will find it the cheapest rental base in the region.

Around Grand Staircase–Escalante National Monument

Best Places to Stay

➜ Boulder Mountain Lodge (p157)

➜ Escalante Grand Staircase B&B (p155)

➜ Canyons Lodge (p158)

➜ Kodachrome Basin Campground (p154)

Best Places to Eat

➜ Hell's Backbone Grill (p157)

➜ Sego Restaurant (p159)

➜ Kanab Creek Bakery (p159)

➜ Burr Trail Outpost (p157)

➜ Rocking V Cafe (p159)

Why Go?

Highway 12 brings the vast majority of visitors to Grand Staircase, and you'll find the main visitor centers and services north of the national monument in the towns of Boulder and Escalante. Nearby Kodachrome Basin State Park features hiking and biking trails past petrified geysers and sandstone chimneys, but it's best for pitching a tent – the campground here has showers, which definitely hit the spot after a day scrambling around in the sandy slots.

A full 120 miles from Escalante, at the southwest corner of Grand Staircase off Hwy 89, is cinematic Kanab, another good base for exploring the park and situated nicely between GSENM, Bryce, Zion and the Grand Canyon's North Rim. The remote Paria Canyon-Vermilion Cliffs wilderness area is a must for hardcore explorers and landscape photographers, with tough multiday canyoneering treks and a coveted hike to the world-famous Wave formation.

When to Go
Escalante

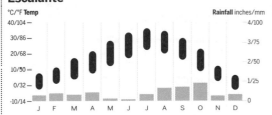

May–Aug
Temperatures soar, thought nights are cool, and traffic is busy.

Mar–Jun, Sep & Oct
Generally pleasant but often unpredictable weather.

Nov–Feb
Snow at higher elevations; canyons are bitterly cold.

Kodachrome Basin State Park

Petrified geysers and dozens of red, pink and white sandstone chimneys – some nearly 170ft tall – resemble everything from a sphinx to a snowmobile at **Kodachrome Basin State Park** (🖉 435-679-8562; https://stateparks.utah.gov/parks/kodachrome-basin; off Cottonwood Canyon Rd, Cannonville; day use per vehicle $8; ☺ 6am-10pm). The park lies off Hwy 12, 9 miles south of Cannonville and 26 miles southeast of Bryce Canyon National Park. Visit in the morning or afternoon, when shadows play on the red rock.

Most sights are along hiking and mountain-biking trails. The moderately easy, 3-mile round-trip **Panorama Trail** gives the best overview. Be sure to take the side trails to **Indian Cave**, where you can check out the handprints on the wall, and **Secret Passage**, a short hike through a narrow slot canyon. **Angel Palace Trail** (1-mile loop, moderate) has great desert views from on high.

Red Canyon Trail Rides (p124), based near Bryce, offers horseback rides.

There are several on-site campgrounds though it may be hard to get a spot. The 26 well-spaced sites at the reservable **Kodachrome Basin State Park Campground** (🖉 800-322-3770; www.reserveamerica.com; Cannonville; tents/RVs $20/30; ☺ Mar-Nov) have showers, full hookups for RVs and shade from juniper trees. The **Bryce View Campground** (🖉 435-679-8562; https://stateparks.utah.gov/parks/kodachrome-basin/bryce-view-campground/; Kodachrome State Park Rd, Henrieville; tent & RVs $20; ☺ Mar-Nov) has 11 reservable sites with fire rings, vault toilet and water tap. Bring your own provisions;

PARK RESOURCES
....

Paria Canyon-Vermilion Cliffs Wilderness (https://www.blm.gov/visit/paria-canyon-vermilion-cliffs-wilderness)

Coral Pink Sand Dunes National Park (https://stateparks.utah.gov/parks/coral-pink)

Kodachrome Basin State Park (https://stateparks.utah.gov/parks/kodachrome-basin)

Escalante Petrified Forest State Park (https://stateparks.utah.gov/parks/escalante-petrified-forest)

---

there is a small **camp store** in the park but supplies are limited.

Escalante

POP 800 / ELEV 5600FT

Your gateway to the north side of the Grand Staircase–Escalante National Monument (GSENM), Escalante is a mix of ranchers, old-timers, artists and post-monument-creation outdoors-lovers. The town itself doesn't exude character, but a friendly selection of lodgings and restaurants make it a decent base camp. Numerous outfitters make this their base for hiking excursions, and you could, too. At the head of several park back roads, it's not far from the most popular GSENM hikes.

◎ Sights & Activities

The GSENM provides most of the attraction for the area; hikes off Hwy 12 and Hole-in-the-Rock Rd are within 12 to 30 miles' drive.

Reserve ahead to rent 4WD vehicles at **High Adventure Rentals** (🖉 435-503-9263; www.highadventurerentals.com; 85 W Main St; 4-hr off-road vehicle rental from $210; ☺ 8am-5pm).

Escalante Petrified Forest State Park   PARK
(🖉 435-826-4466; https://stateparks.utah.gov/parks/escalante-petrified-forest; 710 North Reservoir; day use $8; ☺ 8am-10pm) Two miles west of town, the centerpiece of this state park is a 130-acre lake. Hike uphill about a mile on an interpretive route to see pieces of colorful petrified wood, millions of years old. Follow another short interpretive trail for further examples. The sites at the campground are reservable; showers available.

⌲ Tours

Excursions of Escalante   ADVENTURE
(🖉 800-839-7567; www.excursionsofescalante.com; 125 E Main St; all-day canyoneering $175; ☺ 8am-6pm) For area canyoneering and climbing trips, Excursions is the best; it does hiker shuttles and guided photo hikes, too. Has an on-site cafe.

Escalante Outfitters   ADVENTURE
(🖉 435-826-4266; www.escalanteoutfitters.com; 310 W Main St; natural history tours $45; ☺ 7am-9pm) A traveler's oasis, this store sells area books, topographic maps, camping and hiking gear, and is attached to a cafe. Reputable guided hikes, fly-fishing, natural-history tours and mountain bike rentals available.

DON'T MISS

HIGHWAY 12
....

Arguably Utah's most diverse and stunning route, **Highway 12 Scenic Byway** (www.scenicbyway12.com) winds through rugged canyonland, from near Capitol Reef southeast past Bryce Canyon – linking several national parks on a 124-mile journey. See how quickly and dramatically the land changes from wooded plateau to red-rock canyon, from slickrock desert to alpine forest, as it climbs over an 11,000ft mountain. Highlights include the switchbacks and petrified sand dunes between Torrey and Boulder. Also, the razor-thin Hogback Ridge between Escalante and Boulder is pretty stunning too.

Take time to stop at the many viewpoints and pullouts, especially at Mile 70, where the Aquarius Plateau lords over giant mesas, towering domes, deep canyons and undulating slickrock, all unfurling in an explosion of color.

Escape Goats   ADVENTURE
(☑435-826-4652; www.escalantecanyonguides.com; 310 W Main St; day hike $150) Take an evening tour or day hike to dinosaur tracks, slot canyons and ancient sites. There's also fully catered backpacking trips (three days $750) including gear. Recommended.

Utah Canyon Outdoors   ADVENTURE
(☑435-826-4967; www.utahcanyonoutdoors.com; 325 W Main St; slot canyon hikes from $140; ⊘8am-6pm Wed-Mon) Guided day hikes, multiday supported treks, hiker shuttles and a small outdoors store.

🛏 Sleeping

**Escalante Petrified Forest
State Park Campground**   CAMPGROUND $
(☑435-826-4466; www.reserveamerica.com; 710 North Reservoir; sites $28; ⊛⊛) This 22-site, reservable campground has water, picnic tables, fire pits and restrooms with wonderfully hot showers. It's 2 miles northwest of town along Hwy 12. RV sites with hookups.

Circle D Motel   MOTEL $
(☑435-826-4297; www.escalantecircledmotel.com; 475 W Main St; r $80-115; ⊛🐾🐕) We love the little library of guidebooks and hiking information in the rooms. The friendly proprietor goes out of his way to accommodate guests at this partially updated, older motel. Room microwaves and minifridges are standard.

**Escalante Outfitters
Bunkhouse Cabins**   CABIN $
(☑435-826-4266; www.escalanteoutfitters.com; 310 W Main St; tent sites from $8, cabins $55-150; 🐕⊛) Pitch a tent or rent a rustic, but heated, teeny-tiny log cabin (linens included, shared bathroom, no air-conditioning) in a shady yard. Picnic tables and grills available.

Rainbow Country Bed & Breakfast   B&B $
(☑435-826-4567, 800-252-8824; www.bnbescalante.com; 586 E 300 S; r $99-124; ⊛🐾) Good trail advice and big home-cooked breakfasts. This split-level house on the edge of town is not flashy, just comfortable – with a big TV lounge (no room TVs), guest refrigerator and outdoor hot tub.

Escalante Grand Staircase B&B   B&B $$
(☑435-826-4890; www.escalantebnb.com; 280 W Main St; d $150; ⊛🐕) A wonderful find, with eight spacious rooms sporting individual entrances, skylights and porches. Rooms feature landscape murals with Western motifs. Tom, the host, provides vast quantities of coffee and extensive trail information, with helpful binders containing photos and directions.

Canyons B&B   INN $$
(☑435-826-4747, 866 526-9667; www.canyonsbnb.com; 120 E Main St; d $160; ⊘Mar-Oct; ⊛🐕) A self-catered lodging where upscale cabin-rooms with kitchenette use and porches surround a shaded terrace and gardens. Owners speak Russian and Spanish.

Slot Canyons Inn   INN $$
(☑866-889-8375, 435-826-4901; www.slotcanyonsinn.com; 3680 W Hwy 12; r $175-240, cabin $312; ⊛@🐕) An architectural showpiece on the edge of the desert; upscale all the way.

🍴 Eating

**Escalante Mercantile
Natural Grocery**   MARKET $
(☑435-826-4114; 210 W Main St; ⊘9am-7pm Mon-Sat, 10am-5pm Sun) A well-stocked natural grocer, better with dry goods than produce.

Griffin Grocery   MARKET $
(☑435-826-4226; 30 W Main St; ⊘8am-6pm Mon-Sat) The only full-selection grocery in town.

OFF THE BEATEN TRACK

4WD ADVENTURES

Looking for even more 4WD adventure than the cross-monument drives offer? You have options.

Hell's Backbone Rd Loops a gravel-strewn 48 miles off Hwy 12 between Boulder and Escalante. The original mule-mail route crosses rugged Box-Death Wilderness area. The highlight is a single-lane track atop an impossibly narrow ridge.

Smoky Mountain Rd A challenging, 78-mile dirt-and-gravel road between Escalante and Big Water visitor center. It's passable by 4WD vehicle only (preferably with high clearance). The prime destination is Alstrom Point, 12.5 miles from Hwy 89, a plateau-top vantage with stunning views that include Lake Powell.

Old Sheffield Rd (or Spencer Flats) Undulates for 3 sand-and-gravel miles through desert, slickrock formations and canyons. Some great backcountry camping is to be found out here too. The road leaves Hwy 12, 6 miles east of Escalante.

Circle D Eatery   AMERICAN $$
(☑435-826-4125; www.escalantecircledeatery.com; 475 W Main St; mains $11-26; ☉7am-9:30pm, limited hours Nov-Feb) Has attentive service and satisfying burgers using local beef on fresh jalapeño buns, served with shoestring fries. Smoked meats are a specialty, but there are also pastas, salads and hearty breakfasts.

Cowboy Blues   AMERICAN $$
(☑435-826-4577; 530 W Main St; sandwiches & mains $9-26; ☉11:30am-10pm) Family-friendly meals here include BBQ ribs, steaks and daily specials like burritos or meatloaf. Has a full bar.

ℹ Information

Cell-phone reception is spotty. For local info, see http://escalanteut.com. Services are limited from November through March.

Escalante Interagency Visitor Center (☑435-826-5499; www.fs.usda.gov/recarea/dixie/recarea/?recid=24978; 775 W Main St, Escalante; ☉8am-4:30pm daily Apr-Sep, Mon-Fri Oct-Mar) *The* source for information about area public lands; jointly operated by the BLM, the USFS and NPS. Ask here about trails, road conditions and camping.

Kazan Memorial Clinic (☑435-826-4374; 65 N Center St; ☉9am-5pm Mon, Wed & Fri) Limited medical care; the closest hospital is in Panguitch.
Wells Fargo ATM (250 W Main St; ☉24hr)

Boulder

POP 222 / ELEV 6675FT

A tiny slice of heaven and a great base to explore the surrounding desert wilderness. Until 1940, this isolated outpost received its mail by mule – it's still so remote that the federal government classifies it as a 'frontier community.' Its diverse population includes artists, ecologists, farmers and cowboys. Though only 32 miles south of Torrey on Hwy 12, you have to traverse 11,317ft-high Boulder Mountain to get here. Note that pretty much all services shut down November through March.

◎ Sights & Activities

Anasazi State Park Museum   MUSEUM
(☑435-335-7308; https://stateparks.utah.gov/parks/anasazi; Main St/Hwy 12; admission $5; ☉8am-6pm Mar-Oct, 9am-5pm Nov-Feb) This petite museum protects the Coomb's Site, excavated in the 1950s and inhabited from AD 1130 to 1175. The minimal ruins aren't as evocative as some in southeastern Utah, but it's well worth seeing the re-created six-room pueblo and excellent exhibits about the Ancestral Puebloan peoples. Get backcountry road updates and backcountry permits at a seasonal information desk staffed by rangers.

Dixie National Forest   PARK
(☑435-865-3700; www.fs.usda.gov/dixie) North of Boulder, the Escalante District of this 2-million-sq-acre forest has trails and campgrounds, including a few up on Boulder Mountain.

⚐ Tours

Earth Tours   HIKING
(☑435-691-1241; www.earth-tours.com; day tours from $150; ☀) Choose from half- and full-day area hikes and 4WD trips into the backcountry in and around Bryce, Escalante, Boulder Mountain and Capitol Reef. Keith will pick you up at your hotel in Torrey or Boulder.

Escalante Canyon Outfitters   HIKING
(ECO; ☑888-326-4453, 435-691-3037; www.ecohike.com; 2520 South Lower Deer Creek Rd; ☉Mar-Nov) Started by cofounder of the Southern Utah Wilderness Alliance, Grant Johnson, ECO has well-regarded

multiday treks with a canyonland or archaeological-site focus.

Hell's Backbone Ranch & Trails
HORSEBACK RIDING

(☑435-335-7581; www.bouldermountaintrails.com; off Hell's Backbone Rd; 2hr ride $60) Head across the slickrock plateau into **Box–Death Hollow Wilderness Area** (☑435-826-5499; www.fs.usda. gov/recarea/dixie/recarea/?recid=70912) or up the forested mountain on two-hour to full-day area horseback rides. Or perhaps you'd prefer a multiday camping trip or cattle drive?

🛏 Sleeping

Boulder Mountain Guest Ranch
LODGE $

(☑435-335-7480; www.bouldermountainguest ranch.com; off Hell's Backbone Rd; r $80-115, cabins $115-125, tipi $55; ☺mid-May–Oct; ✸☎) This giant log lodge is in a peaceful 160-acre wilderness with trails, a waterfall and outfitter-led hikes and activities. Think rustic, with a happy hippie vibe. Bunk and queen rooms enjoy a communal atmosphere; out-cabins are more private. The dining room has chef-cooked meals at breakfast and dinners use garden produce.

Pole's Place
MOTEL $

(☑435-335-7422, 800-730-7422; www.polesplace utah.com; 465 N Hwy 12; r from $85; ☺late Mar-Oct; ✸) Run by a fourth-generation local, this nicely kept motel has quiet, decent rooms without wi-fi. There are local menus and historical news clippings to peruse in each room. Limited TV.

★Boulder Mountain Lodge
LODGE $$

(☑435-335-7460; www.boulder-utah.com; 20 N Hwy 12; r/apt/ste from $120/205/260; ✸@☎✸) Watch the birds flit by on the adjacent 15-acre wildlife sanctuary and stroll through the organic garden – Boulder Mountain Lodge has a strong eco-aesthetic. It's an ideal place for day-hikers who want to return to high-thread-count sheets, plush terry robes, spa treatments and an outdoor hot tub. The on-site Hell's Backbone Grill is a southern Utah must-eat.

🍴 Eating

★Burr Trail Outpost
CAFE $

(☑435-335-7565; http://burrtrailoutpost.com; cnr Hwy 12 & Burr Trail Rd; dishes $8-18; ☺7:30am-7pm; ☎) Sip organic coffee and scoff down scrumptious homemade cookies and cakes before or after browsing the art gallery and gift shop at this homey cafe welcoming hikers off the Burr Trail.

Hills & Hollows Country Store
MARKET $

(☑435-335-7349; 840 Hwy 12; ☺9am-7pm, gas 24hr; ☎) Groceries and organic snacks available year-round, though hours may be limited November through February.

★Hell's Backbone Grill
MODERN AMERICAN $$

(☑435-335-7464; www.hellsbackbonegrill.com; 20 N Hwy 12, Boulder Mountain Lodge; breakfast $10-16, lunch $9-21, dinner $16-38; ☺7am-11pm Mar-Nov; ✎) 🌿 Earthy preparations of Southwestern dishes include gorgeous salads made from organic garden produce and braised beef in rich preparations. While this restaurant, a pioneer in sustainable eating and mindfulness, has garnered regional fame, not all dishes are winners – the tofu is a dud. Breakfasts remain satisfying, and there are lunchboxes for hikers. Dinner reservations are a must.

ℹ Information

Most of the town's businesses close November through March, when heavy snow sets in.

The tiny town has no visitor center, but info is available online at www.boulderutah.com.

Anasazi Tourist Information (☑435-335 7382; Hwy 12, Anasazi State Park Museum; ☺9am-5pm mid-Mar–mid-Nov) BLM and other public-land trail and camping information.

Kanab

POP 4500 / ELEV 4925FT

Vast expanses of rugged desert surround the remote outpost of Kanab. Look familiar? Hundreds of Western movies were shot here. Founded by Mormon pioneers in 1874,

---

DON'T MISS

KIVA KOFFEEHOUSE

Just past the Aquarius Plateau, you reach this **singular coffeehouse** (☑435-826-4550; www.kivakoffeehouse. com; Hwy 12, Mile 73; baked goods $4-8; ☺8:30am-4:30pm Wed-Mon Apr-Oct) whose round structure was built directly into the cliffside. Floor-to-ceiling glass windows, separated by giant timber beams, overlook the expansive canyons beyond. Stop by for barista coffee and yummy baked goods.

Kanab was put on the map by John Wayne and other gun-slingin' celebs in the 1940s and '50s. Just about every resident had something to do with the movies from the 1930s to the '70s. You can still see a couple of movie sets in the area and hear old-timers talk about their roles.

Kanab sits at a major crossroads: Grand Staircase–Escalante National Monument (GSENM) is 20 miles away, Zion 40 miles, Bryce Canyon 80 miles, Grand Canyon's North Rim 81 miles and Lake Powell 74 miles. It makes a good base for exploring the southern side of GSENM and Paria Canyon–Vermilion Cliffs formations such as the Wave (p160). Coral Pink Sand Dunes State Park (p160) is a big rompin' playground to the northwest.

◉ Sights & Activities

★ Best Friends Animal Sanctuary   WILDLIFE RESERVE
(☑435-644-2001; www.bestfriends.org; 5001 Angel Canyon Rd, Hwy 89; ◷8am-5pm; 🖈) **FREE** Kanab's most famous attraction is outside of town. Surrounded by more than 33,000 mostly private acres of red-rock desert 5.5 miles north of Kanab, Best Friends is the largest no-kill animal rescue center in the country. The center shows films and gives facility tours four times a day; call ahead for times and reservations. The 1½-hour tours let you meet some of the more than 1700 horses, pigs, dogs, cats, birds and other critters on-site.

Parry Lodge   HISTORIC HOTEL
(☑435-644-2601; www.parrylodge.com; 89 E Center St; ◷movies 8pm Sat Jun-Aug) **FREE** Built in the 1930s, this historic hotel was once movie central. Stars stayed here and owner Whit Parry provided horses, cattle and catering for the sets. There are nostalgic photos, and old Westerns play out back in the **Old Barn Playhouse** (◷shows 8pm) **FREE**, summer Saturday nights.

Little Hollywood Land Museum   MUSEUM
(☑435-689-0706; www.littlehollywoodmuseum. org; 297 W Center St; ◷7:30am-11pm Apr-Oct, 10am-5pm Nov-Mar) **FREE** Wander through a bunkhouse, saloon and other buildings used in Western movies filmed locally, including *The Outlaw Josey Wales,* and learn some tricks of the trade (such as low doorways to make movie stars seem taller). This classic roadside attraction sells all the Western duds and doodads you could care to round up.

☞ Tours

★ Dreamland Safari   TOURS
(☑435-644-5506; www.dreamlandtours.net; 4350 E Mountain View Dr; 3hr slot canyon tour $90) Hikes with naturalist tour guides to gorgeous backcountry sites and slot canyons reached by 4WD. It also offers nature photography and multiday backpacking trips.

Paria Outpost   ADVENTURE
(☑928-691-1047; www.paria.com; Mile 21, Hwy 89, Big Water; tours from $175) Friendly, flexible and knowledgeable. Offers guided horseback rides in Grand Staircase–Escalante National Monument, as well as 4WD tours and guided hikes.

Windows of the West Hummer Tours   ADVENTURE
(☑888-687-3006; www.wowhummertours.com; 208 S 300 E; tours from $99) Personalized backcountry excursions (two hours to full-day) to slot canyons, petroglyphs and spectacular red-rock country.

✸ Festivals & Events

Western Legends Roundup   FILM
(☑435-644-3444; www.westernlegendsroundup. com; ◷Aug) The town lives for the annual Western Legends Roundup in late August. There are concerts, gunfights, cowboy poetry, dances, quilt shows, a film festival and more. Take a bus tour to all the film sites.

🛏 Sleeping

Hitch'n Post Campground   CAMPGROUND $
(☑435-644-2142; www.hitchnpostrvpark.com; 196 E 300 S; tent/RV sites with hookups $23/35, camping cabins $45-50; 🛜🖥) Friendly 17-site campground near the town center; has laundry and showers.

★ Canyons Lodge   MOTEL $$
(☑435-644-3069; www.canyonslodge.com; 236 N 300 W; r from $169; 🌼@🛜🐾🖥) 🐾 A renovated motel with an art-house Western feel. There's a warm welcome, free cruiser bikes and good traveler assistance. In summer, guests enjoy twice-weekly live music and wine and cheese by the fire pit. Rooms feature original artwork and whimsical touches. Recycles soaps and containers.

Quail Park Lodge   MOTEL $$
(☑435-215-1447; www.quailparklodge.com; 125 N 300 W; r from $149; 🌼@🛜🐾🖥) With Schwinn cruiser bicycles and a postage-stamp-size pool, retro pervades all 13 rooms

at this refurbished 1963 motel with surprisingly plush rooms. Mod cons include free phone calls, microwaves, minirefrigerators and complimentary gourmet coffee.

Purple Sage Inn
B&B $$

(☑ 435-644-5377; www.purplesageinn.com; 54 S Main St; r $135-165; ❋ 🐕) A former Mormon polygamist's home, this later became a hotel, where Western author Zane Grey stayed. Now it's a B&B with exquisite antique details. Zane's namesake room – with its quilt-covered wood bed, sitting room and balcony access – is our favorite.

Canyons Boutique Hotel
BOUTIQUE HOTEL $$

(☑ 435-644-8660; www.canyonshotel.com; 190 N 300 W; r/ste from $159/239; ❋🐕❋) From the architecture to appointments, this inn is a modern-day remake of period Victoriana. Ethan Allen furnishings, gas fireplaces and jetted tubs grace every room, but it all looks a little stiff in these parts.

The Flagstone Boutique Inn & Suites
MOTEL $$

(☑ 435-644-2020; www.theflagstoneinn.com; 223 W Center St; r from $159; ❋🐕) A fully refurbished upscale motel. All rooms have full kitchens and accessories to enjoy a cup of coffee. Forget your idea of dusty old motels: there are king beds, flat-screen TVs and sleek style here.

🍴 Eating

★ Kanab Creek Bakery
BAKERY $

(☑ 435-644-5689; www.kanabcreekbakery.com; 238 W Center St; mains $6-16; ⊙ 6:30am-5pm Tue-Sun) For fancy-pants pastries and gourmet breakfasts, this is your first (and only) stop. Croissants, *boules* (tiny pieces of chocolate-covered truffle), baguettes and rye bread are baked daily. Try the Jerusalem *shakshuka*, a cast-iron skillet of eggs in a rich pepper sauce. For lunch there's roast chicken and paella baked in the wood-fired oven.

Escobar's
MEXICAN $

(☑ 435-644-3739; 373 E 300 S; mains $7-14; ⊙ 11am-9:30pm Sun-Fri) Sometimes it feels like all of Kanab is stuffed into this busy, family-run restaurant with swift service and XL portions. Start with the complimentary homemade chips and salsa then move on to a green chili burrito and a chilled mug of beer.

Peekaboo Kitchen
CAFE $

(☑ 435-689-1959; www.peekabookitchen.com; 233 W Center St; mains $10-18; ⊙ 7am-2:30pm Tue-

OFF THE BEATEN TRACK

BIG WATER

About 56 miles from Kanab, this small town with little more than a convenience store is known because of the dinosaur finds (and polygamist residents) in the area. The **Big Water visitor center** (p152) has great paleontology exhibits, which include a replica of a dig, various bones found in the monument (including the 13ft tail of a duckbill) and a spectacular 9ft × 45ft mural by expert dinosaur painter Larry Felder. Dinosaur tracks are fairly common in the area.

The south end of **Smoky Mountain Rd** emerges at Big Water. The nearest town of consequence, Page, Arizona, is 17 miles southeast, and is the access point for Lake Powell and Antelope Canyon.

Sun, 5-9pm Tue-Sat; 🚗) A godsend to green diets, this cafe goes big on vegetarian and vegan dishes, salads and beet chips. The artisan pizzas are pretty good too. Breakfast options include lattes, eggs Benedict served in artichokes, and pumpkin flapjacks. If you are bone tired, it can also deliver.

★ Sego Restaurant
MODERN AMERICAN $$

(☑ 435-644-5680; www.segokanab.com; 190 N 300 W; mains $14-26; ⊙ 6-10pm Mon-Sat) If Kanab is aspiring to be the next Sedona, this boutique hotel-restaurant will fast-track things. Gorgeous eats range from foraged mushrooms with goat cheese to noodles with red-crab curry and a decadent flourless torte for dessert. There are also craft cocktails and local beers. Hours may be expanding. Reserve ahead: there are few tables.

Rocking V Cafe
AMERICAN $$$

(☑ 435-644-8001; www.rockingvcafe.com; 97 W Center St; lunch $8-18, dinner $18-48; ⊙ 11:30am-10pm Thu-Mon; 🚗) Fresh ingredients star in dishes like hand-cut buffalo tenderloin and chargrilled zucchini with curried quinoa. Local artwork decorating the 1892 brick storefront is as creative as the food. Off-season hours vary.

🛍 Shopping

Willow Canyon Outdoor Co
SPORTS & OUTDOORS

(☑ 435-644-8884; www.willowcanyon.com; 263 S 100 E; ⊙ 7:30am-8pm) It's easy to spend hours sipping espresso and perusing the eclectic books here. Before you leave, outfit yourself

WORTH A TRIP

THE NORTH RIM

A solitary stunner, the North Rim of the Grand Canyon is a very accessible day trip, 81 miles south of Kanab on Hwy 89A. At 8000ft, the North Rim is about 10°F (6°C) cooler than the South – even on summer evenings you'll need a sweater. All services are closed from mid-October through mid-May, although the road usually stays open through November. Also, Arizona does not observe daylight-saving time, so in summer it's one hour behind Utah time. For a complete destination rundown, pick up a copy of Lonely Planet's *Grand Canyon National Park*.

with field guides, camping gear, USGS maps, hiking clothes and gas for your camp stove. Off-season hours vary.

ℹ Information

Kanab has several grocery stores, ATMs, banks and services.

BLM Kanab Field Office (☎435-644-1200; www.blm.gov/office/kanab-field-office; 318 N 1 E; ⊗8am-4:30pm)

Kane County Office of Tourism (☎435-644-5033; www.visitsouthernutah.com; 78 S 100 E; ⊗8am-8pm Mon-Fri, 9am-6pm Sat-Sun)

Kane County Hospital (☎435-644-5811, emergency 911; www.kchosp.net; 355 N Main St; ⊗24hr) The closest medical facility to

Kanab City Library (☎435-644-2394; www.kanablibrary.org; 374 N Main St; ⊗10am-5pm Mon & Fri, to 7pm Tue-Thu, to 2pm Sat; 🛜) Free internet and wi-fi access.

Coral Pink Sand Dunes State Park

Restless winds shift giant Sahara-like sand dunes across half of this 3700-acre **state park** (☎435-648-2800; www.stateparks.utah.gov/parks/coral-pink/; Sand Dunes Rd; day use/camping $8/20; ⊗day use dawn-dusk, visitor center 9am-9pm Mar-Oct, 9am-4pm Nov-Feb). For lovers of the strange, it's worth the 24-mile, 90-minute round-trip off Hwy 89 to see the shocking coral-colored hills.

The pinkish hue results from the eroding red Navajo sandstone in the area. Since 1200 acres of the park are devoted to ATVs, it's not necessarily a quiet experience. The visitor center has displays and water. Follow the

half-mile interpretive dune hike to the 265-acre conservation area closed to off-highway vehicles (OHV).

The same winds that shift the dunes can make tent camping unpleasant at the 22-site **campground** (☎435-648-2800; https://utahstateparks.reserveamerica.com; 12500 Sand Dune Rd, Kanab; tent/RV sites $20/40). It has toilets and hot showers; no hookups. Reservations are essential on weekends.

Paria Canyon-Vermilion Cliffs Wilderness Area

With miles of weathered, swirling slickrock and slot-canyon systems that can be hiked for days without seeing a soul, it's no wonder that this wilderness area is such a popular destination for hearty trekkers, canyoneers and photographers. Day-hike permits cost $5 to $7 and several are very tough to get. Remember that summer is scorching; spring and fall are best – and busiest. Beware of flash floods.

Trailheads lie along House Rock Valley Rd (4.7 miles west of the Paria Contact Station); it's a dirt road that may require 4WD. Inquire with rangers.

◉ Sights & Activities

The Toadstools   LANDMARK

(Hwy 89A) This wander gives passersby a taste of the harsh Utah desert and cool rocks. The thin sand trail meanders through the scrub-brush, desert boulders and hoodoos about 1 mile to the first toadstool, a sandstone rock in the form of, you guessed it, a toadstool. Slanting, late-afternoon light is best for catching the shape and depth of the eerie features. The unmarked trailhead sits at a small parking area 1.4 miles east of the Paria Contact Station.

Coyote Buttes North   HIKING

(☎435-688-3200; www.blm.gov/programs/recreation/permits-and-passes/lotteries-and-permit-systems/arizona/coyote-buttes; Hwy 89A, Paria Canyon-Vermilion Cliffs Wilderness Area; permit $7) The Coyote Buttes are regarded as one of the most beautiful and unique geologic environments in the US. It follows that the most coveted of hiking permits are the 20 issued per day by lottery, granting access to the trail-less expanse of slickrock leading to a spectacular natural formation known as **The Wave**. Directions are only given to the lottery winners, who embark on a magical

6.5-mile, five-hour round-trip hike within the Coyote Buttes North section of the park, among swirling, striped slickrock.

To enter the draw, you must have a permit for Coyote Buttes North, purchased in advance, online or in person. Ten permits per day are issued to online applicants and the other 10 go to walk-ins at the GSENM Kanab Visitor Center, the day before hiking. Note that overnight permits are also reservable for **Paria Canyon** and Coyote Buttes South, up to four months in advance, but do not include access to Coyote Buttes North and the Wave.

Apply for permits online at https://www.blm.gov/az/paria/index.cfm?usearea=CB.

Coyote Buttes South   HIKING
(www.blm.gov/programs/recreation/permits-and-passes/lotteries-and-permit-systems/arizona/coyote-buttes; Hwy 89A, Paria Canyon-Vermilion Cliffs Wilderness Area; permit $5) If you want to see related slickrock formations but are finding it hard to get a permit for Coyote Buttes North, an alternative is to explore Coyote Buttes South. Permits are in less demand and can be obtained online between four months and one day in advance at https://www.blm.gov/az/paria/index.cfm?usearea=CB.

A 4WD is absolutely required if you plan to explore the park's deep-sand access roads. Ask rangers for directions.

Wire Pass to Buckskin
Gulch Hike   HIKING
(www.blm.gov/visit/search-details/16450/2; day permit $6) Wire Pass (3.4-mile round-trip) is a great slot-canyon day hike within the Paria Canyon-Vermilion Cliffs Wilderness Area. Descend a sandy wash to where the gorge becomes a slot canyon, shoulder-width in places. You'll scramble down a few boulder-choked sections, and under logs jammed 50ft overhead, before reaching a wide alcove with what was likely an ancient granary ledge; look for the petroglyph panel on the far end.

Wire Pass dead-ends at the confluence with Buckskin Gulch. Stop here (1.2 miles along) or continue exploring the Buckskin slot canyon as far north or south as you like. Note that at times there may be water in one or both of the canyons.

The parking lot is 8 miles south along House Rock Valley Rd.

Buckskin Gulch to
White House Hike   HIKING
(www.blm.gov/visit/buckskin-gulch; day permit $6) This 16-mile backpack within the Paria Canyon-Vermilion Cliffs Wilderness Area starts at the Buckskin Gulch trailhead and ends at White House trailhead. It travels through one of the longest continuous slot canyons on the planet. Those overnighting must obtain a backcountry permit online in advance or from the BLM Kanab Field Office.

🛏 Sleeping

Overnight backcountry camping permits are required and can be reserved in person from the GSENM Visitor Center (p152). In the backcountry, use of human-waste carryout bags (aka wag bags) is encouraged; the Paria Contact Station provides them for free.

Stateline Campground   CAMPGROUND
(House Rock Valley Rd, Kanab) FREE On the Utah/Arizona state line, this attractive, small campground is the most central for Wire Pass or North Coyote Buttes. Its four spots are first-come, first-served, with picnic tables, fire pits and pit toilets. It's 1 mile south of the Wire Pass trailhead, 9.3 miles south of Hwy 89. The clay road can be impassable when wet.

White House Campground   CAMPGROUND $
(☎ 435-644-4600;   www.blm.gov/visit/search-details/256924/1; off Hwy 89, Paria Contact Station; tent sites $5) This primitive campground along the Paria River is frequently used as the endpoint of a Buckskin Gulch trip or the beginning of a Paria Canyon trip. The five walk in sites have pit toilets, but no water and few trees. It's 2 miles down a dirt road behind the contact station, at the White House trailhead.

ℹ Information

In-season info and permits are picked up at **Paria Contact Station** (☎ 435-644-1200; www.blm.gov/visit/paria-contact-station; Mile 21, Hwy 89; ⊙ 8am-4:30pm mid-Mar–mid-Nov), 44 miles east of Kanab. Rangers at the **BLM Kanab Field Office** are in charge of permits from November 16 through March 14.

ℹ Getting There & Away

Trailheads for most routes are along House Rock Valley Rd (4.7 miles west of the contact station), a rugged dirt road, passable only in dry weather.

Capitol Reef National Park

Best Views

➡ Panorama Point (p205)

➡ Sunset Point (p170)

➡ Cohab Canyon trail overlooks (p167)

➡ Rim Overlook (p168)

Best Places to Stay

➡ Fruita Campground (p174)

➡ Torrey Schoolhouse (p176)

➡ Lodge at Red River Ranch (p176)

Why Go?

In this forgotten fold of the Colorado Plateau, you'll find slot canyons that appear as cathedrals cut from the earth, and giant cream-colored domes that arc into perfectly blue skies that hold little fluffy clouds.

Capitol Reef doesn't make it onto many Utah national-park itineraries, lending it a carefree air that promises wide-open vistas, limited crowds (relatively speaking) and plenty of adventurous activities, from hiking through canyons and up to overlooks to dusty-bottoming your way out on rugged 4WD tracks. Or you can simply take in the history and geology that reveals itself in petroglyphs and early Mormon settlements, sandstone streaks and hoodoo towers, and a labyrinth of canyons that stretch back millions of years.

The park's centerpiece is the lazily curving Fremont River and the Waterpocket Fold, a 100-mile buckle in the earth's crust that stymied early explorers.

Driving Distances (miles)

	Capitol Reef National Park (Visitor Center)	Moab	Salt Lake City	Torrey
Moab	145			
Salt Lake City	225	235		
Torrey	10	155	215	
Zion National Park (Springdale Entrance)	190	345	310	180

Entrances

The usual approach to Capitol Reef is to wind over Boulder Mountain on Hwy 12, then turn onto Hwy 24 near tiny Torrey. You'll pass scenic viewpoints, historic sites and hiking trailheads. South of the visitor center, the park's main scenic drive starts near Fruita, running 8 miles south.

Alternatively, the partly paved Burr Trail is a beautifully scenic back door to Capitol Reef's wonders and is easily accessed from the town of Boulder, and in the park via Notom-Bullfrog Rd.

Coming from Moab, you are likely to take I-70, turning southwest onto Hwy 24, where you pass the worthwhile Goblin Valley State Park.

Hwy 24 cuts through the central section of this long, thin national park, which was dubbed a reef by early explorers, as it blocked their way west like a reef blocks a ship's passage.

To the north of Fruita lies Cathedral Valley with its moonscape of towering monoliths. This is the least-visited corner of the park. Several unpaved roads, accessible mainly by 4WD or high-clearance vehicle, go through the north. The easiest route is the Cathedral Rd.

DON'T MISS

Stay up late to watch the night sky. Summer ranger programs occasionally include star talks. And thanks to the remote location, with pitch-black skies cut only by the Milky Way and a confetti of a million stars, the park was awarded the status of an 'International Dark Sky Park'.

When You Arrive

➡ Pay your entrance fee at the self-service kiosk and save your receipt, which is valid for seven days.

➡ Unlike most national parks, there's no entrance station. Just follow Hwy 24 to the visitor center where you can pick up information, get tips on hikes, sit in on a quick ranger talk, fill your water bottles and watch a short orientation film.

➡ The nearest gas stations are in Torrey (11 miles west) and Hanksville (37 miles east).

➡ Always tell someone where you will be hiking and when you plan to return, watch out for flash floods, and bring a gallon of water per person per day.

NATIVE NAME

The Navajo once called this colorful landscape of tilted buttes, jumbled rocks and sedimentary canyons the Land of the Sleeping Rainbow.

Fast Facts

➡ **Entrance fee:** Vehicle/motorcycle/individual $15/10/7

➡ **Total area:** 381 sq miles

➡ **Elevation:** 5500ft

➡ **Average high/low temperature (at Fruita) in July:** 92°F/65°F

Reservations

You can reserve a site at the Fruita Campground from March through October. Book well ahead.

Resources

➡ **Capitol Reef National Park** (www.nps.gov/care)

➡ **Capitol Reef Natural History Association** (www.capitolreefnha.org)

➡ **Canyoneering USA** (www.canyoneeringusa.com)

➡ **Utah.com** (www.utah.com)

➡ **Wayne County Tourism Office** (www.capitolreef.org)

CAPITOL REEF NATIONAL PARK

Capitol Reef National Park

N

0 ——— 20 km
0 ——— 10 miles

HICKMAN BRIDGE

Scuttle up red-rock cliffs and over slickrock to stand underneath this gorgeous natural bridge. (p166)

GOBLIN VALLEY STATE PARK

Head outside Capitol Reef for Gothic towers, wicked formations and amazing canyoneering in this off-the-beaten-track state park. (p177)

Temple Mt Rd

Goblin Valley Rd

Goblin Valley State Park

Upper Cathedral Valley Overlook

Cathedral Valley

Glass Mountain

Corral Canyon

Muddy Creek

Moa (95m

Richfield (40mi); Hwy 89 & I-70 (40mi)

Upper South Desert Overlook

Lower South Desert Overlook

Temple of the Sun
Temple of the Moon

The Hartnet

24

Hanksville

Fremont River

Loa   Lyman
24

Fishlake National Forest

Capitol Reef National Park

95

Bicknell

Hickman Natural Bridge
Panorama Point & Goosenecks Overlook

Petroglyphs

Caineville

Capitol Dome

Torrey

Visitor Center

Fruita
Cohab Canyon

24

Orientation Pullout

Fremont River

Gifford Homestead

Slickrock Divide

The Tanks

Notom

CAPITOL DOME

Capitol Reef is known for its enormous Navajo sandstone domes, one of which resembles the US Capitol building as it appeared to settlers in 1850. (p171)

12

Capitol Gorge

Dixie National Forest

Pleasant Creek

Oak Creek

Sandy Creek

PETROGLYPHS

Marvel at the evocative and rather expressionistic petroglyphs left by the Fremont and Ancestral Puebloan people throughout the park. Some of the best are along Hwy 24. (p171)

FRUITA

Pluck apples, peaches and cherries in this historic orchard right in the middle of the park. (p173)

12

Bitter Creek Divide (5650ft)

Upper Muley Twist Canyon

Waterpocket Fold

Strike Valley

Boulder

Circle Cliffs

Strike Valley Overlook

King Bench

The Post

Henry Mountains

Burr Trail Switchbacks

The Gulch

Lower Muley Twist Canyon

Escalante

Grand Staircase – Escalante National Monument

Halls Creek

Bullfrog Creek

Hansen Creek

Tropic (30mi); Bryce Canyon National Park (38mi); Panguitch (58mi)

Escalante Canyons

Escalante River

Circle Cliffs

Moody Creek

Halls Overlook

Ticaboo

COHAB CANYON

Scale the Waterpocket Fold in search of secret slot canyons and skyscraping lookouts. (p167)

Peek-A-Boo Slot Canyon

Glen Canyon National Recreation Area

Halls Creek Narrows

Lake Powell   Bullfrog

🥾 DAY HIKES

🥾 Grand Wash

Duration 45 minutes–1½ hours

Distance 4.4 miles round-trip

Difficulty Easy

Start/Finish Grand Wash trailhead, at end of 1.3-mile-long dirt spur road off Scenic Dr, 3.4 miles south of the visitor center

Nearest Town Torrey

Transportation Private

Summary Capitol Reef's most dramatic canyon is worth visiting just to walk between the sheer walls of the Narrows. Avoid this hike if rain threatens, as the wash is prone to flash floods.

Start from the parking lot at the end of the Grand Wash spur road. It's an easy stroll up the packed-sand wash from the parking area. Look for seasonal wildflowers such as reddish Indian paintbrush, shrubby white-flowering Apache's plume and stalky, yellow-flowering prince's plume. The canyon's walls inch closer and closer together until, about 1.25 miles from the trailhead, you reach the **Narrows**, where the 80-story canyon is just 15ft wide – a thrilling sight. The canyon walls shrink and spread out again as the flat trail approaches Hwy 24. Return the way you came, or arrange for someone to pick you up on Hwy 24, around 4.5 miles east of the visitor center (look for a trailhead marker on the south side of the highway, where there's a small gravel pull-off).

🥾 Capitol Gorge

Duration 1–2 hours

Distance 2 miles round-trip

Difficulty Easy–moderate

Capitol Reef – Day Hikes

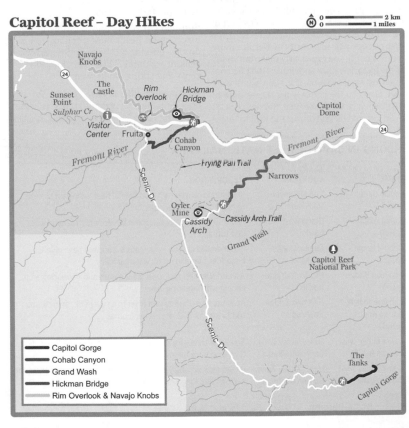

Capitol Gorge
Cohab Canyon
Grand Wash
Hickman Bridge
Rim Overlook & Navajo Knobs

Start/Finish Capitol Gorge trailhead, at end of 2.4-mile-long dirt spur road off Scenic Dr, 8 miles south of the visitor center

Nearest Town Torrey

Transportation Private

Summary Leave your car behind for an easy canyon ramble past historic petroglyphs, then scramble up to hidden water pockets. Avoid this flood-prone route if rain threatens.

Half a century ago, Capitol Gorge was the primary automobile route through the Waterpocket Fold. Pioneers first brought wagons through in the late 19th century, and the route remained in use until 1962. Today the sheer canyon walls are stained with desert varnish, which stands out in dramatic contrast to the red rock. Keep your eyes peeled for bighorn sheep, which have been successfully reintroduced in the park.

About 0.25 miles from the trailhead, you'll reach a scoured panel of ancient Fremont **petroglyphs**. A quarter-mile further, look up to see the **Pioneer Register**, a collection of carved names and dates that go back to the first pioneer passersby in 1871. Despite more recent graffiti, you can clearly make out many of the historic names and dates. Don't be confused by signatures on the right-hand wall, back closer to the petroglyphs. These date to 1911, when a US Geological Survey (USGS) team lowered its leader over the wall to incise the party's names – vandalism by today's standards.

Just over 0.8 miles from the trailhead, bear left and follow signs to the **Tanks**, which lie atop a fairly steep 0.2-mile spur. These giant potholes, or water pockets, hold significant volumes of water much of the year. They were invaluable to early settlers and remain so for animals, so don't drink from or disturb them. When you're rested and ready, head back the way you came – the onward wash trail crosses park boundaries onto private land.

Hickman Bridge

Duration 1–2 hours

Distance 1.8 miles round-trip

Difficulty Easy–moderate

Start/Finish Hickman Bridge trailhead, off Hwy 24, 1.9 miles east of the visitor center

Nearest Town Torrey

Transportation Private

Summary If you've only got time for one hike, Capitol Reef's most popular trail is diverse, offering a canyon and desert-wash walk to a natural bridge, plus long sky views and spring wildflowers.

This popular hike is easy enough for anyone from kids to grandparents to enjoy. Since the route is largely exposed, it's best

HIKING IN CAPITOL REEF NATIONAL PARK

NAME	START LOCATION	DESCRIPTION
Cohab Canyon (p167)	Cohab Canyon trailhead	In a hidden canyon high atop Capitol Reef, sidle past slickrock to head-spinning overlooks.
Grand Wash (p165)	Grand Wash trailhead	Flat trail passing between sheer 80-story-high canyon walls just 15ft apart.
Capitol Gorge (p165)	Capitol Gorge trailhead	Sheer-walled canyon wash featuring ancient petroglyphs, historical sites and secret watering holes.
Hickman Bridge (p166)	Hickman Bridge trailhead	Ascend over slickrock, past giant domes and a towering arch, ending with sweeping views.
Rim Overlook & Navajo Knobs (p168)	Hickman Bridge trailhead	Ascends from the Fremont River to an overlook, then climbs higher still for 360-degree panoramas.
Lower Muley Twist Canyon (p168)	Lower Muley Twist Canyon trailhead	Scramble through a sky-high red-rock canyon just 10ft wide, then loop back through a gulch.
Upper Muley Twist Canyon (p169)	Upper Muley Twist Canyon trailhead	Rugged backcountry loop featuring arches, sculpted sandstone narrows and long views of Waterpocket Fold.

 Wildlife Watching   *Flush Toilets*   *Views*   *Great for Families*

to hike it in the early morning. Cairns mark some of the route, which starts off the same way as the longer, more strenuous hike to the Rim Overlook and Navajo Knobs. Pick up a self-guided Hickman Bridge nature trail brochure at the trailhead, which corresponds to numbered signposts along the route.

Starting from the Fremont River – this is an agricultural-grade river, so you can swim here but be wary of depth and current and don't take any gulps – the trail ascends a red-rock cliff via a few easy switchbacks. As you cross an open area of desert vegetation strewn with volcanic black rocks, the highway vanishes behind giant white sandstone domes. A short spur leads to a tiny **archaeological site** where you can inspect the foundations of Fremont culture pit houses. During April and May look for scarlet claret cup and pink-flowering prickly pear cacti blooming beside the path.

The trail soon drops into a wash, where you can rest in a shady alcove before ascending over slickrock to **Hickman Bridge**, having gained 400ft in elevation from your start. While this chunky yellow arch can be tricky to spot from afar, the trail loops right beneath it for a marvelous appreciation of its mass. Hike counterclockwise and bear left beyond the arch to keep following the trail's loop. Pause to look over the rim and downriver to Fruita, an oasis of green.

🏃 Cohab Canyon

Duration 1–2 hours

Distance 1.7 miles

Difficulty Moderate

Start Cohab Canyon trailhead, off Scenic Dr, 1.2 miles south of the visitor center

Finish Hwy 24, 1.9 miles east of the visitor center

Nearest Town Torrey

Transportation Private

Summary Often overlooked, this trail deters crowds with a steep climb at the beginning, but exploring a hidden canyon and the views from atop Capitol Reef are worth every sweaty step.

If you're with people whose ability or interest in hiking isn't as great as yours, leave them to laze by the river or tour Fruita's historic sights while you tackle this climb with killer views. Starting across the road from Fruita Campground, just south of the Gifford Homestead, this trail makes a steep 0.25-mile initial ascent atop a rocky cliff. From there it levels out through a desert wash, beside which small slot canyons nestle. You'll pass more striking geologic features on your way through sheltered but windy Cohab Canyon itself, which protects piñon and juniper trees (and lizards!).

CAPITOL REEF NATIONAL PARK DAY HIKES

DIFFICULTY	DURATION	ROUND-TRIP DISTANCE	ELEVATION CHANGE	FEATURES	FACILITIES
moderate	1-2hr	1.7 miles one way	400ft	🏜️🔭	
easy	45min-1½hr	2.2 miles one way	25ft	👪	
easy-moderate	1-2hr	2 miles	125ft	🏜️👪	
easy-moderate	1-2hr	1.8 miles	400ft	🔭👪	🚻
difficult	4-6hr	9.4 miles	1600ft	🔭🧗	🚻
difficult	1-2 days	17 miles	1000ft	🔭🧗	▲
difficult	1-2 days	15 miles	1100ft	🔭🧗	▲

🧗 Rock Climbing   ▲ Backcountry Camping

About 1.1 miles from the trailhead, a short but steep spur trail veers off left to climb to two **overlooks** of Fruita and the orchards. After about 0.25 miles of switchbacks, this spur trail splits into separate branches heading toward the southern and northern overlooks – visiting both before returning to the main trail adds just over a mile to this hike. This is a good turnaround point if you'd rather do just a 3.2-mile out-and-back hike, instead of a one-way shuttle hike over to Hwy 24.

The main trail continues threading its way through Cohab Canyon. It ascends to a junction with the **Frying Pan Trail**, a moderately difficult route that leads atop an escarpment for panoramic views, including of Cassidy Arch, before connecting with the Cassidy Arch Trail, which drops into the **Grand Wash** 4 miles from Cohab Canyon; add another mile if you take the worthwhile side trip to the arch. Otherwise, from the Frying Pan Trail junction, the main trail switchbacks down to Hwy 24, ending almost opposite the Hickman Bridge trailhead, around 2 miles east of the visitor center.

🏃 Rim Overlook & Navajo Knobs

Duration 4–6 hours

Distance 9.4 miles round-trip

Difficulty Difficult

Start/Finish Hickman Bridge trailhead, off Hwy 24, 1.9 miles east of the visitor center

Nearest Town Torrey

Transportation Private

Summary This slickrock route to twin bumps of Navajo sandstone perched on the precipitous western edge of Waterpocket Fold yields unsurpassed views. A steep, strenuous climb offers little shade and no water.

Start hiking from the **Fremont River** along the popular Hickman Bridge Trail, but after 0.3 miles, fork right at the signed junction – you'll leave most of the crowds behind. Follow cairns along much of this dry-wash and slickrock route, which sidles around Capitol Reef's giant white domes. Pause at the well-marked **Hickman Bridge Overlook**, south of the trail. Blending in amid the surrounding rock, this natural bridge is visible across a small canyon at eye level with the overlook.

🏃 Overnight Hike
Upper Muley Twist Canyon

DURATION 1–2 DAYS
DISTANCE 15 MILES
DIFFICULTY DIFFICULT
START/FINISH UPPER MULEY TWIST CANYON TRAILHEAD, OFF BURR TRAIL
NEAREST TOWN TORREY
TRANSPORTATION PRIVATE

The upper canyon is less dramatic than the lower, but offers easier terrain and expansive views atop the fold. You'll pass arches and sculpted sandstone narrows along this hike, too.

Though you can approach Upper Muley as a long, difficult day hike, it's better to spend two days and enjoy the scenery. Most people camp near the Rim Trail junction, then hike the Rim Trail Loop without a pack. Don't enter this flood-prone canyon if there is *any* chance of rain in the weather forecast.

To reach the trailhead, drive 3 miles west of the intersection with Notom-Bullfrog Rd on the Burr Trail, then turn right onto the signed side road to Strike Valley Overlook. Alternatively, from Boulder follow the mostly paved Burr Trail, driving just over 2 miles on graded dirt to the turnoff above the switchbacks. With a high-clearance 4WD vehicle, you can usually drive the first 3 miles of this hike to the Strike Valley Overlook trailhead.

From the Upper Muley Twist Canyon trailhead, walk along the gravel wash and head generally northwest. The canyon is wide and the wash level for the 3-mile hike to the Strike Valley Overlook trailhead. The 0.5-mile round-trip jaunt to the ❶ **overlook** is worth the energy, especially if you set down your pack at the trailhead.

Upper Muley Twist Canyon narrows 0.5 miles past the overlook, as steep red sandstone cliffs to the east turn in toward the wash. About 1.2 miles further you'll see ❷ **Saddle Arch**, visible near the rim of the west wall. A sign on the east side of the wash marks the beginning of the Rim Trail Loop. Follow cairns up the canyon's east side, being prepared for some rock scrambling and climbing uphill.

In about 15 or 20 minutes, you'll reach a broad bench capped with juniper trees and ❸ **camping** spots. Avoid treading on the crumbly cryptobiotic soil. If you want a view, but don't mind potentially high winds and not having any shade, camp at the saddle where the trail crests the fold. The Rim Trail Loop is slippery when wet, so use caution. From the potential campsites, follow cairns up to the east rim for spectacular views. A sign at the top points back down to the Canyon Route, which you'll be following later. You may find several sandy potential campsites nearby, too.

Follow the ridge north to a high point for views along the fold to the grand white domes near the visitor center, 35 miles away as the turkey vulture flies. After around 2 miles of roller-coaster ridge hiking, the trail plunges toward Muley Twist Canyon. Several cairned routes lead to the canyon floor, each requiring tricky scrambling. Turn down-canyon (south) and stay high, close to the east wall. After passing some wonderful hat-shaped formations, the trail swings east away from the ❹ **Narrows** below. Several deep potholes serve as water-storage tanks.

Beyond the gap in the west wall, the trail returns to the canyon floor. A quarter-mile down-canyon, the cairned trail climbs the east wall again, though in dry periods you may be able to continue along the canyon floor. After about 2 miles you'll pass Saddle Arch, high on the west wall, soon after which a sign for the Rim Trail Loop signals the end of your loop. After closing the loop, the high, red canyon walls wax low and golden as you retrace your steps to the Strike Valley Overlook trailhead, 1.7 miles away, and another 3 miles south to the Upper Muley Twist Canyon trailhead.

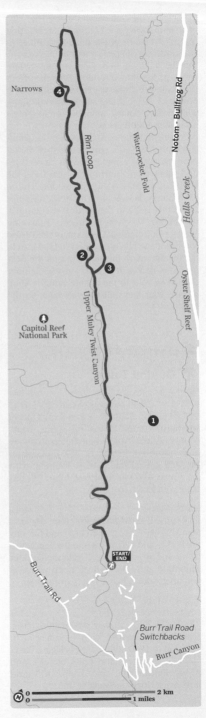

Onward, the trail zigzags along the edge of a south-facing side canyon, a pattern that repeats for much of the remaining hike. As you continue climbing, you'll wind past the mouths of three more side canyons before reaching the **Rim Overlook**, 2.3 miles from the trailhead. Gorgeous views encompass a profile of the fold and its north end, along with mesas, domes, mountains and Fruita more than 1000ft below.

After climbing up and down more sandstone pitches, you'll pass between cliffs (on your right) and a radio repeater tower, and find yourself on a broad ledge that faces the **Castle**, a large, eroded, freestanding chunk of Waterpocket Fold. The trail rambles along this ledge to the northwest edge of a west-facing, W-shaped canyon. Following cairns, you'll climb the west rim of the W and soon spot the **Navajo Knobs** (6980ft), twin bumps that mark the high point on the next promontory. Watch your step as you clamber over loose rock to the double summit, then retrace your steps all the way back to the trailhead.

🏃 OTHER ACTIVITIES

🏃 Guided Tours

⭐**Hondoo Rivers & Trails**   ADVENTURE
(☑435-425-3519; www.hondoo.com; 90 E Main St, Torrey; tours $120-175; ⊙8am-8pm) One of southern Utah's longest-operating backcountry guides, Hondoo specializes in horseback riding, but also offers 4WD tours, shuttles and guided hiking trips. Half-day trips (by horse, 4WD or foot) cost $120; full-day trips with lunch cost $175.

Earth Tours   HIKING
(☑435-691-1241; www.earth-tours.com; day tours from $150; 🐾) Choose from half- and full-day area hikes and 4WD trips into the backcountry in and around Bryce, Escalante, Boulder Mountain and Capitol Reef. Keith will pick you up at your hotel in Torrey or Boulder.

**Capitol Reef
Backcountry Outfitters**   ADVENTURE
(☑435-425-2010; www.backcountryoutfitters. com; 2975 Chadburn Rd, Torrey; ⊙9am-5pm) In addition to 4WD and hiking packages, Backcountry Outfitters also rents bicycles and ATVs. Shuttles and guided bike, ATV and horseback rides are available, too.

Driving Tour
Highway 24

DURATION 1–4 HOURS
DISTANCE 22 MILES ONE WAY
START TORREY
FINISH ORIENTATION PULLOUT
NEAREST TOWN TORREY

This easy, winding route gives you a taste of everything that Capitol Reef offers: striking geology, dramatic desert overlooks, ancient Native American petroglyphs, early Western settlers' sites and hiking trails for stretching your legs.

From Torrey, head east into Capitol Reef on Hwy 24. There is no entrance station; driving this route is free. Be sure to stop at turnouts along the way to read interesting geologic interpretive panels. Then pull over at ❶**Chimney Rock**, the towering reddish-brown rock formation 7 miles east of Torrey. If you're in great shape, consider hiking the strenuous 3.6-mile loop for wide-open clifftop views of Capitol Reef.

A half-mile east of Chimney Rock, turn right toward ❷**Panorama Point** (just a short walk from the road, it's best visited at sunset) and drive 0.8 miles along a graded dirt road to the ❸**Gooseneck Overlook**. An easy 0.1-mile walk from the parking area over rock slabs takes you to this viewpoint above Sulphur Creek, which twists through the canyon in elegant S-curves. Though the observation platform is fenced in, much of the area around it is open – watch your little ones! From the parking area it's an easy 0.4-mile stroll to ❹**Sunset Point**, where the ambient light on the cliffs and domes is best for photographers in the late afternoon.

Another 2.4 miles further east on Hwy 24, you'll arrive at the well-signed turnoff to Capitol Reef's ❺**visitor center**, just north of the Fruita Historic District and the paved ❻**Scenic Drive**. Rising majestically just north of this junction is the snaggle-toothed ❼**Castle**; an interpretive panel details its geologic history.

East of the visitor center, Hwy 24 skirts the Fremont River, the surrounding rock growing paler and more yellow as you approach the park's Navajo sandstone domes. Peer through the windows of the historic ❽**Fruita school**, 0.8 miles east of the visitor center, before stopping at the

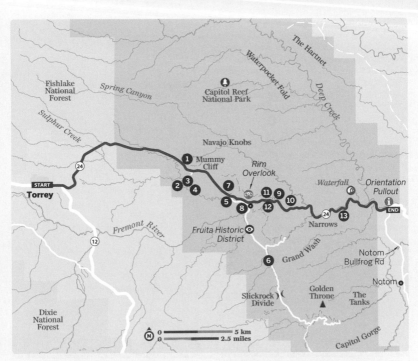

9 **ancient petroglyphs** 0.2 miles further east. Created by the Fremont Culture, these carvings helped convince archaeologists that the Fremont culture was distinct from that of Ancestral Puebloans. The boardwalk is wheelchair-accessible. Bring binoculars or a camera with a zoom lens.

Stop at the turnout 0.8 miles east of the petroglyphs for views of **10** **Capitol Dome**, a giant sandstone dome that vaguely resembles the US Capitol, as it appeared in 1850. This parking area beside the Fremont River is where you'll find the trailheads for **11** **Hickman Bridge** and the more strenuous Rim Overlook and Navajo Knobs route. On the south side of Hwy 24 is an alternate trailhead

for **12** **Cohab Canyon**, while 2.7 miles further east is the end of the Grand Wash.

About 4 miles east of Hickman Bridge, on your right, stop to peer through the window of the one-room 1882 **13** **Behunin Cabin**, once home to a Mormon settler's family of 13. On the north side of the highway, 0.7 miles east of the cabin you'll pass a waterfall. Swimming is not allowed here; numerous accidents and even drownings have occurred. At the park's eastern orientation pullout, just over 9 miles from the visitor center, are restrooms and an information kiosk. It's on the north side of the intersection with Notom-Bullfrog Rd.

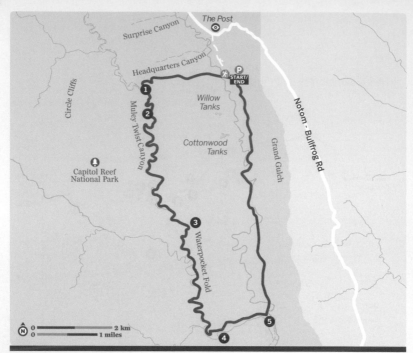

Overnight Hike
Lower Muley Twist Canyon

DURATION 1–2 DAYS
DISTANCE 17 MILES
DIFFICULTY DIFFICULT
START/FINISH LOWER MULEY
TWIST CANYON TRAILHEAD, OFF
NOTOM-BULLFROG RD
NEAREST TOWN TORREY
TRANSPORTATION PRIVATE

This loop follows the dramatic lower canyon through narrow red walls, then returns through grasslands broken up by colorful hills.

Be sure to check with rangers about current conditions and the weather forecast as this hike is dangerously flood-prone. Less than 3 miles south of the Notom-Bullfrog Rd/ Burr Trail junction, 35 miles south of Hwy 24, a well-signed road leads right from the Post. The trailhead is at the southwest edge of the parking lot.

The first mile is steep and exposed, with narrow drop-offs and ledges. From the parking area, follow the well-marked trail west up Waterpocket Fold's red, sloping back. After about an hour of steady climbing, the trail hits sand and the canyon's red walls come into view to the northeast. You'll level out and cross a **1** sandy area strewn with vegetation. Leaving the wash, the trail bears south to lower **2** Muley Twist Canyon, staying high on the canyon's east side, then cutting gently to the canyon floor, about 2 miles from the trailhead.

Sheer red Wingate sandstone walls tower 300ft on both sides. The hike now starts to follow a familiar pattern – from riverbed to high ground and back again – as the canyon twists south. After passing two gaps in the west wall, you'll reach a **3** big side canyon to the northeast, home to several good campsites. Back in the main canyon, the trail soon turns from sand to sandstone and continues straight where the main canyon swings west. Mount a **4** sandy plain to more campsites.

Eventually you'll reach the canyon's narrows, where the 800ft walls are less than 10ft apart at points – narrow enough to 'twist a mule.' Soon afterward the canyon ends where its riverbed flows toward **5** Halls Creek. At this point, cairns mark the return route north to the Post trailhead.

🏃 Cycling

The park's mostly paved **Scenic Drive** satisfies beginners and intermediates, while experienced mountain bikers love **Cathedral Valley Loop** (Caineville Wash Rd), though it becomes a muddy mess when wet. Capitol Reef Backcountry Outfitters rents bikes.

🏃 Horseback Riding & Pack Trips

If you're bringing your own stock, backcountry permits for horse-packing trips are free, but special use regulations apply. Reservations are required at least two weeks in advance to use the Post corral, off Notom-Bullfrog Rd. For the lowdown, visit www.nps. gov/care/planyourvisit/horsepack.htm.

🏃 Four-Wheel Driving

Four-wheel-drive roads crisscross Capitol Reef. Don't even consider attempting any of the 4WD trails without a suitable vehicle. If you don't have a 4WD, you can rent a Jeep from around $160 per day from **Thousand Lakes RV Park** (☑435-425 3500, 800-355-8995; www.thousandlakesrvpark.com; Hwy 24; tent/RV sites $20/40, camping cabins $39-109; ☺Apr-Oct; 🛜🏊).

🏃 Swimming

Only wade in wide, calm sections of a creek or river when there's no threat of a flash flood. Currents can be strong in bigger rivers. Across Hwy 24 from the Chimney Rock parking area, an easy, level trail leads to **Sulphur Creek**. Near the visitor center, you can hike a mile up Sulphur Creek to a large **wading pool** shaded by cottonwoods. You can also wade along **Pleasant Creek** from the end of the park's Scenic Dr. The **Fremont River** is an agricultural-grade river, meaning there are pesticides etc running through it. It's safe for swimming, but you don't want to drink unfiltered water from it.

🏃 Ranger Programs

From May to September the park offers free public programs, including ranger talks, guided walks and evening shows at Fruita Campground's amphitheater.

🏃 Rock Climbing

Technical rock climbing is allowed without permits. Note that Wingate sandstone can flake unpredictably. Follow clean-climbing guidelines, and take all safety precautions. For details, check with rangers or see www. nps.gov/care.

🏃 Fishing

Fishing is permitted in the Fremont River and its tributaries with a valid Utah fishing license. Get one online at https://wildlife. utah.gov/utah-licenses.html.

Alpine Anglers FISHING
(☑435-425-3660; www.alpineadventuresutah. com; 310 W Main St, Torrey; day trip fly-fishing $225) Guided fishing trips and multiday excursions that include both horseback riding and fishing.

Fremont River Guides FISHING
(☑435-491-0242; www.flyfishingsouthernutah. com; 135 E Main St, Torrey; half-/full-day trips from $175/350) Go fishing on the Fremont River or Boulder Mountain.

⊙ SIGHTS

🏠 Fruita Historic District

Offering welcome respite from the menacing red-rock desert, the **Fruita Rural Historic District** (pronounced like 'fruit') is a green valley filled with mature, shade-giving cottonwoods and fruit-bearing trees. The first Mormon homesteaders arrived in the 1880s, and Fruita's final resident left in 1969.

The park now maintains more than 3000 mostly cherry, apricot, peach, pear and apple trees planted by early settlers, and if you visit between June and October you can eat ripe fruit straight from the trees for free (there's a nominal fee for any fruit taken from an orchard). To learn what's in season, ask at the visitor center or call ☑435-425-3791.

You're welcome to pick fruit from any unlocked orchard during designated harvest times; just follow the ranger-posted instructions at the gates. Pick only mature fruit and leave the rest to ripen. You may not climb the trees, but ladders and handheld fruit pickers are available. Near the orchards is a restful **picnic area**, where deer roam and you'll hear birdsong in the trees, a rarity in the desert.

Displays at the **Gifford Homestead** (⊙8am-5pm Mar-Oct), just over a mile south of the visitor center, reveal the day-to-day world of a typical Mormon settlers' homestead. At the small store you can buy ice cream, artisan breads and preserves made from the orchard fruit. Don't miss purchasing one of the famous pies – up to 13 dozen are sold daily, and they usually run out!

A short way back up the main road is the old **blacksmith shop**, though it's little more than a shed with period equipment inside (press a button to hear Dewey Gifford, the town's last resident, reminisce about life in Fruita). Nearby is the family-oriented **Ripple Rock Nature Center** (⊙1-5pm late May–mid-Aug; 🐾) **FREE**.

South of Fruita Campground the historic district ends, yielding to a trail alongside the Fremont River and the continuation of the park's **Scenic Drive**.

Fremont Petroglyphs   ARCHAEOLOGICAL SITE
(www.nps.gov/care/learn/historyculture/fremont. htm; Capitol Reef National Park) Just east of the visitor center (p175) on Hwy 24, look for the parking lot for freely accessible petroglyphs; these are the rock-art carvings that convinced archaeologists that the Fremont Indians were a group distinct from the

Ancestral Puebloans. Follow the roadside boardwalk to see several panels.

🛏️ SLEEPING & EATING

Ask at the visitor center about current road conditions before heading out to the remote, primitive and little-visited Cathedral Valley and Cedar Mesa campgrounds. The nearest motel lodgings are in Torrey. Visitors can get snacks at the general store in the park.

Fruita Campground   CAMPGROUND $
(📞435-425-3791; www.recreation.gov; Campground Rd, Teasdale; sites $20) This terrific 71-site campground sits under mature cottonwood trees alongside the Fremont River, surrounded by orchards. Book well in advance in order to secure a campsite here from March through October. A handful of sites remain first-come, first-serve if you want to try your luck. There is water and an RV dump, but no hookups or showers.

Cedar Mesa Campground   CAMPGROUND
(📞435-425-3791; www.nps.gov/care/planyour visit/primitivecampsites.htm; Notom-Bullfrog Rd; ⊙year-round) **FREE** These five first-come, first-served free sites lack water, but have pit toilets, fire grates and picnic tables, as well

CAMPGROUNDS IN & AROUND CAPITOL REEF

CAMPGROUND	LOCATION	DESCRIPTION
Sunglow (p176)	Forest Rd 143	Small USFS campground outside Bicknell, west of Torrey; can be a local hooligans' hangout.
Goblin Valley State Park (p177)	Goblin Valley Rd	Isolated campground with tin-roofed picnic shelters and showers but no hookups.
Cathedral Valley (p175)	cnr Hartnet & Cathedral Rds	Primitive backcountry campground near scenic rock formations; access road may require high-clearance 4WD vehicle.
Singletree (p176)	Hwy 12	Cooler, forested USFS campground high on Boulder Mountain; seasonal opening dates depend upon snowfall.
Sandcreek RV Park (p44)	Hwy 24	Small, family-run roadside RV park with log cabins near Torrey's town center; horse corral available.
Thousand Lakes RV Park (p173)	Hwy 24	Sprawling roadside RV park with above-average amenities including a playground, horseshoe pits and self-service laundry.
Cedar Mesa (p174)	Notom-Bullfrog Rd	Primitive backcountry campground; during dry season, dirt access road may be accessible by standard vehicle.
Fruita (p174)	Campground Rd, Teasdale	Shady in-park campsites near fruit orchards and a river; often full, so arrive early.

 Drinking Water   *Flush Toilets*   *Ranger Station Nearby*   *Great for Families*   *Dogs Allowed (On Leash)*

as great views east along the fold. They're 30 miles south of Hwy 24.

Cathedral Valley Campground CAMPGROUND (☑435-425-3791;www.nps.gov/care/planyourvisit/ primitivecampsites.htm; cnr Hartnet & Cathedral Rds; ☺year-round) **FREE** The drive here, 40 miles from the visitor center (p175), requires a high-clearance vehicle and may demand 4WD. Six first-come, first-served free campsites have no water, but there are pit toilets, fire grates and picnic tables.

★**Mesa Farm Market** MARKET **$** (☑435-456-9146; www.mesafarmmarket.com; Hwy 24, Caineville; ☺7am-7pm Mar-Oct; ☑) ⬤ Stop in Caineville at Mesa Farm Market for straight-from-the-garden organic salads, juices, goat's cheese and freshly baked artisan bread from an outdoor stone-hearth oven.

Duke's Slickrock AMERICAN **$** (☑435-542-2052; www.dukesslickrock.com; 275 E Hwy 24, Hanksville; mains $10-18; ☺7am-10pm) If you're entering Capitol Reef from the east, take a lunch break at the friendliest cowboy grill this side of the swell. The food is straightforward and filling, the service is great, and there's a tipi tent site out back.

ⓘ Information

The park is open year-round. Just south of Hwy 24, the **Capitol Reef Visitor Center** (☑435-425-3791; www.nps.gov/care; cnr Hwy 24 & Scenic Dr; ☺8am-6pm Jun-Aug, 8am-4:30pm Sep-May) is also the park's headquarters. It's the only source for information in the park. Rangers and volunteer staff offer advice and can help you plan hikes and backcountry trips. The **Capitol Reef Natural History Association** (☑435-425-4106; www. capitolreefnha.org) runs the center's bookstore, which stocks topographic maps. Pay phones and recycling bins are available at the visitor center and Fruita Campground. Cell-phone reception is spotty to nonexistent throughout the park.

For all other tourist information and services, the gateway town of Torrey is about 11 miles west of the visitor center, near the intersection of Hwys 12 and 24. Hanksville (37 miles east) has restaurants, gas and lodging.

Capitol Reef Country Travel Council (☑800-858-7951, 435-425-3365; www.capitolreef. org; Junction Hwys 12 & 24) Information about Capitol Reef and Hwy 12.

ⓘ Getting Around

Capitol Reef has no public transportation system. Aside from Hwy 24 and Scenic Dr, park routes are dirt roads that are bladed only a few times a year. In summer you may be able to drive Notom-Bullfrog Rd and the Burr Trail in a regular

NO OF SITES	ELEVATION	OPEN	RESERVATION REQUIRED?	DAY FEE	FACILITIES
7	7200ft	May-Oct	no	NA	🗑🏕🍴
24	5100ft	year-round	yes	NA	🗑🚻🚼👫♿🐕🚐
6	7000ft	year-round	no	NA	🐕
13	8600ft	May-Sep	yes	NA	🗑🐕🚐
24	6900ft	Apr-Oct	yes	NA	🗑🚻👫🐕🏪🍴📞🚐
61	6900ft	Apr-Oct	yes	NA	🗑🚻👫🐕🏪🍴🚐
5	5600ft	year-round	no	NA	🐕
71	545ft	year-round	yes	NA	🗑🚻🚼🚻🐕📞🔥🚐

🏪 Grocery Store Nearby   🍴 Restaurant Nearby   📞 Pay-phone   🔥 Summertime Campfire Program   🚐 RV Dump Station

passenger car. Remote regions like Cathedral Valley will likely require a high-clearance 4WD vehicle. Check weather and road conditions with rangers before heading out.

Bicycles are allowed on all park roads but not trails. Cyclists and hikers can arrange drop-off/pick-up shuttle services ($1 to $2 per mile) with Hondoo Rivers & Trails (p170) in Torrey.

AROUND CAPITOL REEF

Torrey

POP 362 / ELEV 6830FT

With shy pioneer charm and quiet streets backed by red-rock cliffs, Torrey is a relaxing stop. A former logging and ranching center, its mainstay now is outdoor tourism. Capitol Reef National Park (p163) is only 11 miles east, Grand Staircase–Escalante National Monument is 40 miles south and national forests surround the town. Summer brings a whiff of countercultural sophistication and great dining – but from November to February the town shuts down.

🛏 Sleeping

Singletree Campground　　CAMPGROUND $
(☎877-444-6777; www.recreation.gov; Hwy 12; sites $12-26) The **Fishlake National Forest** (www.fs.usda.gov/fishlake) runs this basic 13-site tent and RV campground at an elevation of 8600ft on forested Boulder Mountain, 12 miles south of Torrey along Hwy 12. There's drinking water, vault toilets and an RV dump station.

Sunglow Campground　　CAMPGROUND $
(☎877-444-6777; www.recreation.gov; Forest Rd 143, Bicknell; campsites $30) Often windy, this USFS campground tucked back amid red-rock cliffs has reservable tent and RV sites. It offers drinking water, picnic tables and flush toilets. Look for the turnoff from Hwy 24, just east of Bicknell.

Austin's Chuckwagon Motel　　MOTEL $
(☎435-425-3335; www.austinschuckwagonmotel. com; 12 W Main St; r from $69, 2-bedroom cabins from $149; ☺Mar-Oct; ❉🐾🐕🐾) Rustic wood buildings ring the pool and shady grounds here at the town center. Good-value-for-money motel rooms have sturdy, basic furnishings; cabins also have kitchens. The on-site general store, deli and laundromat are a bonus.

Cowboy Homestead Cabins　　CABIN $
(☎888-854-5871; www.cowboyhomesteadcabins. com; Hwy 12; cabins $99-109; 🐾🐕) Rustic, pine-paneled roadside cabins with kitchenettes, 3 miles south of Torrey. The cabins have a sofa sleeper and can sleep a family.

★**Torrey Schoolhouse B&B**　　B&B $$
(☎435-633-4643; www.torreyschoolhouse.com; 150 N Center St; r $135-160; ☺Apr-Oct; ❉🐾) Ty Markham has done an exquisite job of bringing this rambling 1914 schoolhouse back to life as a B&B. Antiques and country elegance contrast with the fascinating black-and-white photos of classes starting from a century back. Enjoy a full gourmet breakfast before hiking.

★**Lodge at Red River Ranch**　　INN $$
(☎435-425-3322; www.redriverranch.com; 2900 W Hwy 24, Teasdale; r from $199; @🐾) In the grand tradition of Western ranches, the great room here has a three-story open-beam ceiling, timber walls and Navajo rugs. Details are flawless – from the country quilts on high-thread-count sheets to the cowboy memorabilia in the fine-dining room. Wander its 2000-plus acres, or enjoy the star-filled sky from the outdoor hot tub. No room TVs. Just west of Torrey.

Broken Spur Inn & Steakhouse　　MOTEL $$
(☎435-425-3775; www.brokenspurinn.com; 955 E Hwy 24; r from $129; ☺Mar-Nov; 🅿❉🐾🐕🐾) Spacious hilltop motel rooms are set back from Torrey's busy highway junction. Soak sore muscles in the glass-enclosed heated swimming pool or Jacuzzi. Has a pet fee.

Capitol Reef Resort　　RESORT $$
(☎435-425-3761; www.capitolreefresort.com; 2600 E Hwy 24; r $159-189, cabins & tipis from $249; 🅿❉🐾🐕) One of the closest resorts to the Capitol Reef National Park (p163), this large resort-style complex flirts with modern cowboy style. Tipis and Conestoga wagons offer something different (if only in theory); they're quite luxuriant. It feels somewhat corporate, but the views from the back rooms onto the red rocks are gorgeous and the outdoor heated pool has its obvious appeal.

Muley Twist Inn B&B　　B&B $$
(☎435-425-3640, 800-530-1038; www.muley twistinn.com; 249 W 125 S, Teasdale; r $120-160; ☺Apr-Oct; ❉🐾) Set against a towering red-sandstone dome in a Teasdale neighborhood, this big wooden farmhouse with a wraparound veranda looks small. It isn't.

Casual rooms at the down-to-earth inn are spacious and bright.

✕ Eating & Drinking

**Austin's Chuckwagon
General Store**   MARKET $

(📞 435-425-3335; www.austinschuckwagonmotel.com; 12 W Main St; ☺ 7am-10pm Apr-Oct) Sells camping supplies, groceries, beer and deli sandwiches to go. There's an ATM, showers and laundromat too.

Slacker's Burger Joint   BURGERS $

(📞 435-425-3710; 165 E Main St; burgers $6-10; ☺ 11am-8pm Mon-Thu, to 9pm Fri & Sat) Order an old-fashioned burger (beef, chicken, pastrami or veggie), hand-cut fries (the sweet-potato version is delish) and thick milkshake (in a rainbow of cool flavors like cherry cordial), then enjoy – inside or out – at the picnic tables.

Capitol Reef Cafe   AMERICAN $$

(📞 435-425-3271; www.capitolreefinn.com; 360 W Main St; breakfast & lunch $6-12, dinner mains $10-24; ☺ 7am-9pm Apr-Oct) Whenever possible, this cozy cafe uses local and organic ingredients in its vegetable-heavy dishes.

Rim Rock Restaurant   AMERICAN $$

(📞 435-425-3398; www.therimrock.net; 2523 E Hwy 24; mains $14-34; ☺ 5-9:30pm Mar-Nov) Grilled steaks, pasta and fish come with a million-dollar view of red-rock cliffs. Arrive before sunset for the best show. There's a full bar.

★ Cafe Diablo   TEX-MEX $$$

(📞 435-425-3070; www.cafediablo.net; 599 W Main St; mains $22-40; ☺ 3-9pm; 🖉) One of southern Utah's best, with outstanding, highly stylized Southwestern cooking, including vegetarian dishes that burst with flavor. Think stuffed poblano peppers with quinoa and red chili mole (a sauce of complex spices), Mayan tamales and ribs with pomegranate-chipotle glaze. Book ahead.

**Robber's Roost Books
& Beverages**   CAFE

(📞 435-425-3265; www.robbersroostbooks.com; 185 W Main St; snacks $3-6; ☺ 8am-6pm May-Oct; 🖉) Linger over a latte and a scone on comfy couches by the fire at this peaceful cafe-bookstore with bohemian bonhomie.

☆ Entertainment

Entrada Institute   PERFORMING ARTS

(www.entradainstitute.org; ☺ Sat Jun-Aug) This nonprofit has an artist-in-residence program and offers cowboy poetry and other performing arts events, mostly at Robber's Roost Books & Beverages (p177).

Goblin Valley State Park

A Salvador Dalí–esque melted-rock fantasy, a valley of giant stone mushrooms, an otherworldly alien landscape or the results of a cosmological acid trip? No matter what you think the stadium-like valley of stunted hoodoos resembles, one thing's for sure – the 3654-acre **Goblin Valley State Park** (📞 435-275-4584; www.stateparks.utah.gov/parks/goblin-valley; Goblin Valley Rd, off Hwy 24; per car $15; ☺ park 6am-10pm, visitor center 8am-5pm) is just plain fun.

A few trails lead down from the overlooks to the valley floor, but after that there's no path to follow. You can climb down, around and even over the evocative 'goblins' (2ft- to 20ft-tall formations). Kids and photographers especially love it. Its 19-site **campground** (📞 800-322-3770; http://utahstateparks.reserveamerica.com; Green River; tent & RV sites/yurts $30/$100) books up on most weekends. West of the park off Goblin Valley Rd is Bureau of Land Management (BLM) land, with good, free dispersed camping, but no services (stay on designated roads).

To get to Goblin Valley from Capitol Reef's visitor center, follow Hwy 24 east for about 38 miles to Hanksville. From there, head north 19.5 miles. Look for a signed turnoff on the west side of the highway, from where a paved road leads 5 miles west, then 7 miles south to the park's entrance station. **Little Wild Horse Canyon**, 7 miles west of Goblin Valley, is a suitable hike for beginners, offering plenty of serpentine twists that can be combined with a return via Bell Canyon on an 8.2-mile circuit.

Some of Utah's most famous canyoneering routes are found in the area in and around Goblin Valley State Park. The **San Rafael Swell** and **Robber's Roost** areas are top spots for experts. Watch for flash floods, go with a guide if you're a novice, and try not to get lost.

On the west side of Canyonlands, Robber's Roost's Bluejohn Canyon is now one of the most famous canyoneering routes in the world. It gained infamy in 2003, when Aaron Ralston spent 127 hours here pinned to a boulder before finally amputating his arm. His ordeal has been captured in books and the media, as well as in the 2010 movie *127 Hours*. The biggest mistake he made: not telling anybody where he was going.

Canyonlands National Park

Best Hikes

➡ Grand View Point Trail (p186)

➡ Mesa Arch (p184)

➡ Upheaval Dome Overlook Trail (p186)

➡ Aztec Butte Trail (p182)

➡ Slickrock Trail (p186)

➡ Lathrop Canyon (p183)

Best Views

➡ Grand View at Island in the Sky (p186)

➡ Horseshoe Canyon's Great Gallery (p194)

➡ Dead Horse Point State Park (p192)

➡ The Maze (p193)

Why Go?

Rugged, otherworldly, untamed and at times impenetrable, Canyonlands offers up some of the most remote hiking, cycling and rafting in all of Utah's national parks. This is desert solitude at its best.

Scorched red rocks, resplendent layers of sandstone, buttes and sun-crested canyons shape the landscape's curves, while below in the serpentine canyons of the Green and Colorado Rivers, you'll find a wonderworld of gleaming water, forgotten box canyons, foaming white water and delicate desert fauna that blooms ever so daintily with spring rains.

Grand adventures here can last 10 days, while smaller-scale pursuits can be had from the main entrances at the Needles and the aptly named Island in the Sky. Head to the edge of this tortuous rift in the earth's crust - if you look hard enough you might just see the curve of our firmament as it cascades with nonstop momentum to the west.

Driving Distances (miles)

	Canyonlands National Park (North Entrance)	Canyonlands National Park (South Entrance)	Capitol Reef National Park (Visitor Center)	Moab
Canyonlands National Park (South Entrance)	100			
Capitol Reef National Park (Visitor Center)	155	220		
Moab	30	75	145	
Zion National Park (East Entrance)	325	370	180	315

Entrances

The Colorado and Green Rivers divide the park into four separate and distinct areas called 'districts' by the National Park Service (NPS) – the three main areas are Island in the Sky, the Needles and the Maze.

Island in the Sky and the Needles feature visitor centers, developed campgrounds and paved roads to scenic overlooks, as well as dirt roads and hiking trails. The less-visited Maze and Horseshoe Canyon, an unconnected unit northwest of the Maze, offer only 4WD-accessible dirt roads, hiking trails and primitive campgrounds.

No roads cross the park. Instead, well-marked secondary spurs from two major highways access Canyonlands' districts.

Island in the Sky is the most developed district. To get there from Moab, drive north on Hwy 191 about 30 minutes to Hwy 313; both roads are paved.

The Needles District lies about 85 miles (2¼ hours) southwest of Moab via paved Hwys 191 and 211.

The Maze is about 130 miles from Moab (3½ hours), accessible along dirt roads off Hwy 24; take Hwy 191 north to I-70 then west to Hwy 24 south. Horseshoe Canyon also lies off Hwy 24 via dirt roads, about 120 miles (2½ hours) from Moab.

DON'T MISS

Boating Canyonlands is a singular experience that will stay with you for a lifetime. The upper sections of the Green and Colorado Rivers offer flatwater that is perfect for kayaks, canoes and paddleboards. At their confluence, the rivers form Cataract Canyon, one of the gnarliest stretches of Class III to V white water in Utah.

When You Arrive

→ Canyonlands is open year-round.

→ Admission to the Island in the Sky and Needles districts, good for seven days, costs $30/25/15 per car/motorcycle/individual.

→ There is no fee to enter the Maze.

→ Consider purchasing a Southeast Utah Parks Pass ($55), for admission to Arches and Canyonlands National Parks and Natural Bridges and Hovenweep National Monuments for a year.

→ Reserve your backcountry permit in advance through the NPS Backcountry Permits Office (p195).

→ There is no food, gas, firewood or ice in the park.

→ Water is limited, so bring your own.

→ Arrange tours ahead of time with a Moab operator.

PARK POLICIES & REGULATIONS

→ No ATVs allowed. Other 4WD vehicles, mountain bikes and street-legal motorcycles are permitted on dirt roads.

→ Backcountry campfires are allowed only along river corridors; use a fire pan, burn only driftwood or downed tamarisk, and pack out unburned debris.

→ Free or clean-aid rock climbing is allowed, except at archaeological sites or on most named features marked on US Geological Survey (USGS) maps. Check with rangers.

→ New regulations require bear-proof food canisters and human waste removal in some backcountry areas; check with the park for details.

CANYONLANDS NATIONAL PARK

Fast Facts

→ **Total area.** 527 sq miles
→ **Elevation:** 5800ft
→ **Average high/low temperature in July:** 118°F/51°F

Resources

→ **Canyonlands National Park** (www.nps.gov/cany)
→ **Canyonlands Natural History Association** (www.cnha.org)
→ **Friends of Cedar Mesa** (www.friendsofcedarmesa.org)

Canyonlands National Park

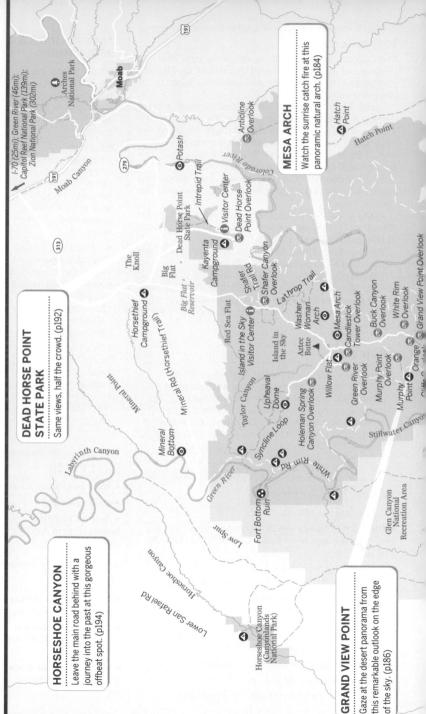

HORSESHOE CANYON

Leave the main road behind with a journey into the past at this gorgeous offbeat spot. (p194)

DEAD HORSE POINT STATE PARK

Same views, half the crowd. (p192)

MESA ARCH

Watch the sunrise catch fire at this panoramic natural arch. (p184)

GRAND VIEW POINT

Gaze at the desert panorama from this remarkable outlook on the edge of the sky. (p86)

I-70 (25mi); Green River (46mi); Capitol Reef National Park (139mi); Zion National Park (302mi)

Moab

Arches National Park

Moab Canyon

Potash

Colorado River

Anticline Overlook

Hatch Point

Hatch Point

Intrepid Trail

Visitor Center

Dead Horse Point Overlook

Dead Horse Point State Park

The Knoll

Big Flat

Big Flat Reservoir

Kayenta Campground

Shafer Trail Rd

Shafer Canyon Overlook

Lathrop Trail

Horsethief Campground

Mineral Rd (Horsethief Trail)

Red Sea Flat

Island in the Sky Visitor Center

Island in the Sky

Washer Woman Arch

Mesa Arch

Candlestick Tower Overlook

Buck Canyon Overlook

White Rim Overlook

Grand View Point Overlook

Mineral Point

Taylor Canyon

Upheaval Dome

Aztec Butte

Willow Flat

Green River Overlook

Murphy Point Overlook

Murphy Point

Orange

Labyrinth Canyon

Mineral Bottom

Syncline Loop

Holeman Spring Canyon Overlook

White Rim Rd

Stillwater Canyon

Green River

Low Spur

Fort Bottom Ruin

Glen Canyon Recreation Area

Lower San Rafael Rd

Horseshoe Canyon

Horseshoe Canyon (Canyonlands National Park)

0   10 km
0   5 miles

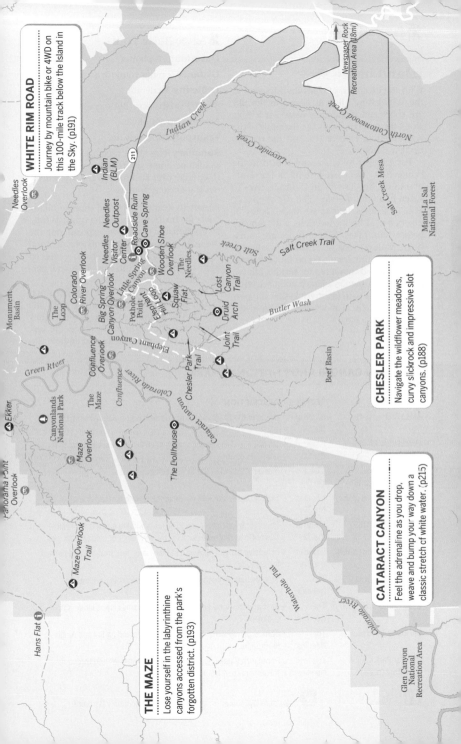

WHITE RIM ROAD

Journey by mountain bike or 4WD on this 100-mile track below the Island in the Sky. (p191)

THE MAZE

Lose yourself in the labyrinthine canyons accessed from the park's forgotten district. (p193)

CHESLER PARK

Navigate the wildflower meadows, curvy slickrock and impressive slot canyons. (p188)

CATARACT CANYON

Feel the adrenaline as you drop, weave and bump your way down a classic stretch of white water. (p215)

Needles Overlook

Indian Creek

Newspaper Rock Recreation Area (18mi)

211

Indian (BLM)

Needles Outpost

Roadside Ruin

Cave Spring

Lavender Creek

North Cottonwood Creek

Salt Creek Mesa

Manti-La Sal National Forest

Needles Visitor Center

Little Spring Canyon

Wooden Shoe Overlook

The Needles

Salt Creek

Salt Creek Trail

Colorado River Overlook

Big Spring Canyon Overlook

Pothole Point

Elephant Hill

Squaw Flat

Lost Canyon Trail

Druid Arch

Butler Wash

Monument Basin

The Loop

Confluence Overlook

Elephant Canyon

Chesler Park Trail

Joint Trail

Beef Basin

Green River

Canyonlands National Park

The Maze

Confluence

Colorado River

Cataract Canyon

Ekker

Maze Overlook

The Dollhouse

Panorama Point Overlook

Maze Overlook Trail

Hans Flat

Waterhole Flat

Colorado River

Glen Canyon National Recreation Area

🚶 DAY HIKES

Island in the Sky

With the exception of trails that descend to the White Rim, hikes at Island in the Sky are short and moderately easy. For a hike along the mesa top, walk the first mile of the west-trending **Wilhite Trail**, off the road to Upheaval Dome.

For a longer hike, descend 1000ft to the White Rim. The easiest route is the **Murphy Loop**, but it's still an 11.3-mile, five- to seven-hour round-trip. The **Gooseberry Trail** (5.4 miles, four to six hours) is for fit hikers only. Check conditions with rangers before long hikes. Where trails are indistinct, walk on rock or in sandy washes to avoid damaging fragile cryptobiotic crusts.

Canyonlands has a rep for serious hiking, but Island in the Sky offers a good selection of short trails with great vistas that are perfect for families. For a workout, do a few easy hikes in a day.

🚶 Aztec Butte Trail

Duration 1–1½ hours

Distance 2 miles round-trip

Difficulty Moderate

Start/Finish Aztec Butte trailhead

Nearest Town Moab

Transportation Private

Summary This short ascent of a Navajo sandstone dome yields stellar views; it's a steep hike over slickrock to the top. Check out the ancient granaries.

Be sure to wear rubber-soled shoes or hiking boots for traction. Stay on the trails, as fragile cryptobiotic crust is widespread atop the dome. In summer bring plenty of water and wear a wide-brimmed hat, as the exposed butte offers no shade. In winter the trail may be icy and impassable.

The first half-mile cuts across grassland to the base of the dome. Cairns mark the ascent. The second half-mile is moderately strenuous. The butte levels off at the top, revealing panoramic views and endless sky.

HIKING IN CANONLANDS NATIONAL PARK

NAME	REGION	DESCRIPTION
Mesa Arch (p184)	Island in the Sky	Island in the Sky's most famous arch is gorgeous at sunrise.
Grand View Point Trail (p186)	Island in the Sky	No place in Canyonlands offers such a sweeping view; watch for passing condors.
Upheaval Dome Overlook Trail (p186)	Island in the Sky	Marvel at Island in the Sky's geologic mystery.
Aztec Butte Trail (p182)	Island in the Sky	Skitter up slickrock to an ancient Native American granary.
Neck Spring (p183)	Island in the Sky	This solitary stream canyon attracts wildlife and fills with wildflowers in springtime; look for the remnants of pioneer ranching.
Lathrop Canyon (p183)	Island in the Sky	Extensive canyon hike with stellar views; less trodden and perfect for solitude.
Pothole Point Trail (p189)	The Needles	Stop by natural potholes to spot tiny swimming organisms.
Cave Spring Trail (p187)	The Needles	Past an abandoned cowboy camp, this trail climbs ladders up slickrock.
Slickrock Trail (p186)	The Needles	Semiloop trail with views of the Needles and La Sal and Abajo Mountains.
Chesler Park Loop & Joint Trail (p188)	The Needles	Popular trek passing grasslands and pinnacles and threading through narrow fractures.

  Views   *Wildlife Watching*   *Backcountry Camping*

Look for the small, ancient **granary**, evidence of an Ancestral Puebloan culture, a likely precursor to modern-day Hopis and Zunis. A small spur trail leads to more ruins. This is the only archaeological site at Island in the Sky.

🥾 Neck Spring

Duration 2½ hours

Distance 6 miles round-trip

Difficulty Moderate

Start/Finish Shafer Canyon Overlook parking area

Nearest Town Moab

Transportation Private

Summary Good for solitude seekers, this stream canyon attracts wildlife and fills with wildflowers in springtime. Look for the remnants of pioneer ranching.

Perhaps because it isn't cliffside, this loop trail attracts fewer hikers. Following the sign in the **Shafer Canyon Overlook parking area**, it crosses the street and descends Taylor Canyon to Neck and Cabin Springs. The initial trail is an old roadbed built in the 1800s by ranchers to bring livestock to water. Hitching posts, water troughs and pipes are still visible (please leave them in place).

Descending slightly, the trail reaches **Neck Spring**. If you stay quiet here, you may see animals (mule deer, chipmunks and bighorn sheep) approaching for a drink. The moisture makes it an ideal climate for Gambel oak, maidenhair fern and Fremont barberry.

Leaving the alcoves, start to climb to white sand hills before reaching **Cabin Spring**, with a cabin, troughs and corrals near the site. A short, steep ascent climbs over sandstone. Follow the cairns to the mesa top, where the trail crosses the main road and continues 0.5 miles along the rim of Shafer Canyon to the parking lot.

🥾 Lathrop Canyon

Duration 2½ hours–2 days

Distance 5 miles to rim, 22 miles to Colorado River

DIFFICULTY	DURATION	ROUND-TRIP DISTANCE	ELEVATION CHANGE	FEATURES	FACILITIES
easy	30min	0.5 miles	100ft		
easy	1-1½hr	2 miles	50ft		
easy-moderate	1-1½hr	0.8-1.8 miles	50-200ft		
moderate	1-1½hr	2 miles	225ft		
moderate	2½hr	6 miles	300ft		
moderate	2½hr-2 days	5-22 miles	2100ft		
easy	45min	0.6 miles	20ft		
easy-moderate	30-45min	0.6 miles	50ft		
easy-moderate	1½-2hr	2.4 miles	70ft		
moderate-difficult	1-2 days	11 miles	520ft		

Great for Families   *Picnic Facilities*

Island In The Sky – Day Hikes

N
0 — 5 km
0 — 2.5 miles

Island in the Sky
Visitor Center
Neck Spring
Shafer Canyon
Overlook
The Neck
Second Overlook — First Overlook
Upheaval Dome
Island in
the Sky   Grays
Pasture
Wilhite Trail
Aztec Butte
Holeman Spring
Basin   Mesa
Arch   White Rim Rd
White Rim Rd
Canyonlands
National Park   Colorado River
Green River

— Aztec Butte Trail
— Grand View Point Trail
— Lathrop Canyon
— Mesa Arch
— Neck Spring
— Upheaval Dome Overlook Trail

Grand View Point — Grand View Point
Overlook

Difficulty Moderate

Start/Finish Lathrop Canyon trailhead

Nearest Town Moab

Transportation Private

Summary An extensive hike into the canyon with stellar views. For an easy stroll, consider an out-and-back trip to the rim. Less trodden than other trails, it's perfect for solitude.

A ranger favorite, Lathrop Canyon is one of the few longer trails in this district. If short on time, hike out to the canyon rim for views of the Colorado River and La Sal Mountains.

Follow the level sandy singletrack through the grasslands. It passes over undulating slickrock marked by cairns. Canyon views start here, including a glimpse of a gorgeous bend in the Colorado.

The trail returns to sandy paths and twists along the canyon rim. It then descends steep switchbacks to a boulder-strewn wash that leads to **White Rim Road**. Hikers can follow the spur road down into **Lathrop Canyon**, a descent of 2100ft. Three at-large permits are available for camping below White Rim Rd.

Mesa Arch

Duration 30 minutes

Distance 0.5 miles one way

Difficulty Easy

Start/Finish Mesa Arch trailhead

Nearest Town Moab

Transportation Private

Summary This easy trail leads to Canyonlands' most photographed arch, one of the best places to watch the sunrise – though don't expect to be alone.

As you ascend, notice the trailside cryptobiotic soil, riddled with bubbly minicanyon systems. This is among the healthiest soil of its kind in the park.

A moderately easy walk up a gentle rise brings you to the **arch**, an elegant sweep of Navajo sandstone that dramatically frames the La Sal Mountains. A thousand feet below, the basin extends in layers of red, brown, green and tan. Look carefully in the near distance to spot a narrow green strip of the **Colorado River**. To your left, through the arch, search atop the red spires for **Washer Woman Arch** (so named for its resemblance to a crouching laundress).

BACKPACKING & OVERNIGHT TRIPS

The Needles (p193) is the top district for backpackers. Overnighters might also consider a river trip or a bike tour on the White Rim Rd. Intrepid adventurers can head off into the Maze, or might consider canyoneering near Robber's Roost.

Island in the Sky

Aside from White Rim Rd, which is mostly a biking route, there's just one major backpacking route in the district: the **Syncline Loop** (8.3 miles, five to seven hours), a primitive route requiring some navigational skills. If you're fascinated by Upheaval Dome, or would like a closer look at the Green River, this is a perfect route with lots of places to camp. Since the trail is largely exposed, it gets blazing hot in summer.

Rangers consider this a route and not a trail – the difference is that you will have to pay close attention in places to stay on the path. In fact, most park rescues occur along this stretch, primarily because day hikers underestimate the trail, get turned around and/or run out of water. Pay close attention to trail markers. You'll need a permit to stay overnight.

The Needles

The Needles' popularity can make it difficult to obtain one of the limited-issue backcountry permits necessary for an overnight hike.

In addition to the Chesler Park Loop and Joint Trail (p186), consider the **Confluence Overlook Trail**, a moderate four- to six-hour round-trip hike from the Big Spring Canyon trailhead, from where you can watch the Green River flow into the Colorado – one or the other river may be silty or muddy depending on recent rainfall. Many other hikes connect in a series of loops, some requiring route-finding skills. Among the best are the **Big Spring Canyon** and **Lost Canyon trails**. For gorgeous scenery, the **Elephant Canyon Trail to Druid Arch** is hard to beat. Rock art along the **Salt Creek Canyon Trail** is very much worth a look.

Permits

In addition to the park entrance fee, permits are required for overnight backpacking, mountain biking, 4WD trips and river trips. Designated camp areas abut most trails; open-zone camping is permitted in some places. Horses are allowed on all 4WD trails. Permits are valid for 14 days and are issued at the visitor center or ranger station where your trip begins. Reservations are available online through the NPS Backcountry Permits Office (p195). A few space-available permits may be available same-day, but advanced reservations are essential for spring and fall trips. Costs:

Backpackers $30 per group of seven

General mountain bike or 4WD day-use $30 for up to three vehicles

Needles Area 4WD day-use $10 per vehicle

River trips $30 reservation plus $20 per person fee

Safety Tips & Regulations

➡ Drink at least one gallon of water each day. Water is limited in the backcountry.

➡ Always carry a topo map, adequate clothing and flashlight.

➡ Always tell someone where you are going and when you expect to be back.

➡ Watch for flash floods.

➡ During a lightning storm avoid lone trees and high ridges.

➡ Protect cryptobiotic soil crusts by staying on trails and roads, or by walking on slickrock or washes.

➡ Permits are required for all overnight backcountry trips.

➡ You have to tote your own poop from some campsites. In others, you'll bury it in a 6in hole at least 300ft from a water source.

Resist the temptation to climb on the arch. Climbing is prohibited on most features named on USGS maps. Anyway, the sheer drop below will surely give you a case of the butterflies. Scamper up the rocks for a look down on the arch.

🏃 Upheaval Dome Overlook Trail

Duration 1–1½ hours

Distance 0.8–1.8 miles

Difficulty Easy–moderate

Start/Finish Upheaval Dome parking area

Nearest Town Moab

Transportation Private

Summary With views of a crater and upheaval canyon, this mysterious destination is debated to be the site of a meteor collision or just a strange geological feature.

This trail leads to overlooks of Upheaval Dome, one of the park's great geologic mysteries. Scientists disagree over how the feature formed – some suggest it's a collapsed salt dome, while others posit it was the site of a meteorite strike some 60 million years ago. Looking more like a mound of gray sand, the dome rests in a depression – one doesn't look up to it, but down on it, like a belly button.

It's an easy 0.4 miles to the first overlook. From the parking area, climb to the fork in the trail, bear right and ascend the slickrock to the **viewpoint**. If you find yourself on switchbacks, you've made a wrong turn.

To reach the second **overlook**, return to the fork in the trail and bear left, clambering over slickrock to a final steep descent. Here you'll have a broader panorama of the surrounding landscape. If you're pressed for time, skip the second vantage point. Otherwise, the afternoon light here is magnificent.

🏃 Grand View Point Trail

Duration 1–1½ hours

Distance 2 miles

Difficulty Easy

Start/Finish Grand View Point parking area

Nearest Town Moab

Transportation Private

Summary Easily earned panoramic views from the cliff's edge to the broad mesa below and wide desert beyond; follow cairns and keep to the rocks.

After marveling at 100-mile views from the roadside observation area, take this easy stroll to the point itself for a better perspective of the massive mesa underfoot. Review the interpretive panels for interesting background. To the right of the panels, the trail descends stone steps to a fairly level, easy walk along the exposed rim – watch the little ones!

To the south, scan the skies over Junction Butte for the peregrine falcons that nest atop it.

Scramble atop the rocks at trail's end for spectacular views. The Needles' namesake spires rise to the south, while off to the west lie the Henry Mountains (on Capitol Reef's eastern flank) and distant Boulder Mountain (eastern terminus of the Aquarius Plateau and top step of the Grand Staircase). Glance below to spot the chalky sandstone of White Rim and the placid Green River. If storm clouds start to roll in, particularly from the west, quickly return to your car.

The Needles

Taken collectively, these trails offer an overview of the region's human and geologic history. Unfortunately, none are wheelchair accessible, but you can take on most of them in a day. Cairns often mark sections across slickrock.

If you like long day hikes, the Needles also includes easily accessible backcountry treks you can do in a day.

One quick easy hike is the **Roadside Ruin Trail**, a 0.3-mile loop that takes 30 minutes to walk. It starts out across uneven gravel and finishes over slickrock. Look for a remarkably well-preserved Ancestral Puebloan granary tucked into a gap in the slickrock. If you're here in late spring, keep an eye out for blooming yucca. Otherwise, consider taking the Cave Spring or the Pothole Point trails.

🏃 Slickrock Trail

Duration 1½–2 hours

Distance 2.4 miles

Difficulty Easy–moderate

The Needles – Day Hikes

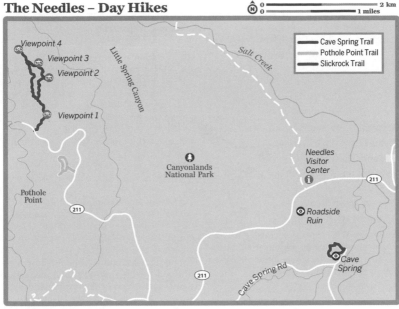

Cave Spring Trail
Pothole Point Trail
Slickrock Trail

Start/Finish Slickrock trailhead

Nearest Town Monticello

Transportation Private

Summary This ridgeline trail is high above the canyons with views below. After ascending gentle switchbacks to slickrock, you'll follow cairns. This semiloop trail is tricky to follow in places.

Brochures available at the trailhead describe four main viewpoints, each marked by a numbered signpost. Keep an eye out during your hike – bighorn sheep are occasionally seen here.

If you're short on time, at least visit Viewpoint 1 for a panorama you simply can't get from the road. Giant red cliffs hang like curtains below high buttes and mesas, the district's namesake needles touch the sky, and the La Sal and Abajo Mountains lord over the whole scene.

Bear right at the 'Begin Loop' signpost to reach Viewpoint 2, where hearty vegetation clings to the desert crust and lines the watercourses. Scamper up the rocks for a primo view. At Viewpoint 3 giant boulders ring Lower Little Spring Canyon, where purple and gray rock layers offer telltale evidence of an ancient shallow sea.

Viewpoint 4 is a high promontory that overlooks Big Spring Canyon, a vast rugged gorge. Watch overhead for birds soaring on thermals. To the north you'll spot Grand View Point at Island in the Sky, perched high atop the red Wingate sandstone cliffs.

On the return path you'll face the needles and spires to the south that define this district. The Abajo Mountains lie beyond.

Cave Spring Trail

Duration 30–45 minutes

Distance 0.6-mile loop

Difficulty Easy-moderate

Start/Finish Cave Spring trailhead

Nearest Town Monticello

Transportation Private

Summary Kids love this short hike for the cowboy artifacts, ladders and slickrock scampers. There are also prehistoric pictographs to view.

Pungent sagebrush marks this trailhead at the end of a well-maintained, mile-long dirt road. Hikers will first reach an abandoned cowboy camp with miscellaneous remnants left by cowboys in the 19th and 20th

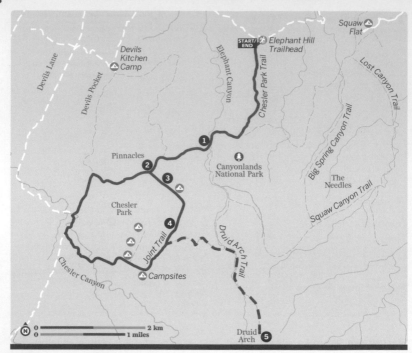

Overnight Hike
Chesler Park Loop & Joint Trail

DURATION 1–2 DAYS
DISTANCE 11-MILE LOOP
DIFFICULTY MODERATE OVERNIGHT HIKE,
MODERATE–DIFFICULT DAY HIKE
START/FINISH ELEPHANT HILL TRAILHEAD
NEAREST TOWN MONTICELLO
TRANSPORTATION PRIVATE

With ample ups and downs, this loop gives great perspective on the Needles.

Among Canyonlands' most popular backcountry treks, these combined routes cross desert grasslands, pass striped pinnacles and thread through tall hairline fractures. Though the trails aren't flat, elevation changes are mild and infrequent. You won't find any water. For most hikers, the *Trails Illustrated Needles District* map ($10) should suffice, but if you're inclined to wander, carry a 7.5-minute USGS map.

Park at the Elephant Hill trailhead, 3 miles from Squaw Flat Campground via a gravel 2WD road. From the parking area, the trail climbs to a bench, then undulates over slickrock toward rock spires. The next section is typically where people make a wrong turn. Cross the wash at the T-junction and follow signs to Chesler Park (*not* Druid Arch), descending 300ft along switchbacks into **1 Elephant Canyon**. Continue to follow signs along the canyon floor.

The final 0.2 miles to the **2 Chesler Park Viewpoint** climbs 100ft, topping out on the rocky pass amid spires 2.9 miles from the trailhead. This marks the beginning of the 5-mile **3 Chesler Park Loop**. Five campsites lie southeast of the junction.

The next morning, leave your backpack at the campsite and explore the claustrophobia-inducing **4 Joint Trail**, where the fractured rock narrows to 2ft across in places; the trail junction lies to the south, about midway around the Chesler Park Loop. Pause just east of the Joint Trail for stellar views of the towering pinnacles. On the southwest section of the loop, you'll follow a half-mile stretch of a 4WD road. If staying two nights, take the side trip to **5 Druid Arch**.

centuries. The trail continues beneath a protruding rock lip, then through 6ft sagebrush to **Cave Spring**, one of few perennial water sources in the Needles. Look for the rust-colored pictographs painted on these walls more than 1000 years ago.

From Cave Spring you'll climb **two ladders** up the slickrock for wraparound views of rock formations, steppes and mesas. The trail has awesome views of rock spires and the La Sal Mountains.

After crossing the undulating sandstone, the trail drops into a wash and returns to the trailhead.

🚶 Pothole Point Trail

Duration 45 minutes

Distance 0.6-mile loop

Difficulty Easy

Start/Finish Pothole Point trailhead

Nearest Town Monticello

Transportation Private

Summary This short loop across slickrock explores the microcosmic ecosystems of potholes. It features views of distant cliffs, mountains and rock formations similar to those along the Slickrock Trail.

The slickrock along this trail features naturally occurring dimples that collect water during rainstorms. To the naked eye, these potholes appear to be nothing more than mud puddles, but closer inspection reveals tiny organisms that must complete their life cycles before the water evaporates. Keep hands and feet out of the potholes, since these organisms are fragile. Though this is an excellent walk for contemplative souls and the scientifically inclined, it does lack drama, unless the potholes are teeming with life (which isn't always readily visible). Acrophobes, take heart: you won't have to stroll beside any cliffs.

🚗 DRIVING

Island in the Sky

Two main roads cross the mesa top at Island in the Sky, forming a Y. The Island In the Sky Visitor Center and entrance station sit atop the northeast arm of the Y, Grand View Point is at the foot of the Y, and Upheaval Dome caps the northwest arm.

One primary 4WD route, the White Rim Rd, loops around the district about 1000ft below the mesa top.

🚗 Grand View Point Scenic Drive

Duration 50 minutes

Distance 12 miles

Start Visitor center

Finish Grand View Point

Nearest Town Moab

This is a classic meander down the park's main road (paved) on a mesa top surrounded by cliffs and steep escarpments.

About 0.5 miles south of the visitor center, pull off to the left at the **Shafer Canyon Overlook**, where you can peer down 1000ft. Below is Shafer Trail Rd, the steep access route to the 4WD White Rim Rd.

A quarter-mile ahead you'll cross the **Neck** (slow down for great views), where the ridge narrows to 40ft across – eventually this strip will erode away, further isolating the mesa. The road levels out as it crosses **Grays Pasture**, where you might spot a bighorn sheep.

Just past Grays Pasture, take the left turn for **Mesa Arch**. Doing the easy hike to this arch is worth every step – especially at sunrise when its underside glows a fiery red. The road to Upheaval Dome bears right here.

A mile past the arch, pull off on the right to take in the sheer walls of **Candlestick Tower**. Visible to the southwest is the **Maze** and its many fins and canyons, all capped with white and orange horizontal lines.

Continue 1.5 miles to a turnout for the **Murphy Loop**. From the stunning overlook you'll see more of the Maze and the snaking Green River. The trail forks left just before the overlook.

Back on the road, 0.5 miles further on the left, take the paved walkway to the **Buck Canyon Overlook** for spectacular views of the La Sal Mountains. Another 1.8 miles south is the **White Rim Overlook**, a good picnic spot and starting point for the **White Rim Overlook Trail**, an easy 1.2-mile round-trip hike.

Three-quarters of a mile down the road, just before Grand View Point, the **Orange Cliffs Overlook** offers views west to the

DON'T MISS

NEWSPAPER ROCK

This tiny recreation area, known as **Newspaper Rock State Historic Monument** (Hwy 211, Monticello), showcases a single large sandstone rock panel packed with more than 300 petroglyphs attributed to Ute and Ancestral Puebloan groups during a 2000-year period. The many red rock figures etched out of a black 'desert varnish' surface make for great photos. It's located 50 miles south of Moab, east of Canyonlands National Park on Hwy 211.

Henry Mountains, the last-charted mountain range in the Lower 48. The Orange Cliffs lie southwest, beyond the Maze. Come at sunset when the canyons glow orange in the waning light.

Five hundred feet ahead, the drive ends at Grand View Point, with one of the Southwest's most sweeping views, rivaled only by the Grand Canyon and nearby Dead Horse Point. In the foreground to the southeast, Monument Basin contains spires similar to those in the Needles; to see them, look south. To spot the Maze, follow the Green River from the northwest to the Confluence, where it meets the Colorado. West of the Confluence, the Doll House formations mark the edge of the Maze and the head of Cataract Canyon, one of North America's most intense stretches of white water.

Stand beside the interpretive panel at the overlook and look down at the rock – the south-facing gashes occurred when lightning struck a man here in 2003 (he lived). Off to your right is the Grand View Point Trail.

🚗 Upheaval Dome
Scenic Drive

Duration 30 minutes

Distance 5 miles one way

Start Spur Junction, 6 miles south of the visitor center

Finish Upheaval Dome

Nearest Town Moab

In a few miles, this drive packs in the sights. Visit an ancient granary and peer down on the snaking Green River. Rock scrambling and crater gazing prove a hit with kids.

At the Spur Junction 6 miles south of the visitor center, turn northwest. A quarter-mile from the junction, turn left and drive to the Green River Overlook and Willow Flat Campground. Walk to the overlook for views of the Green River, Orange Cliffs and Henry Mountains. The small mesas in the foreground bear the marks of flash-flood erosion.

Large piñon trees around the parking area are 300 to 400 years old, while most of the blackbrush is more than 100 years old. The hardest thing for such desert plants is simply taking root. Nothing is growing on the parking-lot island, nor is anything likely to for another 50 years. Water and cryptobiotic crust make all the difference by providing nitrogen and a foothold for plants.

Back on the main road, 0.5 miles further on the right, pull over at the Aztec Butte Viewpoint and Trail. Above the parking area is a granary built by Ancestral Puebloans.

About 2 miles ahead on the left (past a twisty section of road), you'll reach Holeman Spring Canyon Overlook, the only point along this drive that offers long views west across the Green River. A mile further, stop at the Whale Rock Viewpoint and Trail. Named for its smooth slickrock hump, Whale Rock lies at the end of an easy, mile-long round-trip hike that gains only 100ft. The path is exposed, so use the handrails.

Three-quarters of a mile ahead, the road ends at the Upheaval Dome parking lot and picnic area. To see the dome, stroll the short trail from the parking area.

The Needles

Be aware that storms wash out roads periodically and any road may be in poor condition. If the weather's been bad, check conditions at the visitor center before heading out.

🚗 Big Spring
Canyon Overlook

Duration 30 minutes

Distance 6.4 miles

Start The Needles Visitor Center

Finish Big Spring Canyon Overlook

Nearest Town Monticello

Grand View Pt & Upheaval Dome Scenic Drives

0 ━━ 2 km
0 ━━ 1 miles

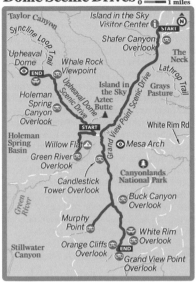

Lovely at sunset, this short spurt goes by cool rock formations and slickrock to finish with gaping canyon views. The road is paved and well maintained. You can bike it, but be careful as the shoulder of the road is narrow.

Stop first at the Roadside Ruin (0.25 miles from the visitor center) and stroll the easy 0.3-mile loop trail to this ancient granary.

Unless you're bound for the 0.6-mile Cave Spring Trail, bear right at the fork in the road and pull over at the Wooden Shoe Overlook, on your left. Scan the cliffs overhead for the namesake rock formation with a tiny arch at its base.

Pass the turnoff for the campground and continue across the wide, even terrain of Squaw Flat. Two miles ahead on the left is a picnic area with shaded tables. The 0.6-mile Pothole Point Trail starts from the small parking lot just west of the picnic area. From here the road curls around the point to the moderately easy 2.4-mile Slickrock Trail.

Just past this trailhead, the road dead ends at the Big Spring Canyon Overlook. Park along the road and walk out on the rocks for a peek into the shallow canyons. Above the rocks rise 100ft formations that look as though they're made of whitish pet-

rified sand dunes. To see the rock spires at Big Spring Canyon Overlook in the best light, visit in the morning – in the afternoon, the sun drops behind them.

🏃 OTHER ACTIVITIES

River rafting, kayaking and canoeing are also possible on the Green and Colorado Rivers. Book trips through Moab agencies.

Island in the Sky

🏃 Four-Wheel Driving & Mountain Biking

Blazed by uranium prospectors in the early 1950s, primitive White Rim Rd circles Island in the Sky. Accessible from the visitor center via steep Shafer Trail Rd, the 70-mile route is the top choice for 4WD and mountain-biking trips. It generally takes two to three days to travel the loop in a 4WD vehicle, or three to four days by bike. As the route lacks any water sources, cyclists should team up with a 4WD support vehicle (there are 4WD rentals in Moab) or travel with an outfitter.

The park service limits the number of motorized vehicles. If you arrive without an overnight permit, call the visitor center about possible cancellations or no-shows. Rangers regularly patrol the route to check permits. Always stay on trails. No ATVs are allowed.

To learn more about the White Rim, pick up *A Naturalist's Guide to the White Rim Trail*, by David Williams and Damian Fagon.

🏃 Kids' Activities

When you arrive at the park, stop by the visitor center (p195) to pick up a Junior Ranger Activity Guide. Once kids complete certain activities, they can return to the visitor center to receive a special certificate and badge from a ranger.

Kids particularly like the Whale Rock and Mesa Arch trails, both easy walks with big payoffs. Keep an eye on your little ones, especially near overlooks, which are often unfenced.

🏃 Ranger Programs

For information about park attractions and insight on its human and geologic history, attend a ranger-led program. April through October, rangers give daily talks at Grand View Point at 10:30am and 11:30am. Talks are given daily at the visitor center at 10:30am and 1:30pm. For additions, check schedules at the visitor center.

The Needles

🏃 Four-Wheel Driving & Mountain Biking

Fifty miles of 4WD and mountain-biking roads crisscross the Needles. Stay on designated routes. Motorists and cyclists must obtain a permit for overnight trips, but not for day-use with the exception of Lavender and Horse Canyons, which require a $5 day-use permit fee; book in advance or check at the visitor center for cancellations, no-shows or leftovers.

All 4WD roads in the Needles require high-clearance vehicles (many off-the-lot SUVs do *not* have high clearance; AWD is not sufficient). Know what you're doing before you set out, or risk damaging your vehicle and/or endangering yourself. Tow-

ing fees can run to about $1000. If you're renting a 4WD vehicle, check the insurance policy; you might not be covered here. For more information, including 4WD routes and road conditions, check with a ranger when you book your permit. No ATVs are allowed.

Several 4WD and mountain-biking trails – formerly cattle roads – lead into the backcountry. **Elephant Hill** is the most technically challenging route in the district, with steep grades and tight turns. The route to the **Colorado River Overlook** is usually moderate in a vehicle and moderately easy on a mountain bike; check at the visitor center first since all conditions are possible. You will want to park and walk the final, steep 1.5-mile descent to the overlook. Following the district's main drainage, the **Salt Creek Trail** is moderately easy for vehicles, but sand makes it not recommended for bikes.

🏃 Kids' Activities

When you arrive at the park, stop by the Needles Visitor Center to pick up a **Junior**

DEAD HORSE POINT STATE PARK

The views at **Dead Horse Point** (☏435-259-2614; https://stateparks.utah.gov/parks/dead-horse/; Hwy 313; park day-use per vehicle $20, tent/RV sites $35/40; ⊙ park 6am-10pm, visitor center 9am-5pm) pack a wallop, extending 2000ft below to the meandering Colorado River, 12,700ft up to the La Sal Mountains and 100 miles across Canyonlands' stairstep landscape. If you thrive on epic landscapes, you won't regret a side trip here.

The turnoff to Dead Horse is on Hwy 313, just 4 miles north of Island in the Sky (Moab is 30 miles away). Toward the end of the drive, the road traverses a narrow ridge just 30yd across. Ranchers once herded horses across these narrows – some were forgotten and left to die, hence the park name. A rough footpath skirts the point for views in all directions. To escape the small (but sometimes chatty) crowds, take one of the short hikes that rim the mesa. Visit at dawn or sunset for the best lighting.

The **visitor center** (☏435-259-2614; http://stateparks.utah.gov/parks/dead-horse; ⊙9am-5pm) features exceptionally good exhibits, shows on-demand videos, and sells books and maps. Rangers lead walks and talks in summer. South of the visitor center, the 21-site **Kayenta Campground** (☏800-322-3770; https://stateparks.utah.gov/parks/dead-horse/the-kayenta-campground/; tent sites/yurts $40/140) provides limited water and a dump station, but no hookups. Reservations are accepted from March to October, but you can often secure same-day sites by arriving early. Fill RVs with water in Moab. Three yurts offer incredible views of the surrounding wilderness.

Mountain bikers should check out the **Intrepid Trail**, an excellent 9-mile singletrack on the rim with great views. Rare for the Moab area, it's flat, so is good for beginners, but its twists and turns keep riders on their toes. Another advantage – at 6000ft it can be cooler than riding in the bottom of a canyon on a hot day. The plateau is known to be 10°F cooler.

Pets are OK on a leash on all hiking trails but not on the Intrepid Trail for bikes.

Ranger Activity Guide. Once kids complete certain activities, they can return to the visitor center to receive a special certificate and badge from a ranger.

Ask at the visitor center about renting a **Master Explorer Day Pack**, which contains binoculars, a magnifying lens and nature guide. Kids especially like the Cave Spring Trail.

🏃 Ranger Programs

From March through October, rangers lead evening campfire discussions. Check schedules at the visitor center when you arrive in the park.

⊙ SIGHTS

Island in the Sky   AREA
(☑ 435-719-2313;   www.nps.gov/cany/planyour visit/islandinthesky.htm;   Canyonlands National Park; vehicle/cyclist $25/10) You'll comprehend space in new ways atop the appropriately named Island in the Sky. This 6000ft-high flat-topped mesa drops precipitously on all sides, providing some of the longest, most enthralling vistas of any park in southern Utah. The 11,500ft Henry Mountains bookend panoramic views in the west, and the 12,700ft La Sal Mountains are to the east. Here you can stand beneath a sparkling blue sky and watch thunderheads inundating far-off regions while you contemplate applying more sunscreen.

The island sits atop a sandstone bench called the **White Rim**, which indeed forms a white border 1200ft below the red mesa top and 1500ft above the river canyon bottom. An impressive 4WD road descends from the overlook level.

The complimentary video at the visitor center (p195) provides great insight into the nature of the park. Remember to keep your park entry receipt – admission to Island in the Sky includes entry to Needles, too.

Overlooks and trails line each road. Most trails at least partially follow cairns over slickrock. Bring lots of water and watch for cliff edges!

The Needles   AREA
(☑ 435-719-2313;   www.nps.gov/cany/planyour visit/needles.htm;   Canyonlands National Park; vehicle/cyclist $25/10) Named for the spires

of orange-and-white sandstone jutting skyward from the desert floor, the Needles District is so different from Island in the Sky that it's hard to believe they're both in the same national park. The Needles receives only half as many visitors as the Island since it's more remote – though only 90 minutes from Moab – and there are fewer roadside attractions (but most are well worth the hike).

The payoff is huge: peaceful solitude and the opportunity to participate in, not just observe, the vastness of canyon country. Morning light is best for viewing the rock spires.

Needles Visitor Center (p195) lies 2.5 miles inside the park boundaries and provides drinking water. Hold on to your receipt: admission includes entry to Island in the Sky.

GPS has limited reception and is best used in conjunction with a map. Likewise, cell phones rarely have reception here. Credit card–operated pay phones outside the visitor center can be used at any hour.

The Maze   AREA
(☑ 435-719-2313;   www.nps.gov/cany/planyour visit/maze.htm;   Canyonlands National Park) A 30-sq-mile jumble of high-walled canyons, the Maze is a rare preserve of true wilderness for hardy backcountry veterans. The colorful canyons are rugged, deep and sometimes completely inaccessible. Many of them look alike and it's easy to get turned around – hence the district's name. (Think topographic maps and GPS.) Rocky roads absolutely necessitate reliable, high-clearance 4WD vehicles. Plan on spending at least three days, though a week is ideal.

If you're at all inexperienced with four-wheel driving, stay away. Be prepared to repair your 4WD and, at times, the road. There may not be enough money on the planet to get you towed out of here. Most wreckers won't even try.

Predeparture, always contact the Hans Flat Ranger Station (p195) for conditions and advice. The station is 136 miles (3½ hours) from Moab, and has a few books and maps, but no other services. Take Hwy 191 north, I-70 west, and then Hwy 24 south. Hans Flat is 16 miles south of Horseshoe Canyon. The few roads into the district are

BEARS EARS NATIONAL MONUMENT

A landscape of lonely desert mesas, dizzying canyon trails and washed-out arroyos, Bears Ears is the youngest national monument in Utah. The area protects tens of thousands of culturally significant sites for Native Americans in the Four Corners, including ancient pictographs, petroglyphs, cliff dwellings, kivas and granaries.

Created in 2016, Bears Ears covers a 1.35-million-acre swath of southeastern Utah, co-managed by the BLM, the Forest Service and five Native tribes. However, in late 2017, just one year after it was formed, the Trump administration controversially submitted a proposal to shrink the national monument by 85%, dividing it into two unconnected parcels: Shash Jáa and Indian Creek. At the time of research, the changes were the subject of pending court cases.

If you visit, you will be largely on your own – there is little to no infrastructure in the park or, indeed, this corner of Utah in general. Make sure you take more water and food than you think you'll need, topo maps, cash for permits, binoculars and a full tank of gas. If you do not have experience navigating the Utah backcountry, think twice before venturing this way. A high-clearance 4WD vehicle is advisable for many of the dirt roads in the area.

Cedar Mesa is the heart of the region, and canyons to explore include Grand Gulch, Slickhorn, Mule and Butler Wash, accessed off Hwys 261 and 95. Further north near the Canyonlands Needles District is Indian Creek, whose challenging sandstone cracks are legendary among rock climbers. If visiting Cedar Mesa, get permits and information at **Kane Gulch Ranger Station** (www.blm.gov/visit/kane-gulch-ranger-station; Hwy 261; day/overnight permit $2/8; ⊙8am-noon Mar–mid-June & Sep-Oct) or the **Monticello BLM office** (☑435-587-1510; 435 N Main St; ⊙7:45am-noon & 1-4:30pm Mon-Fri). Be sure to visit www.friendsofcedarmesa.org to learn more about how to be a respectful visitor in this sacred area.

poor and often closed with rain or snow; bring tire chains from October to April.

The **Maze Overlook Trail** requires that hikers carry at least a 25ft length of rope to raise and lower packs. Camping is at-large, and you'll find several reliable water sources (ask a ranger for locations). You can drive a 2WD vehicle to the North Point Rd junction, 2.5 miles south of Hans Flat, then hike 15 miles to the Maze Overlook.

Horseshoe Canyon   ARCHAEOLOGICAL SITE
(☑435-719-2313; www.nps.gov/cany/planyourvisit/horseshoecanyon.htm; Canyonlands National Park) Way far west of Island in the Sky (p193), Horseshoe Canyon shelters one of the most impressive collections of millennia-old rock art in the Southwest. The centerpiece is the **Great Gallery** and its haunting Barrier Canyon–style pictographs from between 2000 BC and AD 500. The heroic, bigger-than-life-size figures are magnificent. Artifacts recovered here date back as far as 9000 BC.

That said, it's not easy to get to. The gallery lies at the end of a 6.5-mile round-trip hiking trail descending 750ft from a dirt road. Plan on six hours. Rangers lead hikes here on Saturday and Sunday from April through October; contact the Hans Flat Ranger Station for times. You can camp on Bureau of Land Management (BLM) land at the trailhead, though it's really a parking lot. There is a single vault toilet, but no water.

From Moab the trip is about 120 miles (2¾ hours). Take Hwy 191 north to I-70 west, then Hwy 24 south. About 25 miles south of I-70, past the turnoff for Goblin Valley State Park, turn east and follow the gravel road 30 miles. Hanksville is 45 miles (1½ hours).

🛏 SLEEPING & EATING

Canyonlands' campgrounds in the Needles and Island in the Sky districts are extremely popular. At Island in the Sky sites are first-come, first-served – most visitors sleep in nearby Moab. Visitors can reserve some campsites and all group sites at the Needles.

There are no restaurants in the park. Bring your own provisions and plenty of water.

📖 Island in the Sky

Backcountry camping in the Island is mostly open-zone (not in prescribed areas), but is still permit-limited. Nearby Dead Horse Point State Park also has camping; food, fuel and lodging are available in Moab.

Willow Flat Campground CAMPGROUND $
(📞435-719-2313; www.nps.gov/cany/planyourvisit/camping.htm; Canyonlands National Park; tent & RV sites $15; ⊙year-round) Seven miles from the Island in the Sky Visitor Center, the first-come, first-served, 12-site Willow Flat Campground has vault toilets but no water or hookups. Bring firewood and don't expect shade. Arrive early to claim a site during spring and fall.

📖 The Needles

Backcountry camping, in prescribed areas only, is quite popular, so it's hard to secure an overnight permit without advance reservation. Monticello (34 miles) and Moab (80 miles) are the nearest full-service towns.

Store your food in your car or hang food in a stuff sack in the backcountry – campground ravens and small animals are notorious for getting into everything, including coolers.

BLM Campgrounds CAMPGROUND $
(📞435-259-2100; www.blm.gov/utah/moab; Hwy 24; sites free-$6) There are several free BLM campsites outside the Needles (p190) entrance, including Superbowl and Bridger Jack.

Squaw Flat Campground CAMPGROUND $
(📞435-719-2313; www.nps.gov/cany/planyourvisit/camping.htm; Canyonlands National Park; tent & RV sites $20; ⊙year-round) You can reserve sites at this 26-site campground 3 miles west of the Needles Visitor Center between mid-March and June, and September and October (the rest of the year it's first-come, first-served). It has flush toilets and running water, but no showers and no hookups. Opt for side A, where many sites (12 and 14, for example) are shaded by juni-

per trees and cliffs. Maximum allowable RV length is 28ft.

Needles Outpost CAMPGROUND $
(📞435-979-4007; Hwy 211; tent & RV sites $20; ⊙Apr-Nov) If Squaw Flat is full, the dusty private campground at Needles Outpost is an alternative. Shower facilities are $3 for campers, $7 for noncampers. An on-site store sells limited camping supplies, gasoline and propane. The lunch counter and grill (open 8:30am to 4:30pm) serves sandwiches and burgers.

ℹ Information

There are several information centers. **Island in the Sky** (📞435-259-4712; www.nps.gov/cany; Hwy 313; ⊙8am-6pm Mar-Oct, 9am-4:30pm Nov-Feb) and the **Needles** (📞435-259-4711; Hwy 211; ⊙8am-6pm Mar-Oct, 9am-4:30pm Nov-Feb) have visitor centers. Many of the official park brochures are available online, while the Indian Creek website (www.friendsofindiancreek.org) has information on Moab-area climbing and conservation. The information center in **Moab** (p266) also covers the park.

Canyonlands NPS Headquarters (📞435-719-2313; www.nps.gov/cany; 2282 SW Resource Blvd, Moab; ⊙8am-4:30pm Mon-Fri)

Hans Flat Ranger Station (📞435-259-2652; www.nps.gov/cany; Recreation Rd 777, Hanksville; ⊙8am-4:30pm)

NPS Backcountry Permits Office (📞reservations 435-259-4351; https://canypermits.nps.gov/index.cfm; 2282 SW Resource Blvd, Moab; permits $10-30; ⊙8:30am-noon Mon-Fri)

The **Canyonlands Natural History Association** (Map p210; 📞800-840-8978, 435-259-6003; www.cnha.org; 3031 S Hwy 191) has some good info on local history and runs the bookstore.

ℹ Getting There & Around

The easiest way to tour Canyonlands is by car. Traveling between districts takes two to six hours, so plan to visit no more than one per day.

Overlooks are easy enough to reach. To explore further you'll need to contend with difficult dirt roads, great distances and limited water resources. Speed limits vary but are generally between 25mph and 40mph.

Outfitters in Moab have hiker shuttles and run rafting, hiking, biking and 4WD tours in the park.

Arches National Park

Best Hikes

➡ Balanced Rock (p204)

➡ The Windows (p204)

➡ Landscape Arch (p200)

➡ Fiery Furnace (p200)

➡ Delicate Arch (p202)

Best Views

➡ Delicate Arch Viewpoint (p202)

➡ The Windows (p204)

➡ Landscape Arch (p200)

➡ Courthouse Towers Viewpoint (p202)

➡ La Sal Mountains Viewpoint (p202)

Why Go?

With the highest density of rock arches anywhere on earth, Arches National Park offers up a whimsical escape that pushes you to jump, gasp, leap and skip. Simply put, it's magic.

Located just a hop away from Moab, this diminutive park is quite user-friendly, making it a great spot for families, people with disabilities and hikers looking for big views. These views do sometimes come at a price, as the park can get downright overrun on weekends. Get up early, visit weekdays and consider some of the longer hikes to really explore the richness of this national treasure.

While there are more than 2000 arches here, top bucket-list sights include Delicate Arch, Balanced Rock and the Windows. Go further afield with canyoneering trips into the sandstone labyrinths of the Fiery Furnace or Devils Garden. Seeing the sun set or rise over these vainglorious arches, fins, bridges and spires is exhilarating and sublime.

Driving Distances (miles)

	Arches National Park	Bryce Canyon National Park	Canyonlands National Park (North Entrance)	Capitol Reef National Park (Visitor Center)	Moab
Bryce Canyon National Park	270				
Canyonlands National Park (North Entrance)	25	280			
Capitol Reef National Park (Visitor Center)	140	120	155		
Moab	5	270	30	145	
Zion National Park (East Entrance)	310	75	325	180	315

Entrances

The park entrance and visitor center are accessed 5 miles northwest of Moab off Hwy 191. Most people drive it, but you can get here on a paved bike trail as well.

Past the visitor center, you climb into the park proper, where you'll find 22 miles of paved roads – most sights lie on or alongside the pavement. Crowds are often unavoidable. Parking areas overflow at peak times (weekends, spring through fall).

Every year the park takes new measures to handle the problem. At the time of publication Arches was strongly considering implementing a new traffic management plan, for which you would need to **book a peak-season entrance ticket** up to six months in advance. If approved, the system will begin as early as 2019.

For now, the best strategy is to arrive at the park before 7am, when crowds are sparse and the temperatures not so bad; or visit in the evening after 7pm. If you can't find a designated parking spot at one place, continue to the next. To keep drivers from parking in dangerous or sensitive areas, rangers have stepped up ticketing for illegally parked cars. Also, drive carefully; accidents occur when drivers focus on the scenery, not the road – an easy trap to fall into at Arches.

DON'T MISS
....

A guided hike through the Fiery Furnace, one of the signature hikes of the park, takes you into a wild mousetrap of sandstone desertscapes. You need to be fit because you'll be clambering over rock, through canyons and around boulders. Access is extremely limited, so reserve ahead. If that just ain't your thing, make sure you check out both Landscape Arch (the longest arch in Arches National Park, measuring 306ft from base to base) and Delicate Arch.

When You Arrive

➡ Arches is open year-round.

➡ A Southeast Utah Parks Pass, good for admission to Arches and Canyonlands National Parks and Natural Bridges and Hovenweep National Monuments for a one-year period, costs $55.

➡ Bring your own water and lunch. There is no food in the park. Bring a gallon of water per person per day in the summer.

➡ The video at the visitor center gives an excellent (though slightly overdramatized) view on the park's geological history.

ARCHES NATIONAL PARK

PARK POLICIES & REGULATIONS
....

Most standard national parks policies apply here. Pets are not allowed on any of the hiking trails or in the visitor center. You can take them out on the leash at the campground, overlooks or pullouts along the paved scenic drive. Backcountry, climbing and canyoneering permits are available online and at the visitor center.

Fast Facts

➡ **Entrance fee (valid 7 days):** Vehicle/ motorcycle/individual $30/25/15

➡ **Total area:** 119 sq miles

➡ **Elevation:** 4085ft

➡ **Average high/low temperature (at the visitor center) in July:** 100°F/87°F

Reservations

A new traffic-management plan is currently under consideration, which would require visitors to book peak-season tickets (April to October; maximum 2000 vehicles daily) up to six months in advance. Approximately 25% of tickets will be held for same-day reservations. Visitors on foot or bicycle would not need to reserve tickets.

Resources

➡ **Arches National Park** (www.nps.gov/arch)

Arches National Park

DEVILS GARDEN

Dance with the devil on the park's longest trail, stopping along the way to enjoy spectacular views of eight arches. (p200)

FIERY FURNACE

Head out on a ranger-guided trek through this perplexing and mind-defying sandstone maze. (p200)

DOUBLE O ARCH

Double your fun with a hike out to these twin arches. (p200)

LANDSCAPE ARCH

Tramp your way out for views of North America's longest natural arch at 93.3m. (p200)

Yellow Cat Flat

Fin Canyon

Private Arch

Devils Garden Primitive Loop

Wall Arch (fallen)

Dark Angel
Double O Arch

Devils Garden

Navajo Arch
Pine Tree Arch
Partition Arch
Tunnel Arch
Landscape Arch

Clover Canyon

Skyline Arch

Devils Garden Campground

Broken Arch

Sand Dune Arch

Salt Valley

Salt Wash

Fiery Furnace Viewpoint

Salt Valley Overlook

Fiery Furnace

Wolfe Ranch

Delicate Arch (4829 ft)

Delicate Arch Viewpoint

Arches National Park

Panorama Point

Klondike Bluffs

Tower Arch

Marching Men

Eye of the

Arches National Park Rd

(1mi);
I-70 (16mi)

5 km
2.5 miles

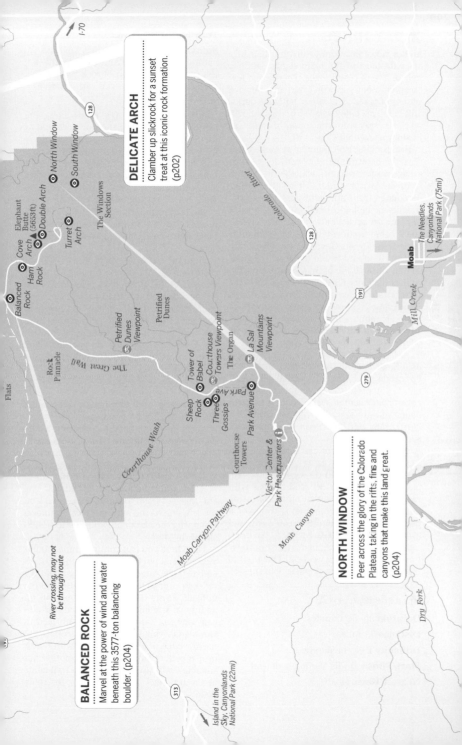

DELICATE ARCH

Clamber up slickrock for a sunset treat at this iconic rock formation. (p202)

BALANCED ROCK

Marvel at the power of wind and water beneath this 3577-ton balancing boulder. (p204)

NORTH WINDOW

Peer across the glory of the Colorado Plateau, taking in the rifts, fins and canyons that make this land great. (p204)

River crossing, may not be through route

Island in the Sky, Canyonlands National Park (22mi)

Flats

Rock Pinnacle

The Great Wall

Courthouse Wash

Balanced Rock

Ham Rock

Cove Arch

Elephant Butte (5653ft)

Double Arch

North Window

South Window

The Windows Section

Turret Arch

Petrified Dunes Viewpoint

Petrified Dunes

Sheep Rock

Tower of Babel

Three Gossips

Courthouse Towers Viewpoint

The Organ

La Sal Mountains Viewpoint

Park Avenue

Courthouse Towers

Visitor Center & Park Headquarters

Moab Canyon Pathway

Moab Canyon

Dry Fork

Mill Creek

Colorado River

Moab

The Needles, Canyonlands National Park (75mi)

I-70

128

191

279

128

313

🚶 DAY HIKES

Arches is geared more to drivers than hikers, with most of the main sights within a mile or two of paved roads. There are a few exceptions, but you won't find an extensive system of trails as at other national parks. Still, you can enjoy several hikes that will take you away from the sound of traffic, at least for a few hours.

Backpacking isn't popular at Arches, but if you're determined, you can do so with a backcountry permit, available in person from the visitor center. There are neither designated trails nor campsites. Due to the fragility of biological soil crusts, the park discourages backcountry treks. The closest you'll come to an established backcountry route is the **Devils Garden Primitive Trail**.

If you're fit and would like to join a guided hike through the narrow sandstone labyrinth at the **Fiery Furnace** (www.nps.gov/arch/planyourvisit/fiery-furnace.htm; permits adult/child $6/3; ☉ Mar-Oct), you can make reservations up to six months in advance at www.recreation.gov. On rare occasions tours may be offered outside the reservation system. If so, tickets for these tours are sold in person on a first-come, first-served basis at the visitor center up to seven days in advance. Buy tickets (in person only, adult/child $10/5) at the visitor center. Walks run 2½ to three hours and are generally offered twice daily (morning and afternoon) April through September.

While park rangers are discouraging it, accomplished hikers can explore the Fiery Furnace unguided. To do so, you must still pay a fee, watch a video and discuss with rangers how to negotiate this confusing jumble of canyons before they'll grant you a permit. Permits are limited to 50 a day, and usually sell out, so go early.

Arches is wildly popular and stays busy through Thanksgiving weekend. One tip is to try sunrise hiking (less popular than sunset).

🚶 Landscape Arch

Duration 30–60 minutes

Distance 2.1 miles

Difficulty Easy–moderate

Start/Finish Devils Garden trailhead

Nearest Town Moab

Transportation Private

Summary Among the world's longest natural stone spans, Landscape Arch is a spectacular ribbon of rock reached via a moderate gravel trail with spurs of interest.

Landscape Arch lies 0.8 miles along the Devils Garden trail at the northern end of the main park road. Along the trail, don't miss the short spurs (0.5 miles) to Tunnel and Pine Tree Arches. To make it more of a full-day hike, continue to Dark Angel spire or do the entire Devils Garden Primitive Trail. Before setting out, fill up with water at the trailhead parking lot. If you can, try to walk this trail in the morning, when it's much more pleasant than in mid-afternoon heat.

From the trailhead, you'll thread through sandstone fins that stand on end like giant wedges. A third of a mile in, bear right at the fork and head downhill to **Tunnel Arch** (on your right) and the 45ft **Pine Tree Arch** (on your left). High on a cliff, aptly named Tunnel Arch looks like a subway tube through the Entrada sandstone. In contrast, Pine Tree Arch is meaty, with a bulbous frame around its gaping middle. Look for the gnarled namesake juniper, which juts from the base of the window.

As you approach **Landscape Arch** along the main trail, the terrain opens up, revealing long views to distant ridges and a vast expanse of sky. In the past visitors could hike right beneath the elegant 306ft sweep of desert-varnished sandstone, longer than a football field. But in 1991 a 60ft slab of rock fell from the arch, nearly killing several hikers. When you notice the cracks on the left side of the arch, it's easy to understand why the National Parks Service (NPS) closed the trail.

From here you can continue on a moderately difficult out-and-back hike to the trail's end at **Dark Angel** spire, adding about 3.4 miles to your journey. You can also add the difficult **Devils Garden Primitive Trail**, an additional stretch of 4.3 miles that includes cool views of sandstone fins. Both lead to **Double O Arch**, where you'll negotiate the narrow edge of a sandstone fin with a 20ft drop on either side. (This rocky route is not suitable for little ones.) Pick up a trail guide at the trailhead or ask a ranger for route details.

Arches National Park – Day Hikes

N 0 ▬▬▬▬▬▬ 4 km
0 ▬▬▬▬▬▬ 2 miles

Legend:
- Balanced Rock
- Delicate Arch
- Landscape Arch
- Sand Dune & Broken Arches
- The Windows

Wall Arch
Landscape Arch
Clover Canyon
Salt Wash
Broken Arch
Devils Garden Trailhead
Sand Dune Arch
Fiery Furnace
Arches National Park Rd
Delicate Arch (4829 ft)
Wolfe Ranch
Arches National Park
(4WD Only)
Willow Flats
Willow Flats Rd
Rock Pinnacle
The Great Wall
Windows Rd
Balanced Rock
Elephant Butte (5653ft)
North Window
Turret Arch
South Window
Colorado River
128

🏃 Sand Dune & Broken Arches

Duration 15–30 minutes to Sand Dune Arch, 30–60 minutes to Broken Arch, 2 hours for complete loop

Distance 0.4 miles (Sand Dune Arch), 1.2 miles (Broken Arch), 2.4 miles (complete loop)

Difficulty Easy–moderate

Start/Finish Sand Dune Arch parking area

Nearest Town Moab

Transportation Private

Summary A varied walk that leads through rock fins (giving a taste of the Fiery Furnace), cool sand dunes and slickrock, this is a good place to take the kids.

From the Sand Dune Arch parking area, follow the trail through deep sand between narrow stone walls that are the backmost fins of **Fiery Furnace**. In less than 0.25 miles you'll arrive at **Sand Dune Arch**, which looks something like a poodle kissing a polar bear. Resist the temptation to climb or jump off the 8ft arch.

From here you can bear left to return to your car or bear right across open grassland en route to 60ft Broken Arch. At the next fork (the start of the loop trail), grasses give way to piñon pines and junipers along a gentle climb to **Broken Arch**. The treat here is the walk *through* the arch atop a slickrock ledge. Wear rubber-soled shoes or boots, or you may have trouble climbing to the arch.

When you're ready, return to the parking area or continue north to Devils Garden Campground. The route follows cairns over slickrock, passing through stands of desert pines. Watch for new arches forming near the trail. If you're staying at the campground, you can join the loop trail there.

From the campground spur it's another 0.5 miles back to the start of the loop trail.

This is a good trail for kids, especially the first section, though savvy adult hikers may find it too tame.

🏃 Delicate Arch

Duration 2–3 hours

Distance 3 miles

Difficulty Moderate–difficult

Start/Finish Wolfe Ranch

Nearest Town Moab

Transportation Private

Summary A shadeless ascent to a bowed sandstone arch that Edward Abbey likened to cowboy chaps. Follow rock cairns on slickrock and mind yourself on exposed heights.

The trail to Delicate Arch may seem interminable on the way up, but the rewards are so great that you'll quickly forget the toil – provided you wear rubber-soled shoes or boots and drink a quart of water along the way (there is no shade). You won't be alone – this is the most popular long hike at Arches.

Start out behind **Wolfe Ranch**, where a short spur trail leads to a small **petroglyph panel**. The trail is wheelchair-accessible to the petroglyph panel. Illustrations showing people on horseback were probably authored by the nomadic Utes, who adopted riding after the arrival of the Spanish.

Past the panel, the trail climbs a series of small switchbacks, soon emerging onto a long, steady slickrock slope. (This hill is visible from the trailhead, as are the tiny figures trudging up the slickrock like pilgrims.) Take your time on this stretch, especially on hot days. If you keep a steady pace, plan on making it to the top in 45 minutes.

As you approach the arch, the trail skirts a narrow slickrock ledge that may be daunting for those afraid of heights – yet it's worth pushing on to round the final corner. To your right, a broad sandstone amphitheater opens up below, and **Delicate Arch** crowns its rim, framing the 12,700ft La Sal Mountains in the distance. Circle the rim to the base of the arch, which sits atop a saddle that drops precipitously on either side. (If you bypass the bowl and bear left, it's possible to clamber high atop large flat rocks for a different perspective – and fewer people.)

Driving Tour
Arches Scenic Drive

DURATION 2½ HOURS
DISTANCE 43 MILES, INCLUDING SPURS
START VISITOR CENTER
END VISITOR CENTER
NEAREST TOWN MOAB

Hitting all the highlights, this paved drive visits Arches' strange forms and flaming desert landscapes. It's packed with photo ops and short walks to arches and iconic landmarks.

From the ❶ **visitor center**, the steep road ascends Navajo sandstone, once ancient sand dunes. Stop at the ❷ **Moab Fault Overlook**. Interpretive panels explain the geology.

A mile ahead, stop at ❸ **Park Avenue**, where you can take a walk past a giant rock fin that calls to mind a row of New York City skyscrapers.

Half a mile past Park Avenue, stop at the ❹ **La Sal Mountains Viewpoint**. This laccolithic mountain range developed underground during volcanic activity, then rose to the surface, fully formed, some 24 million years ago. If the scenery looks familiar, many of the driving scenes in the film *Thelma & Louise* were shot in Arches.

As you descend toward the ❺ **Courthouse Towers Viewpoint**, look left for the ❻ **Three Gossips**, towers that resemble three figures sharing a secret. From the viewpoint turnout, look up at the monoliths. These walls were probably once connected by arches since fallen away, particularly at ❼ **Sheep Rock**. Just ahead in ❽ **Courthouse Wash**, stands of bright-green cottonwood trees offer dramatic proof of how water can transform the parched desert into an oasis. About 1.5 miles further, on the right, the undulating landscape at ❾ **Petrified Dunes** was once a vast sweep of sand dunes. (Technically, the dunes aren't 'petrified,' as they contain no carbon, the determining element in petrification.)

After a 3-mile ascent, you'll arrive at the 3577-ton ❿ **Balanced Rock**, which teeters precariously atop a narrow stone pedestal. Pull over and take the 15-minute loop trail, then turn right onto Windows Rd,

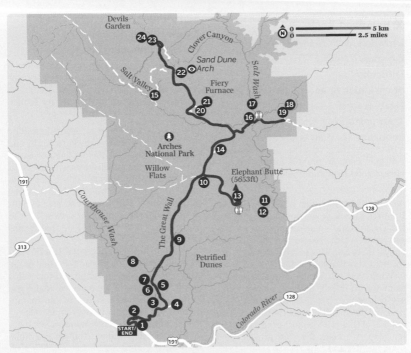

a 5-mile round-trip spur. You'll find pit toilets beside the parking lot at road's end.

Take the easy, short walks to ⑪ **North** and ⑫ **South Windows** and to ⑬ **Double Arch**. It's hard to grasp the immensity of these gigantic marvels until you're beside them. If you want a long view of the vast surrounding landscape but are short on time, head to North Window and stand right beneath it.

Back on the main road, stop at ⑭ **Panorama Point**. The 360-degree view includes an overlook of ⑮ **Salt Valley**, a onetime salt dome that collapsed when water washed away the salt. Interpretive panels explain the geology.

Two and a half miles past the Windows spur, turn right on the signed spur to ⑯ **Wolfe Ranch** and Delicate Arch. Pull into the first parking lot (which includes pit toilets) and take the short, easy walk to the primitive 1907 cabin, with its juniper-log walls and shale roof. ⑰ **Salt Wash**, which is wet year-round, runs from the cabin to the Colorado River. If you're lucky, you may spot a river otter. Cross the footbridge for a surprisingly close look at a small petroglyph panel, incised by Ute people sometime after the year 1600 (look but don't touch, as oils from fingers deteriorate

the rock). If you're up for a strenuous hike, climb the trail to ⑱ **Delicate Arch**, the park's premier hike. Otherwise, continue driving to the ⑲ **Delicate Arch Viewpoint**, 1 mile beyond the Wolfe Ranch turnout.

Two short trails lead to views of the arch, which has also been nicknamed the 'Schoolmarm's Breeches' and the 'Cowboy Chaps.' Follow the crowds to the right for an easy 50yd walk to the lower view, or bear left for a moderately strenuous 0.5-mile hike and 200ft ascent to the better view.

Return to the main road, turn right and drive 3 miles to the ⑳ **Salt Valley Overlook** for a perspective down to Wolfe Ranch and Salt Valley, then pull off again at the ㉑ **Fiery Furnace**. A short walk between split-rail fences leads to the overlook, from which you can peer between the giant fins of Entrada sandstone – at sunset they resemble flames in a furnace.

From here the main road skirts past the Fiery Furnace and the ㉒ **Sand Dune Arch trailhead** to road's end at the ㉓ **Devils Garden trailhead**. Refill your water bottle and picnic before taking the moderately easy walk to ㉔ **Landscape Arch**, the span of which is longer than a football field. Drive out the way you came, omitting the spur roads.

🚶 Balanced Rock

Duration 15–20 minutes

Distance 0.3 miles

Difficulty Easy

Start/Finish Balanced Rock parking area

Nearest Town Moab

Transportation Private

Summary The draw is a boulder as big as a naval destroyer, teetering on a spindly pedestal. Loop around the formation to have a good look at the forces of erosion at work.

A 3577-ton boulder atop a leaning pedestal, **Balanced Rock** shoots from the earth like a fist. The pedestal is made of soft Dewey Bridge mudstone, which erodes faster than the rock above. Eventually, this pedestal will snap, and the boulder will come crashing down.

While you can see the formation clearly from the trailhead, the loop allows you to grasp its actual size (55ft to the top of the pedestal, 128ft to the top of the rock). On the outside of the trail look for yucca, an important desert species that can provide food, soap, needles and rope.

There is wheelchair access to the viewpoint.

🚶 The Windows

Duration 30–60 minutes

Distance 0.6 miles

Difficulty Easy

Start/Finish The Windows trailhead

Nearest Town Moab

Transportation Private

Summary A gravel loop trail makes an easy climb to three massive arches (North and South Windows and Turret Arch). Take the alternative, slightly longer return for a back view of the two windows.

One of the park's most heavily trodden paths, this trail leads directly to North and South Windows and offers a terrific view of Turret Arch. Rangers lead interpretive talks here from spring through fall; if you're interested, check the bulletin board at the parking area. The trail forks about 500ft from the lot. Bear right for a close look at **Turret Arch** along a short loop that rejoins the main trail.

The left fork climbs to the **North Window**. Stand beneath this arch for one of the park's best views, taking in red-rock cliffs and Castle Valley in the distance. Above you is the giant smooth sweep of the mature arch, supported by a base of lumpy Dewey Bridge mudstone. **South Window** sits higher than North Window. Though tempting, keep off the arch (climbing or walking on any arch with an opening of 3ft or more is prohibited).

Two trails lead back to the parking lot from here: the wide, graded main trail and the narrow primitive trail. The latter heads east and then north, with great views and a brief respite from the crowds. Follow the cairns.

HIKING IN ARCHES IN NATIONAL PARK

NAME	START LOCATION	DESCRIPTION
Balanced Rock (p203)	Balanced Rock parking area	A precariously poised boulder perched atop a narrow rock spire.
Delicate Arch (p202)	Wolfe Ranch	Arches' premier hike ascends slickrock to the iconic Delicate Arch.
Landscape Arch (p200)	Devils Garden trailhead	Short walk to one of the world's longest spans, with side hikes to smaller arches.
Sand Dune & Broken Arches (p201)	Sand Dune Arch parking area	Varied route that passes the Fiery Furnace fins and grasslands, threads through an arch and crosses slickrock.
The Windows (p203)	The Windows trailhead	Gravel loop that goes beneath three massive arches that frame stunning views.

 Views   *Drinking Water*   *Backcountry Camping*

OTHER ACTIVITIES

Arrange guided climbing, hiking and canyoneering trips through Moab tour operators.

Rock Climbing

Climbing is allowed only on unnamed features. Routes require advanced techniques. No permits are necessary, but ask rangers about current regulations and route closures. For guided canyoneering into the Fiery Furnace (p200), contact an outfitter in Moab.

Ranger Programs

Rangers lead several activities from spring through fall, most notably the **Fiery Furnace guided hike** (by reservation) in summer; you can also reserve online. Ask when you get here about other ranger talks and programs.

Kids' Activities

When you arrive at the park, stop by the visitor center and pick up a Junior Ranger Activity Guide. Once kids complete certain activities, they can return to the visitor center to receive a special certificate and badge. Kids can also get an Explorer Pack on loan with stuff to do throughout the park. Keep kids on trails to protect the delicate desert ecosystem.

SLEEPING

There's stiff competition for camping in the park but there are plenty of campgrounds throughout the region and lodging galore in Moab.

Devils Garden Campground   CAMPGROUND $
(877-444-6777; www.recreation.gov; Arches National Park; tent & RV sites $25) Surrounded by red rock and scrubby piñons, the park's only campground is 19 miles from the Arches National Park Visitor Center. From March to October, sites are available by reservation. Book months ahead.

Facilities include drinking water, picnic tables, grills and toilets, but no showers (for those, try a place in Moab). RVs up to 30ft are welcome, but generator hours are limited; no hookups.

Information

There are no places in the park to buy prepared food, groceries or supplies. For all services, drive to Moab.

Arches canyoneering and climbing permits are available online (https://archespermits.nps.gov) or at the visitor center.

Arches National Park Visitor Center (435-719-2299; www.nps.gov/arch/planyourvisit/hours.htm; Arches National Park; 7:30am-5pm) Watch the informative video, check ranger-led activity schedules and pick up your **Fiery Furnace** (p200) tickets here.

Grand County Emergency Coordinator (435-259-8115) Search and rescue coordinator.

Getting Around

The only way to see Arches is by bicycle, private vehicle, on foot or as part of an organized tour, like **Moab Adventure Center** (p216) and **Adrift Adventures** (p214).

DIFFICULTY	DURATION	ROUND-TRIP DISTANCE	ELEVATION CHANGE	FEATURES	FACILITIES
easy	15-20min	0.3 miles	20ft		
moderate-difficult	2-3hr	3 miles	480ft		
easy-moderate	30min-1hr	2.1 miles	50ft		
easy-moderate	2hr	2.4 miles	140ft		
easy	30min-1hr	0.6 miles	140ft		

 Great for Families   *Picnic Sites*   *Restrooms*

ARCHES NATIONAL PARK OTHER ACTIVITIES

Moab

Best Hikes & Bikes

➡ Whole Enchilada (p207)

➡ Klondike Bluffs Trail (p208)

➡ Corona Arch Trail (p208)

➡ Fisher Towers Trail (p208)

➡ La Sal Mountains (p209)

➡ Moonflower Canyon (p210)

Best Places to Stay

➡ BLM Hwy 128 Campgrounds (p217)

➡ Up the Creek Campground (p217)

➡ Sunflower Hill Inn (p222)

➡ Sorrel River Ranch (p222)

➡ Cali Cochitta (p219)

Why Go?

Doling out hot tubs and pub grub after a dusty day on the trail, Moab is southern Utah's adventure base camp. Mobs arrive to play in Utah's recreation capital – from the hiker to the four-wheeler, the cult of recreation borders on fetishism.

Starting in the 1950s, miners in search of 'radioactive gold' – uranium – blazed the network of back roads that laid the groundwork for this 4WD mecca. Neither mining nor the hundreds of Hollywood films shot here have influenced the character of Moab as much as the influx of fat-tire, mountain-bike enthusiasts.

The town becomes overrun from March through October. The impact of all those feet, bikes and 4WDs on the fragile desert is a serious concern. People here love the land, even if they don't always agree about how to protect it. If the traffic irritates you, just remember – you can disappear into the vast desert in no time.

Driving Distances (miles)

	Arches National Park	Bryce Canyon National Park	Canyonlands National Park (North Entrance)	Capitol Reef National Park (Visitor Center)	Moab
Bryce Canyon National Park (Park Entrance)	270				
Canyonlands National Park (North Entrance)	25	280			
Capitol Reef National Park (Visitor Center)	140	120	155		
Moab	5	275	30	145	
Zion National Park (East Entrance)	310	75	325	180	315

History

Settlement in this area was resisted by the region's Native American peoples, and it wasn't until the late 1870s that Moab was founded by Mormon ranchers and farmers.

The next population surge occurred during the Cold War climate of the 1950s, when the federal government subsidized uranium mining, and Moab's population tripled in three years. In search of 'radioactive gold,' miners bladed a network of primitive roads, unwittingly laying the groundwork for the region to become a 4WD mecca half a century later. The miners also left ponds of radioactive tailings, residue from the mineral extraction process. Though uranium mining bottomed out in the 1980s, salt and potash mining continue, as does drilling for natural gas in the surrounding area, which remains a contentious issue.

Yet nothing has had as much influence on Moab's current character as the humble mountain biker. In the mid-1980s, an influx of fat-tire enthusiasts discovered the challenging and scenic slickrock desert and triggered a massive surge in tourism that continues unabated.

◎ Sights

Moab Giants   AMUSEMENT PARK
(☑ 435-355-0288; www.moabgiants.com; SR 313, 112 W; adult/family $22/70; ⊙ 10am-6pm; ☻) This paleo-amusement park features giant life-size replica dinosaurs, walking trails, 3D videos that might even bring you to a fourth dimension in some sections, information on dino tracks and more. It might be garish for some, but with a $10-million initial investment, it's certainly entertaining.

Museum of Moab   MUSEUM
(☑ 435-259-7985; www.moabmuseum.org; 118 E Center St; adult/child $5/free; ⊙ 10am-6pm Mon-Sat Apr-Oct, noon-5pm Mon-Sat Nov-Mar) Regional exhibits feature everything from paleontology and geology to uranium mining and Native American art.

Moab Museum of Film & Western Heritage   MUSEUM
(☑ 866-812-2002; https://redcliffslodge.com/property/moab-museum-film-western-heritage/; Mile 14, Hwy 128; ⊙ 8am-10pm) FREE Head out to the Moab Museum of Film & Western Heritage, based at Red Cliffs Lodge (p222), 15 miles north of town, to see Hollywood memorabilia from films shot locally; there are also historical displays on area ranches.

🏃 Activities

Mountain Biking

Moab's mountain biking is world-famous. Challenging trails ascend steep slickrock and wind through woods and up 4WD roads. People come from everywhere to ride the famous Slickrock Trail (p208) and other challenging routes. If you're a die-hard, ask about trips to the Maze (p193). Bike shop websites and www.discovermoab.com/biking.htm are good trail resources, or pick up *Above & Beyond Slickrock*, by Todd Campbell, and *Rider Mel's Mountain Bike Guide to Moab*.

Follow BLM guidelines, avoid all off-trail riding and pack everything out (including cigarette butts). Spring and fall are the busiest seasons. In summer you'd better start by 7am; otherwise the heat is searing.

★ Whole Enchilada   MOUNTAIN BIKING
(☑ 435-259-2444; http://grandcountyutah.net/650/Whole-Enchilada-Trail; Sand Flats Recreation Area, Sand Flats Rd) Accessed from the top of Geyser Pass at 10,600ft, this masterpiece combines the Burro Pass, Hazard County, Jimmy Keen, UPS, LPS and Porcupine Rim trails, offering everything from high-mountain descents to slickrock. It's a full-day affair for advanced riders, with 7000ft of vertical drop and 26.5 miles of trails.

Bar-M Loop   MOUNTAIN BIKING
(http://discovermoab.com/family-bar-m-loop/) Bring the kids on this easy, 8-mile loop skirting the boundary of Arches National Park (p195) with great views and short slickrock stretches. Connect from here to the more advanced Moab Brands trails.

Klonzo   MOUNTAIN BIKING
(www.utahmountainbiking.com/trails/klonzo.htm) Accessed from Willow Springs Rd, this area offers a mix of flowing beginner, intermediate and advanced terrain.

Gemini Bridges   MOUNTAIN BIKING
(www.utahmountainbiking.com/trails/gemini.htm) A moderate, full-day downhill ride past spectacular rock formations, this 13.5-mile one-way trail follows dirt, sand and slickrock. Located about 7 miles north of Moab on Hwy 191.

Moonlight Meadow Trail   MOUNTAIN BIKING
(www.utahmountainbiking.com/trails/moonlight.htm) Beat the heat by ascending La Sal Mountains to 10,600ft on this moderate 10-mile loop among aspens and pines (take it easy: you *will* get winded).

Moab Region

N 0 ___ 5 miles
0 ___ 10 km

FISHER TOWERS

Take in the inspiring views of Castle Valley as you hike through canyons to these eroded sandstone monoliths caked in the region's red mud. (p209)

WHOLE ENCHILADA MOUNTAIN BIKE TRAIL

Bust your butt on a gargantuan feast for adrenaline gluttons. (p207)

MAIN STREET

Grab a pint of local beer and relax in the fun restobars after a long day's adventure. (p223)

BLM HWY 128 CAMPGROUNDS

Go rustic at a low-key campsite shaded by canyon walls while the Colorado River rushes nearby. (p217)

MATHESON WETLANDS PRESERVE

Check out flocks of over 200 species of shore birds, raptors and waterfowl, as well as aquatic mammals like beaver, muskrat and river otters. (p211)

THE COLORADO RIVER

Honor the sun and river gods atop a paddleboard, kayak or raft on this main artery of the region. (p213)

Slickrock Trail
MOUNTAIN BIKING

(☑435-259-2444; http://grandcountyutah.net/654/Slickrock-Bike-Trail; Sand Flats Recreation Area, Sand Flats Rd; car/cyclist $5/2) The iconic slickrock trail that's way harder than you'd think – and way too crowded. A 12.7-mile round-trip, half-day route for experts only.

Klondike Bluffs Trail
MOUNTAIN BIKING

(www.utahmountainbiking.com/trails/klondike.htm) Intermediates can learn to ride slickrock on this 15.6-mile round-trip trail, past dinosaur tracks to Arches National Park. Mostly blue and black trails. Get here by going on Hwy 191 to Mile 148, exiting to Klondike Bluffs.

Magnificent 7
MOUNTAIN BIKING

(www.utahmountainbiking.com/trails/magnificent7.htm) Accessed north of Moab on Hwy 313 (13 miles in from the turnoff), this offers some of the most exposed terrain in Moab, found on the 20 miles of advanced trails.

Navajo Rocks
MOUNTAIN BIKING

(www.utahmountainbiking.com/trails/navajorocks.htm) By the north entrance to Canyonlands, this intermediate area has good sandstone terrain that rides well even when wet. There are seven trails, connecting over 22 miles.

Park to Park Trail
CYCLING

A paved-road bike path travels one way from Moab into Arches National Park (p207; 30 miles), or you can turn off and follow the Hwy 313 bike lane to the end of Canyonlands' Island in the Sky park (35 miles). On Hwy 128, it follows the Colorado River to Grandstaff Trail (p211).

★ Rim Cyclery
MOUNTAIN BIKING

(☑435-259-5333; www.rimcyclery.com; 94 W 100 N; ☺8am-6pm) Moab's longest-running family-owned bike shop not only does rentals and repairs, it also has a museum of mountain-bike technology, and rents cross-country skis in the winter.

Poison Spider Bicycles
MOUNTAIN BIKING

(☑800-635-1792; www.poisonspiderbicycles.com; 497 N Main St; bike rentals per day from $60; ☺8am-7pm) Friendly staff are always busy helping wheel jockeys map out their routes. Well-maintained road and suspension rigs for rent.

Rim Tours
CYCLING

(☑435-259-5223; www.rimtours.com; 1233 S Hwy 191; tours from $85, ☺9am-5pm) Well-organized and well-supported bike trips cover territory all across southern Utah. Trips range from half-day to four-day supported tours,

including rental of sparkling Santa Cruz full-suspension 29ers. Day trips depart at 7am; reserve ahead.

Chile Pepper Bike Shop
MOUNTAIN BIKING

(☑888-677-4688; www.chilebikes.com; 702 S Main St; bike rentals per day from $60; ☺8am-6pm) This shop rents bikes; checking bikes out at 4:30pm with returns the next day at 1pm means you could potentially get two rides in. It also repairs bikes, dishes out local trail beta and has plenty of maps.

Western Spirit Cycling Adventures
CYCLING

(☑800-845-2453; www.westernspirit.com; 478 Mill Creek Dr; 4-day trips from $950; ☺9am-5pm) Canyonlands' White Rim, Bryce to Zion and nationwide multiday tours.

Hiking

There are remarkable hikes in the BLM (Bureau of Land Management) and national forest land surrounding Moab, with a fraction of the visitors received by the big walks in the national parks. Carry plenty of water, stick to trails, and wear insect repellent between spring and early summer to repel aggressive gnats.

Corona Arch Trail
HIKING

(https://utah.com/hiking/arches-national-park/bowtie-corona-arches) To take in petroglyphs and two spectacular, rarely visited rock arches, hike the moderately easy Corona Arch Trail, the trailhead for which lies 6 miles up Potash Rd (Hwy 279). Follow cairns along the slickrock to **Bowtie** and **Corona Arches**. You may recognize Corona from a well-known photograph in which an airplane is flying through it – this is one big arch!

The 3-mile walk takes two hours.

Fisher Towers Trail
HIKING

(https://utah.com/hiking/fisher-towers-trail) The Fisher Towers Trail takes you past these towering sandstone monoliths, the tallest of which rises 900ft. The west-facing monoliths get quite hot in the afternoon, so wait for sunset, when rays bathe the rock in color and cast long shadows. (Bring a flashlight; many lingering hikers have ended up stuck on the trail in the dark.)

The moderate-to-difficult 2.2-mile (one-way) trail lies off Hwy 128, 21 miles northeast of Moab; follow signs.

La Sal Mountains
HIKING

(http://discovermoab.com/la-sal-mountains/; La Sal Mountain Loop) To escape summer's heat, head up Hwy 128 to the Manti–La Sal National Forest lands, in the mountains east of

Moab

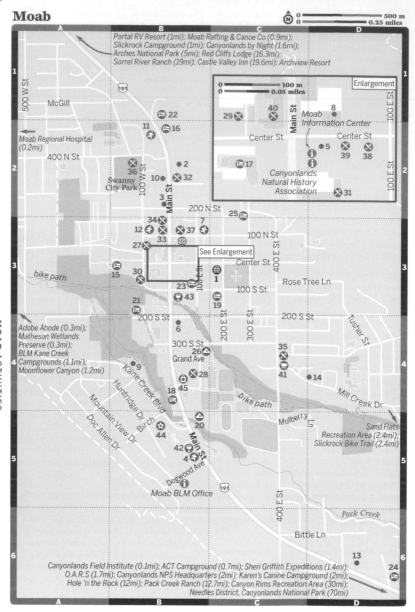

Portal RV Resort (1mi); Moab Rafting & Canoe Co (0.9mi);
Slickrock Campground (1mi); Canyonlands by Night (1.6mi);
Arches National Park (5mi); Red Cliffs Lodge (16.3mi);
Sorrel River Ranch (19mi); Castle Valley Inn (19.6mi); Archview Resort

McGill

Moab Regional Hospital
(0.2mi)

400 N St

Swanny
City Park

Enlargement

Main St

Moab
Information Center

Center St

Center St

Canyonlands
Natural History
Association

200 N St

100 N St

Center St

Rose Tree Ln

See Enlargement

bike path

100 S St

200 S St

200 S St

Tusher St

Adobe Abode (0.3mi);
Matheson Wetlands
Preserve (0.3mi);
BLM Kane Creek
Campgrounds (1.1mi);
Moonflower Canyon (1.2mi);

Kane Creek Blvd

Huntridge Dr

Birch

300 S St

Grand Ave

Mountain View Dr

Doc Allen Dr

bike path

Mill Creek Dr

Mulberry

Sand Flats
Recreation Area (2.4mi);
Slickrock Bike Trail (2.4mi)

Main St

Dogwood Ave

Moab BLM Office

Pack Creek

Bittle Ln

MOAB ACTIVITIES

Moab, and hike through white-barked aspens and ponderosa pines.

Moonflower Canyon   HIKING

(www.blm.gov/visit/moonflower-canyon-recreation-area) If you're short on time, take the easy 1-mile round-trip hike along Moonflower Canyon, a shaded stroll on mostly level ground that ends at a sandstone bowl beneath hanging gardens. A perennial stream makes this hike a cooler, less dusty alternative. The trailhead lies 1.2 miles from town

Moab

MOAB ACTIVITIES

along Kane Creek Rd. Look for petroglyphs at the parking area.

Grandstaff Trail   HIKING
(Hwy 128) This moderately easy trail includes a 2.5-mile walk (five miles round-trip) along a stream. Scoot down a shaded side canyon to find petroglyphs, then continue to the 243ft-wide **Morning Glory Natural Bridge**, at a box canyon. Plan on three to four hours. The trailhead is 3 miles north of Moab.

Hidden Valley Trail   HIKING
For a moderate-to-difficult rim hike above Moab, try the Hidden Valley Trail, which meanders through a pristine hanging valley in the Behind the Rocks Wilderness Study Area. The trailhead is on BLM land at the end of Angel Rock Rd. Plan on taking four to six hours.

Matheson Wetlands Preserve   BIRD-WATCHING
(☑ 435-259-4629; www.nature.org; 934 W Kane Creek Blvd; ☉ dawn-dusk) **FREE** The Nature Conservancy oversees the 890-acre preserve just west of town. You can spot over 200 species of bird in this wetlands area. There are

also chances of seeing beaver, muskrat and river otter.

Driving
People come from around the world to drive in Utah, using Moab as their hub. Here you'll find scenic drives for every taste: from paved desert highways perfect for RVers to vertical slickrock trails for four-wheeling, adrenaline junkies.

★ **Colorado River Scenic
Byway (Hwy 128)**   SCENIC DRIVE
(https://utah.com/scenic-drive/upper-colorado-river) This curvy 31-mile drive follows the winding Colorado River through gorgeous red-rock country of mesas, rock walls, alfalfa fields and sagebrush. Extend the trip with the La Sal Mountain Loop Road (p212).

Drive north on Main St/Hwy 191 and turn right (east) onto Hwy 128. The road winds through red-rock canyons along the Colorado River's serpentine course, which is why it is known in the area as 'the river road.' Arches National Park lies on the north side of the river for the first 15 miles.

Six miles from Hwy 191 you'll reach **Big Bend Recreation Site**, where you can picnic by the river. Eleven miles further on, you'll pass the La Sal Mountain Loop Rd turnoff and **Castleton Tower**, a narrow 400ft spire that rises above Castle Valley and is one of the area's most iconic rock climbs. Across from Castleton, the **Priests and Nuns Pinnacles** shoot up in a graceful line. At mile marker 21, the Fisher Towers rise almost as high as the Eiffel Tower (at 900ft; Titan is the tallest).

Ten miles ahead, you'll reach the **Dewey Bridge** site. Built in 1916, it was among the first spans across the Colorado. The bridge was destroyed by accidental fire in 2008 and its future is currently in limbo due to the high cost of reconstruction. Park near the site to watch rafters running downriver.

When ready, return to Moab or double back to the La Sal Mountain Loop Rd. I-70 lies 13 miles north.

La Sal Mountain Loop Road SCENIC DRIVE
(http://discovermoab.com/la-sal-mountains/) This 67-mile route through Manti–La Sal National Forest runs from the scorching desert into cool green woodlands. Though paved, it's narrow and lacks any guardrails.

When the desert gets too hot to handle, take this route through Manti–La Sal National Forest and let it whisk you to where you can camp, bicycle, hike or sit by a stream and listen as wind ruffles the aspens. Snow closes the road between November and March. Allow three to four hours off-season.

About 15 miles northeast of Moab, off Hwy 128, the La Sal Mountain Loop Rd (aka Castle Valley Rd) climbs southeast into the national forest, up switchbacks (a problem for large RVs) into the forest. Four miles from the turnoff, look to your left for the spires known as the Priest and Nuns, as well as Castle Rock. The route winds past junipers and piñon pines, followed by scrub oaks and, finally, alpine slopes of majestic pines, firs and white-barked quaking aspens. Here, high above canyon country, you'll gain a fresh perspective on the vastness of the Colorado Plateau.

At the crest, you can turn left on a dirt spur road and climb 5 miles further to the picnic area and campground at Warner Lake (p218). For information on hiking and camping, check with national forest rangers. From the Warner Lake spur junction, the loop road descends to Hwy 191, 8 miles south of Moab.

Potash Road SCENIC DRIVE
This 15-mile scenic desert drive passes mining remnants on the way into dry country with soaring rock walls and solitude. Petroglyphs, dinosaur tracks and arches are highlights.

Three miles north of Moab, off Hwy 191, the paved Potash Rd (Hwy 279) skirts south along the Colorado River. It's named for a potash extraction plant at road's end. Just past the turnoff you'll pass a radioactive tailings pond from Moab's uranium-mining days, while midroute, stunning natural beauty abounds. Such are the region's contradictions.

Highlights include Wall Street (p216; for rock climbers), Native American petroglyph panels (look for signs), dinosaur tracks (bring binoculars for a better look), a 1.5-mile hiking trail to **Corona Arch**, and **Jug Handle Arch**, 3ft wide but 45ft high. Also find the Potash Dock put-in for float trips down the Colorado. Past the potash plant, the road continues as a rough 4WD track into Canyonlands' Island in the Sky (p193) district, linking with Shafer Trail Rd.

Hurrah Pass SCENIC DRIVE
(www.visitutah.com/attraction/hurrah-pass/) The 33-mile Hurrah Pass offers jaw-dropping vistas of the Colorado River, Dead Horse Point and Grand View Point. Drivers can continue on but the road gets rougher and is best for 4WD vehicles; 4WD is mandatory beyond the pass.

This route starts out west along paved Kane Creek Rd, off Hwy 191 in Moab, soon passing petroglyph sites and a rock-climbing area. The pavement yields to gravel as you enter Kane Springs Canyon. About 10 miles in you must ford the creek, which, depending on the weather, may be impassable; 4WD is recommended.

After 15 miles you'll reach 4470ft Hurrah Pass. The stupendous scenery includes views up to Dead Horse and Grand View Points. South of the pass the road descends toward the Colorado River, with views of the potash plant on the opposite bank (look for the fields of blue). Explore the desert, and when ready, double back to Moab or continue south on Lockhart Basin Rd toward Canyonlands' Needles district.

From Lockhart Basin Rd the road is much more difficult (4WD is mandatory) and often confusing, eventually emerging about 50 miles south on Hwy 211, just east of the Needles. Contact the BLM for maps and information if you want to do the whole route.

Canyon Rims SCENIC DRIVE
(https://utah.com/canyon-rim) A lovely out-of-the-way 54-mile drive to the Needles and Anticline Overlooks, with great views of the

Needles and Hurrah Pass, this route is accessible to cars and buses.

The BLM-administered Canyon Rims Recreation Area (p218) lies south of Moab, west of Hwy 191 and east of Canyonlands National Park. If you've already visited the area's other major overlooks (eg Dead Horse and Grand View Points) and have time, this byway makes a good day trip. It's also a fine detour on the way to or from the Needles. Don't fret if you miss it, however. The area is especially popular with hikers, campers and all-terrain-vehicle (ATV) enthusiasts. For more information, contact the BLM or stop by the Moab Information Center (p224).

Turn west off Hwy 191, 32 miles south of Moab. The paved road leads 22 miles west to the Needles Overlook, a great panorama of the national park. About two-thirds of the way to the overlook take the spur, where a gravel road stretches 16 miles north to the Anticline Overlook, a promontory with awesome views of the Colorado River, Meander Canyon and Hurrah Pass Rd below.

Rafting

Whatever your interest, be it bashing through rapids or gentle floats for studying canyon geology, rafting may prove to be the highlight of your vacation. Rafting season runs from April to September; jet-boating season lasts longer. Water levels crest in May and June.

Most local rafting is on the Colorado River, northeast of town, including the Class III to IV rapids of Westwater Canyon (p215), near Colorado; the wildlife-rich 7-mile Class I float from **Dewey Bridge to Hittle Bottom** (no permit required); and the Class I to II **Moab Daily**, the most popular stretch near town (no permit required; expect a short stretch of Class III rapids).

Rafters also launch north of Moab to get to the legendary Class V rapids of **Cataract Canyon** (NPS permit required). This Colorado River canyon south of town and the Confluence is one of North America's most intense stretches of white water. If you book anything less than a five-day outfitter trip to get here, know that some of the time downstream will be spent in a powered boat. Advanced do-it-yourself rafters wanting to run it will have to book a jet-boat shuttle or flight return.

North of Moab is a Class I float along the **Green River** that's ideal for canoes. From there you can follow John Wesley Powell's 1869 route. (Note that additional outfitters operate out of the town of Green River itself.)

Visitors can choose from full-day float trips, white-water trips, multiday excursions and jet-boat trips. Day trips are often available on short notice, but overnight trips should be booked well ahead. Know the boat you want: an oar rig is a rubber raft that a guide rows; a paddleboat is steered by the guide and paddled by passengers; motor rigs are large boats driven by a guide (such as jet boats).

Do-it-yourselfers can rent canoes, inflatable kayaks or rafts with required personal flotation devices and accessories. Rentals are discounted for multiday jaunts.

Without permits, you'll be restricted to mellow stretches of the Colorado and Green Rivers; if you want to run Westwater Canyon or enter Canyonlands on either river, you'll need a permit. Contact the Moab BLM Office (p224) or NPS Backcountry Permits Office (p195) respectively. Reserve equipment, permits and shuttles way in advance.

WORTH A TRIP

DETOUR TO MONUMENT VALLEY

From Moab, skirt south on Hwy 191 for stellar desert scenery. Two hours, or 100 miles, south of Moab, the pinprick-sized **Bluff** (www.bluff-utah.org), a historic town surrounded by red rock, makes a good base. From here, hike the new Bears Ears National Monument (p192), drive the rugged hairpin turns of the **Moki Dugway** (30 miles) or the surreal **Valley of the Gods**, or visit **Natural Bridges National Monument** (www.nps.gov/nabr; Hwy 275; 7-day pass per vehicle $10, tent & RV sites $10; ⊘24hr, visitor center 8am-6pm May-Sep, 9am 5pm Oct-Apr), a white-sandstone canyon with a scenic, paved 9-mile loop perfect for pedaling. But nature's grand slam is **Monument Valley Navajo Tribal Park** (⊘435-727-5870; www.navajonationparks.org; per 4-person vehicle $20; ⊘drive 6am-7pm Apr-Sep, 8am-4:30pm Oct-Mar, visitor center 6am-8pm Apr-Sep, 8am-5pm Oct-Mar; ℗), where a 17-mile unpaved driving loop circles reddish mesa formations that sprout like earthen giants. A favorite for Hollywood shots, it's in the Navajo Indian Reservation, 47 miles south of Bluff. Camping is $10 per site.

RAFTING TOURS

Outfitters on guided tours take care of everything, from permits to food to setting up camp and shuttling you back to town.

Navtec Expeditions ADVENTURE
(☑ 435-259-7983; www.navtec.com; 321 N Main St; full-day rafting trips $170; ☉ 7am-6pm) Comprehensive rafting excursions, including Cataract Canyon, combo hiking and 4WD trips.

OARS TOURS
(☑ 800-346-6277; www.oars.com; 2540 S Hwy 191; full-day rafting trips from $99; ☉ 8am-7pm) Has a permit for Canyonlands National Park and runs single- or multiday combination hiking and rafting tours.

Sheri Griffith Expeditions RAFTING
(☑ 800-332-2439; www.griffithexp.com; 2231 S Hwy 191; river trips from $85; ☉ 8am-6pm) Operating since 1971, this rafting specialist has a great selection of river trips on the Colorado, Green and San Juan Rivers – from family floats to Cataract Canyon rapids, and from a couple of hours to a couple of weeks.

Canyon Voyages Adventure Co ADVENTURE
(☑ 800-733-6007; www.canyonvoyages.com; 211 N Main St; full-day rafting trips from $95) In addition to half- to five-day mild white-water and kayaking trips, Canyon organizes multisport excursions that include options like hiking, biking, paddleboarding and canyoneering. Kayak, canoe and outdoor equipment rental available.

Adrift Adventures ADVENTURE
(Tag Along Expeditions; ☑ 800-874-4483; www. adrift.net; 378 N Main St; full-day rafting trips from $74) This one-stop shop offers a little of everything: flat-water jet-boat rides, white-water rafting, land safaris, horseback riding, scenic flights, skydiving and more. Ask about jet-boat return support for Cataract Canyon trips, multisport packages, plus Arches National Park bus tours.

Moab Rafting & Canoe Co KAYAKING
(☑ 435-259-7722; www.moab-rafting.com; 420 Kane Creek Blvd; trips from $99; ☉ 9am-5pm) Small company with guided and self-guided canoe and raft trips.

RAFTING WITHOUT A GUIDE

Good outfitters provide complete information to help you plan a self-guided trip. Reserve equipment, secure permits and book shuttles far in advance. Without a permit, you'll be restricted to several mellow stretches of the Colorado and Green Rivers, but if you want to run Class III and IV rapids in Westwater Canyon or enter Canyonlands on either river, you'll need a permit.

Permits may be solicited a year in advance. Check the river permits link on www.discovermoab.com, or contact the Moab BLM Office (p224) or the NPS Backcountry Permits Office (p195) directly. Backcountry permits are issued at the appropriate visitor center. Strict rules govern sanitation and fires, depending on where you raft; confirm regulations with the appropriate agency.

To rent a raft, canoe or kayak, contact Canyon Voyages. For canoe rentals, call Moab Rafting & Canoe Co.

For shuttles to or from the rivers, call Roadrunner Shuttle (p224). To get back from the Confluence, you must book a jet-boat shuttle in advance; try Adrift Adventures.

Colorado River Northeast of Moab Boating the 36 miles of river northeast of Moab from Westwater Canyon to Takeout Beach takes two to five days. This section is divided

---

ⓘ CHOOSING A BOAT & RIVER

Outfitters ply the rivers in a variety of boats. Resembling a rowboat, an **oar rig** is a rubber raft that a guide rows downriver. Also made of rubber, a **paddleboat** is steered by a guide and paddled by passengers. Not technically a raft, a **motor rig** is a large boat driven by a guide (**jet boats** fall into this category). While this is the quickest way downriver, speed isn't so conducive to slowly soaking up desert landscapes. You can also float in a **kayak**, **inflatable kayak**, **paddleboard** or **canoe**.

Rapids are rated on a scale from one (I) to six (VI), with Class I being still water and Class VI an unnavigable waterfall. Class II rapids are good for novices and families with little kids. Class III are thrilling, while Class IV are borderline scary, depending on your perspective. Class V rapids are technical and dangerous.

Top white-water runs include Cataract Canyon and Westwater. Labyrinth Canyon, Meander Canyon and the Colorado River from Dewey Bridge to Takeout Beach are top flat-water paddles.

THE SCOURGE OF THE COLORADO

As you float down the Colorado, notice the dense stands of wispy-looking trees. Tamarisk, also called salt cedar, is an ornamental tree that was imported to the US in the 19th century and later planted along the river for erosion control. It has since taken over the banks of the Colorado and is choking the waterway.

A single large tamarisk transpires 300 gallons of water *a day*. Some estimates place the species' combined water consumption as high as one-third of the river's overall flow. If that water were returned to the river, the Colorado might again reach the sea. They also increase alkaline levels in water, making it harder for other native species to survive.

The good news? In Death Valley, California, land managers have almost entirely eradicated tamarisk stands, and once-threatened wetlands are rebounding. As you cross the bridge into Moab, and elsewhere along the Colorado, look for charred tree stumps and scorched riverbanks – evidence of the local eradication effort by fire (and herbicides). Biologists are now introducing beetles to eat the tamarisks, a potentially risky move that could reduce tamarisk stands by 70% to 80%.

into three distinct stretches. All fall within the jurisdiction of the BLM. Take Hwy 128 from Moab, which roughly parallels the river, making put in and take out a breeze.

If you're seeking serious white water, **Westwater Canyon** is the place. The first canyon along the Colorado in Utah, Westwater boasts Class III and IV rapids through the oldest exposed layer of rock on the planet. Most people make the 17-mile trip in one long day (10 hours) from Moab, though some choose to camp and make it a two-day trip. Most outfitters offer both options. A BLM permit is required.

Like mellow water and just want to float along? **Dewey Bridge to Hittle Bottom** is a 7-mile section of flat water with great scenery and wildlife-watching. One stretch passes through a bird sanctuary. No permit required.

Also known as Fisher Towers, or simply as the Daily, **Hittle Bottom to Takeout Beach** is the most popular stretch of river near Moab, perfect for novices who aren't ready for Westwater. Families can safely bring small children without boring their teens. The Daily offers mostly Class I and II rapids, with one short section of Class III known as White's Rapid (Class IV at high water, when it's not recommended for kids). Camp at riverside BLM campgrounds. No permit is required.

Colorado River Southwest of Moab (Meander Canyon) This 48-mile section takes three to five days, starting at Potash Dock and ending at Spanish Bottom. The flat-water trip from Potash Dock to the Confluence (where the Green and Colorado Rivers meet) moves slowly on the wide river. It's a scenic trip, good for mellow souls or novice boaters. You can put in at Moab Dock to lengthen the trip

by 15 miles, but since it parallels the highway this section is usually skipped.

A mile and a half north of the Confluence, you'll reach the **Slide**, a moderate rapid that you can portage. In the 4-mile stretch from the Confluence to Spanish Bottom, eddies and whirlpools kick in as you approach Cataract Canyon (*do not* miss the take out). An NPS permit is required to enter Canyonlands. (For a half-day flat-water paddle, put in at Moab and take out at Gold Bar; for a full day, take out at Potash.)

Cataract Canyon The Class V rapids of Cataract Canyon are legendary. Twenty-six rapids churn and roil over this 14-mile stretch where the Colorado squeezes through narrow canyons. Trips down the Cat are extremely technical and dangerous; there's no room for error. Though a jet boat can do it in a day, it is well worth taking your time, camping on beautiful beaches and finding harmony with the natural pace of the river.

This 112-mile trip takes from three days to a week, starting at Moab and ending in Hite. The intensity of the rapids fluctuates hugely, depending on snowmelt and drought. Many fail to realize that you have to float on flat water quite a ways to reach the canyon (rafts put in at Potash or Mineral Bottom), and once through the rapids, you'll wind up on flat Lake Powell – though you'll be so high on adrenaline, you probably won't even notice. Peak flow runs mid-May to mid-June. An NPS permit is required; reserve through the NPS.

Green River (Labyrinth & Stillwater Canyons) 'Discovered' by John Wesley Powell during his famed expeditions, this flat-water stretch down the Green is ideal for canoes. You'll pass rock art along the scenic route.

Start at Green River State Park and end at Mineral Bottom (68 miles) or Spanish Bottom (124 miles); the trip takes between three and nine days.

Take out at the Confluence or use extreme caution en route to Spanish Bottom, lest you get sucked into Cataract Canyon. An NPS permit is required south of Mineral Bottom.

Four-Wheel Driving

The area's primitive back roads are coveted by 4WD enthusiasts. You can rent or take group 4WD tours, or 'land safaris,' in multipassenger-modified, six- to eight-person Humvee-like vehicles. Note that rafting companies may have combination land/river trips.

Off-road utility vehicles like Rhinos and Mules (seating two to four), or four-wheelers (straddled like a bicycle) are available for rent. Personal 4WD vehicles and ATVs require an off-highway vehicle (OHV) permit, available at the visitor center. Outfitter hours shorten between November and February.

The Moab Information Center (p224) has good free route info, as well as *Moab Utah Backroads & 4WD Trails* by Charles Wells, and other books for sale. Canyonlands National Park also has some epic 4WD tracks.

If you go four-wheeling, stay on established routes. The desert looks barren, but it's a fragile landscape of complex ecosystems. Biological soil crusts can take up to a century to regenerate after even one tire track (really).

If you rent a 4WD vehicle, *read the insurance policy* – it may not cover damage from off-road driving and will likely carry a $2500 deductible. Check when you book. Whenever possible, rent a relatively new vehicle.

The week before Easter the annual Jeep Safari takes place.

Dan Mick's Jeep Tours — DRIVING
(☑ 435-259-4567; www.danmick.com; 3-person tours from $300) Private Jeep tours and guided drive-your-own-4WD trips with good ol' boy Dan Mick. A highly regarded local operation.

Coyote Land Tours — DRIVING
(☑ 435-260-3056; www.coyotelandtours.com; adult/child $59/39) Popular daily tours in a bright-yellow Mercedes-Benz Unimog off-road vehicle (seats 12); call ahead. Your badass driver, John Marshall, is certified as an Emergency Medical Technician, off-road driver and US Marshal desert tracker.

Moab Adventure Center — ADVENTURE
(☑ 866-904-1163; www.moabadventurecenter.com; 225 S Main St; half-day tours from $85) The open-

air, canopy-topped land safaris offered here are popular. This megacenter also arranges (alone or in combination) rafting trips, Jeep rental, horseback riding, rock climbing, guided hikes, scenic flights and even Arches National Park bus tours.

Horseback Riding

Rates for horseback riding generally range from $80 for a three-hour ride to $100 for a four-hour outback ride. Kids must be eight years old or older.

Red Cliffs Lodge — HORSEBACK RIDING
(☑ 435-259-2002; www.redcliffslodge.com; Mile 14, Hwy 128) In Castle Valley, 15 miles north of town, Red Cliffs Lodge provides horseback trail rides (March to November), offered mornings and evenings. If you book a multisport rafting trip that includes horseback riding, you'll still be coming here.

Rock Climbing & Canyoneering

Climb up cliffsides, rappel into rivers and hike through slot canyons with local outfitters, who have the inside scoop on the area's lesser-known gems.

West of town, **Wall Street** (Potash Rd) gets crowded on weekends and is an excellent spot to meet other climbers. It's about the only sport-climbing area nearby. Trad climbers will know **Indian Creek**, off Hwy 211 on the way to Canyonlands' Needles district, for its legendary crack climbing. **Castle Valley** serves up a number of classic desert towers on the solid Wingate sandstone layer. Canyoneering expeditions offer chances to rappel into slickrock canyons and hike through cascading water.

For a guidebook to climbs, we recommend Fred Knapp's *Classic Desert Climbs*.

Moab Desert Adventures — OUTDOORS
(☑ 804-814-3872; www.moabdesertadventures.com; 39 East Center St; half-day tours from $85; ⊙ 7am-7pm) Top-notch climbing tours scale area towers and walls; the 140ft arch rappel is especially exciting. Canyoneering trips are also available.

Desert Highlights — ADVENTURE
(☑ 435-259-4433,; www.deserthighlights.com; 50 E Center St; half-day canyoneering trips from $105) Canyoneering and pack raft trips here are big on personal attention. Offers trips to some worthy, little-known destinations.

Gear Heads Outdoor Store — SPORTS & OUTDOORS
(☑ 888-740-4327; www.gearheadoutfitters.com; 471 S Main St; ⊙ 8:30am-6pm) Stock up on all

the outdoor gear you need, including climbing ropes, route guides, books and water-jug refills. The knowledgeable staff are quite helpful.

Skydiving & Air Tours

Redtail Aviation   SCENIC FLIGHTS
(☑435-259-7421; http://flyredtail.com; 94 Aviation Way, Suite F; aerial tours from $179; ⊘8am-5pm) Fly high above Arches, Canyonlands, Lake Powell, San Rafael Swell, Monument Valley and more.

Skydive Moab   ADVENTURE SPORTS
(☑435-259-5867; www.skydivemoab.com; 114 W Aviation Way; tandem dives from $189; ⊘7am-8pm) Skydiving and base-jumping with stunning desert views.

⚘ Festivals & Events

Moab loves a party, and throws them regularly. For a full calendar, consult www.discover moab.com.

Skinny Tire Festival   SPORTS
(www.skinnytireevents.com; ⊘early Mar) Road cycling festival with four rides in superscenic locations around Moab, including the parks.

Jeep Safari   SPORTS
(www.rr4w.com; ⊘Apr) The week before Easter about 2000 Jeeps (and thousands more people) overrun the town in the year's biggest event. Register early; trails are assigned.

Moab Free Concert Series   MUSIC
(www.moabfreeconcerts.com; Swanny Park; ⊘5:30-9pm Fri) [FREE] A concert series that coincides with the Farmers Market (p223). For concert details, inquire at the Moab Information Center (p224).

Moab Music Festival   MUSIC
(☑435-259-7003; www.moabmusicfest.org; ⊘Aug-Sep) World-class classical musicians converge on the landscape of the Utah Canyonlands region.

Moab Folk Festival   MUSIC
(www.moabfolkfestival.com; ⊘Nov) 🎵 Folk music and environmental consciousness combine. This festival is 100% wind-powered, venues are easily walkable and recycling is encouraged.

🛏 Sleeping

Prices drop by as much as 50% outside March to October; some smaller places close November through March. Most lodgings have hot tubs and mini-refrigerators, and motels

have laundries. Cyclists should ask whether a property provides *secure* bike storage, not just an unlocked closet.

Though there's a huge number of motels, they are often booked out. Reserve as far ahead as possible. For a full lodging list, see www.discovermoab.com.

Vacation condo and home rentals are big here. Check out aggregators to save big on condos mostly located south of town. Many include pools, kitchens and living rooms. **Moab Utah Lodging** (☑800-505-5343; www. moabutahlodging.com) is a good local source for vacation rentals.

🛏 Camping

Make reservations when possible. During busy holiday weekends all of the campgrounds around Moab are full. For more information and options, visit the Moab Information Center (p224) or check the online links at www.moab-utah.com and www.dis covermoab.com.

Up the Creek Campground   CAMPGROUND $
(☑435-260-1888; www.moabupthecreek.com; 210 E 300 S; tent sites 1/2 people $25/32; ⊘Mar-Oct) There's something about this shady, tent-only grove with flower beds, lush lawns and recycling that fosters a sense of community. The 20 sites are within walking distance of downtown. Showers are included, but are also available to nonguests for $6; no fires.

BLM Hwy 128 Campgrounds   CAMPGROUND $
(☑435-259-2100; http://discovermoab.com/blm-campgrounds/; Hwy 128; tent sites $15; ⊘year-round) The best place to stay to beat the heat (other than in the La Sals) is along the Colorado River on Hwy 128. Vegetation and the canyon walls provide shade at these 12 BLM campgrounds along a 28-mile stretch of the river. Each includes fire rings and vault toilets but not water. First-come, first-served. Only group reservations accepted.

ACT Campground   CAMPGROUND $
(☑435-355-0355; www.actcampground.com; 1536 S Mill Creek Dr; tent site $25, RV site $44-49, r $69; ⊘year-round; P❄🐾🛜🐕) 🎵 Check out the first commercial straw-bail building in the state of Utah at this roadside RV park, campground and learning center, all in one. There's a very cool community kitchen and learning center, where the owners hope to put on presentations on desert ecology and biology. We only wish it were a little further from the road.

Canyonlands Campground
CAMPGROUND $

(☑ 435-259-6848; www.canyonlandsrv.com; 555 S Main St; tent sites $41-46, RV sites with hookups $60, camping cabins from $85; ☺ year-round; ✳ 🛜 🐾) Located right in town, the quiet sites here are shaded by old-growth trees. Includes showers, laundry, store, small pool and playground. Rates are slightly higher for events and holidays.

BLM Kane Creek Rd Campgrounds
CAMPGROUND $

(http://discovermoab.com/blm-campgrounds/; Kane Creek Rd; tent sites $15; ☺ year-round) Just west of Moab, five first-come, first-served campgrounds, with 105 sites total, are found along Kane Creek. Sites have vault toilets and fire rings.

Warner Lake Campground
CAMPGROUND $

(☑ 877-444-6777; www.recreation.gov; off La Sal Mountain Loop Rd; tent sites $10; ☺ Apr-Oct) When it's 100°F (38°C) in Moab, the La Sals may be a balmy 75°F (24°C) by day and downright chilly at night. Warner Lake Campground sits up high at 9400ft and is one of several developed campgrounds that provides water.

Horsethief Campground
CAMPGROUND $

(☑ 435-259-2100; www.blm.gov/visit/horsethief-campground; Mile 11, Hwy 313; tent sites $15; ☺ year-round) If you are headed to Dead Horse Point (p192) or Island in the Sky (p193), this attractive campground is a great option, and cooler than lower-elevation spots. There are 55 sites with picnic tables, vault toilets and grills. Bring water. It's first-come, first-served. RVs are OK. Just up the road, Cowboy Camp has seven walk-in tent sites (Mile 18).

Canyon Rims Recreation Area
CAMPGROUND $

(☑ 435-259-2100; www.blm.gov/visit/canyon-rims-rec-area; Hwy 191; day/week pass per car $5/10, tent sites $15; ☺ year-round) This oft-overlooked recreation area lies 30 miles south of town,

---

DOG LODGINGS

••

Useful for park visitors (pets are not generally allowed beyond paved areas), Moab's best kennel is **Karen's Canine Campground** (☑ 435-259-7922; https://karensk9campground.wordpress.com; 2781 Roberts Dr), where Fido is another one of mom's brood. It has a kiddie pool, shade canopies and a play area. Call ahead.

---

just west of Hwy 191. It's remote but well toward the Needles (p193). Two developed campgrounds have well-spaced sites in desert vegetation.

The 17-site **Wind Whistle Campground** lies off a paved road 8 miles west of Hwy 191, while the 10-site **Hatch Point Campground** is on the gravel road to the Anticline Overlook, 32 miles south of Moab. When other campgrounds are full, these spots are a good bet, with drinking water (March through October), fire rings and pit toilets. Only group reservations are accepted.

Goose Island Campground
CAMPGROUND $

(☑ 435-259-2100; www.blm.gov/visit/goose-island-campground; Hwy 128; campsites $15) Ten no-reservation riverside BLM campgrounds lie along a 28-mile stretch of Hwy 128 that parallels the Colorado River northwest of town. The 19-site Goose Island, just 1.4 miles from Moab, is the closest. Pit toilets, no water.

Slickrock Campground
CAMPGROUND $

(☑ 435-259-7660; www.slickrockcampground.com; 1301½ N Hwy 191; tent sites $29-39, RV sites with hookups $53-59, cabins $69; ☺ Mar-Nov; ✳ 🛜 🐾 🐕) North of town. Tent sites have canopies; RV sites have 30-amp hookups only. Nonguest showers $3; also has hot tubs, heated pool and a store.

Portal RV Resort
CAMPGROUND $

(☑ 435-259-6108; www.portalrvresort.com; 1261 N Hwy 191; RV sites with hookups $71.50; ☺ year-round; 🛜 🐕) The best place for luxury RVers, with long pull-throughs. Has showers, spa, laundry, store and dog run.

Sand Flats Recreation Area
CAMPGROUND $

(www.blm.gov/ut/st/en/fo/moab/recreation/campgrounds/sand_flats_recreation.html; Sand Flats Rd; tent & RV sites $15; ☺ year-round) At the Slickrock bike trailhead, this mountain-biker special has 120 nonreservable sites, fire rings and pit toilets, but no water and no hookups.

Under Canvas Moab
CAMPGROUND $$$

(☑ 801-895-3213; www.undercanvas.com/camps/moab/; Mile 138, Hwy 191; luxury tents from $199; ☺ Mar-Oct) This 'glamping' option gives you rustic canvas tents with some laudable creature comforts – the pimped-out suites even have flush toilets and sitting areas – just like a Victorian explorer (kinda). There's a community bonfire at night and you have excellent views onto Arches from the 40-acre compound.

🛏 Lodging

Kokopelli Lodge   MOTEL **$**
(☑ 435-259-7615; www.kokopellilodge.com; 72 S
100 E; r from $89; ✳ 🛜 🛝) Retro styling meets
desert chic at this great-value budget motel.
Amenities include a hot tub, a BBQ grill and
secure bike storage.

Adventure Inn   MOTEL **$**
(☑ 435-259-6122;   www.adventureinnmoab.com;
512 N Main St; r from $105; ⊘ Mar-Oct; ✳ 🛜) Go
for the economy rooms at this great little in-
die motel, which sports spotless rooms (some
with refrigerators) and decent linens, as well
as laundry facilities. There's a picnic area on-
site and the owners prove helpful.

Desert Hills   B&B **$**
(☑ 435-259-3568; www.deserthillsbnb.com; 1989
S Desert Hills Lane; r from $129; ✳ 🛜) Get away
from the traffic in town at this homey B&B
in a suburban neighborhood. The four simple
rooms have log beds, pillow-top mattresses
and minifridges – and come with friendly,
personal service.

Big Horn Lodge   MOTEL **$**
(☑ 435-259-6171; www.moabbighorn.com; 550 S
Main St; r from $138; ⊖ ✳ 🛜 🛝) With a kitschy
Southwestern-style facade and cozy interiors
paneled with knotty pine, this two-story motel is a strong bet. Service is taken serious-
ly and there are loads of extras (including a
heated swimming pool inches from the road,
refrigerators and coffee makers).

Inca Inn   MOTEL **$**
(☑ 435-259-7261; www.incainn.com; 570 N Main St,
r from $79; ⊘ Feb-Nov; ✳ 🛜 🛝) This small mom-
and-pop motel has old and slightly dark rooms
with small double beds that are plenty clean.
There's a teeny-tiny pool out front.

Lazy Lizard Hostel   HOSTEL **$**
(☑ 435-259-6057; www.lazylizardhostel.com; 1213
S Hwy 191; dm/s/d $12/32/36, cabins $37-58;
P ✳ @ 🛜) This hippie hangout is popular
with European travelers and the noncar set.
Located behind A-1 storage, it has frayed
couches, worn bunks, a small kitchen and a
peaced-out patio. The little cabins out back
are the way to go.

★ Cali Cochitta   B&B **$$**
(☑ 888-429-8112; www.moabdreaminn.com; 110 S
200 E; cottages $175-225; ✳ 🛜) Charming and
central, these adjoining brick cottages offer
snug rooms fitted with smart decor. A long

wooden table on the patio makes a welcome
setting for communal breakfasts. You can also
take advantage of the porch chairs, hammock
or backyard hot tub in the Zen garden.

3 Dogs and a Moose   B&B **$$**
(☑ 435-260-1692; www.3dogsandamoosecottages.
com; 171 W Center St; cottages $145-320; ✳ 🛜 🛝)
Lovely and low-key, these four downtown
cottages make an ideal base camp for groups
and families who want a little socializing in
situ. The style is French country meets playful
modern. Even better, you can pick your own
tomatoes in the landscaped yard, where there
are also hammocks, a bike wash, a grill and
a hot tub.

Gonzo Inn   MOTEL **$$**
(☑ 800-791-4044; www.gonzoinn.com; 100 W 200
S; r from $199; ✳ @ 🛜 🛝 🛝) Less an inn than
a chain-style motel spruced up with retro-'70s
steel accents and sleek cement showers, the
Gonzo Inn is friendly, and we love the loca-
tion off the main drag. No fear and loathing
here, it caters well to cyclists, with a bicycle
wash and repair station as well as a laundry.
Rooms have refrigerators and coffee makers.

Red Moon Lodge   B&B **$$**
(☑ 512-565-7612;   www.redmoonlodge.com;   2950
Old City Park Rd; d from $140; ⊘ Feb-Oct; 🛜) ✎
Tucked alongside a creek bed with tall cottonwoods, this round house is Moab's most
sustainable stay. There are organic breakfasts,
solar power and sustainable xeriscaping. Fanning out on a stone patio, rooms feature firm
beds, attractive woven rugs and solid furniture. There are no phones or TV. Instead imbibe the Zen spirit, explore the grounds and
stretch out on the yoga platform.

Castle Valley Inn   B&B **$$**
(☑ 435-259-6012;   www.castlevalleyinn.com;   424
Amber Lane, off La Sal Mountain Loop; r & cabins
$135-235; ✳) For tranquility, it's hard to beat
this top option off La Sal Mountain Loop Rd,
15 miles north of Moab. With cozy quilts and
handmade aspen furniture, rooms (in the
main house or new bungalows) sit amid apple,
plum and apricot orchards. Bungalows offer
full kitchen and grill; there's also an outdoor
hot tub. Ideal for cycling Castle Valley.

Pack Creek Ranch   RANCH **$$**
(☑ 888-879-6622; www.packcreekranch.com; off
La Sal Mountain Loop; cabins $175-255; 🛜 🛝) This
hidden Shangri-la's log cabins are tucked beneath mature cottonwoods and willow trees
in the La Sal Mountains, 2000ft above Moab.

CAMPGROUNDS IN & AROUND MOAB, CANYONLANDS & ARCHES

CAMPGROUND	LOCATION	DESCRIPTION
Arches National Park		
Devils Garden (p204)	Arches National Park	Trailside, with picnic tables & grills but few amenities; extremely popular, book far in advance.
Canyonlands National Park		
Needles Outpost (p195)	Hwy 211	Dusty, private campground outside the Needles; hot showers but lagging service.
Squaw Flat (p195)	The Needles	Popular, exceptionally pretty sites located trailside with some shade & slickrock.
Willow Flat (p195)	Close to Island in the Sky	On a dirt road near the Green River Overlook, close to trails; few amenities; popular.
Moab		
ACT Campground (p217)	S Mill Creek Dr	Sustainable, forward-thinking campground right in town, with hookups, showers, shared kitchen & fire rings.
Archview Resort & Campground (p224)	Hwy 191	Shadeless but has wi-fi, grills & pool; 10 minutes from downtown.
Canyonlands Campground (p218)	Main St	RV village complete with pool & playground; shade for tents; central.
Portal RV Resort (p218)	Hwy 191	Upscale RV resort, with pool, wi-fi and grassy tent sites; borders golf course.
Slickrock (p218)	Hwy 191	Well maintained, with air-conditioned cabins, tent canopy.
Up the Creek (p217)	E 300 South	Nice tent-only campground with picnic tables & shade; in center of town.
Around Moab		
BLM Campgrounds (p217)	Hwy 128	10 popular campgrounds along Colorado River; buggy if without breeze.
BLM Kane Creek Rd Campgrounds (p218)	Kane Creek Rd	Just west of Moab, with fire rings & toilets.
Hatch Point Recreation Area (p218)	Canyon Rims	Dirt-road campground with fire rings & pit toilets by Anticline Overlook.
Horsethief (p218)	off Hwy 313	Mesa-top sites that are open but well spaced & attractive; bring water.
Kayenta (p192)	Dead Horse	Near trails; good sites with picnic tables, fire rings & grills.
Under Canvas Moab (p218)	Hwy 191	Skip the tent & set up in this luxury spot just north of town, with fire rings, toilets, canvas tents.
Sand Flats Recreation Area (p218)	Sand Flats Rd	Sandstone setting with pit toilets; near Slickrock Bike Trail; bring water.
Warner Lake (p218)	off La Sal Mountain Loop Rd	High-altitude lake sites with picnic tables in national forest.
Wind Whistle (p218)	Canyon Rims Recreation Area	Dirt road access, scenic & less crowded, with picnic tables & pit toilets.

 Drinking Water   *Flush Toilets*   *Ranger Station Nearby*   *Great for Families*   *Dogs Allowed (On Leash)*

MOAB

NUMBER OF SITES	ELEVATION (FT)	OPEN	RESERVATIONS AVAILABLE?	FACILITIES
52	5200	year-round	yes	
20	5100	Apr-Nov	yes	
26	5100	year-round	no	
12	6000	year-round	no	
40	5100	year-round	yes	
77	4026	Mar-Nov	yes	
140	4026	year-round	yes	
80	4026	year-round	yes	
200+	4026	Mar-Nov	yes	
20	4026	Mar-Nov	yes	
n/a	4000	year-round	groups only	
105	5100	year-round	yes	
10	5900	year-round	groups only	
56	5800	year-round	no	
21	6000	year-round	Mar-Oct	
n/a	5100	Mar-Oct	yes	
120	4500	year-round	no	
20	9500	Apr-Oct	no	
17	6000	year-round	groups only	

 Grocery Store Nearby   *Restaurant Nearby*   *Pay-phone*   *Summertime Campfire Program*   *RV Dump Station*

MOAB

Most feature fireplaces; all have kitchens and gas grills (bring groceries). No TV or phones. Edward Abbey is among the artists and writers who came here for inspiration. Amenities include horseback riding and an indoor hot tub and sauna.

★ Sunflower Hill Inn   INN $$$
(☑ 435-259-2974; www.sunflowerhill.com; 185 N 300 E; r $234-309; ❈ 🐾 🛆) Wow! This is one of the best beds in town. A top-shelf B&B, Sunflower Hill offers 12 rooms in a quaint country setting. Grab a room in the cozier cedar-sided early-20th-century home over the annex rooms. All rooms come with quilt-piled beds and antiques – some even have jetted tubs.

Sorrel River Ranch   LUXURY HOTEL $$$
(☑ 877-317-8244; www.sorrelriver.com; Mile 17, Hwy 128; r from $599; ❈ @ 🛆) Southeast Utah's only full-service luxury resort and gourmet restaurant was originally an 1803 homestead. The lodge and log cabins sit on 240 lush acres, with riding areas and alfalfa fields along the Colorado River. Details strive for rustic perfection, with bedroom fireplaces, handmade log beds, copper-top tables and Jacuzzi tubs. There is a two-night minimum stay during busy periods.

Best Western Plus
Canyonlands Inn   MOTEL $$$
(☑ 435-259-2300; www.canyonlandsinn.com; 16 S Main St; r from $248; ❈ 🛆) A comfortable choice at the central crossroads of downtown, this independently owned hotel features ginormous rooms, fitness center, laundry, playground and outdoor pool. It's a little removed from Main St, but you still get a hint of noise.

Red Cliffs Lodge   LODGE $$$
(☑ 435-259-5050; www.redcliffslodge.com; Mile 14, Hwy 128; ste/cabin from $240/340; ❈ 🐾 🛆 🐕) Dude ranch meets deluxe motel. These comfortable rooms feature vaulted knotty-pine ceilings, kitchenettes with dining tables, and private (though cramped) patios, some overlooking the Colorado River. Larger rooms are ideal for families. Also offers horseback riding and a hot tub, an on-site movie museum for Western buffs, and wine tasting. Pets are allowed and horse boarding is available.

✖ Eating

There's no shortage of places to fuel up in Moab, from backpacker coffeehouses to gourmet dining rooms. Pick up the *Moab Menu Guide* (www.moabmenuguide.com) at area lodgings. Some restaurants close or operate on variable days from December through March.

★ Milt's Stop & Eat   BURGERS $
(☑ 435-259-7424; 356 Mill Creek Dr; mains $4-14; ☺ 11am-8pm Tue-Sun) Meet greasy goodness. A triathlete couple bought this classic 1954 burger stand and smartly changed nothing. Heaven is one of their honest burgers made from grass-fed Wagyu beef, jammed with pickles and fresh lettuce, a side of fresh-cut fries and a creamy butterscotch milkshake. Be patient: the line can get long. It's near the Slickrock Trail (p208).

EklectiCafé   AMERICAN $
(☑ 435-259-6896; 352 N Main St; breakfast & sandwiches $5-10; ☺ 7am-2:30pm Mon-Sat, to 1pm Sun; 🐾 🐕) Soy-ginger-seaweed scrambled eggs anyone? This wonderfully quirky cafe lives up to its eclectic name with its food choice and decor. Come for organic coffee, curried wraps and vegetarian salads. Dinner served some weekend evenings.

Love Muffin   CAFE $
(☑ 435-259-6833; www.lovemuffincafe.com; 139 N Main St; mains $7-11; ☺ 7am-2pm; 🐾 🐕) Early-rising locals buy up many of the daily muffins – like the Breakfast Muffin, with bacon and blueberries. Not to worry, the largely organic menu at this vibrant cafe also includes creative sandwiches, breakfast burritos, quinoa bowls and inventive egg dishes such as the Verde, with brisket and slow-roasted salsa.

Jailhouse Café   BREAKFAST $
(☑ 435-259-3900; 101 N Main St; breakfast $11-14; ☺ 7am-noon Mar-Oct) The eggs Benedict here is hard to beat but the line goes deep on weekends. Whole-grain waffles and ginger pancakes are other temptations. In a former jailhouse, with patio seating.

Crystal's Cakes and Cones   ICE CREAM $
(☑ 435-259-9393; 26 Center St; ice cream from $3; ☺ noon-9pm) For a little piece of Americana, queue up at this popular ice creamery. Though the ice cream isn't locally made, local teenagers serve ever-growing lines with a smile.

Sabaku Sushi   SUSHI $$
(☑ 435-259-4455; www.sabakusushi.com; 90 E Center St; rolls $6-11, mains $13-22; ☺ 5pm-midnight Tue-Sun) The ocean is about a million miles away, but with overnight delivery from Hawaii, you still get a creative selection of fresh rolls,

catches of the day and a few Utah originals at this small hole-in-the-wall sushi joint. Go for happy hour (5pm to 6pm on Wednesdays and Thursdays) for discounts on rolls.

Arches Thai
THAI $$
(📞435-355-0533; https://archesthai.com; 60 N 100 W; mains $8-22; ⊙11am-9pm Wed-Mon; 🍴) This large dining room is geared up to serve, with a pleasant, ample space and good-value lunches that come with soup and crab wontons. With options for tofu, seafood or organic chicken in typical curries and noodle dishes. Also serves Vietnamese pho.

Cowboy Grill
AMERICAN $$
(📞435-259-2002; http://redcliffslodge.com; Mile 14, Hwy 128, Red Cliffs Lodge; breakfast & lunch $10-16, dinner mains $14-32; ⊙6:30-10am, 11:30am-2pm & 5-10pm) Incredible sunset Colorado River views are to be had from the patio or from behind the huge picture windows here. Oh, and the hearty, all-American meat and seafood dishes are also quite good.

Singha Thai
THAI $$
(📞435-259-0039; 92 E Center St; mains $14-20; ⊙11am-3pm & 5-9:30pm Mon-Sat, 5-9:30pm Sun; 🍴) Ethnic food is as rare as rain in these parts, so locals pile into this authentic Thai cafe for curries and organic basil chicken. Service is sleepy and the ambiance generic, but if you're hot for spice, it delivers.

Eddie McStiff's
AMERICAN $$
(📞435-259-2337; www.eddiemcstiffs.com; 59 S Main St; mains $10-22; ⊙11:30am-midnight Sun-Thu, to 1am Fri & Sat; 🍺) Though it's as much taproom-bar as restaurant, the burgers and pizzas (gluten-free available) are almost as popular as the beer here. Salad topped with grilled salmon hits the right note after too many burgers on the road. Occasional live music brightens the night.

Spoke on Center
AMERICAN $$
(📞435-260-7177; www.thespokemoab.com; 5 N Main St; mains $9-20; ⊙11am-10pm) This burger joint sprawls over two stories of semi-industrial open-concept dining space. It serves skillet-plated burger combos and substantial sides. Come dinner, check out the big-dog options like chicken alfredo or grilled salmon with quinoa salad.

★Desert Bistro
SOUTHERN US $$$
(📞435-259-0756; www.desertbistro.com; 36 S 100 W; mains $20-60; ⊙5:30-11pm Wed-Sun) Stylized preparations of game and fresh, flown-in seafood are the specialty at this welcoming

white-tablecloth restaurant inside an old house. Think smoked elk in a huckleberry glaze, pepper-seared scallops and jicama salad with crisp pears. Everything is made on-site, from freshly baked bread to delicious pastries. Great wine list, too.

River Grill
MODERN AMERICAN $$$
(📞435-259-4642; www.sorrelriver.com/dining/; Mile 17, Hwy 128, Sorrel River Ranch; breakfast $10-16, lunch $12-18, dinner $30-50; ⊙7am-3pm & 5-10pm Mar-Oct, 8-10am & 5:30-7:30pm Nov-Feb) For romance, it's hard to beat the wraparound veranda overlooking red-rock canyons outside Moab. Dine on heirloom tomato soup, wedge salad and chili-rubbed pork tenderloin served with buttery polenta. The New American menu changes seasonally, but expect seared steaks, succulent rack of lamb and the freshest seafood flown in.

Self-Catering

Moonflower Market
HEALTH FOOD $
(📞435-259-5712; www.moonflower.coop; 39 E 100 N; ⊙8am-8pm; 🍴) Nonprofit health-food store with great picnic supplies, including takeout sandwiches, and loads of community info.

Moab Farmers Market
MARKET $
(📞435-881-9060; www.moabfarmersmarket.com; 400 N 100 W; ⊙5-8pm Fri May-Oct) Local farms vend their summer produce in Swanny City Park, with free concerts.

City Market & Pharmacy
MARKET $
(📞435-259-8971; 425 S Main St; ⊙6am-11pm) Moab's largest grocery store, with sandwiches and salad bar to go.

🍸 Drinking & Nightlife

Woody's Tavern
BAR
(📞435-259-3550; 221 S Main St; ⊙11am-midnight) Full bar with pool tables and a great outdoor patio; live music Friday and Saturday in season.

Moab Brewery
BREWERY
(📞435-259-6333; www.themoabbrewery.com; 686 S Main St; ⊙11:30am-11pm; 🍺) Choose from a list of nine microbrews made in the vats just behind the bar area. The vast and varied menu is more impressive than the food itself. Be aware that service isn't a strong suit.

Dave's Corner Market
COFFEE
(📞435-259-6999; 401 Mill Creek Dr; ⊙6am-10pm) Sip shade-grown espresso with locals at this corner convenience store.

MOAB DRINKING & NIGHTLIFE

ESSENTIALS

For fresh spring water, take Hwy 191 north to Hwy 128 east and continue 100 yards to **Matrimony Springs** (Hwy 128), on the right. Gear Heads (p216) offers free filtered water.

You can wash your whites at **Moab Laundry Express** (✆435-259-5626; www.moablaundry.com; 471 S Main St; ⊙24hr; ☎). Up the Creek Campground (p217) has tidy and clean showers, also available at **Archview Campground** (✆435-259-7854; www.moab-utah.com/archview/archview.html; Hwy 191; tent site $37-45, RV site from $53, cabin $70-115; ⊙Mar-Nov; ☎⊛), Canyonlands Campground (p218) or Poison Spider Bicycles (p208).

☆ Entertainment

**Moab Arts &
Recreation Center**   HEALTH & FITNESS
(✆435-259-6272; www.moabrecreation.com; 111 E 100 N; ◉) The rec center hosts everything from yoga classes to contra dance parties and poetry gatherings.

Canyonlands by Night & Day   THEATER
(✆800-394-9978; www.canyonlandsbynight.com; 1861 N Hwy 191; adult/child from $69/59; ⊙Apr-Oct; ◉) Start with dinner riverside, then take an after-dark boat ride on the Colorado, with an old-fashioned light show complete with historical narration. It also offers day tours and magic shows.

Slickrock Cinemas 3   CINEMA
(✆435-259-4441; 580 Kane Creek Blvd) First-run movies.

❶ Information

Cell phones work in Moab but not in river canyons.

EMERGENCY

Grand County Emergency Coordinator (✆435-259-8115) Search and rescue.
Moab Regional Hospital (✆435-719-3500; http://mrhmoab.org; 450 W Williams Way) For 24-hour emergency medical care.
Police (✆911; 217 E Center St)

INTERNET ACCESS

Grand County Public Library (✆435-259-1111; www.moablibrary.org; 257 E Center St; ⊙9am-

8pm Mon-Fri, to 5pm Sat; ☎) Easy 15-minute free internet; register for longer access or use the wi-fi. Has great local map resources.

POST

Post Office (✆435-259-7427; 50 E 100 N; ⊙8am-5pm Mon-Fri, 9am-1pm Sat)

TOURIST INFORMATION

BLM Office (✆435-259-2100, permits 435-259-7012; www.blm.gov/ut/st/en/fo/moab.html; 82 E Dogwood Ave; ⊙7:45am-4:30pm Mon-Fri) While most people head to the visitor center, you can get pamphlets and ask about basic camping and BLM use issues here.
Canyonlands Natural History Association (p195) Sells area-interest books and maps online, and at national park visitor centers.
Moab Information Center (✆435-259-8825; http://discovermoab.com/visitor-center/; 25 E Center St; ⊙8am-7pm; ☎) Excellent source of information on area parks, trails, activities, camping and weather. Extensive bookstore and knowledgeable staff. Walk-in only.
Moab Happenings (www.moabhappenings.com) Free publication also available online with events listings.
Utah Mountain Biking (www.utahmountainbiking.com) Descriptions of all the major biking areas.

❶ Getting There & Around

Canyonlands Airport (CNY; ✆435-259-4849; www.moabairport.com; off Hwy 191), 16 miles north of town, receives flights from Salt Lake City. **Boutique Air** (✆855-268-8478; www.boutiqueair.com) flies to Salt Lake City and Denver. Major car-rental agencies, such as **Enterprise** (✆435-259-8505; www.enterprise.com; N Hwy 191, Mile 148; ⊙8am-5pm Mon-Fri, to 2pm Sat), have representatives at the airport.

There are a number of bike paths in and around town; the Moab Information Center can offer a map guide.
Coyote Shuttle (✆435-259-8656; www.coyoteshuttle.com) On-demand Canyonlands Airport and river shuttles. Biker/hiker shuttles meet at the **Chile Pepper Bike Shop** (p208).
Roadrunner Shuttle (✆435-259-9402; www.roadrunnershuttle.com) On-demand Canyonlands Airport, hiker-biker and river shuttles.
Elevated Transit (✆888-353-8283; www.elevatedtransit.com; Moab to Salt Lake City airport $70) Daily service from Blanding to the south to Salt Lake City. Stops in Monticello, Moab and Green River, continuing to Price, Provo, downtown Salt Lake and the Salt Lake City airport.

Understand Utah's National Parks

The Parks Today

In December 2016, when then-President Obama created Bears Ears National Monument, Utah found itself back at the center of a long-simmering controversy that was about to boil over: how should the vast tracts of public land in the American West be managed? Set aside for recreation and environmental and cultural preservation, or sold off to private interests to promote economic growth in local communities and at the state level?

Best on Film

Thelma & Louise (1991) This road-trip story of the enduring female spirit was shot in Arches and Monument Valley.
127 Hours (2010) This Danny Boyle film recounts the gruesome real-life story of Aron Ralston's harrowing ordeal in the Utah backcountry, where he was trapped by a boulder for 127 hours, eventually cutting off his own arm to save his life.
Footloose (1984) While it was shot up north in Utah County, who can forget Kevin Bacon's angst-filled dance in an abandoned silo.

Best in Print

Desert Solitaire (Edward Abbey; 1968) Provocative and hilariously cranky to boot, this ethereal tale of conservation chronicles the author's experience as a ranger at Arches.
Under the Banner of Heaven (Jon Krakauer; 2003) Perhaps the most high-profile book ever written on Utah. It's a compelling exposé of extremist polygamist groups and a provocative look at the state's oft-troubled history.
Refuge: An Unnatural History of Family and Place (Terry Tempest Williams; 1991) Written by a Mormon, naturalist and environmentalist, this story explores the intimate and sensual landscapes of Utah's land and people.

The Public Lands Controversy

With so much public land – over 60% of Utah's land is controlled by the federal government – it's not surprising that land use and stewardship is a contentious issue. Open a newspaper or listen in on the chatter at the local diner and you'll soon see that this is the singular thread that dominates the political and environmental debates seen across the state – and throughout much of the West.

In December 2017, just one year after the creation of Bears Ears, the Trump administration declared its intent to shrink the new monument by 85%, further fanning the flames of national discord. And no wonder – Bears Ears has come to represent many of the hot-button topics in American political debates: federal versus state power, the undue influence of industry lobbyists among politicians, racism, and climate change versus natural resource extraction.

But despite the controversy surrounding Bears Ears, there has actually always been bipartisan consensus on the need to protect the area: the sticking point remains how much land, and who gets control. The monument, under Obama's original proposal, splits management between the Bureau of Land Management (BLM; thus allowing grazing rights for ranchers and ATV use on designated trails, both sore points for environmentalists), the US Forest Service, and a coalition of five Native American tribes, who had long petitioned the government for its creation. Bears Ears is the location of some 100,000 Native American archaeological and cultural sites, some dating back to the 11th century, and looting and degradation have steadily increased over the past decade.

Utah representatives Jason Chaffetz and Rob Bishop had previously introduced a bill in Congress that would protect some of the area in exchange for developing the rest for natural mineral and gas extraction and, critically, voiding the federal government's power to create any future monuments in seven Utah counties. Neither Republicans, Democrats nor the Native American coalition got behind the bill, however.

Taking a Stand

Following President Trump's election, Utah senator Orrin Hatch's office submitted a redrawn proposal of the Bears Ears and Grand Staircase–Escalante boundaries to Secretary of the Interior Ryan Zinke, in order to facilitate the extraction of all natural gas, oil, coal and uranium deposits. Secretary Zinke, after his much-debated review of 27 US national monuments, ultimately recommended that the president significantly reduce the size of both Utah monuments per Senator Hatch's recommendations.

Native Americans immediately condemned the declaration as yet another betrayal by the American government and proceeded to take the federal government to court (where the case is likely to stay for some time). But even before the legal battle had begun, recreationalists, running the gamut from hikers, athletes, hunters and anglers to the rapidly growing outdoor industry, had taken their own stand.

In a pointed letter, Patagonia founder Yvon Chouinard condemned the government's preference for industry profit on public lands, reminding naysayers that the outdoor recreation industry contributes $12 billion annually and 122,000 jobs to the state. Patagonia's subsequent boycott of Salt Lake City's huge Outdoor Retailer Show took the rest of the outdoor industry with them. Within days, the convention pulled out of Utah permanently, relocating to Colorado.

Loved to Death?

Regardless of the political battle, one thing is clear – everyone loves American national parks. Visitation is up record numbers (almost doubling in many parks) and federal funding is down, putting a considerable strain on the most popular destinations. In Zion, for example, the challenges are numerous: traffic jams to enter the park in summer can be up to an hour long. There are only 1200 parking spots, yet some 10,000 daily visitors. And then there are the toilets – like parking spots, there simply aren't enough of them.

Zion installed a park shuttle system in 2000 to ease traffic congestion, but even that is under severe strain, with some 6.3 million riders in 2017. Finding a solution to increased visitation has not been easy: proposals have included increasing entrance fees by over 100% during peak season, installing a reservation system for entrance to the park, or, alternatively, installing a permit system for entrance to certain trails. As of 2018, no decisions had been made.

UTAH POPULATION:
3.1 MILLION

UTAH AREA:
82,169 SQ MILES

NATIONAL PARKS VISITORS:
10.2 MILLION

VISITOR SPENDING IN UTAH:
$8.4 BILLION

if 100 people come to Zion...

55 would use the South Zion Canyon entrance
33 would use the East (tunnel) entrance
12 would use the Kolob Canyons (Northwest) entrance

seasonal visitation - Zion (% of annual visitors)

Jan-Mar 11
Apr-Jun 34.5
Jul-Sep 36
Oct-Dec 17.5

population per sq mile

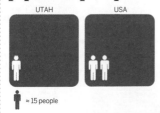

UTAH   USA

≈ 15 people

History

The human history of Utah and its vast public lands entangles itself in a cryptic knot of exploitation, conservation, compassion and avarice. This desolate desert plateau gave rise to dinosaurs and ancestral Native American civilizations, Mormon settlers and cowboy outlaws, uranium prospectors and new-era conservationists driven to protect this unique corner of wilderness. The history of the US and the West has left an imprint, but it's the traces of Utah's indigenous peoples and original mavericks that resonate today.

First Peoples

It's not definitively known when humans first arrived in the Southwest. Most likely, nomadic peoples migrated from Asia across a land bridge between Siberia and Alaska, making their way south between 23,000 and 10,000 years ago. Some models posit subsequent migrations by boat. We know that they arrived by 10,000 BC, as archaeologists have dated spearheads found among the remains of woolly mammoths and other ice-age mammals. However, Native American creation stories say that the people have always been here, or that they descended from the spirit world.

However they arrived, these early groups were primarily skilled hunters. By 8500 BC, most large prehistoric mammals were extinct – some possibly hunted to that fate, though many were unable to adapt to the drying glacial climate. This led to what scholars call the Desert Archaic period, which lasted roughly from 6500 BC to AD 200. The term 'Desert Archaic' refers as much to the period's hunter-gatherer lifestyle as it does to an ecosystem or block of time.

As a survival method, hunting and gathering proved remarkably adaptive and resilient in the Southwest. Early Desert Archaic peoples lived nomadically in small, unconcentrated groups, following the food supply of seasonal wild plants and such small animals as rabbits. Shelters were temporary, and caves were often used. These people became skilled at basketry, a functional craft for groups on the move.

Eventually, late Desert Archaic peoples established semiregular settlement patterns and started to cultivate crops such as primitive corn, beans and squash. By AD 200 several distinct cultures had emerged.

Guide to Rock Art of the Utah Region (2000), by Dennis Silfer, is an authoritative overview of current scientific knowledge about prehistoric indigenous cultures, offering detailed, if somewhat dated, descriptions and explanations of rock-art sites.

TIMELINE	250 million BC	60 million years ago	23,000 BC– 10,000 BC
	Triassic Period of the Mesozoic Era, dinosaurs evolve, southern Utah's plateau country is a shallow sea off the western edge of the earth's giant supercontinent known as Pangea.	Start of the Cenozoic Era – or Age of Mammals. Seismic activity and the movement of continental plates uplifts the entire Colorado Plateau, creating the Grand Staircase and Rocky Mountains.	Groups of nomadic hunters and gatherers migrate from Asia over the Bering Strait land bridge to North America. Competing theories suggest continual migration by boat.

Ancestral Puebloans dominated the Colorado Plateau, which encompasses southern Utah, southwest Colorado and northern portions of Arizona and New Mexico. They were once called the Anasazi – a Navajo word meaning 'ancient enemy' – by archaeologists, but Ancestral Puebloans is now the preferred term, since contemporary tribes believe they are descended from these ancient peoples.

Ancestral Puebloans dominated the Colorado Plateau from around 200 BC to AD 1500, though in southern Utah they left a few centuries earlier, around AD 1200. There's no consensus over why Ancestral Puebloans abandoned the area when they did. It was likely a combination of drought, soil erosion, disease and conflict with other groups over dwindling resources.

Ancestral Puebloans adopted irrigated agriculture, became highly accomplished basket-makers and potters, and believed in a complex cosmology. They are best known for their cliff dwellings, pueblo villages and kivas (ceremonial underground chambers). While southern Utah contains far fewer of these ancient structures than surrounding states, it does boast abundant Ancestral Puebloan rock art. Hovenweep National Monument and Cedar Mesa are your best bet to see these dwellings.

Living in southern Utah concurrently were the Fremont people, who migrated from the north and continued a seminomadic existence, preferring hunting and gathering to farming and villages. They abandoned the area around the same time as the Ancestral Puebloans, and their distinctive rock art is also widespread.

Southern Paiutes & Spaniards

Southern Paiute tribes began emerging around AD 1100. Comprising a dozen or so distinct bands, Paiute territory extended from California's deserts east to Colorado, and from Utah's Great Basin south to Arizona's Painted Desert. The Kaibab Paiutes lived near what is now Zion National Park. Today, their tribal reservation surrounds Pipe Spring National Monument on the northern Arizona Strip.

Generally speaking, Southern Paiutes followed the same survival strategy as Desert Archaic peoples – migrating with the seasons, hunting small animals, gathering wild plants and tending a few modest crops. A staple of their diet was the piñon, or pine nut, and they continued the tradition of fine basketry. Their shelters and even their clothes often weren't made to last more than a season.

Southern Paiutes lived largely in peace for more than 500 years. No one coveted the unyielding land they called home, yet they found abundance in it. Deer were plentiful, the winters around present-day St George were mild, and in summer they fished mountain lakes. Ever-growing numbers of Europeans on the continent didn't know of them, and gold-hungry

Stephen Trimble's hefty tome *The People: Indians of the American Southwest* (1993) stitches together tribal histories and modern realities by letting Native Americans, including Utah's Southern Paiutes and Colorado River tribes, speak for themselves.

6500 BC–AD 200	200 BC–AD 1200	1100	1776
Desert Archaic cultures occupy southern Utah. These nomadic hunter-gatherers become adept at catching small game and adapting desert plants to new uses, including making baskets.	Ancestral Puebloans develop a vibrant culture, with pueblos, cliff dwellings and ceremonial centers spread across the Colorado Plateau; distinct Fremont Culture arises contemporaneously.	Southern Paiute tribes emerge in the Colorado Plateau region, spreading all the way to present-day California, flourishing for the next 700 years until the arrival of explorers and settlers.	In search of a shortcut from Santa Fe to California, the Domínguez-Escalante expedition is the first non–Native American group to explore the Colorado Plateau.

16th-century Spanish conquistadors like Coronado never penetrated the Colorado Plateau's rugged territory.

Then, in 1776, the same year the US declared its independence from Britain, the Domínguez-Escalante expedition encountered the Kaibab band of Southern Paiutes while skirting the western edge of the Colorado Plateau. In the first recorded European impressions of them, Silvestre Vélez de Escalante, a Franciscan friar and Spanish Catholic missionary, described 'a large number of people, all of pleasing appearance, very friendly and extremely timid.'

The Spanish expedition had two goals: to open a communication route from Santa Fe to California and to spread Christianity among indigenous peoples. But the expedition never made it further west, nor

WRITTEN ON THE LAND

Anywhere in southern Utah you may encounter it: the pecked outlines of human figures and animals, painted handprints, squiggled lines etched into desert varnish. Rock art is mysterious and awesome, and always leaves us wondering: who did this and why? What were they trying to say?

Dating from at least 2000 BC to as late as the 19th century AD, rock art in Utah was once called 'a wilderness Louvre' by *National Geographic*. The rock art found in southern Utah has been attributed to every known ancestral and modern people, from ice-age hunters and Desert Archaic nomads to contemporary Native American tribes. One way archaeologists track the spread of ancestral cultures is by studying their distinctive rock-art styles, which tend to be either abstract or representational, both zoomorphic and anthropomorphic. Representational rock art is usually more recent, while abstract designs appear in all ages.

The top spot to view rock art is the Great Gallery at Horseshoe Canyon (p194) in Canyonlands. Other fine examples are found in every national park and across BLM and public lands.

Preservation

➡ Do not disturb or remove any artifacts or features at the site.

➡ Do not trace, repaint, remove graffiti or otherwise touch or apply any materials to the rock art.

➡ Stay back at least 10ft from all rock-art panels, using binoculars or a zoom lens for better views.

➡ Do not climb the cliffs above rock-art sites, as that could let loose a rockslide that would damage the site.

➡ Minimize the number of vehicles you bring to rock-art sites, and do not hike off-trail or build campfires nearby.

1839	1847	1848	1850
After fleeing arrest in Missouri, Mormon founder Joseph Smith leads his followers to Nauvoo, Illinois, where a temple and town are built beside the Mississippi River.	Mormons fleeing religious persecution in the east start arriving in Salt Lake City. Over the next two decades, more than 70,000 Mormons will migrate to Utah.	The Mexican–American War ends with the 1848 Treaty of Guadalupe Hidalgo; Mexico cedes much of the present-day Southwest, including parts of Utah, to the USA.	US federal government establishes the Territory of Utah after denying Latter-Day Saints leader Brigham Young's proposal for a more expansive State of Deseret (Mormon for 'honeybee').

did Spain fund the establishment of any Utah missions. Afterward, the Southern Paiutes were left mostly, but not entirely, alone. Some of the Spanish Trail trading route had been cut, and occasional trappers wandered through, as did strange diseases and even Ute and New Mexican slave traders, who often kidnapped Paiute children to sell for horses and goods elsewhere.

By the early 19th century the Southern Paiutes could weather the passing wagon trains, which trampled grasses and crops, but smallpox and measles were decimating them. By mid-century, before they'd ever had to fight or strike a deal with a Mormon missionary settler, some Southern Paiute populations had dwindled by two-thirds.

Paiute, Ute, Goshute, Shoshone and Navajo people all live in modern-day Utah. The Uintah and Ouray Reservation is located in the northeast, and is the second-largest Native American reservation in the United States. In the southeast, don't miss a day of horseback riding, hiking or shopping in the Navajo Nation, the largest Native American reservation in the US. Festivals celebrating Native American traditions mostly happen in the summer.

Arrival of the Mormons

In 1847 Brigham Young and party reached a point near Utah's Great Salt Lake. Fleeing persecution for their beliefs back east, the Mormons were charged by their prophet Joseph Smith to find a place out west where they could build a heavenly city on earth. They were looking, in other words, for what Southern Paiutes had long enjoyed – the solitude and freedom from interference this harsh land provided. As the story goes, Young sat upright out of his sickbed long enough to say, 'This is the right place. Drive on.'

The Mormons were not your average pioneers, and Young was not an average leader. The plan was to build an independent nation, a theocracy outside the boundaries of the USA. Within a year, however, the rapidly expanding country caught up with them. The 1848 Treaty of Guadalupe Hidalgo turned the Mexican territory into a US possession, and the concurrent discovery of gold in California attracted streams of passing miners. With the miners came Manifest Destiny, the nationalistic belief that the US was ordained by God to stretch from 'sea to shining sea,' from the Atlantic to the Pacific Oceans. Utah would not remain isolated for long.

In 1850 the Territory of Utah was established, with Young as territorial governor. If Young despaired over the political fate of his beloved State of Deseret, he didn't let on. Instead, he aspired to settle an empire larger than Texas as fast as he could. He sent Mormon pioneers in all directions to plow, irrigate and farm the desert into submission, which they did. The Mormons succeeded because they were zealously dedicated to their

To learn more about the 1776 Domínguez-Escalante expedition and read excerpts from Escalante's own diary, track down *Pageant in the Wilderness* (1972), by Herbert Bolton; it's one of the first authoritative accounts.

HISTORY ARRIVAL OF THE MORMONS

1854–58	1861	1863	1865–67
The Mormons send missionaries to convert the Southern Paiutes, a Mormon militia group massacres 120 immigrants. Mormon missionary Nephi Johnson becomes the first non–Native American to enter Zion.	Nicknamed Utah's Dixie, the experimental farming community of St George is founded during the Mormon Church's Cotton Mission days; scarce drinking water makes life difficult. The Civil War kicks off.	Isaac Behunin and his sons are the first Mormons to settle Zion Canyon, building a cabin and clearing some farmland. Behunin is credited with naming Zion Canyon.	Utah's Black Hawk War reaches its peak, with fighting between Mormon settlers and Ute, Paiute and Navajo tribespeople; Native American resistance does not end until 1872.

faith, tempered by their journey to Utah along the Mormon Trail, and organized. They attacked the land as a cohesive group, fired by visions of God, not gold.

Everywhere they went in southern Utah, Mormons displaced Paiutes, appropriating water sources and the most desirable land. In an apparent contradiction, the Mormons also 'adopted' the Paiutes and gave them the only practical support they would receive, which they came to depend on. The *Book of Mormon* claims that Native Americans are one of Israel's lost tribes, so bringing them back into the fold was considered an important Mormon mission, even as racist attitudes toward indigenous peoples prevailed.

The end result for the Paiutes turned out to be much the same as for Native American tribes elsewhere in the Southwest – that is, cultural disenfranchisement, the loss of traditional hunting grounds and access to water sources, and a population decimated by foreign diseases and indentured servitude.

The University of Utah Press (www.uofupress.com) and the national parks' cooperative natural history associations are your best sources of new history books, covering eras from indigenous tribes to Spanish explorers and Mormon settlers.

A Massacre, a War & Statehood

With their modern-day prophets, the practice of 'celestial marriage' (that is, polygamy) and theocratic territorial government, Mormons were perceived as a threat by federal authorities and everyday US citizens, whom the Mormons called Gentiles. In the 1850s, tensions ran high, and minor clashes were common. On September 11, 1857, in the mountains outside St George, building religious hysteria and fear of a federal invasion led a Mormon militia – possibly with the enlisted help of local Paiutes – to slaughter 120 innocent California-bound pioneers. Details of the Mountain Meadows Massacre are still debated today, but the incident confirmed the government's worst fears, prompting the US Army to surround and subdue Salt Lake City that same year.

No one was killed and hardly a shot fired in the so-called Mormon War, which had two main repercussions: it instituted a secular government in Utah, beneath which the religious hierarchy continued to operate for a decade or more; and it curtailed territorial ambitions, reducing the size of Utah. Through the Civil War and beyond, the territory petitioned for statehood, but it was continually denied, even as states around it were accepted. Animosity between Mormons and the federal government lingered, with polygamy as the sticking point. Finally, in 1890 the Mormon Church officially repudiated polygamy and asked its followers to do the same. Six years later Utah won statehood.

A Tale of Two Explorers

In their efforts to be self-sufficient, the Mormons established several missions in southern Utah in the 1850s and '60s: the Iron Mission, centered

1869	1870	1872	1878
First transcontinental railway line is completed north of Salt Lake City. John Wesley Powell successfully descends the Colorado River and begins a geologic survey of southern Utah.	Mormon pioneer Ebenezer Bryce and his family settle near Bryce Canyon, which he famously calls 'a hell of a place to lose a cow.'	John Wesley Powell returns to southern Utah and explores Zion Canyon, calling it by the Paiute name Mukuntuweap, meaning 'straight canyon.' Yellowstone National Park is formed.	Mormons permanently settle in the Moab region. (Ute tribespeople violently thwarted a previous effort in the 1850s.) Agriculture and grazing quickly become the economic mainstays.

around Cedar City, mined ore and smelted iron for construction; while the Cotton Mission, centered around St George, grew cotton for Mormon use and export. Neither mission was ultimately successful. However, the Mormons also sent missionaries south to convert the Southern Paiutes, and its success was largely due to Jacob Hamblin, who arrived in 1854.

Dubbed the 'Mormon Leatherstocking,' Hamblin gained the respect and trust of some Native American tribes across the Southwest. He said he believed that he always told the truth, listened and never shed Native American blood, he would be safe. Hamblin became a peacemaker who negotiated important treaties and, with Native American assistance, explored the Colorado Plateau as no non–Native American had before him, serving as an ambassador of the Mormon Church, including to the Hopi mesas and the Navajo Nation.

In 1869 one-armed Civil War veteran and geologist John Wesley Powell became famous for being the first to descend the length of the Colorado River through the Grand Canyon. Unlike Hamblin, Powell's motivation was not religious, but to survey and explore the land and peoples of southern Utah for science. Thanks to his passion and rigor, Powell and his survey teams' geologic and ethnological work largely forms the basis of what we know about early southern Utah today. In 1870 Hamblin secured Powell's second expedition a welcome among Southern Paiutes. As Hamblin had done, Powell demonstrated respect and earned both safe passage and practical assistance from the Southern Paiutes. You can track Powell's expeditions in Canyonlands, Zion, Grand Staircase–Escalante National Monument and Lake Powell National Recreation Area.

With spare prose and uncommon insight, Western writer Wallace Stegner captures the early history of Utah and the Mormons in The Gathering of Zion: The Story of the Mormon Trail (1964) and Mormon Country (1942).

Taming Zion's Wilderness

Earlier indigenous peoples undoubtedly knew and entered Zion Canyon, for they left evidence on the rocks, but to the Kaibab Paiutes it was a place to be avoided, particularly after sunset. Mysterious and foreboding, the canyon was seen as inhabited by trickster gods who were capricious, even willfully malicious. The first non–Native American to enter Zion Canyon was Nephi Johnson, a Mormon pioneer who came south with Jacob Hamblin on a mission. In 1858, at the behest of Brigham Young, Johnson explored the upper reaches of the Virgin River, looking for good places to settle. One can only imagine what he must have felt as he entered Zion Canyon alone, his Paiute guide waiting safely behind.

Mormons didn't settle in the canyon until 1863, when Isaac Behunin and his sons built the first cabin and cleared some farmland. Behunin is credited with naming Zion Canyon, saying that 'A man can worship god among these great cathedrals as well as in any man-made church.' When Brigham Young visited in 1870, he disagreed with the assessment. Whether due to the arduous journey or the forbidden tobacco Behunin

In Massacre at Mountain Meadows (2008), Ronald Walker and Richard Turley unflinchingly examine one of the darkest incidents in Mormon pioneer history. For another viewpoint, read journalist Jon Krakauer's Under the Banner of Heaven (2003).

1889	1890	1896	1916
Wild West outlaw Butch Cassidy, the son of Mormon immigrants, flees to southern Utah to hide out after robbing a bank in Telluride, Colorado.	Mormon president Wilford Woodruff signs a manifesto that officially ceases the practice of polygamy; plural marriage is still practiced today among fundamentalist groups in rural Utah.	Utah is admitted to the Union as the 45th state after territorial politicians agree to explicitly ban the practice of polygamy in the new state constitution.	President Woodrow Wilson authorizes the establishment of the National Park Service (NPS); Methodist minister Frederick Vining Fisher visits Zion Canyon. The US enters WWI a year later.

was growing, Young proclaimed it 'Not Zion,' a name that stuck among Mormons for years.

After his first famous Colorado River expedition, John Wesley Powell returned to southern Utah and explored Zion Canyon in 1872. Powell called it Mukuntuweap, the Paiute word for 'straight canyon' or 'straight-up land.' But it was Clarence Dutton, a poet-geologist in Powell's employ, who captured its grandeur. Upon seeing the canyon in 1875, Dutton wrote: 'In coming time it will, I believe, take rank with a very small number of spectacles, each of which will, in its own way, be regarded as the most exquisite of its kind which the world discloses.'

In a 1908 official report, a government surveyor first suggested preserving Zion Canyon as a monument. President Taft signed the proclamation creating Mukuntuweap National Monument in 1909. Methodist minister Frederick Vining Fisher toured the canyon in the company of a Latter-Day Saints bishop in 1916, giving names to many of the famous rock formations, including Angels Landing and the Great White Throne. In 1919 the monument's name and designation were officially changed by Congress, and thus Zion National Park was born.

Within a year, park visitation doubled to about 3700 people – hardly crowded, but still a lot considering road conditions and its remote location. To better facilitate tourism to southern Utah, a railroad spur was extended to Cedar City in 1923. Zion Lodge opened two years later,

> For more historical context on John Wesley Powell and his groundbreaking work, read Wallace Stegner's fascinating book *Beyond the Hundredth Meridian: John Wesley Powell and the Second Opening of the West* (1953).

LATTER-DAY SAINTS

Self-proclaimed prophet Joseph Smith was born in Vermont in 1805. The child of mystics, Joseph came of age just as a widespread religious revival movement, called the Second Great Awakening, was feverishly beginning to take hold of the country. Religious revival camp meetings were a common sight, especially in rural towns and on the Western frontier.

Smith claimed to have received his first heavenly visit at age 18, when the angel Moroni revealed to him the location of golden tablets buried in the woods near his home in New York. This was three years after God told him in a vision that all churches currently in existence were false. The angel Moroni returned three more times, once a year. After the fourth visit, Smith was allowed to take the golden tablets home and, using 'stone spectacles' provided by the angel, read and transcribe the indecipherable word of God.

Three years later, in 1830, these revelations were published as the *Book of Mormon*, and the Church of Jesus Christ of Latter-Day Saints was established, with Smith as its charismatic leader. There's much more to the story of the Mormon faith – which thanks to globetrotting missionaries is one of the world's fastest-growing religions, with over 15 million members. If you're curious, just open the *Book of Mormon;* there's one in every hotel room in Utah. St George in Southwest Utah is a great town in which to explore Mormonism in greater depth.

1919	1923	1927	1928
Already national monuments, both Zion and the Grand Canyon officially become national parks; a dirt road to the Grand Canyon's North Rim is built from Kanab, Utah.	Union Pacific Railroad is extended to Cedar City; building begins on Bryce Canyon Lodge, made of local timber and stone and designed by Gilbert Stanley Underwood.	Laborious and often-dangerous construction starts on the Zion–Mt Carmel Hwy, which opens three years later, bringing more tourists to southern Utah.	Named after Mormon settler Ebenezer Bryce, Bryce Canyon becomes Utah's second national park; over 25,000 tourists arrive that year, often en route to and from the Grand Canyon.

accommodating railway tourists following the 'Grand Circle' route around the Southwest. In 1930 the Zion–Mt Carmel Hwy and its tunnel were completed, offering a paved route into and through Zion, bringing in over 55,000 tourists that year.

Bryce Canyon

Historically overlooked, Bryce Canyon nestles alongside the Paunsaugunt Plateau, the latter's name derived from a Paiute word meaning 'home of the beavers.' Fur trappers like Jedediah Smith who roamed the area in the early 19th century made no mention of Bryce's striking scenery, and nor did Spanish traders. During his 1869 survey, John Wesley Powell stuck to the rivers and passed right by. Captain Sutton, a member of Powell's survey, described the distant terrain as seeming 'traversable only by a creature with wings.'

Mormons scouts arrived at Bryce Canyon in the 1850s as they searched the entire Paunsaugunt Plateau for arable land. In the mid-1870s a small group settled in the adjacent valleys, which seemed well suited for grazing livestock. Among the latter was Ebenezer Bryce, who stayed in the area for five years, building an irrigation ditch and a road into the canyon. Bryce moved his family south to Arizona in 1880, but left behind in the canyon his name and the now famous epithet, 'It's a hell of a place to lose a cow.'

Like Zion Canyon, Bryce was popular among railway tourists and conservationists at the turn of the 20th century, though it was more difficult to reach. It wasn't until 1915, when JW Humphrey became the founding supervisor of Utah's Sevier National Forest that Bryce's fate would be sealed. In 1916 Humphrey brought in photographers to take the first pictures of the spectacular canyon for a promotional article that appeared in a Union Pacific Railroad publication. Word got out.

In 1919, the same year Zion became a national park, the state legislature recommended that Bryce also be protected. Four years later President Harding established Bryce Canyon National Monument. In 1928 Bryce became Utah's second national park. Throughout the 1920s, construction of Bryce Canyon Lodge, another Union Pacific Railroad 'Grand Circle' Southwest touring stop, was carried out using locally quarried stone and harvested timber.

Beneath These Red Cliffs: An Ethnohistory of the Utah Paiutes (2006), by Ronald L Holt, with a foreword by tribal chairwoman Lora Tom, is an unflinching tale of indigenous survival, from Western occupation to tribal restoration.

A Capital Wonderland

Capitol Reef's European-American history dates back to 1872, when Mormon settlers first planted fruit trees along the banks of the Fremont River near the town of Junction. Once their trees flourished, the settlers renamed the town Fruita. Over the next decades, Torrey resident Ephraim Pectal sought to promote interest in 'Wayne Wonderland,' a nickname

1933	1936	1941–45	1950s
During the Great Depression, President Roosevelt creates the Civilian Conservation Corps in Utah, who plant more than three million trees in Utah over the next decade.	After five years of arduous construction, Boulder (Hoover) Dam is finished at the Nevada–Arizona state line near Las Vegas, with serious implications for the flow and volume of the Colorado River.	During WWII Utah becomes an important state for defense operations, including military bases, mineral mining and arms manufacturing.	After getting a master's degree in philosophy, writer and political activist Edward Abbey works as a seasonal ranger at Arches National Monument, laying the groundwork for his memoir *Desert Solitaire*.

given to the Waterpocket Fold, which lies in Wayne County. Soon after being elected to the state legislature in 1933, Pectal lobbied President Franklin D Roosevelt to establish what he dubbed 'Wayne Wonderland National Monument.' In 1937 President Roosevelt signed a proclamation creating the mercifully renamed Capitol Reef National Monument.

Despite Depression-era improvements completed by the Civilian Conservation Corps, Capitol Reef National Monument was mostly neglected by the federal government for the next two decades. The first official park ranger didn't even arrive until 1958. But the nationwide 'Mission 66' national parks renewal project brought a host of new tourist facilities to serve over 145,000 annual visitors by 1967. In 1971 Congress finally made Capitol Reef a national park.

The Making of Moab

An expansive, well-researched history is *The Proper Edge of the Sky: High Plateau Country of Utah* (2002), by Edward Geary, who stitches together in telling detail the ongoing relationship of people and the land.

It wasn't until 1878 that Mormons permanently settled in the Moab region. (Ute tribespeople had violently thwarted a previous effort in the 1850s.) Agriculture and grazing quickly became the economic mainstays, although the new railroad that bypassed Moab in 1883 dealt a serious blow to this frontier community. Ranchers used much of the land in what is now Canyonlands National Park as winter pasture for grazing herds, a practice that continued through to 1975.

In the early 20th century, local residents, including the editor of Moab's first newspaper, touted southern Utah's geologic wonders, finally attracting the attention of the Rio Grande Western Railroad. Recognizing the potential of Arches as a tourist destination, the railroad lobbied the government for federal protection. In 1929 President Hoover established Arches as a national monument.

During the Cold War era of the 1950s, when the federal government subsidized uranium mining, Moab's population tripled in three years. By the early 1960s, Arches superintendent Bates Wilson started lobbying for further protection of southeastern Utah's natural resources, calling for the establishment of a 'Grand View National Park.' In 1964 President Johnson established Canyonlands National Park. In 1971 Congress declared Arches a national park too, and expanded the boundaries of Canyonlands to what they are today.

Rock climbers, hippies, rafters, mountain bikers and off-road enthusiasts have shaped the surrounding desert over the years, making this an adrenaline-sports capital.

Exploitation vs Conservation

The amount of arable land in Utah is less than 5%, and in southern Utah that figure is less than 1%. What farmland there is and towns there are depend entirely on rivers. The rain that falls in the desert is hardly enough

1962	1963	1964	1989
Utah's all-weather state Hwy 24 through the Fremont River canyon is finally finished and paved, opening up the Capitol Reef region to burgeoning tourism.	Controversial Glen Canyon Dam is finished and artificial Lake Powell begins to form, eventually covering up ancestral Native American sites and stunning rock formations.	Canyonlands National Park is set aside by Congress, after a lobbying and public-opinion campaign jump-started by Arches National Monument superintendent Bates Wilson. In 1971 both are made national parks.	Introduction of the Red Rock Wilderness Act, controversial landmark legislation that sees over 9 million acres of Utah designated wilderness. The act has yet to pass.

to work up a good spit. Twentieth-century development has been slow to recognize and adapt to these facts, however. Politicians have dammed countless rivers across the Southwest to try to control and divert their flow and create power: the Colorado River has been dammed twice, by Hoover Dam in 1936 and Glen Canyon Dam, among the world's largest, in 1963. Public works projects have repeatedly failed, often spectacularly and expensively, and yet the attempts continue. And still no Eden.

Throughout the busy Beehive State, mining has experienced various heydays – from the great silver mines of the 19th century to modern coal, oil and mineral mining, especially to support WWII military operations. In the 1950s the federal government subsidized uranium exploration, spurring more Cold War–era mining operations in southern Utah, especially around Moab. Though these efforts unearthed little of the radioactive element, mining roads further opened this once-remote landscape to recreational tourism and encouraged settlement. At the same time, all of this extraction has exacted a high toll on the slow-healing desert.

Today, southern Utah's desert settlements are well established, and politics demands that they be supported, even as the economic and environmental costs keep growing. At the same time, many people – both outsiders and those who have made their homes in this seemingly inhospitable place – have long recognized the rare beauty of these lands and made efforts to preserve them. In fact, the first paintings of such Western landmarks as the Grand Canyon and Zion Canyon, by Albert Bierstadt and Thomas Moran, were instrumental in sparking the US conservation movement during the late 19th century, which in turn brought about the establishment of the National Park Service (NPS) in 1916.

Not everyone wants to see southern Utah's remaining wilderness protected. Established by President Clinton in 1996 and administered by the Bureau of Land Management (BLM), Grand Staircase–Escalante National Monument is southern Utah's most controversial federal land grab. Many of Utah's Republican majority believed the president was 'appeasing his Sierra Club constituents' by establishing a monument in a state that had not supported him in either election. Counties in southern Utah sued the federal government, claiming the executive branch lacked jurisdiction to declare a national monument. In 2004 a federal court ruled that the president had acted within his bounds under the authority of the 1906 Antiquities Act, setting the stage for the current showdown between federal versus state power.

Those Who Came Before: Southwestern Archaeology in the National Park System (1993), by Robert and Florence Lister, puts Capitol Reef, Canyonlands and Arches in the greater context of the Colorado Plateau, with striking photographs.

The History of Southern Utah and its National Parks (1950) by AM Woodbury is as much a period piece as a source of reliable history written by a man who lived through the parks' founding.

HISTORY EXPLOITATION VS CONSERVATION

1996	2000	2016	2017
President Bill Clinton establishes Grand Staircase–Escalante National Monument, allowing for some land uses (eg hunting and grazing by permit) not allowed in national parks. Mountain biking continues its rise.	Zion Canyon institutes a mandatory seasonal shuttle system to relieve car congestion and reduce air pollution, eliminating over 5 million pounds of carbon-dioxide emissions annually.	President Obama designates Bears Ears National Monument in southeastern Utah to protect an estimated 100,000 Native American cultural sites.	Secretary of the Interior Zinke and President Trump propose to reduce the size of two national monuments in Utah: Bears Ears (by 85%) and Grand Staircase–Escalante (by 46%).

Geology

Home to all of Utah's national parks, the Colorado Plateau is one of the geologic features that defines the West. No wonder this land of canyons, desert towers and hoodoos so often sits center stage in Hollywood Westerns and Wile E Coyote cartoons. The rise of the plateau, coupled with the effects of a million years of erosion by sand, wind and rivers, is fundamental to understanding the striated geologic history of Utah's national parks.

The Colorado Plateau

The Colorado Plateau extends for 337,000 sq km through portions of Utah, Colorado, New Mexico and Arizona. Evidence of its long-term stability is readily apparent in the horizontal layers of sediment that have changed little from the day they were laid down. But to the west, the thinning and stretching of the earth's crust has been so vigorous that mountain ranges have collapsed onto their sides and entire valleys have fallen thousands of feet. To the east, colliding forces have crumpled the land to form the Rocky Mountains.

Starting out as a shallow basin collecting sediment from nearby mountains, the entire Colorado Plateau was uplifted some 60 million years ago. At that time, the plateau split along deep cracks called faults. Over hundreds of thousands of years, these cracks have eroded to form stupendous cliffs that subdivide the Colorado Plateau into several smaller plateaus. Along the western edge, for example, a line of high, forested plateaus tower 3000ft above desert lowlands and valleys. Nicknamed the High Plateaus by geologist Clarence Dutton in 1880, the term encompasses the flat-topped mesas of Zion and Bryce Canyon National Parks and also Cedar Breaks National Monument.

From an aerial perspective, these lofty plateaus and cliffs form a remarkable staircase that steps down from southern Utah into northern Arizona. Topping this so-called 'Grand Staircase' are the Pink Cliffs of the Claron Formation extravagantly exposed in Bryce Canyon. Below them jut the Gray Cliffs of various Cretaceous formations. Next in line are the White Cliffs of Navajo sandstone that make Zion Canyon justly famous. These are followed by the Vermilion Cliffs near Lees Ferry, Arizona, and finally come the Chocolate Cliffs abutting the Kaibab Plateau and Grand Canyon.

Another way of understanding the Grand Staircase is to visualize that the top layers of exposed rock at the Grand Canyon form Zion's basement, and that Zion's top layers in turn form the bottom layers of Bryce Canyon National Park. Geologically speaking, one can imagine the parks as being stacked on top of each other. Hypothetically, a river cutting a canyon at Bryce would eventually form another Zion Canyon, and then over time create another Grand Canyon.

Armchair explorers can take a virtual field trip to southern Utah, or learn where to find dinosaur tracks, on the Utah Geological Survey's website (http://geology.utah.gov).

A Four-Act Play

Perhaps the simplest way to approach the geologic story of the Colorado Plateau is to think of it as a four-act play. The first act features sedimentation, followed by lithification, then uplift and, finally, erosion. While this is an oversimplification, and there's overlap between the scenes, it offers a framework for understanding the region's geologic history.

More than 250 million years ago, the Colorado Plateau country was a shallow sea off the west coast of the young North American continent (which at the time was merged with other continents into a giant supercontinent known as Pangea). This time period, known as the Paleozoic Era, marked the dramatic transition from primitive organisms to an explosion of complex life-forms that spread into every available niche – the beginning of life as we know it. Fossils, limestone and other sediments from this era now comprise nearly all exposed rocks in the Grand Canyon, and they form the foundation that underlies all of the Colorado Plateau.

At the close of the Paleozoic, the land rose somewhat and the sea mostly drained away, though it advanced and retreated numerous times during the Mesozoic Era (250 million to 65 million years ago). Sedimentation continued as eroding mountains created deltas and floodplains, and as shallow seas and tidal flats left other deposits. Meanwhile, the rise of an island mountain chain off the coast apparently blocked moisture-bearing storms, and a vast Sahara-like desert developed across the region, piling thousands of feet of sand atop older floodplain sediments. Zion's monumental Navajo sandstone cliffs and Arches' soaring spans of Entrada sandstone preserve evidence of mighty sand dunes.

Over millions of years the weight of the accumulated layers (more than 2 miles thick) compacted loosely settled materials into rocks cemented together with mineral deposits – a process called lithification. Sandstone, siltstone and mudstone are each cemented together with calcium carbonate. Variations in particle size and quantities of cement account for these layers' differing strengths – weakly bonded rocks crumble relatively easily in water, while more durable rocks form sheer cliffs and angular blocks.

Then came the uplift. About 60 million years ago North America began a dramatic separation from Europe, sliding west over another part of the earth's crust and leaving behind an ever-widening gulf in the Atlantic Ocean. This movement caused the continent's leading edge to uplift, forever transforming the face of the continent by raising the Colorado Plateau more than a mile above sea level. Though the plateau avoided the geologic turmoil that deformed much of western North America, the forces of uplift did shatter the plateau along fault lines into stair-step subplateaus. Furthermore, the creation of the Rocky Mountains provided headwaters for great rivers that would chisel their way through the newly risen plateau in their rush to the sea, forming the great canyons we see today.

In fact, nearly every aspect of the Colorado Plateau landscape is shaped by erosion. Several factors make the forces of erosion particularly dramatic in the Southwest. First are the region's colorful rock layers themselves. As these layers rose, gravity enabled watercourses to gain momentum and carve through stone, while sporadic rainfall and an arid climate ensured the soft layers would otherwise remain intact. These factors have remained consistent over millennia, enabling fragile hoodoos, fins and arches to develop.

Water is by far the most dramatic shaping force. Flash floods tear through soft rock with immense power, tumbling house-sized boulders down narrow slot canyons and scooping out crumbling sediments like pudding. Those who witness summer thunderstorms will notice how quickly desert waters turn rust-red with dissolving sedimentary rock. Zion's Virgin River has been described as 'a red ribbon of liquid sandpaper' due to its relentless downward gouging.

GEOLOGY A FOUR-ACT PLAY

Challenging *Basin & Range* (1981), by Pulitzer Prize–winning writer John McPhee, is as much about the journey through, as the geology of, the Great Basin, which covers much of western Utah, Nevada and eastern California.

Iconic Formations of Southern Utah

With arches, buttresses, hoodoos, fins, narrows, canyons and spindly wind-whipped towers, Utah offers up iconic glimpses into the earth's violent and fascinating geological history. Here you can travel through time as you journey past layer upon layer of sandstone, gape at delicate arches or just sit and wonder how a river could carve a canyon so deep and so elegant.

POSNOV/GETTY IMAGES ©

1. Island in the Sky (p182)

Here you'll find some of the Canyonlands' best hikes.

2. Chesler Park (p188)

Explore one of the Canyonlands most remarkable formations on the Chesler Park Loop hike.

3. Delicate Arch (p202)

A narrow slickroad ledge leads hikers up to this sandstone archway.

4. Grand Staircase–Escalante National Monument (p138)

There are miles of canyons to explore within this park.

5. The Wave (p160)

Only 20 people a day can explore this unique formation.

DAVID WALL PHOTO/GETTY IMAGES ©

WIN-INITIATIVE/GETTY IMAGES ©

As the rocks' calcium-carbonate cement dissolves in rainwater, it releases sand particles and flows down rock faces, then hardens again as it dries, leaving drippings that look like candle wax – a common feature on rock faces in both Zion and Bryce Canyons. Over time this leaching away of the cement also widens cracks and creates isolated fins that further split and dissolve into hoodoos, windows, arches and other fantastic forms, as seen in all of southern Utah's parks.

In winter, storm erosion works in tandem with another equally powerful force. As rainfall seeps into cracks, it freezes and then expands with incredible pressure (sometimes over 20,000lb per square foot), pushing open crevices and prying loose blocks of stone. At higher elevations such as Bryce Canyon, this freeze–thaw cycle is repeated more than 200 times each year, exacting a tremendous but ultimately beautiful toll on the natural landscape.

Reading the Parks

It's a complex geologic tableau that characterizes the national parks of southern Utah, from Arches to Zion. In a sense it's a remarkably homogenous region, but at the same time, the forces of erosion have carved an amazingly intricate and diverse landscape that's difficult to comprehend. Each park and national monument reveals an astonishing geologic story that goes far beyond the scope of this brief introduction.

Zion National Park

Roadside Geology of Utah (1990), by Halka Chronic, is an invaluable companion for geology buffs, aspiring and otherwise. By the end of your trip, you'll never confuse your Navajo and Entrada sandstones again!

Part of southern Utah's High Plateaus district, Zion sits on the southwest corner of the Colorado Plateau, marking the transition from relatively stable plateau country to the more tectonically active Great Basin. Separating these distinct regions is a long line of cliffs along the Hurricane Fault.

In Zion Canyon, massive cliffs expose over 2000ft of Navajo sandstone, formed by ancient sand dunes. Nowhere else in the world do these rock formations reach such grand heights. Meanwhile, in the park's Kolob Canyons area, sheer cliffs jut abruptly from the Hurricane Fault as if they rose out of the ground just yesterday. The reddish coloration of all of these cliffs is caused by iron oxides. In the more freshly exposed rocks of Kolob Canyons, the red is evenly distributed. More oxides have leached out of Zion Canyon's ancient weathered cliffs, however, leaving the uppermost layers whitish.

Bisecting the national park, the Virgin River continues its steady march – cutting downward about 1000ft every million years – so rapidly, in fact, that side tributaries can't keep up and are left as hanging valleys high on cliff faces. The dynamic interplay between Navajo sandstone and the underlying Kayenta Formation largely shapes Zion Canyon. Through the Narrows, for example, the Virgin River flows entirely between sandstone walls, but where it cuts deeply enough, the river readily erodes the softer shale underneath the sandstone cliffs and dramatically widens the canyon.

Bryce Canyon National Park

Bryce is not a canyon at all, but a series of amphitheaters gouged from the gorgeous Pink Cliffs. The park's central Claron Formation results from soft siltstone and mudstone that settled to the bottom of a giant freshwater lake 60 million years ago. Traces of manganese and iron account for this layer's fetching pink and orange hues. About 15 million years ago, the lakebed lifted, cracking from the stress along countless parallel joints, while further east the Aquarius Plateau rose even higher. The significant valley between the plateau and Bryce was carved by the Paria River, which over the past million years has begun to nip at the park's cliffs.

Bryce features dramatic formations at all stages of development, from newly emerging fins to old weathered hoodoos beaten down into colorful mounds. Runoff along joints on the canyon rim forms parallel gullies with narrow rock walls, or fins, which ultimately erode into the isolated columns known as hoodoos. The layers are so soft that in heavy rains they would quickly dissolve into muddy little mounds, except that siltstone layers alternating with resistant limestone bands give the layers strength as they erode into towering hoodoos. Many hoodoos end up with a cap of harder limestone at their apex, protecting the softer material beneath.

Grand Staircase–Escalante National Monument

This vast, complex region contains examples of nearly every rock type and structural feature found in the Colorado Plateau country. Revealed here are more than 200 million years of geologic history and one of the world's most exceptional fossil records of early vertebrate evolution. The entire period that dinosaurs ruled the earth is preserved in remarkable detail. Grand arches, waterfalls, slot canyons, sculpted sandstone cliffs and challenging terrain make this a memorable place to visit.

The monument encompasses its namesake feature, the Grand Staircase, on its western edge. Over a dozen different geologic layers document Mesozoic seas, sand dunes and slow-moving waters that once teemed with abundant ancient life. Examples range from the lavender, rose, burgundy and peach colors of volcanic ash and petrified forests of the Chinle Formation to the ancient sand dunes preserved in the bluffs of Wingate sandstone at Circle Cliffs.

Few other features characterize this place like the celebrated slot canyons of the Escalante River, carved by fast-moving waters entrenched in resistant sandstone channels that cut downward rather than spreading outward. At their upper ends these canyons modestly wind through the slickrock like tiny veins before feeding into increasingly larger arteries that eventually empty into the Colorado River.

Capitol Reef National Park

Here, along a narrow, 100-mile stretch, the earth's surface is bent in a giant wrinkle, exposing multiple rock formations in tilted and upended strata. It's a unique geological feature of the region, in that the relatively stable Colorado Plateau was twisted and pulled here. This type of step-up feature is known as a monocline, and the Waterpocket Fold is one of the longest contiguously exposed monoclines in the world. Incredibly, the rock layers on the west side have been upended more than 7000ft higher than those to the east. Dubbed a reef by early explorers, who found it a barrier to travel, the fold is capped with bare rounded domes of Navajo sandstone reminiscent of the US Capitol building from the 1850s – hence the name Capitol Reef.

While just a few major canyons cut across the Waterpocket Fold, a baffling maze of side canyons crisscrosses the park in myriad directions. All formed along clefts and other weak points in the rock, where moisture collects (natural pools of water atop the fold account for its name) and eventually scours out ever-expanding gullies. Another sandstone layer, the Wingate Formation, gives the Waterpocket Fold a line of distinctive sheer red cliffs on its west side. A third sandstone layer, Entrada sandstone, forms the freestanding pinnacles and walls of Cathedral Valley.

Other formations add so much color and structural diversity that this park is considered without equal in a region chock-full of geologically impressive parks.

One of the best views of the Grand Staircase lies along Hwy 89A between Kanab, Utah, and Jacob Lake, Arizona, where the steps rise dramatically.

Singing Stone: A Natural History of the Escalante Canyons (1999), by Thomas Fleischner, brings the geology of Grand Staircase–Escalante National Monument into understandable, human terms as it examines the land controversies of the New West.

Canyonlands National Park

Canyonlands is defined by the mighty Colorado and Green Rivers. Although the rivers have already carved through 300 million years of the earth's history, only the oldest 125 million years' worth of rock layers remain – a staggering testament to the power of erosion. When you gaze into the canyon depths from Grand View Point at the Colorado River, you're only looking at the middle slices of a giant geologic cake, with the top layers eaten away and the bottom layers still unseen.

Canyonlands is even more diverse than the Grand Canyon, possessing not just two converging river canyons, but intervening high mesas and a complex landscape of slickrock canyons, spires and arches. Cradled between the Green and Colorado Rivers, the Island in the Sky mesa is a tableland of Wingate sandstone topped with scattered buttes and domes of Navajo sandstone. Below the mesa, slopes plunge 2000ft to the rivers past a shelf of White Rim sandstone partway down. The rivers twist and turn along meandering paths inherited from the Miocene epoch (about 10 million years ago), when the land was still a flat plain.

To the south, you'll find the Needles, where colorful red and white bands showcase a complicated, 250-million-year-old history of retreating and advancing shallow seas. The red layers formed in river flooding after the sea's retreat, while white layers represent ancient beaches and coastal dunes. To the west lies the Maze, an almost incomprehensibly convoluted landscape explored by backcountry adventurers.

In many parts of Utah, red cliffs appear to be stained black by a thick coating of desert varnish. Composed of clay minerals, oxides and hydroxides of manganese and iron, this patina is formed very slowly (even for geological time) and is instrumental in dating rock formations. It also provides the canvas on which many of southern Utah's petroglyphs have been carved.

> Capitol Reef has lots to interest amateur paleontologists, including North America's oldest predinosaur megatrack site, plant megafossils and a 100-million-year-old oyster reef.

Arches National Park

Compared to the other parks, Arches' geologic makeup is relatively easy to understand. Ancient rock layers rose atop an expanding salt dome, which later collapsed, fracturing layers along the dome's flanks. These cracks then eroded along roughly parallel lines, leaving fins of freestanding Entrada sandstone. In the last 10 million years, erosion has removed roughly a vertical mile of rock, carrying away all older materials save for the freestanding fins. This process continues today: even as brittle arches occasionally collapse, new ones are always in the making.

An arch formation is more a matter of happenstance than a predictable pattern, as people pay scant attention to the countless 'almost' arches that crumble into oblivion. But in a few lucky cases, rock slabs flake from the sides of fins in just the right way to create small openings that grow into arches as water seeps into cracks, freezes and dislodges more pieces.

At times the rock itself assists by releasing tremendous internal pressures stored within its layers, which causes more slabs to pop off. The uniform strength and hard upper surfaces of Entrada sandstone are the perfect combination for creating such beautiful arches, and today this park has the world's greatest concentration of natural stone arches.

> Dive deeper into the geology of Utah and the Colorado Plateau, with history, hiking and interactive map features on www.utahgeology.com.

Wildlife

The Colorado Plateau's harsh and arid landscape asks a lot of the plants and animals that make their homes here. Rains are few and far between, habitable terrain is limited, smaller washes evaporate quickly while rivers are separated by hundreds of miles, and the temperature shifts are dramatic. This said, many specialized plants and animals have found remarkable ways to survive and adapt to life on the plateau.

Animals

Wildlife in southern Utah's parklands ranges from nimble bighorn sheep and speedy raptors to scampering lizards and nosy ringtail cats, all scattered across a vast and wild region. Only rarely do animals congregate in large or conspicuous numbers, however. During the hottest days of summer, most animal activity takes place in the early evening or at night, when temperatures drop. Bird-watching is a particularly rewarding activity in southern Utah.

Large Mammals

Mountain Lions

Even veteran wildlife biologists rarely see a mountain lion, though a fair number reside in canyon country. Like their favorite prey, mule deer, mountain lions mostly inhabit forested areas. Reaching up to 8ft in length and weighing as much as 175lb, these solitary animals are formidable predators that rarely bother humans. A few attacks have occurred in areas where human encroachment has pushed hungry lions to their limits, mainly around rapidly growing towns and cities.

A Field Guide to Desert Holes (2002), by Pinau Merlin, is a quirky look at underground critters most visitors usually won't notice in the desert, unless you know where and how to look for them.

Mule Deer

Forests and meadows are the favored haunts of mule deer, which typically graze in the early morning and evening. Uncommon when settlers first arrived, and soon hunted out, mule deer nearly vanished around the turn of the 20th century, then quickly rebounded as their predators were eliminated.

Bighorn Sheep

Like solemn statues, desert bighorn sheep often stand motionless on distant cliff faces or ridgelines, distinguished by their distinctive curled horns. During the late-fall and early-winter breeding season, males charge each other at 20mph and ram horns so loudly that the sound can be heard for miles.

Small Mammals

Chipmunks & Squirrels

Several species of small, striped chipmunks and ground squirrels are ubiquitous in the parks. The white- and brown- or black-striped Uinta chipmunk is especially common along the canyon rim in Bryce and on Zion's forested plateaus. Though it resembles a chipmunk, the golden-mantled ground squirrel lacks facial stripes. Both species scamper through the forest, searching for nuts and seeds. They also beg for handouts, but resist the urge to feed them.

On open desert flats you're more likely to see the white-tailed antelope squirrel, one of the few mammals active during the daytime. Look for its white tail, which it carries over its back like a reflective umbrella, shielding it from the sun as it darts between shady patches. True to its name, the speckled gray rock squirrel nearly always inhabits rocky areas. This large, bold squirrel often visits campgrounds.

Beavers

Some of the first Western explorers to wander across the Colorado Plateau came in search of prized beaver pelts. Limited to the few large rivers, beavers have never been common in southern Utah, but they are frequently sighted, because most visitors flock to the parks' rivers. In Zion their persistent nocturnal gnawing on large cottonwood trees presents something of a quandary. Wire mesh protects the base of some trees, but the park must still address the bigger question of how to restore the original balance of beavers, spring floods and cottonwoods that existed before humans forced the river into its current channel.

Porcupines

To learn some more about Bryce Canyon's prairie-dog community, download the short podcast from the park's official website at www.nps. gov/brca/photosmultimedia/podcasts.htm.

Looking much like an arboreal pincushion, the porcupine spends its days sleeping in caves or the hollows of trees in piñon-juniper woodlands. It's easy to overlook this strange creature, though on occasion you might encounter one waddling slowly through the forest. It's most active at night, when it gnaws on the soft inner wood of trees or pads around in search of flowers, fruit, nuts and berries.

Ringtail Cats

One of southern Utah's most intriguing creatures is the nocturnal ringtail cat, which looks like a masked chihuahua with a raccoon tail. It preys on mice and squirrels, but will eat lizards, birds or fruit in a pinch. Fairly common in rocky desert areas, ringtails may appear around campsites at night, though they are generally timid and secretive.

Wood Rats

Although they bear a superficial resemblance to city rats, wood rats are extraordinary, gentle creatures. The Colorado Plateau's species all share a maddening propensity for stealing small shiny objects like watches or rings and leaving other small objects in exchange – hence the animal's common nickname, the pack rat. Wood rats build massive stick nests (middens) that are used by countless generations. Upon dismantling these middens and examining their contents, biologists have been able to document more than 50,000 years of environmental prehistory in the region.

Birds

Small Birds

The first birds many people encounter are white-throated swifts, which swoop and dive in great numbers along cliff faces and canyon walls. Designed like sleek bullets, these sporty 'tuxedoed' birds seem to delight in riding every wind current and chasing each other in noisy, playful pursuit. Flying alongside the swifts are slightly less agile violet-green swallows, a familiar sight around campgrounds and park buildings. Both species catch their food 'on the wing.'

One bird with a unique call is the blue grouse. This resident of mountain forests vocalizes from the ground and has such a deep call that you almost feel it in your bones. Most sightings occur when a startled grouse erupts from your feet into flight. On rare occasions you may spot a male as it puffs up its chest and drums to attract a female.

The stirring song of the canyon wren is, for many people, the most evocative sound on the plateau. So haunting is the song it hardly seems possible that this tiny rust-red rock-dweller could produce such music. Starting as a fast run of sweet tinkling notes, the song fades gracefully into a rhythmic cadence that may leave you full of longing.

In contrast, the garrulous call of the Steller's jay can grate on your nerves like a loud rusty gate. But this iridescent blue mountain bird makes up for it with wonderfully inquisitive and confiding mannerisms. It often seems to have no fear of humans and eagerly gathers around picnic tables and campsites, hoping for leftovers – keep these birds wild by not giving them handouts or any other encouragement to beg.

Another common forest dweller is Clark's nutcracker, a grey bird with black wings and tail. Its highly specialized diet consists almost entirely of pine nuts, which it pries out of thick pine cones using its downturned bill like a crowbar. These birds may deposit up to 1000 ground caches of nuts in a single year, making its feeding habits integral to the survival and propagation of mountainous pine forests.

Rafters and riverside hikers will almost certainly meet the brilliant blue grosbeak, with its loud, long musical warbles. This migratory bird scours dense thickets for tasty insects and grubs, and males often ascend to high perches to defend their territory. The American dipper is often seen bobbing its head to snap up underwater insects, especially in Zion's Virgin River. This medium-sized gray fellow is North America's only true aquatic songbird, ably swimming in rapidly rushing rivers (without webbed feet!) to feed.

Discover Utah's birds and the best places to spot them on the extensive www.utahbirds.org website. Includes photos, profile checklists and a log of rare sightings.

Large Birds

Of the various owls that reside on the Colorado Plateau, none is as familiar as the common and highly vocal great horned owl, which regularly fills the echoing canyons with its booming 'hoo-hoo hooo hooo' calls. This is among the largest and most fearsome of all raptors, and when one moves into the neighborhood, other owls and hawks hurry on to

WILDLIFE ANIMALS

POTHOLES

A miracle of life unfolds wherever desert rains accumulate in what seem like lifeless, dusty bowls among the rocks. Hiding in the dust are the spores and eggs of creatures uniquely evolved to take advantage of ephemeral water. Within hours of rainfall, crustaceans, insects, protozoa and countless other organisms hatch and start swimming in this brew of life. Though most are microscopic or very small, there are also oddly shaped, 1in to 2in tadpole shrimp that resemble prehistoric trilobites.

Toads and frogs arrive the night after a rain and lay eggs that hatch quickly. Unlike amphibians in other areas, which can take months or years to develop, these tadpoles are champion athletes that emerge from the water in two to three weeks. No matter how productive a pothole may seem, however, its lifespan is limited by evaporation. All too soon, water levels drop, and everything turns to dust again. By then all the organisms have retreated into dormancy to wait for the next drenching rainstorm, which may be months or even years away.

Because each pool is a fragile ecosystem, hikers should exercise special care when they find a pothole. If necessary, remove only a little water, and don't jump or swim in the water, because body oils, sunscreens and insect repellents can harm resident life. These creatures have nowhere else to go! Even when dry, these pools need our attention because the 'lifeless' dust is actually full of eggs and spores waiting to spring into life again.

Wildlife Spotting Guide

Head out into the desert wilderness for glimpses of this unique and delicate ecosystem that includes blooming cacti and living soils, tadpole shrimp, owls and peregrine falcons, lizards, snakes and bugs aplenty, plus a few larger mammals like bighorn sheep, mountain lions and mule deer.

1. Mule Deer
Mule deer frequent park campgrounds and developed areas, often moving upslope to avoid summer heat and returning downslope as winter approaches.

2. Pronghorn Antelope
Pronghorn antelope are North America's fastest land mammals, running at speeds of up to 60mph. Catch them if you can – in a photo, that is – at Bryce Canyon.

3. Bighorn Sheep
Thanks to reintroduction eff orts throughout southern Utah, bighorns are making a slow recovery after hunting and diseases introduced by domestic sheep drove their populations to record lows. Bring binoculars to spot theses sure-footed, cliff -climbing animals. Close sightings are rare and typically brief.

4. Raptors
Rare but beautiful California Condors sometimes are seen soaring through the canyons. Other top raptors include the great horned owl, golden eagle (pictured) and peregrine falcon.

5. Chipmunks and Squirrels
Small mammals are more abundant than their larger cousins, and many types of squirrels (pictured: antelope squirrel), chipmunks and small carnivores can be spotted around park campgrounds and picnic areas and along hiking trails.

6. Big Birds
The most ubiquitous large bird is the common raven (pictured), which seems to delight in making a noisy scene with its raucous calls and ceaseless play. This bird is an especially common sight along roadsides, where roadkill provides it with a steady supply of food.

7. Small Birds
Whether you get a thrill from watching the high-speed dives of white-throated swifts or from hearing the bright songs of canyon wrens (pictured) echoing across the plateau, there's no question that southern Utah's 250-plus bird species are among the region's top highlights.

8. Amphibians and Reptiles
Amphibians and reptiles are uniquely adapted to desert life, and a surprising variety of beautiful and unique species call southern Utah home. Fast-moving lizards (pictured: common collared lizard) skitter and snakes slither throughout the region, while frogs and toads are commonly found around water sources.

2

5

6

7

8

more favorable hunting grounds or run the risk of being hunted down as prey themselves. This bird's glaring face and prominent 'horns' (actually erect tufts of feathers) may startle hikers as it peers down at them from a crevice or dark cavity.

The threatened Mexican spotted owl has garnered considerable media coverage over the years. In California and the Pacific Northwest, this owl nests solely in old-growth forests, which are being logged, and climate change is affecting its habitat in the Southwest. The subspecies that lives on the Colorado Plateau makes its home in Utah's rugged canyons and mountain forests. Sightings are rare – there are only 2000 left in the US – but thrilling.

Commanding vast hunting territories of some 60 sq miles, powerful golden eagles are typically observed in passing as they travel widely in search of jackrabbits and other prey (up to the size of an adult deer). Watch for the characteristic golden tint on the eagle's shoulders and neck. Boasting a 7ft wingspan, it is among the area's largest birds, second in size only to reintroduced California condors. California condors are often confused with common turkey vultures. You can tell these fellow scavengers apart by the coloration on the undersides of their wings. Turkey vultures (or 'TVs') have black wings, with white tips. California condors also have black wings, but with white triangular-shaped patches on their undersides.

Despite their endangered status in recent decades, peregrine falcons thrive throughout the region, especially in Zion Canyon. There they find plenty of secluded, cliffside nesting sites, as well as one of their favorite food items, white-throated swifts, which they seize in midair. Look for the falcon's long, slender wings and dark 'moustache.'

Visitors may be surprised to see wild turkey. Formerly hunted out, this flashy game bird has been making a slow comeback in areas where it's protected, particularly in Zion Canyon. In the spring mating season, males fan out their impressive tails and strut around to impress females.

In *Desert Solitaire*, Edward Abbey recounts how a gopher snake that lived beneath his trailer in Arches National Park seemed to keep the rattlesnakes away.

Amphibians & Reptiles

Amphibians

Bleating choruses of common canyon tree frogs float up from boulder-strewn canyon streams each night. Gray-brown and speckled like stone, these tiny frogs dwell in damp crevices by day, emerging at night (and sometimes late afternoon) to sing beside rocky pools. Occupying a similar habitat is the aptly named red-spotted toad, a small species with red-tipped warts covering its body. Its nighttime song around breeding pools is a high, persistent musical trill.

More secretive, and thus rarely encountered, is the tiger salamander, the region's only salamander. Spending the majority of its life in a burrow, this creature emerges when abundant water triggers its breeding cycle. In order to fully develop, a larval salamander requires a water source, although some larvae never change into the adult form and become sexually mature while still in the larval stage. Coloration varies by region, but most are blackish all over.

Lizards

Perhaps the region's most abundant and widespread reptile is the eastern fence lizard, a small creature you'll probably see perched atop rocks and logs or scampering across the trail. During breeding season, males bob enthusiastically while conspicuously displaying their shiny blue throats and bellies. Females have dark, wavy crossbars on their backs and only a pale bluish wash underneath.

Bold in comparison is the greenish collared lizard, a large-headed species with striking black bands around its neck. This fearsome lizard eats just about every small animal it can overpower. Because it has little to fear, it often perches conspicuously atop large boulders, scanning for movement in all directions. Like most of southern Utah's lizards, it's inactive during the coldest winter months.

You may also encounter the curiously flattened horned lizard, which looks like a spiny little pancake. This lizard's shape is an adaptation to its exclusive diet of ants. In order to survive on this nutrient-poor diet, the horned lizard must eat lots of ants and consequently has an extremely large stomach that lends it its short, round appearance. Its shape also makes it harder for predators to grasp its body.

Snakes

The Colorado Plateau is excellent habitat for snakes, though visitors seldom encounter more than a few resident species. Most common is the gopher snake, easily mistaken for a rattlesnake because it hisses and vibrates its tail in dry leaves when threatened. Sporting a tan body with dark brown saddles, this 6ft to 8ft constrictor preys upon rodents, small birds, lizards and even the offspring of other snakes.

Nothing compares to the jolt of terror and adrenaline prompted by the angry behavior of a rattlesnake. Both humans and wild animals react with instinctive fear, even though rattlesnakes rarely strike unless provoked. These mild-mannered creatures would rather slide away unharmed than provoke a confrontation. A few species reside in the region, but only rarely does a visitor get close enough to tell them apart.

Another snake that keeps its distance is the striped whipsnake. This extremely slender 3ft to 6ft snake moves like lightning when alarmed and can climb into trees and bushes so quickly it seems like it's falling away from you. The snake uses this speed to capture lizards and rodents.

Scientists have documented 16 native species of bats in Canyonlands National Park, accounting for nearly 90% of all bat species found in the entire state.

Fish

The Colorado River and its tributaries were once home to at least 14 native fish species, nearly all of them unique to these waters and highly adapted to extreme conditions. After the introduction of grazing, dams and other artificial changes to the landscape, dozens of introduced species are now outcompeting these native fish.

One representative native species is the threatened Colorado pikeminnow, North America's largest minnow (it can weigh up to 25lb and reach over 3ft in length). Once so abundant that it was pitchforked out of irrigation canals, the pikeminnow is in drastic decline, as many artificial dams block its 200-mile migration route. Three other endangered fish, the humpback chub, bonytail and razorback sucker, suffer similar fates. It's unclear whether they will survive the changes being made to the rivers.

Plants

The Colorado Plateau's complex landscape supports an equally diverse mix of plant species. Many are specific to the plateau, while others are drawn from adjacent biological zones such as the Great Basin, Mojave Desert and Rocky Mountains. Each park and monument boasts a list of hundreds of species, and no two places are alike.

Most species are adapted in some way to the Southwest's arid environment, either lying dormant until rains arrive or toughing it out through dry spells. If you arrive in wet season or after a drenching rain, you may be lucky enough to witness the region in its full splendor, when flowers carpet the landscape in all directions.

What you'll witness more often, however, is the plodding life of plants that struggle to conserve every molecule of precious liquid. Many plants sport hairy or waxy leaves to prevent evaporation, while others bear tiny leaves. At least one common plant, Mormon tea, has done away with water-wasting leaves altogether and relies on its greenish, wiry stems for photosynthesis. Most species have long taproots to penetrate the soil in search of water.

The rapid rate of erosion on the Colorado Plateau also has a profound effect on the area's ecosystems. Unlike other regions, where eroded materials accumulate and cover vast areas with homogenous soils, erosion on the plateau carries sediments away. Plants have nowhere to live except on freshly exposed bedrock, and because each rock layer has its own distinctive composition and chemistry, this profoundly limits the species that can grow there.

Biological soil crust is the living ground cover that forms the foundation of high desert plant life across the plateau. This black crust is dominated by cyanobacteria, but also includes lichens, mosses, green algae, microfungi and bacteria. It's the web that keeps the desert from eroding. Never step on these delicate living features.

LIFE ZONES

Dominating southern Utah's parks, desert scrub is the hot, dry zone below 4000ft where scraggly shrubs cling to life on sandy flats. The most common are low-growing blackbrush, shadscale, Mormon tea and sagebrush. Annual precipitation is likely to average less than 8in, a number that includes winter snows as well, so it isn't very much rain, and most of it ends up running over bare rocks and washing away before plants can even use it.

Another widespread habitat is the open woodland of piñon pine and Utah juniper. Piñon-juniper woodland ('P-J' for short) grows mostly between 4000ft and 7000ft. Due to competition for water, trees are spaced widely here, though they still provide shade for many understory plants, as well as food and shelter for many animals. In some areas the trees grow in distinct lines, following cracks in the rock where water gathers after rain.

Growing in a narrow band between 7000ft and 8500ft, ponderosa pine forest indicates the presence of increased rainfall at higher elevations. In Zion, however, ponderosa pines grow at lower elevations, because porous Navajo sandstone is full of water, demonstrating once again how water dictates where plants can grow in this region. Ponderosa pines thrive in Zion and Bryce Canyon (with a few stands in Grand Staircase–Escalante) but are absent in lower-elevation Capitol Reef, Canyonlands and Arches.

Boreal forest above 8500ft has much in common with Rocky Mountain forests, even supporting many of the same plants and animals. This is a zone of cool, moist woodland and rainfall that exceeds 20in a year, conditions that favor trees like spruce, Douglas fir and quaking aspen. This forest populates a few high mesas in Zion, but the best examples are found at higher elevations in Bryce Canyon, particularly at road's end near Rainbow Point, where stands of ancient bristlecone pines survive.

Due to intensive grazing, the grassland that once covered much of this region has been largely replaced by desert scrub and alien weeds. Early Western explorers' journals describe a lush grassy landscape, though you'd hardly know it today. In areas of deeper sand and soil, where shrubs don't grow well, it's still possible to find pockets of galleta and Indian ricegrass.

Readily available water supports another set of unique habitats, ranging from hanging gardens clustered around cliffside seeps to riparian woodland lining perennial creeks and rivers. The presence of water attracts many plants and animals to these habitats. Monkey flowers, columbines and ferns mark spots where springs flow from sandstone cliffs. Riverbanks that were once home to majestic cottonwood and willow stands are more likely today to harbor highly invasive tamarisk.

Trees

Piñon pines are well known for their highly nutritious and flavorful seeds. These same seeds have long been a staple for Native Americans, and many animals also feast on the seeds when they ripen in the fall. Piñons bear stout rounded cones and short single needles. Together with Utah junipers, piñon pines form a distinctive plant community that covers millions of acres of Southwestern desert. Blue, berrylike cones and diminutive scalelike needles distinguish junipers.

Mingling with piñons and junipers in some canyons is the beautiful little Gambel oak, with its dark green leaves turning shades of yellow and red in fall and adding to the palette of color, particularly in Zion Canyon. Often growing in dense thickets, the oaks produce copious quantities of nutritious, tasty acorns long favored by Native Americans and used to make ground meal, breads, cakes and soups.

To identify the stately ponderosa pine, look for large spiny cones, needles in bundles of three, and yellowish bark that smells like butterscotch or vanilla. Between 20,000 and 12,000 years ago, the Douglas fir was one of the region's dominant species, though today they are restricted to isolated mountaintops and north-facing slopes. This relict of an earlier time dramatically demonstrates how the region's vegetation has changed since the last ice age. It's identified by its single needles and cones with three-pronged bracts on each seed.

Found amid damp mountain meadows, quaking aspen is immediately recognizable by its smooth, white bark and circular leaves. Every gust of wind sets these leaves quivering on their flattened stems, an adaptation for shaking off late snowfalls that would otherwise damage fragile leaves. Aspen groves comprise genetically identical trunks sprouting from a common root system that may grow to more than 100 acres in size. By budding repeatedly from these root systems, aspens have what has been called 'theoretical immortality' – some aspen roots are thought to be more than a million years old.

Rivers and watercourses in this harsh desert landscape are lined with thin ribbons of water-loving plants that can't survive anywhere else. Towering prominently over all others is the showy Fremont cottonwood, whose large, vaguely heart-shaped leaves rustle wildly in any wind. Hikers in the canyons' scorching depths find welcome respite in the shade of this tree. In spring, cottonwoods produce vast quantities of cottony seed packets that fill the air and collect in every crack and crevice. Box elder is another common streamside plant. It issues winged, maplelike seeds and bears trifoliate leaves that resemble those of poison ivy.

Since 1920 the aggressive weedy tamarisk (salt cedar) has largely replaced native streamside plant communities. Though this delicately leaved plant from Eurasia and Africa sports a handsome coat of soft pink and white flowers through the summer, its charm ends there, for it robs water from the soil and completely overwhelms such native species as cottonwood and willow.

A special treat is a visit to the fruit orchards of Capitol Reef, where you can pick apples, peaches and cherries.

Shrubs

Blackbrush covers large tracts of Southwestern deserts. This dark shrub reaches great ages and is only rarely replaced by young seedlings. With wiry stems, shrunken leaves and yellowish-red petal-less flowers blooming only after heavy spring rains, it may look more dead than alive.

Also triggered by spring rains, the common cliff rose (or desert bitterbrush) paints rocky slopes with its white blossoms surrounding yellow stamens. You're likely to 'hear' this plant before you see it, as bees and

Wondering what flower you just saw? Use Arches National Park's online flower database, searchable by month, color and name, or download free plant-finder keys from www.nps. gov/arch/learn/ nature/wildflowers.htm.

Ancient bristlecone pines may be slow growing, but they're believed to be the oldest living single organisms on earth, with some over 5000 years old.

The common desert shrub nicknamed Mormon tea is a species of Ephedra plant, which Native Americans also used for medicinal purposes, including as a stimulating brew.

insects swarm to its acrid-smelling flowers. Though its resinous, leathery leaves taste bitter, deer still munch on the plant in winter.

Narrowleaf yucca is a stout succulent related to agave and century plants. Yuccas favor sandy sites, while blackbrush predominates on thin gravelly soils. Growing in a dense rosette of thick leaves, this plant sends up a 5ft stalk of creamy flowers. A night-flying moth pollinates these flowers; in exchange, the caterpillars eat some seeds. Native Americans used yucca fibers to weave baskets and sandals.

Ripening in summer, the juicy black canyon grape is a tart favorite food of many different kinds of mammals and nearly 100 species of birds. Its vines snake over bushes and rocks in damp canyons, particularly in Zion Canyon, where its maplelike leaves turn yellow, orange and red in the fall.

Another distinctive shrub is greenleaf manzanita, which flourishes in ponderosa pine forests along the rim of Bryce Canyon. It bears reddish-brown bark and equally smooth, quarter-sized leaves. Bees alight on its pale pinkish flowers, while mammals and birds feed on its fruit.

Wildflowers

A surprisingly large variety of wildflowers thrive in the Colorado Plateau's arid, rocky landscapes. While late-winter precipitation and spring snowmelt trigger some plants to flower, many others bloom following midsummer thunderstorms or when temperatures cool in early fall.

Seeps, springs and stream banks host some of the most dramatic flower displays. The brilliant flash of monkey flowers amid greenery comes as something of a shock for hikers who've trudged across miles of searing baked rock. These red, yellow and purple flowers with widely flared 'lips' are very tempting to hummingbirds.

Columbines are also common at the seeps and springs, though some species range up into forested areas as well. The golden columbine and crimson-colored Western columbine are most common in wet, shaded canyon recesses. Rock columbine grows amid Bryce Canyon's hoodoos, where its vivid blue flowers stand out against red-rock cliffs. The flowers of both species hold pockets of nectar that attract large numbers of butterflies and hummingbirds.

The showy prince's plume boldly marks selenium-rich desert soils with a 2ft to 3ft stalk of dainty yellow flowers. By using selenium in place of sulfur to manufacture its amino acids, this plant renders itself poisonous to herbivores and grows in soils that other plants can't tolerate. Prospectors once thought of this plant as an indicator of places to dig for uranium, as selenium deposits may naturally occur near uranium. Other wildflowers that do well on dry, gravelly slopes include stalky penstemon and paintbrush varieties, all with bright, showy tubular flowers.

In peak years evening primroses are so abundant that it looks like someone scattered white tissues over the sandy desert. Turning from white to rosy pink, the small flowers open at sunset and close by morning, thus avoiding the day's heat and conserving water. At night large sphinx moths dart from flower to flower, collecting nectar and laying eggs.

Blooming in late spring and early summer, the three-petaled sego lily is another white flowering plant that is also Utah's state flower. Native Americans and early Mormon settlers once harvested the plant's walnut-sized bulbs for food. Don't confuse its small, delicate blooms with the large, showy white flowers of sacred datura, which blooms from spring through fall. This poisonous plant was traditionally used by some indigenous tribes during religious rituals as a potent hallucinogenic, but it can be deadly.

Conservation

Here under the desert stars and up by the devilish hoodoos, the dance of nature is profound, intricate and delicate. The uniquely adapted ecosystems are intimately tied to water, and even the smallest of environmental impacts can create huge change for one of North America's largest intact wildernesses. Top conservation challenges today are increased visitation, mining and resource extraction, land use and management, climate change, invasive species and man-made dams.

Increased Visitation

Over 12.6 million people traveled to Utah's national parks and monuments in 2017 – that's a lot of boots on the ground, paddles in the water and wheels on the trail. And the five national parks are seeing an unprecedented spike in visitation. Zion leads the way, with a 70% increase in tourism since 2010, reaching 4.5 million visitors in 2017.

In a region where life hangs by a fragile thread, the heavy trampling of human feet and off-road vehicles leaves lasting impressions. Desert crusts, wet meadows and riverside campsites are slow to recover from such use, and repeated visits can cause permanent damage. The effects may accumulate so gradually they almost go unnoticed. Scientists at Bryce Canyon estimate that 3% of the vegetation disappears each year from people wandering off trail among the hoodoos – just tiny little bites that build up over time. Petroglyphs are also at risk from idiots leaving graffiti.

The park managers are acutely aware of this and actively try to mitigate visitor impacts wherever possible. Both Zion and Bryce Canyon have developed free public-transit systems and a growing network of pedestrian and bicycle trails as a way of reducing traffic congestion and air pollution. All of southern Utah's parks and concessionaire businesses now encourage and facilitate recycling. Zion's visitor center is a model of smart, sustainable ecobuilding practices that hopefully more national and state parks will imitate in the future, as much as their operating budgets allow.

But visiting national parks is good for the environment, right? Sure it is. More visitation means more visibility and awareness for protecting Utah's wild lands, it means an educated citizenry and it means more funds for the National Park Service (NPS).

If you want to minimize the impacts of your trip, consider riding bikes into the parks or at the very least carpooling, staying on trails, picking up litter and, of course, leaving no trace. The challenge of visitation is not just about air pollution and littering, it's also about noise pollution, light pollution that affects dark skies, and habitat encroachment.

Land Use

Unfortunately, grazing, mining, oil and gas extraction, and military exercises still create scars around southern Utah's parks and monuments. The debate on land use in Utah has become one of the largest hot-button environmental issues in the US West today.

Desert vegetation grows so slowly that even impacts left by early Western prospectors, ranchers and explorers may look fresh, and protected

Edward Abbey is arguably Utah's most famous environmentalist. Check out *The Monkey Wrench Gang* (1975), a mostly fictionalized, raucous tale of 'ecowarriors' and their plan to blow up Glen Canyon Dam, along with the dreamy classic *Desert Solitaire* (1968).

Cadillac Desert: The American West and Its Disappearing Water (1993), by Marc Reisner, is an exhaustively researched, compelling account of the West's most critical issue: balancing development with its most precious resource.

parklands remain damaged by long-ago visitors. Cows have had such a devastating impact on the desert that it no longer functions as the same ecosystem. Only on a few inaccessible mesa tops do fragments of ancestral plant communities survive. Today's dry, brushy desert hardly resembles the landscape that existed even half a century ago, and it's not likely to recover for centuries to come.

Plants that adapt best seem to be invasive weeds, which have quickly overtaken areas damaged by cows and human activities. Introduced plants such as tamarisk, Russian thistle (tumbleweed) and cheatgrass pose a serious problem, as they can force out native plants and animals, creating extensive monocultures. Cheatgrass even alters the chemistry of the soil, possibly rendering it unusable to other plants. And many invasive plants are nearly impossible to remove once they gain a foothold.

Construction of dams and reservoirs throughout the Southwest has radically changed the delicate balance that has sustained life here for millennia. In place of floodplains that once richly nourished riparian and aquatic food chains, dams now release only cold water in steady flows that favor introduced fish species and invasive weeds. In populated areas, the draining of underground aquifers is shrinking the water table and drying up desert springs and wetlands that animals have long depended on during the dry season.

To learn more about the great land debate, check out the Southern Utah Wilderness Alliance (www.suwa. org), a grassroots political organization that's been critical in the land-conservation fight.

Climate Change

The Environmental Protection Agency (EPA) estimates that temperatures in the US Southwest have risen by almost 2°F over the last century. Over the next 100 years, the NPS expects the Colorado Plateau will become hotter and more arid – a 2014 Bureau of Land Management (BLM) report said temps could rise by as much as 2° by 2060 – causing even more extreme droughts. This affects where plants grow, where animals eat, where wildfires burn, and even where people play. Across the Southwest, piñon pine are dying off at an alarming rate as a result of an ongoing drought, animals are changing habits to adapt to changing ecosystems, and the tourism industry is adjusting approaches as changing rain patterns affect river levels, sandstorms affect watersheds, and ski areas and even tourism seasons change as winter temperatures rise.

CRYPTOBIOTIC CRUSTS

One of the desert's most fascinating features is also one of its least visible and most fragile. Only in recent decades have biological soil crusts begun to attract attention and concern. These living crusts cover and protect desert soils, gluing sand particles together so they don't blow away.

Cyanobacteria, among the earth's oldest living lifeforms, start the process by extending mucous-covered filaments that wind through the dry soil. Over time these filaments and the sand particles adhering to them form a thin crust that is colonized by microscopic algae, lichens, fungi and mosses. This crust absorbs huge amounts of rainwater, reducing runoff and minimizing erosion.

Unfortunately, this thin crust is instantly fragmented under the heavy impact of human footsteps, not to mention bicycle, motorcycle and car tires. Once broken, the crust can take up to 100 years to repair itself. In its absence, the wind and rains erode desert soils, and much of the water that would otherwise nourish desert plants is lost. Many of these soils formed during the wet climates of the Pleistocene and may be irreplaceable in today's arid conditions. Tragically, as soon as the crust is broken and soil is lost, grasses will be permanently replaced by shrubs, whose roots fare better in the thinner soils.

Visitors to the Southwest bear a special responsibility to protect these living soil crusts by staying on established trails. Look closely before you walk anywhere – intact crusts form a rough glaze atop the soil, while fragmented crusts have sharp edges.

Survival Guide

Clothing & Equipment

CLOTHING

Modern outdoor garments made from new synthetic fabrics (which are breathable and actively wick moisture away from your skin) are better than cotton or wool. The exception is if you're hiking out of the canyon in midsummer, when cotton is a godsend. Soak cotton shirts or bandannas with water at every opportunity, for the evaporative cooling effect.

To cope with changing temperatures and exertion, layering your clothing is a good way to regulate your body temperature.

For the upper body, the base layer is typically a T-shirt made of synthetic fabric. The second layer can be a lightweight, breathable long-sleeved shirt for sun protection or a synthetic or tech-wool fleece sweater that will keep you insulated. The outer shell consists of a weather-proof jacket that also protects against strong cold winds.

For the lower body, shorts will probably be most comfortable in midsummer, although some hikers prefer long pants – light, quick-drying fabric (eg nylon) is best. Thermal 'long john' type underwear can't be easily removed, and it is not recommended except when conditions are expected to remain very cold all day. Waterproof overpants are an outer shell for the lower body.

Hikers in southern Utah should always carry a wind-proof and waterproof rain jacket and pants that are properly seam-sealed. The jacket should have a hood to keep the rain and wind off your head.

Trail-running or walking shoes with good traction and soft soles are fine over most terrain. If you have bad ankles, consider higher-ankle hiking boots. If you are planning on hiking in water (eg the Narrows), wear breathable shoes, not Gore-Tex, which will trap water inside.

MAPS

If you're driving or taking the shuttle and hiking on frontcountry trails, the glossy fold-out, full-color map and seasonal park newspaper available at national park entrance stations and visitor centers is usually enough to get around. **Bureau of Land Management** (BLM; www. blm.gov) and **United States Forest Service** (USFS; www. fs.fed.us) offices give away or sell maps that cover lands under their jurisdiction. They may not be great maps for general use, but they're indispensable for exploring outside the national parks, where public recreation lands can be a patchwork of different agencies' jurisdictions and private landholdings.

The **United States Geological Survey** (USGS; www.usgs.gov) publishes the standard 1:24,000 (7.5-minute) topographical quadrangle maps, available as free downloads online in PDF format. The level of detail is more than most visitors will need, unless you're planning a backcountry trip. Keep in mind that some USGS map survey information may be outdated, and buying these maps can quickly become expensive if your route extends across multiple quads. You can order print copies ($8 to $9 per quad) directly from the website or look for them at southern Utah's national park bookstores, outdoor outfitters and public lands information offices (see the USGS website for a complete list of local retailers).

National Geographic (http://shop.nationalgeo graphic.com) publishes the *Trails Illustrated* series of waterproof, tear-resistant topographic maps (scale varies from 1:35,000 to 1:70,000), which collectively cover all of southern Utah's national parks, as well as other wilderness areas, including around Moab. Based on USGS maps, but often helpfully marked up with more details for outdoor recreation, these foldable maps ($10 to $12 each) are widely available at national park visitor centers, bookstores and elsewhere. If you're traveling with a handheld GPS, or want to customize trail maps to print out yourself at home,

National Geographic's TOPO! mapping software is a good investment; the Utah state series costs $50.

For driving maps, the *Utah* state highway map is perfectly adequate. It's available free from many tourist information offices. In addition to more detailed regional driving maps, the **American Automobile Association** (www.aaa.com) also publishes an *Indian Country Guide Map* ($15), which covers southern Utah, northern Arizona and the Four Corners area. For a handy driving and motorcycling road atlas, Benchmark Press' *Utah Road & Recreation Atlas* ($23) shows every road in the state, along with land and water features, outdoor recreation areas, campgrounds, trailheads and hundreds more points of interest.

EQUIPMENT

Packs

For day hikes, a daypack will usually suffice, but for multiday hikes you'll need a backpack. Daypacks with built-in hydration systems eliminate the hassle of toting unwieldy water bottles.

Backpacks with a relatively large capacity (between 2500 and 5500 cubic inches, or 40L to 90L) are best for overnight hiking in the backcountry.

Tents

A three-season tent will suffice for most backpacking trips in southern Utah. Ultralight backpackers may opt to ditch the tent and use just the rainfly and footprint (ground tarp).

If you're planning a backcountry trip during winter, then you'll need a four-season tent to keep you sheltered from the snow and harsh windy, wet and freezing conditions.

The floor and the outer shell, or rainfly, should have taped or sealed seams and covered zips to stop leaks. Most hikers find tents of around 4.5lb to 6lb a comfortable carrying weight.

Sleeping Bags

As with tents, three-season sleeping bags will suffice for most campers in southern Utah. Cooler seasons and higher elevations, for example at Bryce Canyon, call for both sleeping bag and a sleeping pad (mat) for insulation from the cold ground.

During the summer, lower desert elevations are usually hot enough to forego a sleeping bag altogether; backcountry campers might consider bringing just a sleeping bag liner or a sheet. Some campers soak a sheet in a nearby river for the evaporative cooling effect to ensure a more soothing sleep.

Down fillings are warmer than synthetic for the same weight and bulk but, unlike synthetic fillings, do not retain warmth when wet. The given figure, for instance 23°F (-5°C), is the coldest temperature at which a person should feel comfortable in the bag (although the ratings are notoriously unreliable).

Self-inflating sleeping mats put an air cushion between you and the ground. More importantly they insulate from the cold. Foam mats are a low-cost but less comfortable alternative.

Stoves & Fuel

The type of fuel you'll use most often will help determine what kind of camp stove is best for you. The following types of fuel can be found in the US, and local outdoor outfitters and camping supply stores can help you choose an appropriate camp stove if you aren't traveling with your own.

Butane, propane and isobutane are clean-burning fuels that come in nonrecyclable canisters and tend to be more expensive. These fuels are best for camping in warmer conditions, as their performance markedly decreases in below-freezing temperatures. Check airline regulations before you bring fuel. You can buy all types of fuel in Utah.

Inexpensive white gas is reliable in all temperatures. It's more volatile than other types of fuel, but overall it's the most efficient and clean-burning type of fuel available in the US.

The most sustainable alternative is renewable denatured alcohol, which burns slowly but also extremely quietly. Lower temperatures mean longer cooking times, so you'll have to carry more fuel with you.

Mountain Biking & Canyoneering

For biking, you can either rent the latest bikes or bring your own. Full-suspension mountain bikes are recommended for most beginners – they're just easier. If you have them, bring cycling shorts and top, repair kits, inner tubes and pumps. Most riders use a small hydration daypack. A good bike lock is nice for overnights in Moab.

It gets cold on rivers. Don't forget warm, dry cloths (in a dry bag – your guide has one if you don't). River sandals are useful when fording waterways or doing water sports. Outside of summer, consider a wetsuit or drytop. You will also need a PFD (personal flotation device) if doing nonguided trips.

Many canyoneering routes require a static rope, rappel device, helmet and harness, plus a wet- or dry suit and dry bag. Always check rental climbing equipment for frays.

For scrambling, consider a soft-soled approach shoe that grips the rock like a gecko.

Directory A–Z

Accessible Travel

➡ The national parks exist for the enjoyment of all, offering opportunities for those in wheelchairs or with hearing, visual or other physical or mental disabilities to experience the wilderness. It may also be possible to obtain a free lifetime America the Beautiful access pass (p262).

➡ Check individual park websites or ask at park visitor centers for up-to-date accessibility guides, details of which are often printed in the parks' free guides.

➡ All of southern Utah's national parks have wheelchair-accessible visitor centers, at least one accessible campsite in their main campground, and a few viewpoints and/or trails that are wheelchair-accessible. Some parks also offer ranger programs for the hearing impaired.

➡ Service animals (ie guide dogs) may accompany visitors on park shuttles, inside museums and visitor centers, and on hiking trails

and in the backcountry (check current regulations to see if permits are required at visitor centers). Ensure your service animal wears its official vest at all times, to avoid any misunderstandings with park rangers or other visitors.

➡ In Zion and Bryce Canyon, park shuttles are wheelchair-accessible and lodges offer wheelchair-accessible rooms compliant with the ADA (Americans with Disabilities Act).

➡ Accommodations outside the parks are required to have at least one wheelchair-accessible room, though few are fully ADA-compliant. More often, these are ground-floor rooms with wider doorways, less furniture, and handles around the tub and toilet. Always ask exactly what 'accessible' means when making reservations.

➡ Some car-rental agencies offer hand-controlled vehicles and vans with wheelchair lifts at no extra charge, but you must reserve them well in advance.

➡ **Access Utah Network** (☑801-533-4636, relay line 711; www.nchpad.org/Directories/Programs/USA/Utah) is a state agency that provides accessibility information for all Utah parks and referrals to other helpful organizations. The nonprofit, Salt Lake City–based **Splore** (☑801-484-4128; www.splore.org; 4029 Main St; ☺9am-5pm Mon-Fri) specializes in providing outdoor activities for those with special needs.

Accommodations

Book accommodations well in advance during the summer, holiday weekends and spring break.

Camping From RVs to the backcountry, Utah is a camper's dream destination. You should always reserve months ahead where possible – particularly for national parks and if you're in an RV.

Hotels Choices are often limited in rural areas, though when available hotels offer the most luxury.

B&Bs These family-run homes generally offer value and personality.

Motels Chain motels line the roadsides everywhere, catering to a range of budgets and comfort levels.

Vacation rentals A great deal for families or groups when available.

B&Bs & Inns

B&B rates often include a home-cooked breakfast,

PRACTICALITIES

Weights & Measures Feet, yards and miles; weights are tallied in ounces, pounds and tons.

Smoking Prohibited in all public buildings, restaurants and malls. Some hotels may still allow smoking – but it's becoming rare.

though in Zion they usually include breakfast vouchers at a restaurant instead to accommodate people who want an earlier start. Minimum stays are common in high season and on weekends. Amenities vary widely, but rooms with TV and telephone are the exception; the cheapest units share bathrooms.

Camping

Camping is unsurprisingly the most popular option when visiting the national parks. You'll need to be on the ball before you arrive, otherwise you risk not finding a site. A few campgrounds are open year-round; most generally open in March or April and stay open until the first snowfall, usually between late October and mid-November. Wildfires can be devastating and because of this campfires are not always permitted – respect the rules.

➡ Campgrounds in state and national parks tend to have flush toilets and sometimes RV dump stations.

➡ Private campgrounds cater more to the RV crowd, with water and electricity hookups, wi-fi internet access, showers and even cable TV.

➡ On national forests (US Forest Service; USFS) and Bureau of Land Management (BLM) land, expect more basic campsites with fire pits, picnic benches, vault toilets and possibly no drinking water.

➡ USFS and BLM lands often allow free dispersed camping. Check websites like www.campendium.com and www.freecampsites.net for free camping locations, or ask at the local ranger office.

➡ The most popular campgrounds fill up fast, especially at national and state parks. Some accept reservations up to six months in advance, while others are strictly first-come, first-served (show up early in the day to claim a site).

➡ State park, USFS and BLM campgrounds might have space when the national parks hang out their 'Campground Full' signs.

➡ For camping reservations in national parks, national forests and other federal recreation lands (eg BLM), contact the **National Recreation Reservation Service** (☎518-885-3639, 877-444-6777; www. recreation.gov). For Utah state park campgrounds, contact **Reserve America** (www.reserveamerica.com; reservation fee $9).

Hotels & Motels

Just about every hotel and motel offers air-conditioned, nonsmoking rooms with a TV and phone. Rooms are often priced by the size and number of beds; rates are usually the same for single or double occupancy. Children are sometimes free. Even if a hotel accepts pets, they will not allow you to leave your pet in the room during the day.

Lodges

Of the national parks in the area, only Zion, Bryce Canyon and the Grand Canyon's North Rim have lodges.

Ranch Resorts

Resorts and guest ranches are often destinations in themselves, with a host of activities on hand. Accommodations range from private cabins to lodges to campsites. You'll find a few ranch resorts scattered outside Zion's east entrance and around Capitol Reef and Moab.

Vacation Rentals

Apartment rentals are not as common in rural Utah as

elsewhere, though they do exist. Access to a kitchen is almost always included.

Activities

Hiking is the activity of choice, but it's just one of many pursuits possible in and around southern Utah's parks. Rock climbing and canyoneering are also huge, while horseback trail rides and 4WD roads are popular activities back down closer to earth. Although the parks aren't great for mountain biking, there are miles of fat-tire trails outside Moab, also a jumping-off point for river-rafting and paddling trips. Winter brings snow play, cross-country skiing and snowshoeing to the mountains.

Climate

The weather in southern Utah can vary wildly from one park or town to the next, even from one day to the next, especially during the unpredictable shoulder seasons of spring and fall. Then there's the summer heat, which routinely hovers above 90°F (32°C). Winter brings snowstorms. Altitude makes a difference in temperature year-round: hikers in Zion Canyon may be sweat-soaked at noon, but campers at Bryce Canyon will shiver in their sleeping bags later that night.

Discount Cards

Park Passes

The **America the Beautiful annual pass** (http://store. usgs.gov/pass; $80) is valid for free admission to all national parks and federal recreation lands for 12 months from when you buy it. Each pass admits four adults and all accompanying children under age 16. Buy the pass online or from any participating federal agency, including at national park entrance stations. Upon entry, be prepared to present your pass along with a photo ID (eg driver's license).

With the **America the Beautiful senior pass** (lifetime fee $80), US citizens and permanent residents 62 or older receive free admission to all national parks and federal recreation lands, plus 50% off select activity fees (eg camping in national parks). The lifetime **America the Beautiful access pass** (free) is for US citizens or permanent residents with a permanent disability; bring documentation if your disability is not readily visible. These discount parks passes must be obtained in person.

EATING PRICE RANGES

The following price ranges refer to a main course on the dinner menu.

$ less than $15

$$ $15–25

$$$ more than $25

Automobile Clubs

Members of the **American Automobile Association** (www.aaa.com) and its foreign affiliates (eg Canada's CAA) qualify for small discounts (usually 10%) on hotels and motels, Amtrak trains, car and RV rentals, chain restaurants and shops, tours and more.

Senior Cards

People over the age of 65 (sometimes 55, 60 or 62) often qualify for the same discounts as students; any ID showing your birth date should suffice as proof of age.

Members of the American Association of Retired Persons, for those 50 years of age and older, often get discounts (usually 10%) on hotels, car rentals and more.

Student Cards

For international and US students, the **Student Advantage Card** (www.student advantage.com) offers 15% savings on Amtrak train and Greyhound bus fares, plus discounts of 10% to 20% at some motels, hotels, chain stores and airlines.

Electricity

120V/60Hz

120V/60Hz

Food

Meals are often an afterthought on a trip to southern Utah's national parks, but gateway towns do provide a decent variety of options, from basic cafeteria eats to upscale Southwestern cuisine. Zion and Bryce Canyon's park lodges offer filling, but just-OK food; their top-end prices and historical atmosphere make them better for a special occasion than everyday dining. The other parks do not offer food (and water is occasionally limited) so bring it with you.

Groceries & Self-Catering

➡ Small grocery stores in park gateway towns usually stock only a limited selection of items, such as canned goods, bread, milk, ice and other staples. If you're driving to southern Utah, you may want to stop off in larger towns and cities like St George and Moab to stock up on groceries – it'll cost less than buying supplies in smaller park gateway towns.

➡ To fill up your cooler, ice is sold at almost every convenience store and gas station, but they may run out on hot summer days. In-room refrigerators are not always a standard amenity at motels and hotels, and they're not available inside park lodges. In all of southern Utah's national parks, you'll find picnic areas and campsites with picnic tables; the latter may have fire pits or grates for cooking.

Insurance

➔ Getting travel insurance to cover any theft, loss or medical problems you may encounter is highly recommended. Some travel insurance policies do not cover 'risky' activities such as motorcycling, skiing or even trekking, so read the fine print. Make sure the policy covers hospital stays and an emergency flight home.

➔ Paying for your airline ticket or rental car with a credit card may provide limited travel accident insurance. If you already have private health insurance or a homeowners' or renters' policy, find out what they will cover and only get supplemental insurance. If you have prepaid a large portion of your vacation, trip cancellation insurance may be a worthwhile expense.

➔ Worldwide travel insurance is available at www.lonelyplanet.com/travel_services. You can buy, extend and claim online at anytime – even if you are already on the road.

Internet Access

➔ Many hotels, motels and private RV campgrounds have either a public computer terminal or offer wi-fi (sometimes free, or costing $10 or more per day); ask when reserving.

➔ In the national parks, wi-fi hot spots are rare (look for unsecured networks near

visitor centers and lodges). Pay as you-go self-service internet terminals are rarely available and can also be slow, unreliable and/or expensive.

➔ Nearby towns and cities usually have at least one copy center offering online terminals (typically $5 to $12 per hour) and wi-fi. Wi-fi abounds at restaurants and cafes.

➔ Public libraries usually offer internet terminals (though these may have time limits and require advance sign-up or waiting in line) and sometimes wi-fi. Out-of-state residents may be charged a small fee for internet terminal use.

Legal Matters

Utah follows most major US national laws. The state's liquor laws are more stringent than most US states. This means beers sold at grocery stores are only of the 3.2% alcohol variety. State-

LIQUOR LAWS

Utah has some of the oddest liquor laws in the country. As with everywhere in the US, you must be 21 to drink legally. But that's where the similarities end.

In Utah, grocery stores sell near-beer (which doesn't exceed 3.2% alcohol content) seven days a week. State-run liquor stores and package agencies sell beer, wine and spirits Monday through Saturday (closed Sunday). In southern Utah you'll find licensed liquor stores and package agencies in St George, Hurricane, Cedar City, Kanab, Panguitch and Moab.

Lounges and taverns only serve near-beer. Stronger drinks are served at restaurants with liquor licenses between 10am and 1am daily, as well as at 'dining or social clubs' that are open to the general public. At restaurants, servers aren't permitted to offer alcoholic drinks or show you a drink menu unless you specifically ask. When you order a drink, you must also order food, but a snack or appetizer will do. Wherever you're doing your drinking, you can only order one drink for yourself at a time. A pitcher of margaritas? Fuhgeddaboutit.

Alcohol is legally prohibited on Native American reservations and cannot be transported on tribal lands, even if you're just passing through.

run liquor stores are generally found in most cities, but you'll be hard-pressed finding any stores in really small towns. Alcohol can't be sold after 1am. Marijuana is illegal here.

LGBTIQ+ Travelers

This is a conservative state, but generally gay and lesbian travelers will feel welcomed. There aren't really any gay bars in remote southern Utah. You'll need to go to Salt Lake or Cedar City for that. PDA is OK.

Maps

If you are on a serious back-country hike, you should use a topographic map, compass and/or GPS.

Money

There are ATMs in Springdale and Zion Lodge (Zion);

INTERNATIONAL VISITORS

All travelers should double-check current visa and passport requirements *before* coming to the USA. For the latest entry requirements and eligibility, consult the Visa section of the **US Department of State website** (http://travel.state.gov) and the Travel section of the **US Customs & Border Protection website** (www.cbp.gov). If you're still in doubt, contact the nearest US embassy or consulate in your home country (visit www.usembassy.gov for a complete list). There are no documentation requirements to move from state to state in the US, and there are no agriculture controls on the Utah borders. You will need to follow local laws, including leaving your marijuana in Colorado and Nevada.

Passports

➡ Under the Western Hemisphere Travel Initiative (WHTI), all travelers (including returning US citizens) must have a valid machine-readable passport (MRP) when entering the US by air, land or sea. An MRP has two lines of letters, numbers and <<< at the bottom of the data page.

➡ MRPs issued or renewed after October 26, 2006, must be e-passports (ie have a digital photo and integrated chip with biometric data). MRPs issued or renewed between October 26, 2005, and October 25, 2006, must have a digital photo or integrated chip on the data page.

➡ The only exceptions to these MRP requirements are for select US, Canadian and Mexican citizens who are able to present other WHTI-compliant documents (eg preapproved 'trusted traveler' cards).

➡ Under the US Department of Homeland Security (DHS) registration program, US-VISIT (www.dhs.gov/us-visit), almost all visitors (excluding, for now, most Canadian and many Mexican citizens) will be digitally photographed and have their electronic (inkless) fingerprints scanned upon arrival; the process typically takes less than a minute.

Visas

➡ Currently, under the US Visa Waiver Program (VWP), visas are not required for citizens of 36 countries for stays up to 90 days (no extensions) if you have an MRP. If you don't have an MRP, you'll need a visa to enter the USA.

➡ Citizens of VWP countries *must* register with the Electronic System for Travel Authorization (ESTA) online (https://esta.cbp.dhs.gov) at least 72 hours before their trip begins. Once approved, ESTA registration is valid for up to two years.

➡ Citizens from all other countries need to apply for a visa in their home country. The process costs a nonrefundable $131, involves a personal interview and can take several weeks, so apply as early as possible.

Panguitch; Bryce Canyon City (Bryce Canyon); Torrey (Capitol Reef); and Moab (Arches). It's always good to have some cash on hand for state park and camping fees.

Credit Cards

Credit cards are almost universally accepted. In fact, you'll find it next to impossible to rent a car, book a hotel room or order tickets over the phone without one. Visa, MasterCard and American Express are most common.

Most ATMs will dispense cash if you use your credit card, but that can be expensive because, in addition to steep service fees, you'll be charged interest immediately. Ask your credit-card company for details and a four-digit PIN number.

Currency Exchange

If you're arriving from abroad, exchange money at the airport or in the nearest city; for example, at a major bank or currency-exchange office such as American

Express. In smaller park gateway towns, exchanging money may be impossible. There are currently no currency-exchange services inside the parks, so make sure you have plenty of US cash and a credit card.

Tipping

Tipping is *not* optional. Only withhold tips in cases of outrageously bad service.

Airport & hotel porters Per bag $2, minimum per cart $5.

Bartenders Per round 10% to 15%.

Guides Not required, but recommended. A good start is $20 per day.

Hotel maids Per night $2 to $5.

Restaurant servers Tip 15% to 20%, unless a gratuity is already charged.

Taxi drivers Tip 10% to 15%.

Opening Hours

Regular business hours are from 9am until 5pm weekdays. In bigger towns, supermarkets may stay open until 8pm or later.

Banks 9am to 5pm Monday to Friday; some also open 9am to 1:30pm Saturday.

Bars Usually from 5pm to 1am daily.

Post offices 8:30am to 4:30pm, possibly Saturday morning (usually 9am to noon).

Restaurants Breakfast is usually served from 7am to 10am, lunch from 11:30am to 2:30pm and dinner from 5pm to 9pm.

Shop hours 10am to 5:30pm Monday to Saturday and noon to 5pm Sunday; malls stay open later.

Post

The **US Postal Service** (www.usps.com) is inexpensive and reliable. You won't find any post offices inside the parks, but visitor-center bookstores, concessionaire shops and lodges may sell stamps. Outside the parks, gateway towns usually have at least one post office, while cities have multiple branches.

Public Holidays

On holiday weekends, especially Memorial Day, Fourth of July and Labor Day in summer, expect the parks to be ridiculously busy, with campgrounds full and all nearby accommodations

booked out weeks, if not months, in advance.

On national holidays, banks, schools and government offices (including post offices) close, and transportation, museums and other services operate on a Sunday schedule. Holidays falling on a weekend are usually observed the following Monday.

New Year's Day January 1

Martin Luther King Jr Day Third Monday in January

Presidents' Day Third Monday in February

Memorial Day Last Monday in May

Independence Day July 4 (aka the Fourth of July)

Labor Day First Monday in September

Columbus Day Second Monday in October

Veterans' Day November 11

Thanksgiving Day Fourth Thursday in November

Christmas Day December 25

Safe Travel

Dehydration is the biggest danger. Brings lots of water (a gallon per person per day in summer) and protect yourself from the sun. Falling down is the other big danger. Bring good walking shoes, watch your step, avoid rockfall areas and don't get close to the rim (people fall off). Use proper safety precautions when out on the water. Wildlife can be both dangerous and annoying. In some areas, flies and mosquitoes are prevalent. In others, be cautious of bears and other big animals. On these wide open roads, try to keep your speed down and watch for crossing wildlife.

Telephone

➡ Cell (mobile) phone and data reception is sketchy at best in southern Utah's national parks and wilderness areas, and varies

depending on your exact location and service provider. In most park gateway towns, cell-phone reception is usually decent, though again it depends on where you are.

➡ Please be considerate of other park visitors when using your cell phone. Being woken up by phones ringing in a neighboring campsite, or listening to someone conduct a loud conversation at a scenic viewpoint, can really tarnish the outdoor experience for everyone in the immediate vicinity.

➡ Public pay phones are found in southern Utah's national parks at campgrounds, lodges and visitor centers. Local pay phone calls cost 50¢ minimum, the cost increasing with the distance and length of call. Increasingly, in-park pay phones are not coin-operated and will only accept credit cards or prepaid calling cards. You're usually better off using a prepaid phonecard, typically sold at park bookstores, concessionaire shops and lodges. Be sure to read the fine print for hidden costs, such as activation fees or connection surcharges for making calls from pay phones.

Time

➡ Utah is on Mountain Standard Time (GMT minus seven hours). When it's noon in Salt Lake City, it's 11am in Los Angeles, 3pm in New York, 8pm in London and 5am (the next day) in Sydney.

➡ Daylight Saving Time (DST) starts on the second Sunday in March, when clocks are set one hour ahead, and ends on the first Sunday in November.

➡ If you're driving to Utah, beware that the state of Arizona (including Grand Canyon National Park) does not observe DST, but the Navajo Nation does. Confused yet? We thought so.

Tourist Information

National park visitor centers and regional public lands information offices are your best bets for parks travel information once you arrive in southern Utah.

The state's official tourism agency, **Utah Travel Council** (www.utah.com), offers loads of free information to help plan a vacation, including downloadable travel e-guides and website sections dedicated to national and state parks, outdoor recreation, annual festivals and events, and more. You'll find a **Utah Welcome Center** (435-673-4542; http://travel.utah. gov; 1835 S Convention Center Dr, Dixie Convention Center; 10am-5pm) in St George.

County and other regional travel bureaus are also helpful:

Capitol Reef Country Travel Council (800-858-7951, 435-425-3365; www.capitolreef.org; Junction Hwys 12 & 24) Covers Capitol Reef and Hwy 12.

Cedar City & Brian Head Tourism & Convention Bureau (Map p96; 435-586-5124, 800-354-4849; www.visitcedarcity. com; 581 N Main St; 8:30am-5pm Mon-Sat;) Area-wide info and free internet use.

Escalante Chamber of Commerce (www.escalanteut. com) Covers Grand Staircase–Escalante National Monument and Boulder.

Garfield County Office of Tourism (435-676-8585, 800-444-6689; www.bryce

canyoncountry.com; 55 S Main Street, Panguitch; 9am-noon & 1-5pm Mon-Fri) Covers Bryce Canyon and Hwy 12.

Kane County Office of Tourism (435-644-5033; www. visitsouthernutah.com; 78 S 100 E; 8am-8pm Mon-Fri, 9am-6pm Sat-Sun) The main source for area information; great old Western movie posters and artifacts on display.

Moab Information Center (Map p210; 435-259-8825; http://discovermoab.com/visitor-center/; 25 E Center St; 8am-7pm;) Comprehensive online resource.

Zion Canyon Visitors Bureau (Map p84; 435-772-3434; www.zionpark.com; 118 Lion Blvd; 9am-5pm Mon-Fri) Offers comprehensive accommodations listings of family-friendly motels and hotels, as well as boutique inns and B&Bs, in the gateway town of Springdale, on UT 9 west of the park.

Volunteering

There are many opportunities to volunteer in and around southern Utah's parks, from one-day projects to longer-term endeavors. Volunteers can do trail maintenance, pull invasive plants, train to be an interpretive ranger or work with youth organizations.

Bureau of Land Management (www.blm.gov/get-involved/volunteers) Apply online or contact the nearest BLM office.

National Park Service (www. nps.gov/volunteer) Apply for the Volunteer in Parks (VIP) program and search for opportunities by park name or state online.

Sierra Club (www.sierraclub. org) Day or weekend service projects and volunteer vacations, including for families, focus on conservation (annual membership $25).

Student Conservation Association (www.thesca.org) Nonprofit organization offers conservation internships that earn academic credit, as well as summer trail-crew work.

Volunteer.gov (www.volunteer. gov) Online searchable database of volunteers for all public lands agencies, including NPS and tUSFS.

Zion Canyon Field Institute (435-772-3264; www. zionpark.org; programs $45-85) Arranges day-long service projects, typically in the Narrows of the Virgin River during summer and fall.

Work

Nearly everyone who works inside the parks is employed by the NPS, the parks' cooperating nonprofit organizations or by park concessionaire businesses. Most employment opportunities are low-paying seasonal jobs that are mostly filled by young people, teachers or retirees. Planning ahead is essential, whether you are applying with NPS or park concessionaires – applications for summer jobs are typically due around December. Getting work for non-US citizens without a work visa is nearly impossible, though under-the-table arrangements may be found.

Transportation

GETTING THERE & AWAY

Most travelers to Utah arrive by air or car, with bus and train running a very distant third and fourth place. Major transportation hubs are Las Vegas and Salt Lake City. You can also fly into Denver or Phoenix, though both are a bit further away. Moab now has direct flights from Denver.

Flights, cars and tours can be booked online at www.lonelyplanet.com/bookings.

Air

Your best bet to get here by air is to fly into Las Vegas, Nevada, or Salt Lake City, Utah. Moab has a direct service from Denver.

Canyonlands Field Airport (www.moabairport.com) Commercial service had just begun when we passed through, with new direct services to Denver.

Denver International Airport (www.flydenver.com) Denver is 5½ hours from both Arches and Canyonlands.

Grand Junction Regional Airport (www.gjairport.com) Small regional airport in western Colorado. Two hours from Arches and Canyonlands.

McCarran International Airport (www.mccarran.com) Las Vegas' airport is three hours from Zion and 4½ hours from Bryce.

Phoenix Sky Harbor International Airport (https://skyharbor.com) Six to seven hours from Zion.

Salt Lake City International Airport (www.slcairport.com) Three to four hours from all of Utah's main parks.

St George Municipal Airport (www.flysgu.com) Small airport one hour from Zion. Closer than the main hubs, but less likely to have good airfare deals.

Land

Most people get here by automobile, either in a rental or their own. There are a few long-haul bus companies, but getting to and around the parks is hard without your own wheels. There are no checks to cross state borders.

Bus

➡ Long-distance buses can get you to major points within the region, but you'll still need to rent a car to get around as public transportation to the parks is nonexistent.

➡ **Greyhound** (Map p92; ☑ 800-231-2222; www.greyhound.com; 1572 S Convention Center, St George) runs buses throughout Utah. There is service to St George and Cedar City for access to Bryce and Zion parks, with routes connecting to Las Vegas, Denver and Salt Lake, to continue on to most major

---

CLIMATE CHANGE & TRAVEL

Every form of transport that relies on carbon-based fuel generates CO_2, the main cause of human-induced climate change. Modern travel is dependent on airplanes, which might use less fuel per mile per person than most cars but travel much greater distances. The altitude at which aircraft emit gases (including CO_2) and particles also contributes to their climate change impact. Many websites offer 'carbon calculators' that allow people to estimate the carbon emissions generated by their journey and, for those who wish to do so, to offset the impact of the greenhouse gases emitted with contributions to portfolios of climate-friendly initiatives throughout the world. Lonely Planet offsets the carbon footprint of all staff and author travel.

US cities. Note that tickets are not sold at the St George bus stop, you'll need to buy them online.

➡ Private shuttles sometimes connect parks with nearby towns, such as Green River to Moab or St George to Zion.

➡ To save money, plan seven days in advance, buy tickets online, travel on weekdays and travel with a companion.

➡ You can take bus tours (p271) of the park, a good alternative if you don't have a car.

Car, Motorcycle & RV

While the quickest way to get to Utah is by plane, the best way to get around is with your own private vehicle. Most destinations cannot be reached with public transportation.

Train

➡ Amtrak (www.amtrak. com) operates two major routes through the area. Use them to reach the region, but not for touring.

➡ The *California Zephyr* runs between the San Francisco Bay Area and Chicago with stops at Green River (50 miles northwest of Moab, no car rental), Grand Junction (western Colorado, with car rental) and Salt Lake City.

➡ The *Southwest Chief* runs from Chicago to Los Angeles,

with stops at Albuquerque in New Mexico, and Flagstaff in Arizona.

GETTING AROUND

Bicycle

➡ Touring southern Utah by bike is a hardy endeavor and best done with the support of an outfitter or tour operator. The **Adventure Cycling Association** (📞800-755-2453; www.adventurecycling. org) provides info on cycling routes, sells bicycle maps and arranges tours. For emergency roadside assistance, join the Better World Club.

➡ Zion Canyon, Bryce Canyon and Capitol Reef have scenic drives open to recreational cyclists. Although national park trails are off-limits to bicycles (except for Zion's Pa'rus Trail), bicycles are usually allowed on any paved or dirt park road.

➡ Bicycle rentals are readily available. Expect to spend $25 to $50 per day for a cruiser or basic mountain bike.

➡ Moab is generally considered the mountain-biking capital of the Southwest. Grand Staircase–Escalante and

the Zion area are also good mountain-biking destinations.

Bus

➡ There is no bus service to or between southern Utah's national parks. However, both Zion and Bryce Canyon offer free seasonal park shuttles that are handy for seeing the main sights and avoiding traffic headaches.

➡ In Zion, the mandatory park shuttle runs from spring through fall, when the canyon's main scenic drive is closed to private vehicles. Another free shuttle route runs through the gateway town of Springdale, connecting with the Zion shuttle. Both routes run frequently. Shuttles do not serve Hwy 9 east of Canyon Junction through the Zion–Mt Carmel Tunnel or the park's more remote Kolob Terrace and Kolob Canyons Rds.

➡ In Bryce Canyon, an optional park shuttle runs from May through September. Although this free shuttle connects the dots between the park's most popular sightseeing spots, as well as the lodge, visitor center, campground and Ruby's Inn tourist complex just north of the park, it does not travel all the way down the canyon's scenic drive, except on twice-daily guided shuttle-bus tours (free).

Car & Motorcycle

There are usually no restrictions on travel by private vehicle in the national parks, although Zion Canyon is only accessible to park shuttle buses from spring to fall. Otherwise, cars and motorcycles are allowed on all public paved and dirt roads inside and outside the parks.

ARE WE THERE YET?

Judging how long it will take to drive from point A to point B in southern Utah is an art form. Some highways drive like dirt roads, some dirt roads like highways, and slow-moving trucks and RVs can impede your progress for miles uphill. Most southern Utah road savvy is only gained through hard-won experience. When in doubt, always plan for it to take longer than you think.

As a rule, if a dirt road is noted as 'good' and passable to passenger cars, you can usually drive an average of 30mph on it, but numerous rough sections and washes will force you to slow to 20mph or even 10mph. The speed limit on state highways is 55mph to 65mph; on the interstates it's 75mph to 80mph.

Automobile Associations

For 24-hour emergency road-side assistance, free maps and travel discounts on lodging, attractions, car rentals and more:

American Automobile Association (AAA; ☑435-652-6920, roadside assistance 800-222-4357; www.aaa.com; 844 W Telegraph St, No. 4, Washington; ☺9am-6pm Mon-Fri) Has a walk-in office in the town of Washington (just on the east side of the greater St George area), and reciprocal agreements with some international auto clubs (eg Canada's CAA). Bring your membership card from home.

Better World Club (www.betterworldclub.com) Eco-friendly alternative auto club that supports environmental causes and offers optional emergency roadside assistance for cyclists. Annual membership (from $60) gets you two 24-hour emergency roadside pickups and transport within a 5-mile radius.

Good Sam RV Club (www.goodsamclub.com) Emergency roadside assistance and towing services for RVs, online route planner and 10% discounts at participating campgrounds.

Driver's License

➡ Visitors may legally drive a car in Utah for up to 12 months with their home driver's license.

➡ If you're from overseas, an International Driving Permit (IDP) will have more credibility with police and simplify the car-rental process, especially if your license doesn't have a photo or isn't written in English.

➡ To legally ride a motorcycle, you'll need a valid US state motorcycle license or a specially endorsed IDP.

Fuel & Repairs

➡ Always start out with a full tank of gas and extra gallons of drinking water, plus food and blankets in case of emergencies.

➡ Gas stations are few and far between in southern Utah. There are no gas stations inside any of the parks, and gas can be expensive in gateway towns. Try to fill up in bigger cities and along interstate highways, where gas is cheaper and stations are often open 24 hours.

➡ For emergency roadside assistance and towing services, join an auto club. In case of any roadside emergencies, keep in mind that cell phones work in most towns and cities, but only in very limited areas of the national parks.

➡ Just outside Bryce Canyon, **Ruby's Inn American Car Care Center** (☑435-834-5232; www.rubysinn.com/bryce-canyon-car-rental; 105 S Main St, Bryce Canyon City; ☺7am-11pm May-Sep, 8am-6pm Oct-Apr) offers full-service repairs for cars, trucks and RVs, although parts are limited and you may have to wait quite a while for all but the simplest of repairs. It also sells standard auto supplies and decently priced gas, and offers a car wash and 24-hour, AAA-approved towing services. Otherwise, your best bets for faster car repairs and finding auto supplies are in St George and Moab.

Insurance

For rentals, always first check your auto-insurance policy or credit card from home to see if you're already covered.

➡ Utah law requires all drivers to carry proof of liability insurance, which covers damage to any property or people you might hit.

➡ Insurance against damage to the car itself, called collision damage waiver (CDW) or loss damage waiver (LDW), costs another $30 or so per day; it may also require that you pay the first $100 to $500 for any repairs. Some credit cards offer reimbursement for collision damage if you pay for the entire rental with that card. There may be exceptions for rentals longer than 15 days, exotic models or 4WD vehicles.

➡ Many rental companies stipulate that any damage a car sustains while being driven on unpaved roads is not covered by the insurance they offer. A few companies prohibit driving off paved roads entirely, even when renting a 4WD vehicle. Clarify this ahead of time if you plan on doing any off-road driving.

Rental

➡ To rent your own wheels, you'll need to be at least 25 years old, hold a valid driver's license and have a major credit card, *not* a check or debit card. A few companies may rent to drivers between 21 and 25 years of age for a surcharge (about $25 per day).

➡ With advance reservations, you should be able to get an economy-size vehicle for around $30 per day, excluding insurance, taxes and fees. Some major car-rental companies, including Avis, Budget and Hertz, now offer 'green' fleets of hybrid rental cars, expect to pay significantly more for these models.

➡ Renting a 4WD vehicle such as a Jeep costs more (from $45 per day). The cheapest places to rent 4WD vehicles are Las Vegas and Salt Lake City, but then you'll be stuck with a higher-priced, fuel-inefficient vehicle for your entire trip. Renting a 4WD locally in southern Utah is more expensive on a daily basis (easily over $100), but may work out cheaper overall if you only need a 4WD for a couple of days.

➡ Car-rental rates usually include unlimited mileage, but hefty surcharges apply for additional drivers and one-way rentals. Child or infant safety seats are required by law (reserve when booking), renting from $10/50 per day/week.

➤ Most companies have rental desks at Salt Lake City, McCarran (Las Vegas) and Denver international airports and Grand Junction regional airport. St George, Cedar City and Moab also have rental locations.

➤ Motorcycle rentals and insurance are not cheap, especially if you have your eye on a Harley-Davidson. Depending on the model, it costs $100 to $250 per day plus taxes. Rental rates usually include helmets, unlimited miles and liability insurance, but collision insurance (CDW) costs extra.

Road Conditions

➤ For highway driving conditions, visit the website of the **Utah Department of Transportation** (www.udot.utah.gov). Every national park provides updates on roads within its boundaries; either visit the park website or call the visitor information numbers. For road conditions outside the national parks, contact the federal agency in charge of that area – most often it's the BLM (Bureau of Land Management) or USFS (US Forest Service).

➤ Overall precipitation is low, but when it does rain, it can wreak havoc. Most common during July and August, short, heavy thunderstorms cause flash floods and turn dirt roads into impassable mud slicks, though they dry quickly. Even the lightest rain can leave desert slickrock and hard clay roads treacherously slippery and too dangerous for any vehicle (including 4WDs) for at least a day or two afterward.

➤ Always check with rangers before driving dirt roads, and watch the skies. Never park your vehicle in a desert wash,

where it could possibly get swept away by a flash flood.

➤ In winter higher elevations have snow, while lower elevations see freezing rain, occasional snow and nighttime temperatures that can turn blacktop roads icy. High-elevation mountain roads may be closed completely from the first snowfall in late October or early November until the snow melts away, usually between April and June.

Road Hazards

Be extra cautious while driving in Utah. It may be tempting to put your vehicle into cruise control and zip down the highway at 80mph without a care in the world, but there is no shortage of hazards, from dust storms and rainstorms to livestock and wildlife.

➤ Be particularly vigilant any time you see a wildlife-crossing road sign, especially at dusk. While hitting a deer is bad enough, hitting an elk, which weighs anywhere from 500lb to 900lb, may very well result in serious injury or death.

➤ Driving too slowly or erratically can be a hazard in the parks. Maintain a reasonable speed on crowded scenic drives. Do not block traffic by suddenly stopping in the middle of the road to take a photo. All of the rules of the road still apply in national parks.

➤ If you're driving an RV or other oversized vehicle, be courteous and don't hog the road – use signposted pullouts to let faster traffic pass.

➤ National park parking lots are renowned for accidents: overloaded vehicles with poor visibility, screaming children causing a distraction, pedestrians who pop up out of nowhere and aggressive drivers trying to snag precious parking spots make for a particularly high collision rate. If you are at

fault in an accident within a national park, not only are you responsible for all damages, but you will also be issued a ticket. Take it slow.

Road Rules

➤ Drive on the right-hand side of the road. The use of seat belts is required for drivers, front-seat passengers and anyone under age 20. Children under eight years old are required to sit in a car seat or booster, unless they are taller than 57in (145cm). Motorcycle helmets are not required for adults over age 18.

➤ The maximum speed limit on major Utah highways is 80mph, but it can be much lower on back roads.

➤ You may make a right turn on a red light after first coming to a full stop, unless signs say otherwise. U-turn laws vary by city; look for posted signs.

➤ It is permissible to talk on your cell phone while driving, but illegal to 'manipulate' your phone (ie dial or text). Get a hands-free setup if you don't already have one.

➤ Strict penalties for driving under the influence (DUI) of drugs or alcohol in Utah include steep fines and jail time. Police can give roadside sobriety checks to assess if you've been drinking or using drugs. You'll fail if your blood alcohol is over the legal limit (0.08%). Refusing to be tested can result in immediate suspension of your driver's license. It is illegal to carry open containers of alcohol inside a vehicle, even when they're empty; store them in the trunk instead.

Hitchhiking

Hitchhiking is never entirely safe anywhere in the world, and we don't recommend it. That said, hitchhiking is sometimes the only way to get between trailheads after an end-to-end hike, if you don't happen to have two cars to shuttle. The rules for hitchhiking in each national park change every year, so ask at the visitor center before you stick your thumb out. Keep in mind that hitch-hiking is usually only allowed at designated roadside pull-outs within the parks.

RVs

RVs remain a popular way to travel around southern Utah. Although the larger models can be cumbersome to navigate and guzzle gas at an alarming rate, they solve transportation, accommo-dation and cooking needs in one fell swoop.

➡ After the size of the vehicle, consider the impact of gas prices, gas mileage, additional mileage costs, insurance and refundable deposits; these can add up quickly. It pays to shop around and read the fine print.

➡ Rental rates vary by size, model and mileage. The base rate for a four-person vehicle can be anywhere from $420 to $1800 weekly in summer, plus 34¢ for each additional mile not included in your package. Get out a good map and calculator to determine if it's practical.

➡ Before heading out, consult http://gorving.com

or www.rvtravel.com for tips galore.

➡ Visit Woodall's (www.woodalls.com) for a thorough RV campground guide.

➡ Some roads in southern Utah are not appropriate for RVs, and a few roads expressly forbid travel by RVs (or sometimes only for models over a certain length). For further details, consult seasonal park newspapers or ask the staff at visitor centers.

➡ RV dump stations and electrical hookups are found at private campgrounds outside the parks. Inside the parks, dump stations may only be available seasonally (if at all) and generator use is usually restricted to certain hours at NPS (National Parks Service) campgrounds, which may not have pull-through sites and may restrict RV camping to vehicles of a certain length only.

➡ Be aware that if you're planning on driving an RV or other oversized vehicle through the Mt Carmel–Zion Tunnel inside Zion National Park, you'll need to pay an escort fee and time your trip during specific hours.

Rental
Adventure Touring RV Rentals (☑877-778-9569; www.adventuretouring.com) Serving Las Vegas and Denver.

Cruise America (☑800-671-8042; www.cruiseamerica.com) Rents RVs and trailers in Salt Lake City, Las Vegas, Denver and other major gateway cities.

Jucy Rentals (☑800-650-4180; www.jucyrentals.com; 5895 Boulder Hwy) Green and purple pop-up camper vans; located in Las Vegas.

Outdoorsy (www.outdoorsy.com) Easy rental-by-owner service.

Tours

Most ranger-guided walk-ing, hiking and shuttle-bus tours of the parks are free; ask at park visitor centers about what's currently being offered. The parks' natural history associations also offer excellent guided tours and field trips.

Region-wide tour oper-ators:

Adventure Bus (☑909-633-7225; www.adventurebus.com)

Backroads (☑510-527-1555; www.backroads.com)

Green Tortoise (☑800-867-8647; www.greentortoise.com)

Road Scholar (☑800-454-5768; www.roadscholar.org; 🐾)

Southern Utah Scenic Tours (☑888-404-8687; www.utahscenictours.com)

Health & Safety

The US healthcare system generally relies on private insurance, though some public healthcare options remain available. If you are traveling from abroad, it's smart to get travel insurance through somebody like World Nomads (www.world-nomads.com), as just a night in a hospital can cost you $10,000.

The key to health and safety are good predeparture preparations and common sense while traveling. While the potential problems may seem frightening, few visitors experience anything worse than a skinned knee. Much of this information covers worst-case scenarios, which can be avoided or at least dealt with more effectively if you're well prepared.

BEFORE YOU GO

If you're planning on doing any hiking, start getting regular physical exercise a few weeks prior to your trip. When possible, visitors from lower elevations and cooler climes should allow at least a day or two to acclimatize before undertaking any strenuous activity in southern Utah's deserts or mountains. And remember the golden rule: if you're going into the backcountry, always let someone know where you are going and how long you plan to be gone. There's even an app for that: www.hiker-alert.com.

Further Reading

Hikers, climbers, backpackers, paddlers and other off-road explorers may want to stuff one of these excellent first-aid guides into their packs.

➡ *Backcountry First Aid and Extended Care* by Buck Tilton (2007). Pocket-sized guide that's compact and lightweight, but info-packed for situations when medical help is over an hour away.

➡ *Wilderness 911* by Eric A Weiss (2007). A step-by-step guide to first aid and advanced care in remote areas when you have limited medical supplies.

➡ *Medicine for the Outdoors* by Paul S Auerbach (2009). Layperson's reference with explanations of wilderness medical problems and practical treatment options.

IN THE PARKS

➡ While crime is not a particular problem in any of the national parks, you should still lock your car, and place any valuables you don't carry with you in the trunk, especially when you park at less-visited trailheads.

➡ For casual park visitors, staying safe and healthy is usually a matter of hydrating properly, being aware of the weather forecast (eg watch for flash floods) and not goofing around near precarious cliffs and canyon rims. Many emergencies arise when visitors overestimate their own physical abilities or underestimate the power of Mother Nature.

➡ When visiting southern Utah, you'll need to be more self-sufficient and prepared for the unexpected than usual. The desert offers innumerable ways to come to a bad end, and people discover new ways all the time.

Medical Assistance

➡ In any emergency, dial ☎911. Unfortunately, if you're injured in rural areas or inside the parks, calling may not be an option; cell phones often don't work outside the major interstate corridors, and canyon walls block signals. Satellite phones and personal locator beacons (PLBs) are your best options in the backcountry.

→ Park rangers with medical training can help visitors who get into trouble, free of charge for basic first aid. For more serious ailments, drive to the nearest hospital emergency room or clinic. Search-and-rescue (SAR) and helicopter evacuations are only for truly life-threatening emergencies. Emergency operations are costly and also put the lives of rangers and other staff at risk.

→ Utah Search and Rescue Assistance (https://secure. utah.gov/rescue) $25 yearly plans and $100 five-year plans work like rescue insurance, and provide much-needed funding to the awesome men and women that rescue your sorry butt from places you probably shouldn't have been. Fishing and boating licenses will also cover costs of search and rescue generally.

Infectious Diseases
Rabies
→ Rabies is a viral infection of the brain and spinal cord that is almost always fatal. The rabies virus is carried in the saliva of infected animals and is typically transmitted through an animal bite, though contamination of any break in the skin with infected saliva may result in rabies. In the US, most cases of human rabies are related to exposure to bats. But rabies may be contracted from any mammal, including squirrels, raccoons and unvaccinated cats and dogs.

→ If there is any possibility, however small, that you have been exposed, you should seek preventative treatment, which consists of rabies immune globulin and rabies vaccine and is quite safe. In particular, any contact with a bat should be discussed with health authorities, because bats have small teeth and may not leave obvious bite

marks. If you wake up to find a bat in your room, especially if you have small children, rabies prophylaxis may be necessary.

Environmental Hazards
Altitude
The rim at Bryce Canyon ranges in altitude from 8000ft to 9000ft above sea level, while Cedar Breaks rises above 10,000ft. A common complaint at high elevations is altitude sickness, characterized by shortness of breath, fatigue, headaches, dizziness and loss of appetite. It sounds benign, but it can actually be quite serious – drink plenty of water and take a day or two to acclimatize before attempting anything strenuous. If symptoms persist, return to a lower elevation. Ibuprofen helps.

Bites & Stings
ANIMAL BITES
→ Do not attempt to pet, handle or feed any wild animal, no matter how cute and cuddly it may look. Most injuries from animals in the parks are directly related to people trying to do just that. For example, squirrels on Zion's Riverside Walk are notoriously aggressive because so many park visitors have illegally fed them.

→ Any bite or scratch by a mammal, including bats and squirrels, should be promptly and thoroughly cleansed with large amounts of soap and water, followed by application of an antiseptic such as iodine or alcohol. Local health authorities should be contacted for possible rabies treatment, whether or not you've already been vaccinated against rabies. It may also be advisable to start an antibiotic, because wounds caused by animal bites and scratches frequently become infected.

SNAKES
→ Despite southern Utah's abundance of venomous snakes, fatalities are rare. Snakebites can usually be prevented by giving the animal space – when you encounter a snake, back away slowly. Most reported snakebites result from people picking up the snake, either out of bravado or mistakenly assuming the animal is dead.

→ If you're bitten by a snake, seek immediate help. Snakebites don't cause instantaneous death, and medical centers usually stock the necessary antivenins.

→ If you're bitten on a limb, a light constricting band above the bite can help. Keep the affected area below the level of the heart, and move as little as possible. What you should not do is wrap the limb in a tight tourniquet, slash or suck the wound, put ice on it or take any alcohol or drugs. Simply stay calm and get to a hospital.

SPIDERS & SCORPIONS
→ There are no particular first-aid techniques for spider or scorpion bites. Some (like tarantula bites) are merely painful, while others (like black widow and scorpion bites) contain venom. Doses are generally too small to kill adult humans, but children face a risk of serious complications.

➡ Cool the wound using cold water or ice, and if you're hiking, return immediately; reactions can be delayed for up to 12 hours, and you may want to call Utah Poison Control (800-222-1222) and seek medical help.

Cold
HYPOTHERMIA

➡ While generally associated with winter hiking at altitude, hypothermia is a real danger in the desert in any season. Even a sudden rain shower or high winds can rapidly lower your body temperature. Symptoms of hypothermia include exhaustion, numbness, shivering, stumbling, slurred speech, dizzy spells, muscle cramps and irrational or even violent behavior.

➡ Hypothermia often strikes people hiking narrow canyons, where they must wade or swim in pools that are frigid even in summer. One such place is Zion's Narrows, where hikers spend most of their time immersed in the Virgin River. Hypothermia is also a danger for campers from fall to spring, when overnight temperatures routinely drop near or below freezing, even in the desert or following mild days in the mountains.

➡ To help avoid hypothermia, don't wear cotton clothes (which dry slowly and provide no insulation when wet). Instead wear synthetics or woolen clothing that retain warmth even when wet. Always carry waterproof layers and high-energy, easily digestible snacks like chocolate, nuts and dried fruit. Canyoneers should wear a wet or dry suit when advised.

➡ To treat hypothermia, take shelter from bad weather and change into dry, warm clothing. Drink hot liquids (no caffeine or alcohol) and snack on high-calorie food. In advanced stages, carefully put hypothermia sufferers in a warm sleeping bag cocooned inside a windproof and waterproof outer wrapping. Do not rub victims, who must be handled gently.

Heat
DEHYDRATION & HEAT EXHAUSTION

➡ You don't need to do much to become dehydrated in the desert – just stand around. If you do engage in an activity, expect water and salts to leave your body at a vastly accelerated rate.

➡ It's very important to both drink water and eat

salty foods when hiking in the desert. The minimum is a gallon of water a day per person, or 16oz every hour while active. Though that may sound like a lot, you'll drink that and more if you're active. Keep a few extra gallons of water in the car. Eating is just as important, however, and is the half of the equation many people forget. Always carry high-energy bars or trail mix.

➡ Dehydration (lack of water) or salt deficiency can cause heat exhaustion. Signs and symptoms of heat exhaustion, which occurs when you lose water faster than your body can absorb it, include nausea, vomiting, fatigue, headaches, dizziness, muscle cramps, heavy sweating and/or cool, clammy skin.

➡ Treat heat exhaustion by drinking, eating, resting in the shade and cooling the skin with a wet cloth and fanning yourself.

HEATSTROKE

➡ Heatstroke, which can be fatal, occurs when your internal cooling mechanism breaks down and your body temperature rises dangerously.

➡ Symptoms include flushed, hot and dry skin (ie sweating has stopped), severe throbbing headaches, hyperventilation and a rapid pulse. Some victims may act in an uncharacteristically bizarre manner, display a lack of coordination and eventually go into convulsions.

➡ Immediate hospitalization is essential. In the meantime, move the victim into the shade, remove clothing and cover with a wet cloth or towel, fan vigorously and seek immediate help. Ice packs can be applied to the neck, armpits and groin.

HYPONATREMIA

➡ Hyponatremia (low sodium blood level) occurs when

WATER PURIFICATION

All groundwater in the desert, whether a river, seasonal stream or sandstone seep, should be considered unsafe to drink and treated accordingly.

Giardiasis and cryptosporidiosis are common intestinal diseases that stem from drinking untreated water. Giardiasis can be treated, but there is no effective treatment for cryptosporidiosis. Both can last for anywhere from a few weeks or months to several years, though neither is typically life-threatening.

The most reliable way to destroy the offending organisms is to boil water. Water purification tablets and portable water filters (0.5 microns or smaller) are good options outside meal times; ultraviolet purifiers are the newest gadget on the market, though they are battery dependent. Drinking water provided at national park visitor centers and campgrounds is reliably safe, unless posted notices indicate otherwise.

you drink a lot of water but don't eat. The excess water essentially flushes electrolytes and nutrients from your body.

➡ Prevention is key: add electrolyte powder or a pinch of sea salt to drinking water.

➡ Symptoms are similar to heat exhaustion (and can become life-threatening if left untreated), including nausea, muscle cramps, headaches and vomiting.

➡ Treatment is to rest in the shade and eat salty foods until the blood's sodium-level balance is reestablished. Rapidly evacuate if the victim's mental status changes.

SUNBURN

➡ You can sunburn quickly in the desert, sometimes in less than an hour, even on a cloudy day. Apply sunscreen (SPF 30 or higher) religiously every morning and reapply throughout the day. Always wear a hat, preferably one with a wide brim.

SAFE HIKING

➡ Hiking into a desert means taking extra precautions to make sure you return safely. This is true whether you plan to be gone an hour or a week. The desert has a way of compounding simple errors in judgment very quickly, and consequences range from unpleasant to grave.

➡ Always tell somebody in advance where you are going and when you expect to be back.

➡ If you do run into trouble, don't panic – sit down (if possible) and regain your cool before making any important decisions.

➡ One little-talked-about risk facing hikers is their own enthusiasm. Respect your limits. Remember that even in the middle of a national park, you're in a remote, wild place. Don't act foolishly by tackling a trail that's above

your skill level. Twisting an ankle or breaking a leg is surprisingly easy.

➡ Depending on where you are when you're injured, it could take several hours or even days before a SAR team can find you and get you to a hospital. Needless to say, if no one knows where you are, or what time to expect you back, they won't even come looking.

➡ Beware of flash floods! Rain falling 50 miles away can cause a flash flood that can wipe you out. Watch the weather carefully, and in emergency, move to higher ground.

Getting Lost

➡ Getting lost is always a danger. Always bring a map (preferably a topographical map) and a compass, and be familiar with prominent landmarks. Handheld GPS units can be helpful, but remember that batteries fail and sometimes it's impossible to get a clear satellite signal when you're inside a canyon.

➡ Always stay on the trail; don't take shortcuts. Not only does this help avoid accidents and injuries from steep drop-offs and hidden hazards, but it makes it easier for potential rescuers to find you. If you do get lost, stay calm and stay put, making your location as visible as possible (eg spread out brightly colored clothing or gear in an exposed place). Use a signal mirror or whistle to alert other hikers that you need help.

Falls & Jumping

➡ Nothing focuses one's attention like the edge of a 2000ft-high crumbling sandstone cliff. The consequences of a fall are self-evident and keep most people from taking unnecessary risks. Yet

people fall to their deaths every year in southern Utah. Cliff edges are sheer and trails along them very exposed. Rocks can be loose and slickrock, when wet, is indeed slick.

➡ There are no guardrails along the parks' hiking trails; watch your children carefully at all times.

➡ The more pernicious danger is carelessness. Most park rescues involve young men who are canyoneering and have fractured their legs while bouldering, leaping off rocks, or jumping into shallow, murky pools.

Flash Floods

➡ Flash floods are an ever-present danger in the desert, as flash floods that drowned seven hikers in Zion's Keyhole Canyon in September 2015 sadly demonstrated. No matter how dry a streambed looks, or how sunny it is overhead, a sudden rainstorm miles away can cause a stream or dry wash to 'flash' in minutes, sending down a huge surge of rock- and log-filled water that sweeps away everything in its path. Flash floods will kill hikers caught in creeks, dry riverbeds and narrow canyons, unless there is an escape route.

➡ Never park or camp in dry washes.

➡ Always check the flash flood warnings at park visitor centers or with the national weather service; this is especially crucial if you're planning on hiking through any slot canyons.

➡ Flash floods are most common during the summer monsoon season (roughly July through mid-September), but they can happen anytime a storm drops heavy rain.

➡ Telltale signs of an impending flash flood include sudden changes in water clarity (eg the stream turns muddy), rising water levels and/or floating debris, and a rush of wind, the sound of thunder or a low, rumbling roar. If you notice any of these signs, immediately get to higher ground (go as high as you can) – the water level doesn't usually increase all at once with one large wave, so you should have a minute or two to escape. If that's not possible, get behind a rock fin.

➡ Do not run down canyon – you can't beat a flash flood. Instead, wait it out; water levels usually drop within six to 24 hours.

Crossing Rivers & Streams

➡ On some backcountry trails, especially popular canyoneering routes, you may have to ford a river or stream swollen with snowmelt that is fast-flowing and cold enough to be a potential risk. Before stepping out from the bank, ease one arm out of the shoulder strap of your pack and unclip the belt buckle and chest compression straps. That way, if you lose your balance and are swept downstream, it will be easier to slip off your pack.

Flora & Fauna

➡ Southern Utah is awash in critters that, if bothered, can inflict a fair bit of pain, including rattlesnakes, scorpions, tarantulas, black widows, wasps and even centipedes. Spiders rarely bite unless harassed, which is also true of rattlesnakes, which like to warm themselves on trails or rock ledges, particularly in the late afternoon.

➡ Avoid shoving your hand beneath logs and rocks or into piles of wood, and never reach blindly over ledges or beneath boulders.

➡ Always shake out your hiking boots before putting them back on.

➡ If you encounter a mountain lion while hiking (extremely unlikely), maintain eye contact and do not look away. Wave your arms or hiking poles above your head to make yourself appear larger, and therefore possibly a threat. Gather young children to your side and stick together. Back away slowly, but resist the

COMMON AILMENTS

Plaguing hikers of all ages in southern Utah, the following may not pose problems if you're prepared.

Blisters

To avoid blisters, make sure your shoes are well worn in before you hit the trail. Your footwear should fit comfortably with enough room to move your toes; shoes that are too big or too small will cause blisters. The same goes for socks: be sure they fit properly and ideally are specifically made for hikers. But take into consideration Utah's extreme temperatures – you don't want to be wearing thick hiking socks if it's hot out. Wet and muddy socks can cause blisters, so even on a day walk, pack a spare pair. Keep your toenails clipped but not too short. If you do feel a blister coming on, treat it sooner rather than later by applying a bit of moleskin (or duct tape).

Fatigue

A simple statistic: more injuries happen toward the end of the day than when you're fresh. Although tiredness can simply be a nuisance on an easy walk, it can be life-threatening on narrow exposed ridges or in bad weather. You should never set out on a walk that is beyond your capabilities on the day. If you feel below par, have a day off or hop on a park shuttle. To reduce the risk of accidents, don't push yourself too hard – take rests every hour or two and build in a good half-hour or hour-long lunch break. Toward the end of the day, take down the pace and increase your concentration. Also eat properly throughout the day; nuts, dried fruit and chocolate are all good, energy-giving snack foods.

Knee Strain

Many hikers will feel the burn on long, steep descents, especially in southern Utah's canyon country. Although you can't eliminate strain on knee joints when dropping steeply, you can reduce it by taking shorter steps that leave your legs slightly bent and ensuring that your heel hits the ground before the rest of your foot. Lightweight hiking poles are effective in taking some of the weight off your knees. Compression bandages may also help.

urge to run, which makes you look like prey. If the lion approaches you, yell loudly, throw rocks and sticks, and fight back by whatever means possible.

➡ Learn to identify poison ivy: serrated leaves that grow in clusters of three and waxy white berries. This toxic plant grows in thickets, preferring moisture-laden canyons. If you think you've been exposed, immediately wash the affected area with soap and water.

Lightning

➡ If a thunderstorm is brewing, avoid exposed ridges or summits. Never seek shelter under objects that are isolated or higher than their surroundings, such as a lone tree. In open areas where there's no safe shelter, find a dry depression in the ground and take up a crouched-squatting position with your feet together; do not lie on the ground. Keep a layer of metal-free insulation, such as a camping pad, between you and the ground. Avoid contact with metallic objects, including backpack frames or hiking poles.

➡ If you're hiking with a group, spread out, keeping at least 50ft between each person. If anyone is struck by lightning, immediately begin first-aid measures such as checking their airway, breathing and pulse, and treat any burns. Prolonged

rescue breathing may be necessary, due to respiratory arrest. Evacuate and get medical help as quickly as possible.

Rockfall

➡ Always be alert to the danger of rockfall, especially after heavy rains. If you accidentally let loose a rock on a trail, loudly warn other hikers below by yelling out 'Rock!' Bighorn sheep, deer and other large animals sometimes dislodge rocks, another reason to be especially vigilant while hiking.

SAFE CYCLING

➡ Newcomers to desert road cycling and mountain biking should pay particular heed to safety. Wear a helmet, carry lots of water and bring high-energy foods. Also pack a map and keep track of your route. Don't start out on rough trails – first get your bearings on easier rides. The vibration from rougher trails can loosen headsets, so be sure to check your fittings.

➡ Expect the best, but prepare for the worst. In addition to extra water and food, carry a windbreaker, a wide-brimmed hat, sunscreen, sunglasses, a patch kit, tools and matches. Avoid riding alone, and always tell someone where you're going. The desert is

DON'T HORSE AROUND!

Day hikers may encounter horses and mules, which always have the right of way. If you're hiking when horseback riders or a mule train approaches, stand quietly on the inner side of the trail, turn your pack away from the animals (lest one bumps your pack and knocks you off balance) and listen for directions from the lead rider.

unforgiving and should never be underestimated.

➡ Road cyclists must adhere to traffic regulations and should use caution along heavily trafficked roads, especially during the busy summer season. On Zion Canyon's Scenic Drive, cyclists must pull over and allow park shuttle buses to pass.

➡ Although not required by Utah law, always wear a helmet as well as bright colors to improve your visibility to drivers. Emergency roadside assistance for cyclists is offered by the Better World Club (www.betterworldclub.com).

Behind the Scenes

SEND US YOUR FEEDBACK

We love to hear from travelers – your comments keep us on our toes and help make our books better. Our well-traveled team reads every word on what you loved or loathed about this book. Although we cannot reply individually to your submissions, we always guarantee that your feedback goes straight to the appropriate authors, in time for the next edition. Each person who sends us information is thanked in the next edition – the most useful submissions are rewarded with a selection of digital PDF chapters.

Visit **lonelyplanet.com/contact** to submit your updates and suggestions or to ask for help. Our award-winning website also features inspirational travel stories, news and discussions.

Note: We may edit, reproduce and incorporate your comments in Lonely Planet products such as guidebooks, websites and digital products, so let us know if you don't want your comments reproduced or your name acknowledged. For a copy of our privacy policy visit lonelyplanet.com/privacy.

WRITER THANKS

Greg Benchwick

This was an amazing adventure thanks to my research assistants: Sarah Senderhauf and the indomitable Violeta Benchwick. A huge debt of gratitude to the National Parks Service, especially Zach Alan who took the time to describe every hike in Bryce Canyon National Park. Thanks as always to my co-writers and editors. And to the men and women who fight fearlessly to preserve our national parks and public lands from destructive and greedy forces. RESIST!

ACKNOWLEDGEMENTS

Climate map data adapted from Peel MC, Finlayson BL & McMahon TA (2007) 'Updated World Map of the Köppen-Geiger Climate Classification', Hydrology and Earth System Sciences, 11, 163344.

Cover photograph: Hikers on the Navajo Loop Trail, Bryce Canyon National Park, Danita Delimont Stock/ AWL ©

THIS BOOK

This 4th edition of Lonely Planet's *Zion & Bryce Canyon National Parks* guide was curated by Christopher Pitts, and researched and written by Christopher, Greg Benchwick, Benedict Walker and Carolyn McCarthy. The previous edition was written by Greg Benchwick, Carolyn McCarthy and Christopher Pitts. This guidebook was produced by the following:

Destination Editor Ben Buckner

Senior Product Editors Grace Dobell, Vicky Smith

Product Editor Ross Taylor

Senior Cartographer Alison Lyall

Book Designer Jessica Rose

Assisting Editors Janet Austin, Anita Isalska, Kate Mathews, Lou McGregor, Lauren O'Connell, Sarah Reid, Maja Vatrić

Cartographer Valentina Kremenchutskaya

Cover Researcher Naomi Parker

Thanks to William Allen, Hannah Cartmel, Joel Cotterell, Evan Godt

Index

Map Legend

Sights
- Beach
- Bird Sanctuary
- Buddhist
- Castle/Palace
- Christian
- Confucian
- Hindu
- Islamic
- Jain
- Jewish
- Monument
- Museum/Gallery/Historic Building
- Ruin
- Shinto
- Sikh
- Taoist
- Winery/Vineyard
- Zoo/Wildlife Sanctuary
- Other Sight

Activities, Courses & Tours
- Bodysurfing
- Diving
- Canoeing/Kayaking
- Course/Tour
- Sento Hot Baths/Onsen
- Skiing
- Snorkeling
- Surfing
- Swimming/Pool
- Walking
- Windsurfing
- Other Activity

Sleeping
- Sleeping
- Camping
- Hut/Shelter

Eating
- Eating

Drinking & Nightlife
- Drinking & Nightlife
- Cafe

Entertainment
- Entertainment

Shopping
- Shopping

Information
- Bank
- Embassy/Consulate
- Hospital/Medical
- Internet
- Police
- Post Office
- Telephone
- Toilet
- Tourist Information
- Other Information

Geographic
- Beach
- Gate
- Hut/Shelter
- Lighthouse
- Lookout
- Mountain/Volcano
- Oasis
- Park
- Pass
- Picnic Area
- Waterfall

Population
- Capital (National)
- Capital (State/Province)
- City/Large Town
- Town/Village

Transport
- Airport
- BART station
- Border crossing
- Boston T station
- Bus
- Cable car/Funicular
- Cycling
- Ferry
- Metro/Muni station
- Monorail
- Parking
- Petrol station
- Subway/SkyTrain station
- Taxi
- Train station/Railway
- Tram
- Underground station
- Other Transport

Routes
- Tollway
- Freeway
- Primary
- Secondary
- Tertiary
- Lane
- Unsealed road
- Road under construction
- Plaza/Mall
- Steps
- Tunnel
- Pedestrian overpass
- Walking Tour
- Walking Tour detour
- Path/Walking Trail

Boundaries
- International
- State/Province
- Disputed
- Regional/Suburb
- Marine Park
- Cliff
- Wall

Hydrography
- River, Creek
- Intermittent River
- Canal
- Water
- Dry/Salt/Intermittent Lake
- Reef

Areas
- Airport/Runway
- Beach/Desert
- Cemetery (Christian)
- Cemetery (Other)
- Glacier
- Mudflat
- Park/Forest
- Sight (Building)
- Sportsground
- Swamp/Mangrove

Note: Not all symbols displayed above appear on the maps in this book

OUR STORY

A beat-up old car, a few dollars in the pocket and a sense of adventure. In 1972 that's all Tony and Maureen Wheeler needed for the trip of a lifetime – across Europe and Asia overland to Australia. It took several months, and at the end – broke but inspired – they sat at their kitchen table writing and stapling together their first travel guide, *Across Asia on the Cheap*. Within a week they'd sold 1500 copies. Lonely Planet was born.

Today, Lonely Planet has offices in Franklin, London, Melbourne, Oakland, Dublin, Beijing and Delhi, with more than 600 staff and writers. We share Tony's belief that 'a great guidebook should do three things: inform, educate and amuse'.

OUR WRITERS

Christopher Pitts

Zion National Park Chris first drove West on a family road trip across the country and immediately fell in love with the star-studded nights. Four years at Colorado College gave him plenty of opportunities to hitchhike to Utah and lug round gallons of water during not-always-sunny spring breaks in the Canyonlands. Seventeen years, several continents and two kids later, he's back in Colorado, traveling I-70 with the rest of the family whenever the opportunity arises. Visit him online at www.christopherpitts.net.

Greg Benchwick

Bryce Canyon National Park Greg has been drifting across the high plains of the Colorado Plateau for most of his life – he calls it a 'true spiritual home'. As a kid, he canoed desolate river canyons with his family, while in his wilder college days he pushed the limits on classic rock-climbing routes like Castleton Tower and the Moonlight Buttress. He's backpacked lost canyons, hitchhiked to Zion, mountain-biked Moab, and found solitude and peace in the lost corners of this desert wonderworld. Greg also wrote the Plan section.

Contributing Writers & Researchers

Carolyn McCarthy The red-rock desert of Utah is a favorite destination for Carolyn. She has contributed to more than 30 titles for Lonely Planet, including *Panama, Trekking in the Patagonian Andes, Argentina, Chile, Colorado, Southwest USA* and national parks guides. Follow her on Instagram @masmerquen. For more information, see www.carolynmccarthy.pressfolios.com.

Benedict Walker A beach baby from Newcastle, Australia, Ben turned 40 in 2017 and decided to start a new life in Leipzig, Germany! Writing for Lonely Planet was a childhood dream. It's a privilege, a huge responsibility and loads of fun! He's thrilled to have covered big chunks of Australia, Canada, Germany, Japan, Switzerland, Sweden and the USA. Come along for the ride on Instagram @wordsandjourneys.

Published by Lonely Planet Global Limited
CRN 554153
4th edition – March 2019
ISBN 978 1 78657 591 3
© Lonely Planet 2019   Photographs © as indicated 2019
10 9 8 7 6 5 4 3 2 1
Printed in Singapore